CHOOSING SIDES
Unions and the Team Concept

BY
Mike Parker
AND
Jane Slaughter

A Labor Notes Book
South End Press
Boston 1988

A Labor Notes Book
Copyright © 1988 by the Labor Education and Research Project
First printing May 1988

Book designed by David McCullough and Elissa Clarke.
Cover designed by David McCullough. Cover photo by Irene Perloff.

Library of Congress Cataloging in Publication Data
Parker, Mike, 1940-
    Choosing sides.

    "A labor notes book."
    Includes bibliographies and index.
    1. Industrial management—United States—Employee participation—Case studies. 2. Automobile industry and trade—United States—Management—Employee participation—Case studies. 3. Automobile industry workers—United States—Job stress—Case studies. 4. Industrial relations—United States—Case studies. 5. Work groups—United States—Case studies. 6. Trade unions—United States—Officials and employees—Attitudes.   I. Slaughter, Jane, 1949-   . II. Title.
HD5660.U5P36   1988   331'.01'12   88-80585
ISBN 0-89608-348-9
ISBN 0-89608-347-0 (pbk.)
Library of Congress Catalog Card Number: 88-80585

Contents

Acknowledgments

Many people felt the need for this book—and we only wish we could have had it in their hands earlier. Some of them helped to make the book possible by sending us material, checking out information, arranging interviews, or providing criticisms and suggestions. As it happens, some who have helped us disagree sharply with our conclusions on many points.

We are grateful to the many workers, too numerous to list here, who contributed their insights and who are quoted in the case studies. The book was enriched by the authors who contributed chapters or sections of chapters: Ellis Boal, Pamela Briggs, Peter Downs, Ronda Hauben, John Junkerman, Bob Kutchko, Nelson Lichtenstein, and Eric Mann.

In addition we would like to thank: Richard Aguilar, Tatsuro Akimoto, Charlie Allen, Steve Babson, David Bensman, Irving Bluestone, Barbara Boylan, Amy Bromsen, Cheryl Buswell-Robinson, Neil Chacker, Dave Chmielewski, Peter Cole, Ben Daankbar, Dick Danjin, Peter Dooley, Donny Douglas, Julie Edgar, Dianne Feeley, Dan G, Al Gardner, Frank Hammer, Steve Herzenberg, Gary Huck, Todd Jailer, Eileen Janadia, Mike Joss, Ron Kassuba, Harry Katz, Pete Kelly, Shelley Kessler, Bob King, Carole Kirby, Phill Kwik, Elly Leary, Mike Leslie, Dan Luria, Linda Manning Myatt, Dan Maurin, Pam McGinnis, Jimmy McWilliams, Kim Moody, Marilyn Morehead, Greg Nicklas, Bruce Nissen, Ken Paff, Bob Parker, Bill Parker, Steve Phillips, Joe Pietrzyk, Ted Pych, Jim Renard, Billy Ridgers, Tom S, Bob Schroeder, John Snow, Wendy Thompson, Jerry Tucker, Peter Unterweger, Rae Vogeler, Tim Wise, Tony Woodley, Jim Woodward, Mike Wunsch, Dave Yao, Dave Yettaw.

We also wish to thank those who helped but for one reason or another feel it necessary to remain anonymous.

Many readers of *Labor Notes* responded generously to our request for funds to help get the book into print. Twenty-two unions made donations:
Aluminum Workers Local 445
American Postal Workers Union Local 4871
Canadian Association of Professional Radio Operators
Canadian Paperworkers Local 855
Canadian Auto Workers
Canadian Auto Workers Local 707
Communications Workers Local 1032
Communications Workers Local 1180
Communications Workers Local 4309
Machinists Local 2740
San Mateo County Central Labor Council
Service Employees Local 616
United Auto Workers Local 160
United Auto Workers Local 438
United Auto Workers Local 594
United Auto Workers Local 599
United Auto Workers Local 977
United Auto Workers Local 1200
Union of Northern Workers
United Paperworkers Local 9
Utility Workers Local 369
Vancouver Municipal and Regional Employees Union.

Particular thanks to UAW Locals 438, 594, and 977, which contributed $500 dollars apiece.

We owe special thanks to Dave McCullough, who designed the book and its cover. Dan La Botz helped out with one of the more difficult sections. Mike Konopacki and Ted Rall contributed original cartoons. Hal Stack, Director of Labor Studies at Wayne State University, helped us with the academic literature and provided us with useful criticism.

Jane is particularly grateful to the staff of *Labor Notes*, who shouldered many of her regular responsibilities so that she could work on the book.

Mike would like to thank his daughter, Johanna Jordan Parker, for her understanding and help, and Margaret S. Jordan for the relationship of trust and support that made it possible to attempt and complete this project, as well as for the many ideas she contributed.

We owe our biggest debt of gratitude to Elissa Clarke, author of the *Labor Notes* book, *Stopping Sexual Harassment*. In our three-person team, Elissa was a dedicated team leader—our organizer and editor. In addition, her mastery of a bug-filled computer publishing system made this book as current as possible. We would not like to attempt another book without her.

Mike Parker   *Jane Slaughter*

A Foreword from Victor Reuther

Today the employers, taking advantage of a political climate reminiscent of the anti-union twenties, are attempting to undermine collective bargaining as we have known it for the last 50 years, and to sap the strength of our unions. The corporations' attack on the unions is not primarily a frontal assault in the form of union busting—though that goes on, too. Rather the employers' attack on the unions is taking the form of an ideological assault, a battle for the minds of union members.

The corporations are attempting to undermine the unity and solidarity of the workers on the plant floor and in the union to draw workers into a mythical partnership. They offer the enticing illusion that the worker will have a voice in management. The cutting edge of this battle for the mind of the worker is the "team concept." That is why this book is not merely important, but crucial for the future of U.S. labor unions.

It is, of course, not the first time that management has tried this kind of mind-bending. In the 1920's John D. Rockefeller, Jr. called for "employee representation" and Charles Schwab, the head of U.S. Steel, promoted "constructive cooperation." Employee representation was intended to keep the unions out of the factories.

Today, faced with a unionized workforce, the employer wants to undermine the union and undercut the contract, and has a variety of strategies to do so. For example, there are "model" agreements such as the GM Saturn plant's team concept contract, really a return to "enterprise" unionism as opposed to a national union with a national agreement. The Saturn-type agreement pits state against state, community against community, and local union against local union, as each attempts to offer greater concessions to the company. In 1937 the UAW rejected GM's proposal of "enterprise" unionism, a separate contract for each plant, and demanded a national agreement. Today the union succumbs to the ruse it rejected over 50 years ago.

Meanwhile within the plant the corporations have pushed various cooperation schemes such as the team concept. The team concept is more than a mere gimmick; it is an attempt by management to control not only the worker's behavior on the job, but also the worker's feelings and thoughts. The employer plays upon the worker's desire to use his or her creativity and intellect. The team concept promises the worker that he or she will be something more than a mere factory hand, calls upon him to think, and asks him to cooperate with management.

But cooperation with management ever so subtly turns into competition with one's fellow workers. In the struggle for productivity and even quality, department is pitted against department, and worker is pitted against worker. What began by appealing to the worker's idealism turns some workers into informers and weakens union solidarity. Often when workers are reluctant to approve the team approach, they are threatened by management with plant closings.

Where the team concept was born and has become dominant, in Japan, workers no longer turn to the union for help. A study called "Consciousness of the People" conducted by the Japanese labor federation Sohyo in March 1986 found that few Japanese workers take their problems to the union any more. Only seven percent said that the person they go to when they have a problem at work is the union steward.

Today U.S. unions are ill prepared to defend themselves from so subtle and insidious a management strategy. Our unions have grown more and more centralized and bureaucratic. Many workers believe the company takes—and the union allows—concessions when they are not really needed. The trade union leadership is not involving the union members in discussion, and so the unions don't seem as relevant to workers as they did in the thirties, forties and fifties. Such unions cannot involve and mobilize their members to take on the new challenge.

The United Auto Workers and other unions have embraced the team concept. Now we frequently find management and the union, arm in arm, singing that old song, "We are all one big happy family here." It seems to be a return to the 1920's: the team leader is just a new age straw boss, and worker flexibility is just another name for the company's right to dispose of the worker as it pleases.

The revitalization and democratization of the unions is essential. Networks of union activists are growing up in response to this challenge. The New Directions movement in the United Auto Workers and the cross-union network associated with *Labor Notes* are examples. They are a way for workers to analyze the attack which is taking place, and develop the strategies to re-

---

Victor Reuther was one of the founders of the United Auto Workers. He was a strike leader in the Flint sitdown strike in 1936 and then became director of organizing in Indiana. He served the union as an organizer, education director, and director of the International Affairs Department and was special assistant to UAW Presidents Walter Reuther and Leonard Woodcock.

spond to it. They are essential steps in restoring leadership accountability to the rank and file. What's more, they can begin to institute the solidarity which is needed to fend off enterprise unionism and the whipsawing of local against local and worker against worker.

Choosing Sides: Unions and the Team Concept reflects the first-hand experience of Mike Parker and Jane Slaughter as former workers in the auto plants, Mike at Chrysler and Ford, and Jane at Chrysler and GM. But perhaps more important, it is an expression of their involvement in the networks of activists associated with *Labor Notes*. Drawing from their own experience as auto workers and from their many contacts among labor union activists, as well as a serious examination of the existing literature, Mike Parker and Jane Slaughter's *Choosing Sides* analyzes the impact of the team concept on workers and their unions better than any academic

study could, and arms the rank and file activist or local union official to respond to management's latest ploy. They mix detailed practical advice with a vision of what could be.

I highly recommend this book to those who want not only to understand what is happening to labor-management relations in this country, but who also want tools to strengthen the unions in their dealings with management. Ultimately this book confirms what many have intuitively understood, that today as in the past, in the struggle between management and union, one must choose sides.

Introduction

This book is written for unionists. Some are facing demands from their employers to implement teams and are deciding on a response. Others are only too familiar with the day-to-day realities of the team concept, but want to better understand it or to know how others have responded. Still other unionists are not immediately confronted with teams, but want to be prepared. *Choosing Sides: Unions and the Team Concept* is meant to be useful to people in all these categories.

The book is divided into three parts. Part I analyzes the team concept in the auto industry, Part II provides background information, and Part III looks at the team concept through the experiences of 15 different companies and plants.

Chapter 1 defines what the team concept package means in practice. Chapter 2 explains the recent history of team concept ideas both in this country and elsewhere, and how the U.S. auto industry came to adopt its version of the team concept. Chapter 3 examines the team concept in its most developed form, a production system we have named "management-by-stress." This chapter demonstrates that, behind the flowery rhetoric, management is demanding profound changes that significantly alter the balance of power on the shop floor. Chapter 4 contrasts management-by-stress to a humanized vision of the workplace, which turns out to be quite different from the team concept. Chapter 5 addresses the question of what unions can do when confronted with management's demands for teams. This chapter offers suggestions for dispelling the myths about the team concept and negotiating a team concept agreement that preserves workers' rights as much as possible. It draws on the experiences of different locals in modifying the worst aspects of team agreements.

Part II provides additional background on aspects of management-by-stress. Chapter 6, by British social psychologist Pamela Briggs, exposes the myths about Japanese labor relations. Chapter 7 looks at the roots of the classification system in the auto industry. In this chapter historian Nelson Lichtenstein draws a parallel between yesterday's straw bosses and today's team leaders. Chapter 8 brings the discussion of classifications up to date, and explores why reduction of classifications is so critical to management-by-stress and so detrimental to workers. Chapters 9 and 10 provide additional details on the setting of work standards and on how management uses the issue of quality.

Part III is composed of 15 case studies of team concept plants. The case studies present a range of the variants of team concept plants—what we describe in Chapter 2 as a "continuum." Some of the case studies focus on a particular aspect of the team concept, while others try to give a more general picture. Chapter 11 on NUMMI (New United Motors Manufacturing, Inc., the joint GM-Toyota venture in Fremont, California) describes a model "management-by-stress" plant. Chapter 12 on GM's Shreveport, Louisiana truck plant describes a plant which came to the team concept via a more subtle route. Each of these plants has become a prototype in its own way. Readers should keep these chapters in mind as they read the other case studies, because we try not to repeat all the details but to highlight important differences or particularly interesting aspects of each plant. The histories are supplemented with contract language and newspaper articles.

Chapter 13, on six Chrysler plants, examines team concept contract language closely.

Chapter 14, on GM's Oklahoma City plant, describes GM's early, non-union approach to the team concept—and how the United Auto Workers fought it.

Chapters 15 and 16 explain how General Motors pressured workers into accepting the team concept in Fairfax, Kansas and Van Nuys, California. These chapters were written by workers from the plants, Bob Kutchko and Eric Mann. The second half of the Van Nuys chapter tells how the local union is now resisting the worst aspects of teams.

Chapters 17 and 18 describe employee selection and training at Mazda and at GM's Wentzville, Missouri plant. The Wentzville chapter is by Peter Downs, recording secretary of UAW Local 2250.

In Chapter 19, we interview a team concept pioneer from one of GM's first team concept plants, who tells why the initial enthusiasm wears off.

Sometimes the team concept is largely superficial rhetoric, as described in Chapters 20 and 21 on GM's Poletown and Orion, Michigan plants. An interesting feature of the Orion experience is the skilled trades' struggle to maintain their lines of demarcation.

Some locals have turned back the company's demands for teams. Chapters 22 and 23, on GM's Pontiac Truck and Bus and Warren Hydra-Matic plants in Michigan, are about successful resistance. The Warren chapter also includes information on an advanced version of team concept—"business teams."

Chapter 24 describes Ford's Hermosillo, Mexico plant. It contains the important lesson that whatever else it may be, team concept is not the magic potion that will make U.S. industry competitive with industry in low-wage countries. The corporations which are pushing team concept in the U.S. are also pushing it on their workforces everywhere else.

Chapter 25, by journalist John Junkerman, describes a non-union team concept factory, Nissan's Smyrna, Tennessee assembly plant. It is interesting to note how Nissan is similar to and how it differs from the unionized management-by-stress plants described in this book, NUMMI and Mazda.

We have tried to make *Choosing Sides* as complete as possible. Each chapter is written so that it stands on its own, and this has made for a certain amount of repetition. We have also included documentation with many case studies, especially contract language, and there is some repetition in this area as well.

We hope that this method has made the information easily accessible.

Team concept challenges many of the fundamental principles as well as the power of the labor movement. We wrote this book because we believe that the future of our children, all working people, and possibly the entire world depends on building a strong labor movement. We hope that *Choosing Sides* is a useful tool in the struggle for workers' rights.

1. What Is Team Concept?

In advertising, *before* and *after* pictures are used to demonstrate miraculous cures for baldness, quick and effortless weight loss, and better-than-new home remodeling. The team concept is sold with much the same approach. Look at the assembly line before teams:

The automobile assembly line moves on at an unrelenting pace. Each worker does one small job on the line over and over. The supervisor acts as if workers were hired from the shoulders down. Good workers come in every day, do their jobs without complaint or error, and go home. Bad workers require constant supervision and harsh penalties to curb absenteeism.

The work is boring and frustrating, and most workers hate their jobs. Workers ignore the problems they see on the line, as any suggestions they do offer are ignored or classified as complaints.

Union rules and hundreds of job classifications prevent management from using people efficiently. Often dozens stand around doing nothing, waiting for a person with the correct classification to do a critical job to get things moving again.

Problems are never settled easily. Union and management spend thousands of hours arguing and processing formal grievances over trivial events.

Customers gripe about quality. Sales fall, profits drop, and workers are laid off.

But never fear, there is a cure. Look at the same plant only months after implementation of the amazing team concept:

Groups of a dozen or so workers work together as teams. Together, they decide how best to do the jobs in their area and meet production goals. When there is a problem, the team meets and figures out a solution. Workers feel involved and look forward to coming to work. With the new attitudes, most disciplinary and production problems disappear. Quality and productivity improve. Management personnel shift from an unpleasant disciplinary role to new creative roles.

Team members are multiskilled or cross-trained so they can help each other out and do different jobs as the situation requires. The teams handle many of the foreman's previous functions, including scheduling and dealing with production problems. Hourly workers called team leaders handle tasks ranging from routine paperwork to training new hires and making job assignments. Foremen become "advisors" or group leaders for several teams.

Dignity and respect are the new bywords. Management respects workers' knowledge, while workers come to understand the real problems faced by the company. Barriers crumble: foremen take off their neckties; time clocks are eliminated; workers and management share the same cafeterias, parking facilities and bathrooms.

Best of all, quality and productivity improve, so the plant becomes more profitable and workers can enjoy increased job security.

Like other before/after advertising, the "before" picture plays on people's fears and insecurities. The "after" picture builds on superficial changes that tap into hopes and fantasies. Unfortunately, just like the baldness cures, team concept in the auto industry does not deliver what it promises. This book will show that while teams may be advantageous to the corporations, they come at a dear price to workers and the union movement.

The team concept is best known in the auto industry because the press has made much of the contrast

---

GM HAS A VISION

In 1987 General Motors ran a series of ads in *Business Week* with the theme: "The vision is paying off."

At the beginning of the decade, the problem was clear. American Industry was in decline. Some short term fixes were possible but competition from lower-wage nations demanded something more—an American industrial renaissance. GM took the challenge...

The great flaw in the assembly line concept is that—followed to its extreme—it tends to exclude the creative and managerial skills of the people who work on the line.

We believe that new technology must be integrated with new social systems in a human partnership. A partnership that gives people authority over machines and responsibility for their work. Once people are put in charge of machines their creativity is unleashed...

The symbols of confrontation [at the GM Fort Wayne Truck plant] have been replaced by the symbols of cooperation. Everyone eats together, parks together, and works together. The people who build vehicles decide a lot of what goes on in the plant. They're involved in choosing the lighting for their areas because they're the ones who need the light. They help determine how jobs will be done because they are the ones who do them...

The president of the local union in Fort Wayne says that there has been a change in the culture of the plant. People now consider their work a craft. They get involved and like being involved. They want even more involvement.[1]

between the floundering U.S. auto industry and the profitable Japanese companies, which seem to have achieved their success through the team concept. The team experiments in humanizing work in Sweden are also attractive to many unionists. The words "teams" and "teamwork" evoke positive images of the Superbowl or of people working together harmoniously to achieve a common goal. Let's have a little team spirit to beat the competition—"Go, U.S. industry! Go!"

By March 1988 the team concept was in use or planned for in at least 17 General Motors assembly plants, in six Chrysler plants, in Ford's Rouge Steel operation and Romeo engine plant, and in all of the wholly or partially Japanese-owned plants (Nissan, Honda, Mazda, Diamond-Star and NUMMI). General Motors has also been actively pushing team concept in its components plants. In plants at several companies, team concept has been installed in certain departments. In still others, key elements of team concept such as fewer classifications have already been bargained. Team concept is projected for use in GM's Saturn project, much ballyhooed as the factory that will revolutionize car production in the United States. And the United Auto Workers explicitly endorsed team concept in the national union contracts signed with Ford and GM in the fall of 1987.

The team concept is growing in other industries as well, although what is meant by "team concept" varies widely from company to company. Companies as diverse as makers of corn syrup and sellers of insurance have been hailed for their bold innovations in labor relations through teams.[2] Electronics, paint, chemical, oil refining, heavy equipment, telephone, motors, photocopying, and high tech companies have all experimented with teams. Some of the better-known corporations which use team concept include AT&T[3], General Electric, Proctor and Gamble, Xerox, Honeywell, Cummins Engine, Best Food, and United Technologies, among others. An executive vice-president of General Electric claims a 40 percent increase in his company's return on investment in the five years since the team concept began at a GE plant in Quebec.[4]

Team concept has also spread into the public sector. There are experiments in public schools in Florida, Tennessee, and Washington state.[5] To many, it may seem that the team concept is an idea whose time has come.

In this book we concentrate on the auto industry. Within the auto industry we focus on assembly rather than parts plants and use the language of the assembly line. Just as auto led the way for other industries in demanding contract concessions and Quality of Work Life programs earlier in the decade, so they are leading the way on the team concept in unionized industry as well. The team concept as it has been defined by the auto industry needs to be studied by unionists everywhere. Both private and public employers in workplaces of every kind are watching the auto industry for lessons.

Stirring in the Rhetoric

On first hearing, the team concept sounds great. Through teamwork—everyone pulling together—we can increase productivity, improve quality, enhance job satisfaction and save jobs. Even allowing for some hype, it sounds too good not to try.

A lot of what claims to be "new industrial relations," however, is nothing more than the old auto in-

---

WHAT'S IN A TEAM?

The team concept starts with the assumption that workers must be interchangeable. Management says that teamwork requires getting rid of classifications and that all team members must learn all jobs on the team.

This use of the word "team" is special and peculiar. Management uses the word because of its positive associations from other areas of life: sports teams, surgical teams, management teams, union leadership teams, and so on.

But in every one of these cases, "teamwork" implies the cooperation of specialists towards a common goal. The qualities that make a good wide receiver in football are not the same as those of a center. The neurosurgeon and the anesthesiologist cannot substitute for one another. Every business management team includes specialists in finance, manufacturing, marketing, and research and development. A good union leadership team includes people with expertise in bargaining, accounting, contract enforcement, labor law, past practice, and labor history. Rarely is one person exceptional in all areas.

In fact, the main place in our language where "team" implies interchangeable members is where it refers to a team of horses—beasts of burden of equal capabilities, yoked together to pull for a common end (determined by the person holding the whip).

WE DON'T NEED A UNION HERE... WE'RE A TEAM, REMEMBER?

dustry trick of passing off last year's model by changing the name plate and adding some tail fins. For example, the following goes on in many traditional auto plants:

On occasion the foreman holds a meeting of his group and announces the week's productivity and scrap figures or discusses the latest safety memo. The foreman's "go-fer" takes care of vacation schedules and work gloves.

Instead we could write:

Hourly workers are organized into teams which meet with their advisor to discuss quality and work procedures. A team leader takes care of vacation scheduling and supplies.

Same plant, same reality. But by stirring in the right rhetoric, we produce instant team concept and brand new industrial relations.

Although it sounds harmless, this fluff aspect of team concept is dangerous because it serves to disguise the fact that important changes *are* happening. In the auto industry the team concept has come to mean a package deal that involves changes that would seem to have nothing to do with teams themselves. Many of the provisions of team concept agreements challenge principles, such as seniority, for which unions have fought in order to protect workers. Other provisions seem to be blank checks to management.

In some plants workers have resisted the imposition of team concept (for example, Chrysler's Newark, Delaware plant or GM's Oklahoma City, Warren Hydra-Matic, and Pontiac Truck and Bus plants). Management, some union leaders, and many outsiders explain workers' opposition as "resistance to change" or "institutional friction."

Both may exist, but it is condescending to dismiss workers' concerns by saying that they have no substance. A brief look at the team concept's record reveals the need for union caution and careful examination at the very least.

First, in recent history teams have been linked with union busting. The team concept was part of General Motors' failed 1970's "Southern strategy" to shift work to right-to-work states and keep out the United Auto Workers. The only two significant auto assembly plants in the U.S. which have kept the union out, Honda and Nissan, are noted for their use of the team concept.

Second, in Japan the team concept is associated with company unions—management-controlled unions whose main job is to implement company policy and boost productivity, rather than represent the needs of their members.

A third cause for pause is that the supposed benefits of teams do not jibe with the line-up of forces involved. Team concept claims to provide workers with dignity, security, and control over their jobs. So why aren't workers aggressively demanding the team concept? In most instances where the team concept has been implemented, it was a management proposal which met opposition from the workforce. In fact, in case after case,

management has openly threatened to move work or even close plants to convince workers to adopt teams.

The Team Package

A look at the team concept shows that these warning signals are worth heeding. When team concept becomes part of a collective bargaining agreement in the auto industry, it means a package deal with many components. These include:

1. A rewritten contract announcing that a new relationship exists between the company and its workforce.

2. Interchangeability, meaning that workers are required or induced (through "pay-for-knowledge") to be capable of doing several jobs.

3. Drastic reduction of classifications, giving management increased control to assign workers as it sees fit. The abolition of classifications and interchangeability in job assignments are the main things management wants when it talks about team concept.

4. Less meaning for seniority. In some cases seniority is explicitly undermined or modified. In other cases, opportunities for exercising seniority disappear. For example, if classifications are eliminated, opportunities to transfer to different classifications by seniority are also eliminated.

5. Detailed definition of every step of every job, increasing management control over the way jobs are done.

6. Workers' participation in increasing their own workload.

7. More worker responsibility, without more authority, for jobs previously performed by supervision.

8. A management attempt to make workers aware of the interrelatedness of the plant's departments and the place of the individual in the whole; an attempt by both union and management to get away from the "I just come to work, do my job and mind my own business" outlook.

9. An ideological atmosphere which stresses competition between plants and workers' responsibility for winning work away from other plants.

10. A shift toward enterprise unionism, where the union views itself as a partner of management.

Some unionists have different visions of what team concept could be—an altogether distinct, more humane "package." In particular, many have heard of the Swedish experiments with teams at Volvo and would like to duplicate something along the lines of what they've heard in their own workplaces.

However, whatever models may be used in other countries, or whatever version American unionists may dream of implementing here, in the auto industry management is implementing its own vision. People with alternative visions of the team concept will do well to understand why the package has turned out the way it has in auto. We believe that the same forces will tend to operate in other workplaces as well.

Happy Days at the Ford Factory *Have you seen a Ford contract ... lately?*

DANZIGER
The Christian Science Monitor

Danziger in The Christian Science Monitor ©1987 TCSPS

Team Concept Spreads

Although initially cautious about committing itself, by 1985 the top UAW leadership had embraced the team concept, in deed if not in word. In particular, the union's vice-president in charge of GM workers, Donald Ephlin, promoted GM's cost-cutting through its version of teams. Having accepted the logic that American auto companies needed to be more competitive, union leaders found themselves in some strange company.

A team concept agreement with General Motors' new Saturn subsidiary was signed by the International Executive Board in July 1985, long before ground had been broken for the Tennessee plant. In 1986 and 1987 the International's Chrysler Department worked to spread a standard version of team concept in half a dozen Chrysler plants. Bargaining committees in many plants, especially at GM, were told by their International representatives that team concept was necessary and that they had better negotiate it or their plant could close.

The auto companies have implemented the team concept in their various plants in one of two ways: 1) by installing it in newly-built plants, with little or no consultation with the UAW, or 2) by threatening to close an existing plant or move work away from it in order to pressure the local union to change its contract.

This latter process is called "whipsawing"—playing one local against another. General Motors in particular has been adept at explicitly dangling the promise of a new model before two plants and letting the local unions decide who would "bid" the lowest. The case studies of Chrysler and of GM's Van Nuys, California and Fairfax, Kansas plants illustrate how whipsawing has functioned.

The UAW's 1987 National Agreements at Ford and GM contained language which many local union leaders believed would encourage the companies to whipsaw even more. In exchange for job security language, both contracts committed the local unions to search for ways to improve "operational effectiveness." Suggested plans included team concept and pay-for-knowledge. Efforts of local joint committees were to be overseen by National Job Security and Operational Effectiveness Committees made up of corporate and International-appointed representatives. Many opponents of the team concept on the local level charged that this language meant team concept had already been decided upon nationally and would be thrust upon the locals one by one.

Faced with whipsawing and with the pro-team concept attitude of the International union, it has been difficult for local union officials who distrusted team concept to come up with a viable defense. In particular

TEAMS IN BRITAIN

In Britain, the introduction of team concept has been accompanied by conscious and hard-nosed union-busting.[6] Some techniques will sound very familiar to American workers, such as the joint venture and vote-till-you-get-it-right. In April 1987, General Motors announced that it would close its van plant in Luton, England. The plant would reopen, however—as a joint venture with Isuzu, under Isuzu management.

The only hitch was that under British law, working conditions could not be changed unless the unions in the plant approved. The new contract GM and Isuzu wanted included team concept with full management flexibility to assign workers and restrictions on union activity. Five times the unions at Luton rejected the proposal, despite GM's insistence that it would close the plant altogether if the unions did not go along. Finally, on the sixth ballot, GM narrowly won the vote.

Another team concept plant is Nissan's assembly plant in Sunderland, in northeast England, opened in 1985.[7] Nissan management insisted that it would recognize only one union at the new plant, de-spite the fact that British tradition is that each plant contain several different unions representing different categories of workers. A strong shop floor stewards system has accompanied this tradition, with the stewards from the different unions meeting together.

To weaken the unions' strength on the shop floor, the "single union" strategy has now become popular among new investors. Nissan forced the various unions to compete for company recognition; British workers call this process a "beauty contest," with each union trying to make itself look most attractive to management. In the case of Sunderland, the Amalgamated Engineering Union (AEU) agreed to "complete flexibility and mobility of employees" and the team concept—and won the contest.

The results appear to have been like those in the U.S., with worker complaints of extreme speedup and a union unwilling or too weak to do anything about it. Indeed, although the AEU is recognized as representative of all the workers, less than one quarter of the plant's workers have joined the union.

---

it has been nearly impossible to build a united strategy to resist team concept.

Given this steamroller effect, many unions will need to figure out how to modify team concept once it's installed. We will discuss some of these ideas in Chapter 5. We will also stress the need for unified action and cross-fertilization of ideas to fight whipsawing.

Notes

1. Series of advertisements in *Business Week*, April-May 1987.

2. See, for example, "Management Discovers the Human Side of Automation," *Business Week*, September 29, 1986.
Also, Labor Relations Today, November-December 1987.

3. For a description of the Communications Workers of America/AT&T team concept experiments, see Greg Nicklas, "Self-Managing Teams and Unions," *The Quality Circles Journal*, International Association of Quality Circles, June 1987.

4. *Toronto Star*, September 30, 1987.

5. NEA Research, "Employee Participation Programs: Considerations for the School Site," National Education Association, Washington, D.C., 1988.

6. An excellent paper analyzing these trends in the British automobile industry is Peter J. Turnbull, "The Limits to Japanisation—Just-In-Time, Labour Relations and the U.K. Automotive Industry," to be published in *New Technology, Work and Employment* in Autumn 1988 (Vol.3, No.2).

7. Stuart Crowther and Philip Garrahan, "Invitation to Sunderland: Corporate Power and the Local Economy," paper for a conference on "Industrial Change in Declining Areas," at Sunderland Polytechnic, April 14-16, 1988.
Also, "Workers quit as low morale hits Nissan Car Plant," *Daily Telegraph*, London, May 6, 1987.
Also, CAITS, *Flexibility: Who Needs It?*, London, 1986.
Also, Rod Hague, "Employment Policy and Industrial Relations in Three Japanese Firms in Northeast England," paper presented at conference on "The Japanisation of British Industry," University of Wales Institute of Science and Technology, Cardiff, September 17-18, 1987.

2. The Background

The team concept did not arise in a vacuum. Spurred by the recession of the early 1980's, declining profit margins, and growing foreign competition, U.S. management looked to reduce costs by cheapening labor. Companies went after both contract concessions, such as wage and benefit changes,[1] and restyled labor relations—notably Quality of Work Life (QWL) programs.[2] To their surprise, they found less resistance from the unions than they had expected. Labor-management cooperation schemes, especially in industries facing heavy competition, became the order of the day.

The auto companies put their faith in another cost-cutting strategy as well—investment overseas. Chrysler, Ford, and GM invested heavily in non-U.S. plants of their own and also in Japanese and Korean auto companies. Ford owns 25 percent of Mazda; GM 40 percent of Isuzu and 50 percent of Daewoo Motors; Chrysler owns 24 percent of Mitsubishi, which in turn owns 15 percent of Korea's Hyundai.[3] The Big Three all market cars produced by their foreign partners. The Big Three are also projected to import 300,000 vehicles and 1.4 million engines per year from Mexico to the U.S. by 1989. There are about 36 Big Three-owned *maquiladora* plants along the Mexican border exporting every type of labor intensive auto part from wiring harnesses to dashboards.[4] It would be appropriate for U.S. auto companies to say, like Pogo, "We have met the foreign competition—and they is us!"

But given their huge investment in the U.S., American companies could not shift all their production overseas overnight. Furthermore, it was still necessary to produce a substantial part of their cars and trucks where they were sold. Japanese companies themselves were opening assembly plants on American soil. U.S. management needed a way to increase productivity at its domestic plants if profits were to meet expectations.

The concessions that American managers had already received from the union—lump sums instead of wage increases, fewer holidays, combined classifications were not enough. But their success thus far indicated to American managers that there was more where the first concessions came from, that more could be wrung out of the workforce.

Two Roads to the Team Concept

Two distinct influences led U.S. managers to embrace the team concept. One is a continuation of the Quality of Work Life programs begun in the late 1970's and early 1980's. Using much of the same rhetoric of "participation" and "respect for the worker," team concept was seen as a continuation and higher stage of

QWL. Often the same people and the same corporate departments assigned to oversee the QWL programs were made responsible for implementing team concept. Like QWL, team concept typically involved the use of consultant firms and nominal involvement of the union in designing the programs.

The second influence was the success of the Japanese auto companies and, in particular, the Toyota-General Motors joint venture in California—New United Motors Manufacturing, Inc. (NUMMI). Team concept was imported along with other Japanese practices, such as "just-in-time" inventory systems, which seemed to explain the Japanese companies' extraordinary productivity.

Initially these two routes led to two different kinds of team concept plants, although by 1988 the two paths were converging. We will examine each of these influences in turn.

The QWL Road

Many of the early QWL practitioners saw teams as an advanced form of employee participation. D.L. Landen, one of General Motors' QWL pioneers, for example, envisioned an evolutionary process.[5] Landen, director of GM's Organizational Research and Development until 1982, held that quality circles represented a step toward employees having organized input into work decisions. Gradually, with the proper direction and training, responsibilities would be shifted downward to the employees, and the role of supervisor would change to being more of a resource person or advisor. The group would become a "semi-autonomous work group."

Developing gradually, the group would then become "totally independent." At this point, Landen says, a major restructuring based on "autonomous work groups" or "business teams" would be possible. The number of supervisors would continue to be reduced through attrition and the experienced supervisors would take on "new responsibilities such as planning, plant-wide problem solving, interfunctional coordination... "

This whole process, Landen argued, would take place because forces of world competition were forcing management (and the UAW) to come to their senses and do things the rational way. QWL practitioners delighted in telling stories of gross mismanagement which occurred simply because managers never thought to ask the workers who were actually doing the work. Once workers' input was allowed, management practices would become more sound and U.S. industry would be back on the fast track of world competition.

In the 1970's and 1980's some companies experimented with what were called "sociotechnical systems (STS)." Essentially STS was a reaction against the standard way of designing work: get the most modern technology, then make the workforce fit the technology. STS advocates argued instead that the proper way was to find the best *combination* of social arrangements—such as teams—with technology. In the jargon: "Jointly optimize the social and technical systems."

In some Western European countries, where the labor movement was willing to exercise its power to achieve workplace reforms, some of the work of STS practitioners reflected a pro-labor orientation. But in the U.S., STS was strictly a management project. STS advocates gained management's ear by promoting it as a productivity fad:

> Early system analyses suggested that sociotechnically designed plants might result in improvements in productivity and responsiveness and smaller workforce complements.[6]

Before the 1980's neither STS nor QWL were taken very seriously by mainstream auto industry management. GM did hope that such programs might prove effective in keeping unions out of its Southern plants. Technocrats in human resources departments were sometimes allowed to use entire plants for work reorganization experiments. But, in general, the QWL ideas were on the fringes. Center stage were new technology, marketing, and financial wheeling and dealing.

It was the 1979-82 recession which provided the impetus for QWL. The auto industry was in a crisis and there was a greater opening for new ideas. But most importantly, the United Auto Workers were on the defensive and management found that QWL programs were an effective means to undermine the union, get cooperation from the union, or get around the union.

A few of the early QWL experiments in union plants went so far as to use teams. In some Ford plants, Employee Involvement groups were organized according to "natural work groups." The Ford Rawsonville, Michigan plant, one of the first to give major local concessions, experimented with teams in some departments in the early 1980's. In 1981 GM instituted teams plantwide at its new Shreveport, Louisiana truck plant and at its Buick Factory 81 in Flint, Michigan.

Although the various plants that came to the team concept via the QWL road differ widely, certain themes emerge. First, the new programs are always advertised as being advantageous to all concerned. Nobody need feel threatened. Even if some job categories are eliminated (as are some levels of supervision in D.L. Landen's vision), job insecurities are soothed by the promise that any reductions will be through attrition.

Second, there is—or was—much confidence that proper training could solve any problem. After all, since the system was rational and ultimately produced the best possible solution, with enough training anyone could learn to overcome habits of the past. Most of the plants have heavily-financed training programs. In part,

the extensive training is used to win workers' allegiance to the team concept.

Third, there are ample provisions for everyone involved—workers, various levels of management, union officials—to "buy into the process" or become "stakeholders." In practice this often means elaborate new structures and highly desirable new jobs created for selected hourly and salaried workers to administer or "facilitate" the team concept. Often these positions become heavily involved in plant politics, and look like possible stepping stones into management. Dozens of joint committees requiring participation of union officers are developed to oversee the team concept operation, many of them requiring "off-sites" or conferences at resort locations. In other words, plenty of perks to spread around.

Fourth, the line between collective bargaining and joint activities, while maintained on paper, becomes blurred.

The Japanese Road

In the early 1980's Japanese companies began to open auto and truck assembly plants in the U.S., initially in an attempt to head off growing protectionist sentiment. Honda had been producing motorcycles in the U.S. since 1980. In 1982 it expanded its Marysville, Ohio operation to produce Honda Accords and four-door Civics. About 3,700 workers were employed. In 1985, Honda added an engine plant 40 miles away in Anna, Ohio.

Nissan opened its plant in Smyrna, Tennessee in 1983 and reached production capacity of light pickup trucks and Sentras with about 2,500 hourly workers.

Both operations duplicated the team organization and management practices used in Japan. All the "associates," as employees were called at Honda, or "technicians," as hourly workers were called at Nissan, shared common parking lots and cafeterias with management. There were "open door" policies to resolve differences.

Both Nissan and Honda claimed to achieve productivity and quality comparable to their Japanese plants. They therefore attracted the attention of American managers.

Management Resists Teams

Although American managers were interested in the Honda and Nissan plants and how they worked, it was still possible to miss their relevance for the rest of the U.S. auto industry. They were "greenfield" (entirely new) plants, each with a carefully selected workforce and substantial training in Japan. Most important, they had no union requiring negotiations or compromise. Surely these plants could not provide working models for an auto industry with long traditions, built-in interests, and unions.

Besides, management at both Honda and Nissan played their cards close to the chest. It was hard to know just what was happening in the plants and how well it was working.

In addition, American managers were doubtful that Japanese methods could be used in the U.S. Racial stereotypes were the explanation—stereotypes which demeaned both Japanese and U.S. workers (see Chapter 7 on myths about the Japanese). One stereotype said that the Japanese were more "docile" and willing to follow orders unquestioningly.[7] Another said that Japanese methods could be applied only in Japan because of its "homogeneous" culture, a culture which stresses values such as hard work and loyalty to the employer. This culture extended to management, which strove for the success of the company rather than individual grand salaries.

The emphasis on "homogeneity" had a strong undertone of racism. The United States, with its mix of races and cultures, was supposedly too "heterogeneous" to use teams. This was a code word for blaming Blacks and Latinos, who make up a sizable proportion of the auto workforce, for the problems American managers perceive in their employees.

Yet a third stereotype included a demeaning view of Japanese intelligence. The Japanese, the cliche went, were good at copying (and maybe this indicated that they were also sneaky), but they were not very imaginative or creative. After all, U.S. managers reassured themselves, the most useful practices we could learn from Japan, such as statistical process control and quality circles, were actually pioneered by Americans such as W. Edwards Deming and Joseph Juran.

And while the American version of teams through QWL had its proponents in every company, mainstream auto management also resisted the QWL version of the team concept. It was one thing to use QWL to co-opt the union. It was quite another to let the QWL advocates go so far as to reorganize the plant. Even in some of the new plants where teams were supposedly designed into the structure from the start, such as GM's Orion and Poletown plants, actual management practice differed little from that in a traditional plant.

The Search for an American Solution

Rather than borrowing from Japan, technology seemed to be the perfect answer. Problems with the "heterogeneous" U.S. workforce could be solved by using technology to organize, discipline, and replace workers. Advertisements in management magazines pointed out that robots never took coffee breaks, never objected to working out of classification, and never complained to their union steward.

GM's much publicized Saturn project was supposed to represent a giant leap forward in technology and in other areas as well, including materials, product design, dealer networks, and even work reorganization, enabling GM to produce an American-built small car that could compete with imports. Ford and Chrysler

soon followed with their own overblown pilot projects, Alpha and Liberty.

GM's new Orion and Poletown assembly plants best exemplify the technology strategy. By installing the very latest technology, GM hoped, with one massive leap, to learn about and establish the assembly plant of the future. In theory there was not a problem that a massive dose of technology could not solve. What would beat the competition was good old American know-how.

By itself, the technology strategy seemed to flop. The inefficiency and poor quality of the Poletown plant made it the symbol of the problems of new technology. These problems gave a new boost to the sociotechnical approach and to proponents of other QWL roads. The reason the technology failed, we were told, was because management hadn't understood that new technology required a different kind of workforce—a workforce that was involved and committed, flexible and multiskilled. And this in turn required a management and a structure which could develop this kind of workforce.

NUMMI Becomes the Model

If there was one single factor which erased management's reluctance to switch to teams, it was NUMMI. In just two years the Fremont, California assembly plant went from "interesting experiment" to *the* success story in U.S. automobile manufacturing. Despite vigorous denials from officials at all the Big Three companies, who hated to look like Johnny-come-latelies, by the end of 1986 NUMMI had become both the standard and the model for the U.S. auto industry, and especially for General Motors.

One reason that NUMMI became the shining star was that the other great hopes were fading. The glow of Saturn was badly tarnished by a steady stream of retreats, modifications, and delays. The technology strategy seemed to have failed, as exemplified by GM's high-tech Poletown plant which was riddled with inefficiency and poor quality. And Orion, which had invested heavily in extensive training and recruitment at start-up, was still at the bottom of GM's productivity list.[8]

In the meantime, NUMMI achieved stellar productivity and quality statistics for the Chevrolet Nova (a version of the Toyota Corolla). NUMMI made American managers sit up and take notice because:

1. The plant achieved massive increases in labor productivity. An internal video tape for GM managers proudly claims that the new plant requires only 14 hours of direct labor to assemble a Nova as against the 22 hours required to produce the J car in the same plant before the merger with Toyota.[9] GM circulates internal weekly comparisons on labor efficiency. The one for the week ending May 11, 1986 shows 21.2 total labor hours per vehicle at NUMMI as compared to about 37 hours at J car plants.[10] GM Vice-President George Eads says of NUMMI, "If GM were to be producing its current level of output at the NUMMI level of efficiency, we could be a company with the same volume of output

and have two-thirds the number of people."[11]

2. Despite the fact that the Nova start-up used new equipment, methods new to the workforce, and a new management—all conditions which create years of quality problems in U.S. manufacturing experience—quality at NUMMI quickly climbed and stayed at the top.

3. NUMMI achieved these feats, not with a new plant, but by taking over a traditional GM assembly plant.

4. The technology of the plant was not particularly advanced.

5. Most of the workforce had worked in the same plant when it was run by General Motors. At that time it had the reputation in management circles of being militant, with plenty of lost time for wildcat strikes, major absentee, drug and alcohol problems, and a lack of concern about product quality. Same workers, even many of the same union leaders, and yet a change in management transformed the plant to one noted for high productivity, cooperation and low absenteeism.

6. All of this was accomplished without a confrontation with the union. Indeed, local and national union leaders are some of NUMMI's biggest public relations boosters. UAW President Owen Bieber wrote:

> The NUMMI difference is that job design and the work process itself—the human technology—are extremely efficient. And NUMMI's productivity, achieved through balanced interaction of humans and machines, is the envy of the entire U.S. industry.[12]

By 1986 General Motors in particular was under terrific pressure to show some fast results. In that year Ford, with less than half of GM's market share, took home higher profits than GM. GM was widely criticized for its look-alike designs and was losing market share to Chrysler and Ford as well as to foreign competition. GM even came in for internal criticism, when board member H. Ross Perot charged that the company was mismanaged. GM was taking a beating in the esteem of the financial community and the media.

Thus GM turned to the NUMMI model as its

DID FORD HAVE A BETTER IDEA?

It is ironic that General Motors has attracted so much criticism from its comrades in big business when, in fact, much of what GM has done is just what the financial analysts ordered.

A few years previous, it had been a popular sport to criticize the auto industry for not investing for the long term, even if it meant short term losses. GM did invest for the long term with its new technology strategy. Technology always involves periods of debugging; the more technology the longer the period. But in 1986 and 1987 much of the criticism of GM management was because its investment in technology had not produced immediate results.

Ford, on the other hand, became Wall Street's darling because of its high profits—regardless of the strategy used to achieve them. Ford experienced heavy losses in the early 1980's and did not have as much money to invest in technology and new plants as GM did. The descendants of Henry Ford turned instead to a strategy of eliminating plants, paring the workforce to the bone, and then working both to capacity. The number of hourly workers at Ford dropped from 192,000 in 1978 to 102,000 in 1987—a cut of 47 percent—while production fell only 13 percent.[15]

A part of these labor savings was accomplished by scheduling immense amounts of overtime; the average hourly Ford employee worked 450 hours of overtime in 1986, nearly nine hours per week. But Ford also cut workers by gaining concessions from frightened local unions. As early as 1981, for example, three Detroit-area plants made significant concessions, such as allowing skilled trades work to be done by production workers, pruning inspectors, and

allowing more outsourcing[16]—all practices which foreshadowed those in the Japanese-owned U.S. plants. Ford's productivity increased 57 percent from 1981 to 1987, and by 1987 Ford's labor costs per vehicle were over $800 less than those at GM.[17] Ford's profit sharing payments of $3,700 per worker for 1987, so popular with its remaining workforce, were partly at the expense of the thousands of Ford workers who had lost their jobs.

In recent years, then, Ford has been able to show larger profits because it is getting more work out of fewer workers and operating at more efficient capacity levels[18]—while introducing the team concept only slowly. When in late 1986 and 1987 GM announced plans to cut capacity by 11 plants and to lay off 33,000 workers, it was beginning to catch up to Ford in the race to get lean and mean.

At the same time Ford is making plans to further squeeze its workforce by turning its attention to the team concept.

In April 1987, after threatening to close the plant, Ford completed negotiations for a local contract at its Romeo, Michigan engine plant. According to a management summary, "The negotiations resulted in the attainment of most of the Engine Division's labor relations wants."[19] The agreement includes production work teams with team members responsible for housekeeping and minor maintenance tasks. There will be no separate absentee replacement or relief operators. Skilled trades will be reduced to two classifications, and the union agreed to the subcontracting of cleaning services and to "cooperate with vendor equipment repairs under extended warranty contracts."

new savior. NUMMI was real and it was now—unlike the promises of the yet-to-be-built Saturn plant or of once-the-bugs-are-worked-out technology. And it was available for close examination by GM management. NUMMI demolished all the excuses that had prevented

John Z. Gelsavage

U.S. managers from using the Honda and Nissan plants as models.

In January 1986 D.D. Campbell, vice-president of GM and director of its CPC Group (in charge of the Chevrolet and Pontiac lines), circulated a document titled "Implementing the NUMMI/Toyota System at a GM Assembly Plant." Campbell urged that "we should spread the better parts of the NUMMI system as rapidly as we can."[13] R.M. Donnelly, manufacturing manager for CPC, headed an internal GM group to develop a "General Motors Production System (GMPS)." A presentation of that production system in November 1986 explicitly took NUMMI as a starting point and proposed that the first step of GMPS training should be in-depth visits to NUMMI.

If General Motors had its NUMMI from which to learn quickly, Ford and Chrysler had their own models. Chrysler is set up to learn from its joint venture with Mitsubishi, Diamond-Star. Ford and Mazda's Flat Rock, Michigan plant have a "special relationship" providing each the opportunity to study the other. When Ford planned to add a stamping unit to its Wayne, Michigan assembly plant, it sent workers to Japan and Mexico for training, not to Ford's established U.S. stamping plants. Models like NUMMI are also spreading rapidly in the auto parts industry through joint ventures, Japanese buyouts, and the establishment of new Japanese-owned parts plants.

For American managers the lessons of NUMMI were clear cut. You could take an ordinary factory with a unionized workforce and, by changing the management (and the contract), get productivity and quality that could compete with the Japanese. Japanese management techniques could be adopted wholesale and made to work in the U.S.

By 1987 this lesson had sunk home. A survey of auto industry executives found that there had been a complete turn-around in their cost cutting plans since 1985. In the earlier survey, automation was seen as the leading method for cutting costs, while management practices—"the management system and how the people work together"— was ranked 14th. By 1987 management practices were seen as the main way to cut costs, while automation had slipped to 17th.[14]

Management-By-Stress

After NUMMI, Japan became the vogue. Everybody who was anybody took trips to Japan to study management techniques. This included top UAW leaders. During negotiations for the 1987 contract, for example, the GM and UAW bargaining teams took a joint two-week study tour of the Japanese auto industry.

Some analysts view the adoption of Japanese methods as the "Japanization" of the U.S. auto industry. Yet, without denying the influence of Japanese industry, the term "Japanization" misses on several points. First, it contributes to the racism that already fogs the issues. Second, as the Japanese-managed plants around the

WHAT ABOUT SWEDEN?

Before Japan became the trend, many unionists had heard of "team production" mainly as a Swedish method. The Volvo factory in Kalmar, Sweden was reported to have found an alternative to repeating the same boring task over and over on an assembly line.

While these differences were exaggerated, they were significant. Team production at Kalmar still uses an assembly line. But rather than the continuous moving chain, car bodies are shuttled from station to station on moving platforms or automatic guided vehicles (AGV's). Each worker's job includes varied tasks and takes longer than a job in a U.S. plant. Workers like the AGV system because it sometimes allows them to build up a "bank" and then take a break.[20] The new Udevall Volvo plant now under construction will use still larger teams and bigger portions of the car will be assembled in each station.[21]

A Canadian union report on Kalmar pointed to the union's involvement in designing the plant and positive features such as low noise level, the control teams had over their immediate environment, and the ability of teams to independently vary their pace of work. The report also suggests that teams may be too isolated from one another and that, in comparison to other Metal Worker local unions, the Kalmar union had a weaker steward structure, lower membership involvement in union education, and a union leadership less willing to challenge management.[22]

Swedish unionists report that although they see advantages in the team system under certain conditions, it has not produced a utopia in the plants. The union maintains its adversarial role.[23] Kalmar management maintains computer control of the AGV's and can cause them to move whether or not a worker is finished with a task. While experimentation with long cycle times continues in other plants, a reorganization of Kalmar in 1984 reduced maximum cycle times from 20 minutes to four minutes.[24]

A 1985 report by a joint industry-union board pronounced Kalmar generally a success but also indicated that it was no final answer from the worker's point of view:

> The overwhelming majority of employees at Kalmar feel that the work organization... is either "good" or "fairly good." The jobs are deemed to be better than those on a traditional assembly line. However, even though the jobs are consistently given high ratings, many employees feel that assembly work gives too little room for the exercise of initiative and personal growth on the job.[25]

In 1986 the board reported that 75 percent of the workers felt they had little or no chance to influence their work.[26]

An important thing to bear in mind is that experiments with teams in Sweden and elsewhere in Western Europe have taken place in a political and social context very different from that in the United States: the workforce in Sweden is 90 percent unionized; "co-determination" in Germany gives unions more input into some policy decisions; the labor movement has more direct political influence through labor parties; workers' rights are better protected by the government; and the government plays a more direct role in industry and in maintaining levels of employment. Often team programs were initiated by the labor movement and reflected labor's confidence in being able to shape and control them—a far cry from the U.S. context where teams are designed by management and advanced as part of a general offensive against a retreating labor movement.

In at least one case, a European company has strongly opposed the team concept. Fiat agreed to raise wages at its newly acquired Alfa Romeo plant in order to get the union to give up teams and return to a traditional assembly line operation, with productivity increases and fewer workers.[27]

But whatever the virtues and problems of this Western European version of team production, it is *not* what U.S. auto companies have been trying to force on their workers. The few cases where U.S. auto management has shown some interest in the Swedish approach have been kept to deadends and side roads. Keith Brooke, one of GM's QWL specialists now working with the Saturn Project, describes a mid-1970's experiment with team production. Instead of using the assembly line, a team of four workers was allowed to lay out their work area and assemble an entire van in one location. The cycle time of the job was about two days. Brooke reports that the workers were so enthusiastic that they would get together on weekends to work out problems. As each van was built the workers put into it a photograph of themselves and a letter with their home phone numbers, inviting the customers to call them if they had any problems. Brooke had no explanation as to why GM dropped the project.[28]

Currently the media is playing up the new Buick Reatta Craft Centre in Lansing, Michigan, which is building a luxury sports car priced between $25,000 and $30,000.[29] Automatic guided vehicles are used, and the cars may remain at work stations for up to 30 minutes. At full running speed the plant will make only seven cars an hour. Each car will take about 82 hours of labor (compared to the target of under 20 in most team concept plants). Yet, despite the fact that neither the product nor the method of work have much in common with other team concept plants, the *New York Times* holds up the Reatta plant as the example of the team concept in the auto industry.[30]

world show (such plants exist in Britain, Mexico, Canada, and Spain, among other countries), the system does not require some special Japanese culture for either management or workers in order to operate effectively. Third, although the system was highly refined in Japan, many of the techniques, especially techniques in process control, were pioneered and developed by Americans and others.

The main point, however, is that the country of origin is not as relevant as the fact that these are *management* methods, adopted by employers of all nationalities for the purpose of squeezing unions and workers of all nationalities. Japanese workers are as much victims of this system as U.S., British, and Mexican workers are now coming to be. We prefer the term *management-by-stress* because, as we show in the next chapter, it describes how the system actually works. Management-by-stress uses stress of all kinds—physical, social, and psychological—to regulate and boost production. It combines a systematic speedup, "just-in-time" parts delivery, and strict control over how jobs are to be done, to create a production system which has no leeway for errors—and very little breathing room.

Management-by-stress (MBS) is becoming the cutting-edge model for U.S. managers in production industries. (They often call it "synchronous manufacturing.") Chapter 3 examines the components of the MBS system, and looks at the theoretical ideas behind it. The case studies of the NUMMI, Mazda and Nissan plants (Chapters 11, 17 and 25) provide examples of the management-by-stress system in its undiluted form.

Differences Among Team Concept Plants

Not all team concept plants are about to become exact duplicates of NUMMI and Mazda. Plants which became team concept earlier on, such as GM's Shreveport, Louisiana or Buick Factory 81 plants, took the "QWL road" to team concept, which we described earlier. It seems that such plants are moving toward a more complete management-by-stress system, but in their own way, rather than implementing it full-blown as NUMMI did. One indication of this is that workers in such plants complain that every year—or every month—management drops more and more of the friendly, "participatory" side of team concept.

In general, the later in the decade that a plant "went team concept," the more management-by-stress features it was likely to incorporate. The Van Nuys, California GM plant, for example, which began team concept in May 1987, based its system on NUMMI's and brought in trainers from NUMMI.

One reason that the QWL road, as opposed to a strict MBS model, still has some influence is the question of company politics. Those who have been in charge of QWL programs have a vested interest. It is embarrassing for the industrial relations experts and human resource managers to admit that they have been wasting their time on the "touchy-feely" QWL-type pro-

grams. They have tried to adapt their QWL rhetoric to fit the reality of what top management wants out of team concept. In that way, they can justify both what they have been doing and why they are still needed. Also, there are a few management people who believe what they say about dignity and will privately admit that they believe conditions at NUMMI to be inhuman.

Secondly, the existence of unions and long-standing traditions in existing plants makes for a different situation from that in greenfield plants. In some cases, management finds it easier to package new programs—such as team concept—with old wrappers—such as QWL—and, at other times, to put new wrappers on the same old stuff. The results, therefore, vary widely. How it all comes out depends on the peculiarities and internal company politics of local plant management, mixed together with the role of the local union, and reinforced or sabotaged by market conditions.

Searching for an "all-American" model, both management and UAW leaders have held up the Shreveport plant as a model when trying to get other plants to adopt the team concept. Since 1985 dozens of delegations of plant managers and local union leaders have taken tours through the Shreveport plant in preparation for team concept negotiations in their own plants. Chrysler managers told local union leaders who toured Shreveport in 1987 that this was the type of plant they were seeking. We have therefore described the Shreveport organization in considerable detail in Chapter 12.

Are team concept plants really operated differently from traditional ones? The answer is not a clear-cut yes or no even in individual cases. Instead it is useful to see these plants as being on a continuum.

At the low end of the continuum, some plants vary only slightly in day-to-day operation from traditional auto plants, with the exception that the union is weaker. Two examples are GM's Poletown and Orion plants.

Towards the middle of the continuum are Shreveport and GM's Fort Wayne, Indiana truck plant, where the team concept substantially affects the plants' "culture" and way of operating, for both workers and management.

At the high end of the continuum—with maximum speed-up and maximum rhetoric about worker participation—are the full-blown management-by-stress plants, NUMMI and Mazda.

Notes_____

1. For a full discussion of contract concessions, see Jane Slaughter, *Concessions and How To Beat Them*, Detroit, Labor Notes, 1983.

2. The development of QWL and its relation to unions is detailed in Mike Parker, *Inside the Circle: A Union Guide to QWL*, Detroit, Labor Notes/South End Press, 1985.

3. United Auto Workers Local Union Press Association, 1986.

4. *International Motor Business*, April 1986, cited in UAW Research Department, *Research Bulletin*, October 1987, pp.2-6.

5. D.L. Landen, "Beyond Quality Circles," D.L. Landen and Associates, February 1982.

6. Harvey F. Kolodny and Barbara Dresner, "Linking Arrangements and New Work Designs," *Organizational Dynamics*, Winter 1986, p.34.

7. In fact, the high productivity of Japanese factories is a product of extremely harsh discipline, a company union, and other sanctions, not willing acceptance by the workforce. See John Junkerman, "We Are Driven," *Mother Jones*, August 1982. The article is also reprinted as part of *Inside the Circle*, cited above.

8. Daniel Luria, "The Relations Between Work Rules, Plant Performance, and Costs in Vehicle Assembly Plants and Parts Production," paper prepared for "The Future of Work in the Automobile Industry," WZB Conference, Berlin, November 1987, p.18.

9. GM Technical Liaison Office, *This is NUMMI*, video tape for GM management, 1985.

10. General Motors, *D-150 Labor Performance Report—Passenger Assembly*, week ending May 11, 1986, No.36.

11. *Detroit Free Press*, June 8, 1987.

12. Owen Bieber, "Updating Labor-Management Relations Is Only Part of the Answer," *The Journal of State Government*, January/February 1987.

13. Internal memo from D.D. Campbell to L.B. Campbell, R.M. Donnelly, A.F. Platt, and D.G. Upton, January 22, 1986.

14. Arthur Anderson and Co., Delphi Survey, cited in Luther Jackson, "U.S. Automaker Work Force Cuts Forecast," *Detroit Free Press*, August 5, 1987.

15. Employment figures from Ford Motor Co.; production figures from *Automotive News Market Data Book*, 1979 and 1987.

16. *Labor Notes*, November 23, 1981.

17. "Ford Tops Big Three in Labor Cost per Vehicle," *Automotive Industries*, November 1987. This figure is *after* GM's labor costs are adjusted to take into account the fact that Ford does much more outsourcing than GM. GM builds 70 percent of every vehicle in-house, Ford 50 percent, and Chrysler only 30 percent. Ford is even more cost efficient than Chrysler, even though Chrysler is the outsourcing champion.

18. See Luria, "The Relations..." for a discussion of the relationship between capacity utilization and productivity measures.

19. "Summary of Understandings—Romeo Engine Plant," circulated among Ford management, n.d.

20. Stefan Aguren, Reine Hansson and K.G. Karlsson, *The Volvo Kalmar Plant: The Impact of the New Design On Work Organization*, The Rationalization Council, SAF-LO (established by the Swedish Employers' Confederation and the Swedish Trade Union Confederation), 1976.
Also, Steve Lohr, "Making Cars the Volvo Way," *New York Times*, June 23, 1987.
Also, Peter Unterweger, UAW Research Department, "Appropriate Automation: Thoughts on Swedish Examples of Socio-Technical Innovation," presentation to Industrial Relations Research Association Conference, Spring 1985.

21. *Automotive Industries*, November 1987.

22. Quality of Working Life Committee of the United Commercial Workers Provincial Council (QFL), *Toward an Improvement in the Working Conditions of Commercial Workers*, Montreal, June 1979.

23. Talk by Ingemar Goeransson, researcher, Swedish Metal Workers Federation, for UAW Local 600, Detroit, August 11, 1987.

24. Christian Berggren, "The Swedish Experience with 'New Work Concepts' in Assembly Operations," paper prepared for "The Future of Work in the Automobile Industry," WZB Conference, Berlin, November 1987, pp.11-14.

25. Stefan Aguren et al., *Volvo Kalmar Revisited*, quoted in Unterweger.

26. Cited in Berggren, p.12.

27. *Ward's Automotive International*, May 1987.

28. Speech to Strategic Planning and Management Forum, Troy, Michigan, September 18, 1986.
Also, Harvard Business School, "General Motors Corporation—Detroit Plant," Case 9-676-072, 1976.

29. John McElroy, "Reatta Craft Centre: Exploring the Low Volume Niche," *Automotive Industries*, November 1987.
Also, Michele Krebs, "Reatta Plant Eyes Bigger Role," *Automotive News*, August 3, 1987.

30. John Holusha, "A New Spirit at U.S. Auto Plants," *New York Times*, December 29, 1987.

3. Management-by-Stress: Management's Ideal Team Concept

Over the last decade, while the U.S. auto industry was in a tailspin, several Japanese automakers established factories in the United States: Honda in Ohio, Nissan in Tennessee, Mazda in Michigan, Mitsubishi in Illinois, and Toyota in California. These plants achieved stellar productivity and quality figures using management techniques imported from Japan. Toyota accomplished these numbers in a joint venture with General Motors, using a former GM plant and a United Auto Workers workforce (the joint venture is called New United Motors Manufacturing Inc.—NUMMI). More than any other single plant, NUMMI became the one for U.S. management to watch.

Although management uses the term "synchronous production" to describe this model, we have used the term "management-by-stress" (MBS) because it highlights the way stress serves as the force that drives and regulates the production system. This chapter examines the principles and underlying philosophy of the management-by-stress model.[1] Chapters 11, 17 and 25 on NUMMI, Mazda and Nissan provide more details of its functioning.

It is impossible to understand how a management-by-stress system works without seeing all of its features as interrelated and dependent upon each other. The remarkable productivity figures achieved by NUMMI cannot be attributed to any single policy. Instead management's success story results from a combination of the following:

1. Speedup—ways for workers to do more work in less time.

2. "Just-in-time" (JIT) organization of inventory and production.

3. Extensive use of outside contracting.

4. Technology designed to minimize indirect labor.

5. Design-for-manufacture—products specifically designed to reduce labor costs.

6. Methods to reduce scrap and rework.

7. Tighter management control.

As we will see, the approach in each of these areas depends heavily on a corresponding and consistent approach in the other areas.

Speedup: Stressing the System

Management-by-stress goes against many traditional U.S. management notions. It even seems to go against common sense. Isn't it logical to protect against possible breakdowns and glitches by stockpiling parts and hiring extra workers to fill in for absentees?

Instead, the operating principle of management-by-stress is to systematically locate and remove such protections. The system, including its human elements, operates in a state of permanent stress. Stressing the system identifies both the weak points and those that are too strong. The weak points will break down when the stress becomes too much, indicating that additional resources are needed. Just as important, points that never break down are presumed to have too many resources, and are thus wasteful.

The *andon* board illustrates how management-by-stress works. *Andon* is a visual display system, usually including a lighted board over the assembly line showing each work station. Most *andon* displays use one or two colors combined with chimes, buzzers or sirens. For illustration purposes, imagine a variation where the status of each station is indicated with one of three lights:

GREEN—production is keeping up and there are no problems.

YELLOW—an operator is falling behind or needs help.

RED—problem requires stopping the line.

In the traditional U.S. operation, management would want to see nothing but green lights and would design enough slack into the machinery and procedures so that an operation would almost always run in the green. Individual managers try to protect themselves with excess stock and excess workers to cover glitches or emergencies. CYA (cover your ass) is considered prudent operating procedure.

But in the management-by-stress production system, "all green" is not a desirable state. It means that the system is not running as fast or efficiently as it might. If the system is stressed (for example, by speeding up the assembly line), the weakest points become evident and the yellow lights go on. A few jobs will go into the "red" and stop the line. Management can now focus on these few jobs and make necessary adjustments.

A NUMMI manager explains the process to workers by comparing it to their experience when the plant was run by General Motors:

> Ever shut the line down? What happened? Everything broke loose. The plant manager, the plant superintendents, assistant superintendents, foremen, general foremen, everybody became unglued. We don't get unglued here. It's a different world. It's OK to shut the line down. It's OK to make a mistake. It's OK to cause a problem because that's an opportunity for us to change something and do something just a little better the next time around.[2]

Once the problems have been corrected, the system can then be further stressed (perhaps by reducing the number of workers) and then rebalanced. The ideal is for the system to run with all stations oscillating between green and yellow.

Stressing the system can be accomplished by increasing line speed, cutting the number of people or machines, or assigning workers additional tasks. Similarly, a line can be balanced by decreasing the resources or increasing the work load at those positions which always run in the green. In management-by-stress systems, extra resources are considered as wasteful as producing scrap.

There is an elegance to the idea that the system "equilibrates" or drives towards being evenly balanced. The logic of the system itself is to move towards what management considers perfection, by constantly readjusting and rebalancing to be ever more efficient. After years of observing waste in traditional plants, some people (workers as well as managers) are attracted to this vision of a smoothly functioning, rational, efficient management system. In engineering terms, it could be described as a tight control system with "fast response inner loops." The only problem is that human beings are the cogs in the system, not transistors, computers, and motors.

Just-In-Time

Just-in-time (JIT) is a "demand-pull" approach to production. This means that an operation does not produce until its product is called for by the next operation. A material handler does not replace stock until the line operation signals that it needs more. A department does not produce until it is signalled from the following department that more is needed. Just-in-time is best known because it allows (or requires) drastic cuts in in-

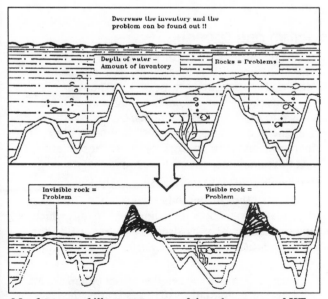

Mazda manual illustrates some of the advantages of JIT. The headline reads: "Decrease the inventory and the problem can be found out!!"

ventories. Instead of stockpiling parts at various points in the production process, management attempts to reduce stockpiles as nearly as possible to zero, and to organize production so that parts will arrive just as they are required.

There are several well-known savings with just-in-time:

1. Interest costs on the value of capital tied up in inventory. Depending on current interest rates, this amounts to between five and fifteen percent of the value of the material in inventory.

2. The cost of warehousing and storing the inventory. This includes the cost of the warehouse space, labor, management, and record keeping, as well as the cost of damage and losses that take place during warehousing. Savings are even higher when delivery is directly to the assembly line, rather than to a receiving dock.

3. Quality control is easier because there are fewer parts in the pipeline. When a part supply runs two days ahead of actual use, if a problem is discovered at the point of use, this means that two days' worth of parts will have to be repaired or discarded. But if parts production is running only minutes ahead of use, a problem can be corrected almost instantly.

By themselves these are powerful reasons for management to adopt JIT. But what about the traditional reasons for inventory? By maintaining inventories or banks, one part of the production system is cushioned from problems in another part—the "just-in-case" method. There is time to fix a problem before it affects the next section of the plant.

Consider an assembly operation under JIT. If a station in the middle stops, downstream operations must quickly stop because they have no supply. Less obvious is that upstream operations must also stop because the finished products have no place to go. Even if there were some place to stack parts, it is a violation of the operating principles of JIT to produce when there is no immediate demand.

These seemingly negative features of JIT become positive under a management-by-stress system. When a single point experiences trouble of any kind—whether difficulty meeting production or quality—there is no hiding. It becomes instantly apparent to all and is likely to affect operations far beyond the immediate trouble spot. Management at all levels will focus attention on the weak spot.

But how to deal quickly with problems allowed to surface through JIT? One option is to add resources to the weak spot. The production system could be designed with "flying squads" available to come to the aid of those workers having a problem.

But the characteristic response under management-by-stress is very different: pressure is allowed to transmit through to production workers, team leaders and lowest level management by making *them* solve the problem and catch up. There is no external assistance until management is satisfied that extraordinary efforts and all the resources available to the team have been used. And, as with the *andon* board, management can use JIT to identify those departments which never have a problem, and then trim their resources or add work until problems do start showing up. "Cushions" have no place in MBS.

The system assumes that pressure is the most effective way to motivate workers. For example, a Mazda manual describes a situation where a tire assembly station builds up a large supply of tires between itself and the installation point on the main line. What seems to be an advantage—that the main line will not have to stop if the tire assembly machine has a problem—is really a disadvantage. The manual explains that with the buffer there is not enough pressure on the operator: "When the trouble which occurred at the tire assembly station is found and corrected, the pressure to find the true cause of the situation is weakened."[3]

Stress, rather than management directives, becomes the mechanism for coordinating different sections of the system. The stress throughout tightly links the different parts to make the system "self-regulating" for management's purposes.

Ideally this means that top management only needs to make a few key decisions about the output required and the system will automatically adjust to produce that output to specifications as efficiently and cheaply as possible. Top management does not have to constantly monitor and direct specific production schedules in every department. Instead management only has to let the entire plant know the general level of planned production. As Yasuhiro Monden says of the Toyota system: "Only the final assembly line needs to be notified of changes in sequence for the entire plant's production to be modified accordingly."[4]

But this can work only if the material handler, supplier department, and supplier company are all firmly committed to deliver "just-in-time" despite any obstacles. In order to maintain this commitment over a long period of time there are penalties for failure. In the case of supplier companies, the penalties are financial. In the case of individual workers, the penalties include attention and pressure from management, reduced perks, undesirable new assignments, and possible discipline. That is why personal stress as well as system stress is required for MBS to keep running smoothly. A relaxed attitude—"I am just doing my job, I don't need to pay attention to anyone else's job"—makes the system inoperable.

That is also why management-by-stress relies so heavily on visual displays of the production system. When everyone can see who is responsible, more pressure can be brought to bear on those who fail to respond to the demands of the system. As Toyota managers put it:

> In the just-in-time production, all processes and all shops are kept in the state where they have no surplus so that if trouble is left unattended, the line will immediately stop running and will affect the entire plant. The necessity for improvement can be easily understood by anyone.[5]

Similarly, equipment breakdowns are clearly of greater consequence under JIT. One result is that there is a much greater emphasis on preventive maintenance. But when breakdowns do occur the system makes them highly visible, and tremendous pressure is put on maintenance workers to make repairs as quickly as possible, sometimes neglecting safety procedures. While this pressure also exists in traditional plants, in MBS plants the reduced number of maintenance workers, the change in job duties, the blurring of lines of demarcation, and the demands of JIT increase the frequency and stress level of "crisis" jobs.

Set-up jobs under JIT also become crisis jobs. Following the principles of JIT means that only small lots are produced at one time. This particularly affects stamping plants where relatively few large presses produce many different parts—but only one kind at a time. Under older systems it might require 24 hours to change a die in a press. Then the press would stamp out a part supply for a week or more before the die was changed for another part. But with the small batches required by JIT, many more die changes are necessary and the pressure is on to reduce the time per change.

There are amazing results. *Automotive Industries* magazine runs an annual die change contest. In 1987 the fastest team used two minutes and 28 seconds from the time the last of the old parts came off the press to the time the first good new part came off. The fastest teams were at the Nissan and Honda plants. Much of this swiftness is accomplished with design changes—major and minor alterations in the presses, dies, parts and tools. But a part of the speed comes from pressure to work quickly.

Taylorism and Speedup

At the turn of the century Frederick W. Taylor championed "scientific management," symbolized by the time-and-motion study "expert" with the stopwatch. Since then management has sought ways to break jobs down to their smallest elements, examine each work element, determine the fastest method to perform an operation, and instruct workers to use those methods. At the same time, unions have found that decent working conditions required limiting Taylorism.

Most of the current industrial relations literature portrays team production, including the versions which depend on management-by-stress, as a humanistic alternative to scientific management. *Business Week* editorializes:

> Such team-based systems, perfected by Japanese car makers, are alternatives to the "scientific management" system, long used in Detroit, which treats employees as mere hands who must be told every move to make.[6]

This is part of the fantasy being constructed around these management-by-stress systems. In fact the tendency is in the opposite direction—to specify every move a worker makes in far greater detail than ever before. The bottom line: far from a repudiation of scientific management, management-by-stress intensifies Taylorism.[7]

In management-by-stress plants, as in traditional plants, team members have very little control over the basic design of their own jobs. Management chooses the processes, basic production layout, and technologies to be used. These in turn largely determine job requirements and design. For example, when GM opened its Fairfax II plant under a new team agreement, workers thought they were going to have input into their job designs. They were surprised when they got called back to find that management had selected their team leaders, who (with industrial engineering) had already broken down the jobs into basic elements and laid the jobs out.

While the jobs are in fact designed by "teams," most of the original members of these teams are engineers, supervisors, and management-selected team leaders. They "chart" the jobs, that is, they break every job down to its individual acts, studying and timing each motion, adjusting the acts, and then shifting the work so that jobs are more or less equal. The end result is a detailed written specification of how each team member should do each job. Jobs are "balanced" so that the difference between *takt* time (number of seconds the car is at each work station) and the job cycle time (number of seconds for a worker to complete all assigned operations) is as close to zero as possible. (See Chapter 9 for a more detailed discussion of work standards.)

As production increases and bugs are worked out there are fewer and fewer changes made in job operations. Workers who are brought onto the team are expected to follow detailed procedures that have been worked over and over to eliminate free time and which specify how each motion is to be carried out. The team member is told exactly how many steps to take and what the left hand should be doing while the right hand is picking up the wrench.

Jobs are to be done in precisely the same way every time by every worker. If the charting calls for holding the part with your right hand and tightening with your left, that is how it must be done. The worker may not change the procedure without permission of a supervisor. The company explains that this is how quality is maintained. Why even chance a possible variation that might result from holding and tightening with opposite hands?

While this may be logical from an engineering point of view, it can be hard on the human element. Short people may find it easier to do a job differently than tall people. Sometimes it is desirable to change the way one is doing a job in the middle of the day to give some muscles a chance to relax and use others. The very rigidity of the system is illustrated by one Mazda team

leader's notion of flexibility: "We make allowances for people who are left handed."

But no matter how well workers learn their jobs, there is no such thing as maintaining a comfortable work pace. There is always room for *kaizen*, or continuous improvement. Whether through team meetings, quality circles, or suggestion plans, if you don't *kaizen* your own job someone else is likely to. The little influence workers do have over their jobs is that in effect they are organized to time-study themselves in a kind of super-Taylorism.

Monden gives an example: management wants to reallocate jobs on a team because five workers are working every second out of a minute and the sixth, worker F, has 45 seconds of waiting time. This waiting time, says Monden,

> should not be disposed of by distributing it equally among the six workers remaining on the line. If it were it would be simply hidden again, since each worker would slow down his work pace to accommodate his share of waiting time. Also, there would be resistance when it came time to revise the standard operations routine again. Instead a return to step 1 is necessary to see if there are further improvements that can be made in the line to eliminate the fractional operations left for F.[8]

Thus changes in a job can never result in more breathing space for team members. Any improvements become the impetus for management to find even more ways to speed up the team. Good-bye, Mr. F.

Appropriating Workers' Knowledge

Contrary to his current-day image, Frederick Taylor realized that workers do have minds and valuable knowledge. He insisted that the first duties under scientific management were

> the deliberate gathering in on the part of those on the management side of all the great mass of traditional knowledge, which in the past has been in the heads of the workmen and in the physical skill and knack of the workmen which they have acquired through years of experience.[9]

Management-by-stress systems seek to utilize a worker's sense of observation, recognizing this as a valuable tool which should not go to waste. Like Taylor, MBS seeks to harness that brain power by asking or even demanding that workers make available their thoughts about the production process. Workers make suggestions, and management may or may not accept those suggestions. But once the suggestion is made the knowledge becomes part of management's power to control every worker on the line.

Management-by-stress does differ from Taylorism in one regard. Taylor thought that he could discover production workers' secret knowlege of the manufacturing process all at once, and that workers would then revert to being nothing but hired hands. MBS managers, on the other hand, know that since workers continue to

MANAGEMENT
CONTEMPLATES
THE "PERFECT WORKER"...

©
'86 HUCK UE
AFTER ROBERT MINOR

JOB
COMBINATIONS
AND
SPEED-UPS

actually do the work, they continue to have knowl-edge about it that management observers do not enjoy—and therefore some power over produc-tion. So the MBS formula is not to try to take all decision-making power off the shop floor, but to shift that small amount that workers do have to lower level management or to those workers who identify with management. There are several elements to this:

1. Lower level management knows the produc-tion process because group leaders (first-level supervi-sors) regularly work the line—something forbidden by union practice in traditional auto plants.[10] (Taylor also advocated that management work on the floor with semi-skilled and skilled workers in order to develop cooperative relations.)

2. Team leaders, who rotate through all jobs and are union members, are often effectively incorporated into management. At NUMMI some 900 workers have taken the 30-hour (unpaid) training course to qualify for a team leader position.[11] Except for the fact that they lack formal powers of discipline, team leaders may have the full range of supervisory responsibilities and often come to think like supervisors. A key part of their jobs is to document worker knowledge for use by the actual supervisors.

3. Within the limits of the basic process and the technology used, group leaders have the main responsi-bility for designing jobs and adjusting them. At NUMMI there is no separate industrial engineering or time-study department. The group leaders and their team leaders have a vested interest in seeing that the ini-tial job design and charting they did during trial-build succeeds, and they are in a position to monitor the work continually.

4. Through charting, jobs are very tightly defined, and workers are not allowed to alter the way in which the job is done. A worker who believes she knows an easier or better way to do a job must share that knowl-edge with the team or group leader in order to get the group leader's approval. Similarly, job rotation under these circumstances forces workers to share their job knowledge with each other and with management. In traditional plants workers often share information with each other voluntarily. The fact that this sharing is vol-untary is a source of dignity and satisfaction. Further, having the choice when and when not to share informa-tion with management provides the worker with some bargaining ability. The choice to share with fellow work-ers allows peer group pressure against those who would be rate-busters.

While there is worker resistance to the tight con-trol over jobs, without union support it is not very pow-erful. Thus in the MBS system management can gather to itself the information about how things actually work in production—information often denied traditional management by its self-imposed or union-imposed isola-tion from the shop floor. This added knowledge allows management to increase its control over the finest de-tails of production. Without this detailed knowledge, at-tempts by management to exert exact control over the work process just couldn't work and the results would be laughable.

Lacking detailed knowledge of the shop floor, traditional management has to back off and allow work-ers some flexibility in how they do their jobs if anything is to be produced. This is not to imply that workers have substantial flexibility under traditional assembly line conditions. Rather, the fact that MBS systems seek to squeeze the tiny amount of worker autonomy and flexibility out of an already rigid system is an indication of the extremes that MBS systems will go to in order to exert discipline and control.

Absenteeism

Another key element in maintaining a taut system is the policy toward absenteeism. At NUMMI and Mazda, there are no extra workers hired as absentee replacements. A team consists of four to eight workers plus a team leader. The team members all have full jobs carefully assigned through the charting system. There is no slack. The team leader has no regular production job but performs an extensive list of assignments, some of which would be handled by the supervisor in a traditional plant. The team leader keeps track of absenteeism and tardiness, distributes tools and gloves, deals with problems of parts supply, and trains team members on new jobs. In addition, the leader helps out when a team member is having difficulty with a job, and fills in when someone needs relief or must go to the repair area to correct a defect.

If a member is absent, normally this means the team leader has to do the production job of the missing member. Then if team members need relief or help they must depend on the group leader (who supervises two to four teams), either to fill in directly on the job or to assign a leader or member from another team to help out.

Again, stress keeps the system functioning. All the difficulties of someone's being absent fall on those who are in daily contact with the absentee—the co-workers and immediate supervisor. The problems are not shifted upstairs by having the Personnel Department hire and maintain a "redundant" workforce to cover for possible absences. No department's budget is hurt by absenteeism. The system makes only the absentee's peers suffer.

Other team members find it harder to get relief when they need it. Because of the way jobs are set up, if

---

OTHER POINTS OF VIEW

This chapter paints an unlovely picture of life in a management-by-stress plant. It contradicts most of what is said in the glowing accounts of the team concept in the popular media. Where do those accounts come from?

Many stories about how workers feel about life in management-by-stress plants are based on reports of company officials, union officers or consultants who have some vested interest in the programs being declared a success. Some very positive descriptions are based on interviews at the time the plant was starting up.[13] As we have described earlier, the working conditions and the role of teams during the start-up period are transformed by the time the lines reach full production speed. Some reports are based on testimony by workers specially selected by the company to meet reporters. The distortions are then compounded by authors who know little about what life is like in a factory.

There is certainly a minority of workers in MBS plants who claim to love their work situations. There are even workers for whom the discipline, regimentation, and hard physical labor of MBS plants fit their personal needs and desires. There are also some workers who have received or hope to receive perks such as trips to Japan or promotions.

But there are several reasons why these accounts do not provide an accurate picture of life in the plants. And they mean even less about how the MBS system would be accepted if spread to still more plants and more workers.

1. Most of the new MBS plants were able to select their workforces from a huge pool of applicants. Over 130,000 applied to Nissan and 96,000 to Mazda. (NUMMI had a more restricted pool but was as selective as possible.) The companies had very careful screening processes, so that the workers at these plants are not a representative sample of working people.

2. The number of active supporters will probably continue to decline as the plants get older. Experience with Quality of Work Life programs shows that in the early stages of these programs workers are usually positive about them and tend to give management the benefit of the doubt, because workers would like to believe the promises of participation and respect.

3. Many workers privately admit to the pressures and the difficult pace—"eight hours of aerobic exercises," some have called it.[14] But they defend the company because it provides them with the only decent paying job they are likely to get. While many fear they will not be able to keep up with the pace when they grow older, they fear even more losing their jobs immediately. They accept the view that if the company were not run essentially the way it is there would be no jobs at all. They also believe that public criticism of the company will hurt sales and threaten their jobs.

4. The sense of fear in MBS plants is striking. The power exercised by supervisors, combined with little sense of either union presence or individual rights, chills the desire to criticize a plant where company loyalty is a priority. Many NUMMI workers have declined to be interviewed by reporters about their experiences in the plant, citing responses of management and fellow workers to previously published interviews.

the person covering the absentee's job has difficulty, it will interfere with the pace of the other jobs. As a result, team members tend to resent the absentee who, given the assumptions of MBS, seems to be the cause of the problem.

The team leader also has limited sympathy for the absent worker because he or she has to replace the absentee in addition to trying to keep up with normal team leader responsibilities. Similarly, an absent worker results in major changes for the group leader, who must now fill in on the line, shuffle people around, and/or lose the managerial services of the team leader.

The system is set up so that any variations in the company-determined operating arrangements place additional stress on those at the bottom. Because the jobs are already hard, survival and self-preservation produce enormous peer pressure against absenteeism. Several workers interviewed at NUMMI commented that they would like to have people who were absent too much removed from their group.

Peer pressure can be a powerful force in the workplace. Most of us have strong needs to be accepted and respected by the people we regard as our peers. In a factory where the discipline of the line increases alienation and a sense of powerlessness, the threat of losing this acceptance and respect is even more compelling. The harder the job is, the more workers depend on one another for even small instances of informal cooperation: moments of relief, humor, psychological support, watching your back, physical assistance, and information.

Management well understands the power of peer pressure and directs it to their own ends. Maintaining a "macho" atmosphere so that workers are made to feel like "sissies" for enforcing health and safety standards is one example. Of course, using peer pressure in this way is not new to MBS. Many group piece rate systems were set up so that workers would get angry at an absent group member because the replacement was not as fast and therefore held back the pay of the whole group. Under MBS, the stakes are raised from bonus payments to being able to survive on the job.

The pressure against absenteeism is reinforced during the hiring process. An applicant's attendance record is one of management's most important considerations in hiring. NUMMI's application form requires workers to specify the number of days missed each year for the previous five years and give reasons for absences in excess of ten days per year. A strict disciplinary procedure with harsh penalties further inhibits absenteeism.

The total system is successful in enforcing attendance. GM claims around two percent unscheduled absenteeism for NUMMI, compared to 8.8 percent for the whole corporation.[12]

Stopping the Line

"Workers can stop the line." This promise is the single feature that has come to symbolize the difference between MBS production systems and "the old way of doing things." The companies present this power as the foundation of their policy of respect for the humanity of workers. Monden says, "It is not a conveyor that operates men, it is men that operate a conveyor."[15]

Exactly how a worker goes about stopping the line differs from plant to plant and even within plants. At NUMMI, for example, "pulling the cord" results in distinctive chimes and flashing lights on the *andon* board. If the cord is not pulled again within a set time to cancel the warning (usually one minute) then the line will stop. In other versions, the worker may have a choice of buttons: yellow to sound the call for help, and red to stop the line. In some variations the worker can restart the line, while other variations require a supervisor to restart it.

The ability to stop the line is powerfully attractive. In the Big Three, a worker did not stop the line unless someone was dying. It didn't matter if a worker couldn't keep up or if scrap was going through. You tried to get the foreman's attention, and he could decide whether to stop the line (rarely) or leave the problem to be picked up or repaired further on (usually). In most plants stopping the line without a really good cause meant discipline. The decision to stop the line represented the boundary between the judgment of workers and the judgment of management.

Under MBS the right to stop the line is supposed to substitute for the cumbersome system of establishing work standards used in traditional auto plants. In traditional plants, the company industrial engineers or time-study experts determine the particular operations and time allotments for each job. The union contract requires employees and union to be notified when a job is to be time-studied, and prohibits management from setting standards under exceptional circumstances or by using exceptionally young, strong, nimble, or well-trained workers. Work standards, once established, cannot be changed arbitrarily except by repeating the contractual procedure. The union has the right to grieve work standards, and these are among the few issues that can be struck over during the life of the contract.

The contract specifies that when a tool, process, or part is changed, the old standards do not apply. Consequently, many jobs are operated without formal production standards. Even then, the worker has more protection than in a management-by-stress plant, because the contract language states that management cannot discipline workers for failing to keep up as long as they are working at a "normal pace." Under these circumstances, management pressures to force higher production could be effectively resisted by the union as "harassment."[16]

"But with the stop cord, why have all these bureaucratic procedures?" the argument goes. There is no need for contractual arrangements to change line speed or the number of tasks on a job if you have a system that trusts the worker. If the worker is making a genuine attempt, but cannot keep up, he just pulls the stop cord. There is—supposedly—no penalty.

This arrangement is written into the NUMMI contract:

> As part of the New United Motors production system, employees are expected to use their best efforts in performing the job within the *takt* time [production time per vehicle] and to alert their Group/Team Leader of production and quality problems. If the problem in production or quality is such that they cannot complete their tasks in the proper manner, they are expected, without being subject to discipline, to pull the cord or push the button to sound the alarm, and ultimately stop the line, alerting a Group/Team Leader of the problem. If the problem is of a recurring nature, the employees will work together to *kaizen* [seek to improve] the operation according to the procedure set forth in Appendix "C."[17]

The NUMMI contract specifically allows for easy change of production standards by the group leader. The union is not involved in the initial setting of such standards. Production standards are specifically not grievable but use a different procedure: if a worker is dissatisfied with a production standard, the first step is to try to work it out with the group leader. If this fails the worker can appeal to the Standardized Work Committee, composed of two management and two union representatives.

During trial-build and training periods "the cord" seems to work for everyone. It helps workers get assistance when problems come up, and it helps keep quality high even through all the problems of establishing a new line. It aids management in identifying problems so they can be quickly resolved.

However, once the job is well defined and most of the bugs are worked out, "the cord" can become oppressive. As the line is speeded up and the whole system is stressed, it becomes harder and harder to keep up all the time. Once the standardized work—so painstakingly charted, refined, and recharted—has been in operation for a while, management assumes any problem is the fault of the worker, who has the burden of proof to show otherwise. NUMMI rules provide for warnings, suspensions, and firing for "failure to maintain satisfactory production levels based on Company performance standards" (see Chapter 11). Stopping the line means the chimes and lights of the *andon* board immediately identify who is not keeping up. The pressure is also on the supervisor.

As a NUMMI manual explains:

> The role of the supervisor is to go to the trouble spot as soon as the *andon* displays the problem and find out what happened. If the line is stopped and there is no safety problem, the supervisor's first priority is to get the line back into operation as fast as possible. Then it is the supervisor's responsibility to find out the real cause of the problem, and take counter measures to make sure that the same problem cannot happen again.[18]

There is good reason for this pressure. An idle assembly line represents enormous costs in equipment and labor. Just-in-time can multiply these costs many times over. The system cannot achieve its legendary productivity if the line is stopping frequently. Thus once the line is up to full operating speed, supervisors do become "unglued" when the line actually stops.

A worker who is having trouble keeping up has four immediate choices, none of them good:

1. He can stop the line. This is likely to attract immediate and unhappy attention from the group leader.

2. He can work "into the hole"—farther down the line from his assigned position—to try to catch up. But it's hard to catch up when you're already working at maximum speed. And, like everything else in management-by-stress, the system uses peer pressure against working in the hole. Because jobs are so tightly charted, a worker who keeps working into another person's area may throw off that worker's pacing.

3. He can signal the team leader for help. But if the team leader has to spend all of her time helping one worker to prevent the line from stopping, then that leader is not available for other workers who might need to go to medical or just need temporary assistance—creating peer pressure again.

4. He can let the job go through uncompleted. Again the system works against it. Workers downstream are certain to pull the cord if they spot an incomplete job from a previous station. Not only does management teach workers over and over that this is their responsibility, but this is one instance when pulling the cord may get the downstream workers a breather at no cost to themselves. And attention is once again drawn to the unfortunate worker who has fallen behind—who has compounded his error by letting unfinished work go through.

Therefore, under the assumptions of MBS, the only solution is for workers to keep up with the line speed with no errors.

Reluctance to pull the cord thus translates into pressure to keep up with the job whatever it takes. Some NUMMI workers use part of their breaks or come in early to "build stock" or get ready for their jobs. When asked why they do it, they insist that there is no management pressure on them. The breaks are their time and they feel better using breaks to make their jobs bearable. But as this practice spreads, and the union does nothing about it, more and more workers will be forced by the system to use personal time to keep up. Thus the high productivity figures are partly the result of effectively forcing workers to work overtime for free.

Others just try to work harder. Some work "in the hole" in hopes of catching up later. A Mazda worker describes the Catch 22 in which a co-worker found herself:

> She had a hard time one day and pulled the stop cord several times. The next day management literally focussed attention on her. Several management officials observed and they set up a video camera to rec-

ord her work. She found herself working further into the hole. She worked into the hole too far and fell off the end of the [two-foot] platform and injured her ankle. They told her it was her fault—she didn't pull the stop cord when she fell behind.

Management is aware of workers' reluctance to pull the cord, although it provides a different explanation. Monden describes a situation in Japan:

> Because the workers' morale is so high, they often fail to stop the line when they should and even enter the next process to complete their assigned operations; i.e. they force themselves to finish their jobs in spite of the supervisors' instructions to stop the line if they are delayed or become tired.[19]

Toyota installed photoelectric cells in some stations to check for failure to complete all operations in the allotted time. Other checking devices include floor mat sensors that are triggered if an operator moves too far from the assigned position. These automatically shut down the line. Initially, workers did not appreciate this further limit on their own autonomy and

> resisted such limited forms of automatic controls because they were forced to complete their jobs within the assigned cycle time. [But after supervisors explained why these controls were necessary] the workers fully accepted the system, quality control improved, and the total time consumed by line stoppages was actually reduced.[20]

Thus with a fairy tale explanation, management installs electronic supervisors and electric tethers and automates the very item—the cord—that was supposed to symbolize workers' power over production.

The Multifunctional Worker

Everything in the management-by-stress system is tied together. A principle of just-in-time is that a worker never produces for stock even if there is nothing else to do. Extra stock is waste, and besides there is no place for it to be stored and no procedure to handle it. It is better for workers and machines to stand idle than to produce in excess of what is immediately needed.

Yet management also cannot allow idle time to be part of the system. Idle time reduces labor productivity. The system is designed so that any idle time is a visual indication that something needs to be adjusted. For example, a worker who can shave a few seconds from his or her cycle time should *not* take the initiative to help out fellow workers or find some task to be done. It is better to stand idle so that management and team members can see that there is some free time which can be assigned a regular task. If management allowed JIT to result in idle time as a normal situation, the value of idle time as a visual indicator would disappear.

If JIT forbids producing in advance, but idle time cannot be tolerated, the only way that the system can work is if production is organized so that jobs can be shifted and adjusted easily without disrupting the production process itself. This is particularly important in the auto industry where both the number of vehicles to be built and the model mix can vary considerably and quickly.

For example, one way to adjust production in a sales downturn is to slow down the speed of the assembly line. Slowing the line creates idle time for each worker. But if management can remove some workers and redistribute the tasks to the workers remaining in the team, most idle time can again be eliminated. The ease and speed with which management can redistribute tasks determines how responsive the plant can be to shifting demand. While all auto plants do this to some extent, the high responsiveness of MBS plants is a major contribution to their high productivity.

This management flexibility to easily redistribute tasks and eliminate idle time requires that:

1. Tasks must be broken down into the smallest units possible.

2. Each task must be well defined so it can easily be reassigned.

3. The skill level required for each task must be as low as possible.

4. Workers must be able and willing to do any task assigned.

5. Tasks must be arranged close together and in a way that decreases non-productive time walking between tasks.

One approach is to mix subassembly jobs with jobs on the main line. Such an arrangement, as illustrated below, allows workers to move from task to task in a circular pattern, reducing non-productive walking time. It also makes it easy for management to shift a task from worker A to worker B for line balancing, or to eliminate one worker and redistribute the tasks to those remaining.

Most significant is the requirement that workers be *able to do* and *movable to* any job management wishes. Management calls it "multiskilling," but this is a misleading term.

The *abilities* required in performing several related jobs of very short duration which have been carefully broken down by the charting process are manual dexterity, physical stamina, and the ability to follow in-

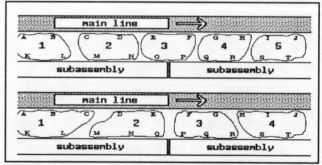

Mixing subassembly jobs with jobs on the main line makes it easy for management to balance the line by eliminating workers.

structions precisely. Even here management is careful to design jobs not to require exceptional amounts of any of these, because they want to be able to assign workers interchangeably. These are not "skills" in the usual sense of requiring training and specialized knowledge. The essence of "multiskilling" is actually the *lack of resistance*, on the part of the union or the individual worker, to management reassigning jobs whenever it wishes, for whatever reason.

During hiring, MBS plants have shown little interest in applicants' skills acquired from previous work and much more interest in attendance records, ability to follow directions, physical stamina, and general attitude toward management. Once hired, the worker does not benefit by learning more marketable skills. Instead, she learns how to carry out a large number of extremely "job-specific" tasks. Each such task requires little training in the sense of learning new skills—rather they require practice in order to learn to do them quickly enough. The issue of multiskilling thus becomes less an issue of training than it is of overcoming any barriers such as union contract provisions, classifications, or traditions that prevent workers from doing more than one job. What training there is focuses more on company procedures and values than on marketable technical skills (see Chapter 8).

Outsourcing

The UAW-NUMMI contract specifies that the company will take "affirmative measures," including "assigning previously subcontracted work to bargaining unit employees capable of performing this work," before laying off any employees. This arrangement, a variant of the system used in Japan, is being interpreted in this way: as long as the company guarantees the jobs of all regular workers, the union will not object to outside contracting (employees of an outside firm do work in the plant, such as cleaning) and outsourcing (parts bought from outside firms). Outside contracting and outsourcing are extensive at both NUMMI and Mazda.[21]

The deal seems to provide job security, but in reality the job security is *less* than if the work were not outsourced and the plant had traditional seniority protections during layoffs. Say the MBS assembly plant has 1,000 workers, and there are 200 workers working at a supplier company nearby making seat cushions. If sales decline, which would normally cause the layoff of, say, 200 assembly workers, the assembly plant is committed to bringing the seat cushion work into the plant, in order to keep those 200 assembly workers on the job. (Whether management would actually follow through on this commitment during a downturn, given the investment required, is another question.) The 200 cushion workers at the supplier company would all lose their jobs, in favor of the assembly workers.

Now let us look at the same situation in a traditional assembly plant of 1,200 workers. This plant includes a cushion room because the union was able to prevent the company from outsourcing the cushion work. When sales decline, the lowest 200 or so workers are laid off, plant-wide. There are still 1,000 workers on the job and 200 on the street—but the laid-off workers have recall rights to their union plant.

The 1,000 MBS workers, who supposedly received job security in exchange for outsourcing, have not gained any more job security in comparison with the 1,000 highest-seniority workers in the traditional plant. All the MBS workers have achieved is to isolate themselves from the cushion workers, who now work for a different company for lower wages and with less job security.

Thus the job security that the deal provides is of the "see no evil" variety. Management divides workers into two tiers—those at the main plant, protected by the union and the paternalism of the company, and those at the supplier plants, usually non-union, who have no protection from layoffs and no supplementary unemployment benefits as the unionized workers do.

In the long run, of course, jobs are lost by attrition even at the main plant.

Union endorsement of this kind of arrangement gives substance to the charge that unions attempt to protect the elite few at the expense of poorer, less protected, workers—who also turn out to be disproportionately women and minorities. Such a policy also makes it all the more difficult for unions to organize the increasing number of non-union supplier plants.

Outsourcing accounts for some of the supposed savings of just-in-time. The assembly plant gets rid of the costs of holding inventory, but the supplier company is forced to maintain inventory (even renting warehouses near the JIT customer) so it can supply exactly when the assembly plant "pulls." Mazda, for example, has plans to rent warehouse space on its Flat Rock, Michigan site to suppliers. The supplier must also inspect its products and bear the costs of delivery directly to the line. Thus inspection, material handling, rework, and clerical jobs are all still being performed. But the work is removed from the bargaining unit and contracted out to the lower paid, typically non-union suppliers.

Often the only economic pressure which constrains management to produce subassemblies in-house is the need to control them very closely. For example, most assembly plants used to have their own cushion rooms for seat upholstery partly because of the need for the right color and style to go in the right car. With greater main plant control over suppliers, the trend in recent assembly plants is to outsource the cushion work. At NUMMI, for example, Hoover Universal delivers the proper color and style seats every few hours. As the procedures for JIT deliveries direct to the line are improved, more and more subassemblies will be outsourced.

Similarly, because the MBS system is built on standardizing and regularizing all work, jobs that do not neatly fit this pattern, like construction work and landscaping, are also contracted out.

Use of New Technology

NUMMI management points with pride to the fact that it has succeeded without the most advanced technology. This has led many, both in management and in the union movement, to see in NUMMI an alternative to the high tech approach to productivity.

At NUMMI Toyota chose a conservative approach to technology because it was dealing with its first plant in the U.S. and a special relationship with General Motors and the United Auto Workers. Even so, while the plant does not represent the cutting edge in new technology, it is not far behind. Mazda is even more modern. In 1986 Nissan management claimed that its Smyrna, Tennessee facility had more robots than any other U.S. assembly plant.[22] Honda has announced elaborate plans to install a new system in its Ohio plant which is supposed to automate 80 percent of vehicle assembly and triple productivity.[23]

Management-by-stress systems have a coherent approach to technology. Automation is not done for its own sake. Labor is divided into two kinds. On the one hand is direct or "value-added" labor. This is direct work on or assembly of materials which increases the value of the product. On the other hand, almost everything else is "non-value added" or indirect labor. This includes material transfer and handling, most inspection, maintenance, and cleaning. There is a heavy emphasis on reducing non-value added labor.

Since the focus is on simplifying, standardizing and regularizing work, any technological change which essentially replaces a production worker with an indirect "non-value added" job is rejected. For example, from an MBS point of view a machine which replaces one production worker but requires an additional electrician to be in the area is a bad idea. Secondly, the automation must increase management flexibility, not decrease it. The approach can be seen in Monden's warning about possible problems with automation:

> Even if the introduction of an automatic machine reduces manpower by 0.9 persons, it cannot actually reduce the number of workers on the line unless the remaining 0.1 person...can be eliminated...
>
> [Automation] often has the undesirable effect of fixing the number of workers who must be employed at a given workplace...regardless of production quantity...
>
> In both respects the introduction of [automation] may actually eliminate the ability to reduce the number of workers—a matter of some concern, since it is always essential to reduce the workforce, especially when demand decreases.[24]

The emphasis in MBS plants, then, is on small automation which improves the functioning of the system—*jikoda* or "autonomation," as it is called at NUMMI and Mazda—rather than on sweeping changes which transform basic manufacturing methods. These terms refer especially to technology which is used to detect production problems and which automatically stops operations. MBS plant engineers, then, concentrate on such changes as installing a photoelectric cell that shuts the line off if a part is not installed properly.

At the same time the MBS system also makes it easier to introduce larger technologies, in two ways. First, by requiring workers to do jobs in very exact ma-

---

SOME NEW TERMS

A number of Japanese terms have become part of the daily language in management-by-stress plants.

Andon—A system of visual displays. The *andon* lighted display board over a work area shows which work stations are not keeping up.

Jikoda—Sometimes used to refer to automation generally, or more specifically to automation which checks for defects and automatically stops the process. Sometimes called "autonomation."

Kaizen—Process of constant improvement. Sometimes used as a verb—to solve a problem or to fix, as in "we have to *kaizen* that machine."

Kanban—The cards attached to parts in Toyota's just-in-time "demand-pull" system. As the parts are used or transferred the *kanban* are removed and used to request (order) replacements. The term is sometimes used to refer to the whole just-in-time system.

Three M's:

Muda—Waste. Scrap production, overproduction, idle time, wasted time, inefficient process.

Muri—Overburden. Overloading a piece of equipment or a person.

Mura—Unevenness. Inconsistent use of a person or machine.

Four S's:

Seiri—Removal of unnecessary material and equipment.

Seiton—A place for everything and everything in its place.

Seiso—Cleaning the equipment and area.

Seiketsu—Practicing the above three to keep the workplace neat and clean.

Takt—Effectively, the amount of time the vehicle is at each operator's station. More generally, calculated by taking number of minutes the line or process is running and dividing by the total production planned. Usually measured in minutes or seconds per unit, it is the inverse of the more traditional measure of line speed in units/hour. Example: if a line is to produce 500 vehicles in a 450-minute (7.5 hour) work day, the *takt* time would be .9 minutes or 54 seconds per unit. The line speed in this case would be just under 67 units per hour.

The Five Why's—Asking "why" at least to five levels to get at the root cause of problems in order to correct them.

chine-like ways, management uses workers as prototype automation. Second, since management can flexibly assign workers to new duties and the system forces "cooperation," many of the usual problems of introducing automation are reduced.

Thus, MBS plants are not likely to be an alternative to high tech plants. While they may not install unproven technologies which require highly skilled operators and maintenance backup to overcome "bugs," MBS plants will very quickly install and modify technologies once they are proven elsewhere.

Design-for-Manufacture

It used to be that cars and other products were designed with only the market in mind. Once designed it was the manufacturing engineer's job to figure out how to mass produce the design as cheaply as possible. Now the idea is to design the product from the very beginning with an eye toward decreasing production costs and minimizing labor required. How the product is designed in large part determines how it is produced. One German estimate is that 70 percent of the cost of the automobile is already determined at the design phase and only a ten percent variation is possible through the whole production phase.[25]

MBS fits particularly well with design-for-manufacture (DFM). The detailed charting process provides design engineers with the kind of data they need to calculate production time into their designs. Similarly, the high degree of flexibility management has in determining exactly how production will be carried out allows for better integration of design and production. Product design is one of those areas of so-called management rights which unions have rarely challenged but must begin to do so. From a worker's vantage point it makes little difference whether a job is lost after production begins, when management designs a robot which can weld two pieces together, or whether a design change eliminates the need to put those pieces together in the first place.

Tighter Management Control

In business circles, proponents of the team concept emphasize that one of its principles is to push decision making and responsibility to the lowest levels of the organization. As we have seen, responsibilities (in the sense of demands on the individual worker) are pushed down as far as possible to the workers on the line. But the power and control which determine how these demands are to be met are pushed down only to the group leader level. Thus it is the group leader who controls the detailed setting of work standards to which the hourly worker must adhere.

Keeping the system stressed is the key to tighter managerial control with fewer managers. If a worker is off the job, slows down, falls behind, or does something incorrectly, the tightness of the system itself makes the lack obvious, even faster than in a traditional plant. Less supervision is needed because management observers are not required to identify trouble spots; the system does this either through visual indication or by breaking down. Management can concentrate on dealing with the trouble spots. As Toyota managers put it:

Control of abnormality becomes easy. It will only be necessary to make improvements by directing attention to the stopped equipment and the workers who did the stopping.[26]

Further, a supervisor gets less interference from the union than under a traditional contract. In the MBS system, job standards are not protected or policed by the union; supervisors can change work standards or work assignments at will. In a traditional plant workers sometimes protest by working to the letter of the rules. There can be no "work to rule" when all the rules are made by the supervisor.

And What About Teams?

In management and union circles, as well as the popular press, the system we have described as management-by-stress is referred to as the "team concept." Yet we have made few references to the functioning of teams. In the actual operation of the plant—as opposed to the ideological hype—"teams" is simply the name management gives to its administrative units. For the most part, if we substituted "supervisor's sub-group" for team and "sub-group leader" for team leader, understanding of management-by-stress would not suffer at all.

There is, however, some reality to the popular notions about teams. Some teams meet and discuss real problems. When the lines move slowly enough workers can and do help each other out. But this is most likely during initial start-up when the "teams" often consist mainly of supervisors, engineers and team leaders. Once the line is up to speed, jobs are specified in detail and each worker can barely keep up with his or her own job, let alone help someone else out. Besides, the system does not like regular initiative or uncharted actions on the line. When the system is running at regular production speed, team meetings tend to drop in frequency. Some workers at NUMMI complain that months pass between team meetings. In other cases team meetings are nothing more than shape-up sessions where quality or overtime information is transmitted to the workers or a supervisor announces changes in assignments.

When management talks to itself about what makes the system work, teams, in the sense of teamwork or team meetings, are rarely mentioned. In his description of Toyota, considered *the* reference by many NUMMI managers, Yasuhiro Monden does not use the term "team" at all. He does describe the mandatory Quality Control Circlés made up of "a foreman and his subordinate workers." In the entire 230-page book explaining the production system, discussion of these circles totals seven pages, and much of this discussion covers the suggestion system and its rewards.

Similarly, John Krafcik, an MIT researcher and a

former quality control engineer at NUMMI, lists teams as one of the reasons for NUMMI's success. But in describing them, Krafcik discusses only the supervisory duties of the team leader ("although a UAW member") and the peer pressure against absenteeism, not any supposed team powers or problem-solving functions.[27]

The Union

Management-by-stress is truly a lean and mean system. In tightly connecting all operations, consciously seeking to strip out all protections and cushions, and making all parts of the system almost instantly responsive to change, management-by-stress becomes a highly efficient system for carrying out management policy.

But these same strengths also create a potential Achilles heel for management. The responsiveness of the system to basic management decisions means that a single miscalculation outside a limited range can bring the system down.

Many of the new management techniques to increase productivity also make unions *potentially* more dangerous. If workers *collectively* take certain actions the system becomes extremely vulnerable. One industry publication contains the warning that with just-in-time, "unions have a lot more power than they did before."[28] The action of workers in one department can immediately affect the entire operation, both upstream and downstream. The visibility used by management to maintain stress also becomes the way that workers throughout the plant know that something is up.

The key word is "collectively." The system easily handles individuals and small groups who resist. The

visual display techniques combined with the appropriation of worker knowledge, the detailed charting of all jobs, the multiskilling, the role of team leaders, and the fact that supervisors regularly work the floor make it relatively easy for management to identify and replace "troublemakers."

But suppose everyone starts pressing the stop button in an organized campaign to let management know that the line speed is too fast or that they need absentee replacements. It is no longer a case of isolated troublemakers, and management can no longer contain the problem. An organized slowdown, sickout, or other job action affecting a sizable minority in a department can disrupt the entire plant. If team members are unified and refuse to cooperate with a management-appointed team leader, the team can effectively force management to appoint a leader of the team's choosing. And if union consciousness is strong and the union backs the team leader, the team leader and team meetings can be used to organize for workers' demands.

While collective action gives power to workers in both traditional and MBS plants, the MBS plants are particularly vulnerable to workers' small scale shop floor actions. But collective action of this kind takes organization—the kind provided both formally and informally by unions.

In MBS plants the union's relationship with management must be settled from the beginning. MBS operates by putting stress on workers. It cannot operate for long with a union that fights stressful jobs and organizes its members to challenge management on the shop floor. For MBS management there are two alternatives: either prevent unionization in the first place, or keep a subdued union which helps prevent any collective action and defuses any sense of solidarity and militancy on the shop floor. There is no room in MBS for a union which sees itself as representing the interests of workers and actively organizes its members to achieve their own interests.

Personal Stress

Applied to the world of inanimate objects, the word "stress" simply means pressure or force. It is neither good nor bad. Increasing stress will tend to cause a piece of metal to deform or break—a desirable result if the metal is being stamped into a fender, but undesirable if the metal is a bridge support. In most mechanical situations, stress can be continuous as long as it is below a certain point.

But stress is much more complicated in human beings. Some forms of stress contribute positively to a person's health. Participation in an aerobic activity, such as running, conditions skeletal and heart muscles by subjecting them to small

INDIVIDUALS CAN BE EASILY HANDLED BY THE SYSTEM

COLLECTIVELY, THE SYSTEM BECOMES MORE VULNERABLE

Ted Rall

doses of stress followed by periods of relaxation. The stress response also helps prepare the body to deal with emergencies. The cascade of physiological changes that takes place when a person is faced with a dangerous situation is often called the "flight or fight" reaction. The increased production of certain hormones allows for exceptional effort, including seemingly "superhuman" feats such as lifting a truck off a trapped co-worker.

Yet stress can also kill. Continued long-term stress over which the individual has no control, when the high hormone levels and other physiological changes become the body's normal state, has well-established links to heart disease, asthma, ulcers, diabetes, depression, drug abuse and alcoholism. Research on animals has shown a direct relationship between "inescapable stress" and suppression of the immune system cells involved in fighting cancer.[29] The primary hormone released in response to stress, cortisol, suppresses the immune function generally and kills certain brain cells.[30] Chronic stress contributes to accidents and family problems. High continued stress levels can be particularly dangerous because a person can believe he or she has "gotten used to" stressful environments even while the body maintains its high reaction to stress.[31]

What kind of jobs generate the greatest stress? Researchers have found that a combination of high job demand and low job control produces the maximum stress.[32] Contrary to the popular belief that stress is the burden of top executives, studies have shown that the most stressful jobs include inspectors of manufactured products, material handlers, public relations workers, laboratory technicians, machinists, laborers, mechanics, and structural-metal craftpersons.[33]

It is not just the work itself which creates stress in management-by-stress plants. For all the public talk about their new job security, interviews with NUMMI workers reveal that fear of the plant closing is uppermost in their minds and often justifies everything that happens in the plant. The fact that the system is so inflexible when it comes to workers' personal needs also generates stress. (What kind of job could I do in this plant if I were injured? How do I get time off for a personal problem?)

Management-by-stress plants often deal with some of the causes of stress through such things as paying attention to tool design. They may also have individual counseling and exercise programs to help relieve some of the symptoms of stress. (Such programs also, of course, can contribute to a "blame the victim" outlook.)

But overall the system itself multiplies personal stress by continually increasing the demands on the individual while reducing personal control.

Respect and Dignity for the Individual

Toyota and NUMMI claim that dignity and respect for the individual are key to their management theory. Toyota managers describe the system as the "respect-for-human" system. Evidence of this respect certainly exists. Visitors to the NUMMI plant are struck by the plant's atmosphere. Workers are addressed using courteous language. The plant is clean and well lit and seems like a nice place to work.

At the same time operation of the plant indicates a very peculiar notion of humanity—that human fulfillment is achieved only by striving for management's goals. Monden displays this management mentality:

> Reductions in the workforce brought about by workshop improvements may seem to be antagonistic to the worker's human dignity since they take up the slack created by waiting time and wasted action. However, allowing the worker to take it easy or giving him high wages does not necessarily provide him an opportunity to realize his worth. On the contrary, that end can be better served by providing the worker with a sense that his work is worthwhile and allowing him to work with his superior and his comrades to solve problems they encounter.[34]

In management-by-stress plants, workers are expected to believe that personal illness or family needs must take second place to perfect attendance. Personal time is at the beck and call of the company. Mazda tells its workers to arrange their personal lives so they can work ten hours every day although management may only assign them eight.[35] Workers' "human" qualities are manipulated so that peer pressure works to achieve management's ends. The view that a paternalistic management endows workers with dignity by reducing the workforce and increasing the workload of those remaining may be a convincing rationalization for the managerial mind. But unions have different goals and need a different definition of human dignity. We look at what humanized working conditions could entail in the next chapter.

Notes

1. We have drawn heavily on the views of Toyota management as described in *Toyota Production System* by Yasuhiro Monden, an industrial engineering book endorsed by senior Toyota managers (Yasuhiro Monden, *Toyota Production System: Practical Approach to Production Management*, Industrial Engineering and Management Press, 1983). We have also used documents and video tapes developed by General Motors for internal management use, as well as training materials developed by NUMMI and Mazda. Finally, and most importantly, we have looked at the day-to-day operation of NUMMI and Mazda by interviewing workers from both those plants.

2. General Motors Technical Liaison Office, *This is NUMMI*, video tape for GM managers, 1985.

3. *MMUC Production System: Concept and Outline*, Mazda Motor Manufacturing (USA) Corporation, 1986.

4. Monden, p.65

5. Y. Sugimori, K. Kusunoki, F. Cho, S. Uchikawa,

"Toyota Production System and Kanban System," 1977, reprinted in Monden, p.211.

6. *Business Week*, August 31, 1987.

7. Two excellent pieces with analyses similar to that presented here are Knuth Dohse, Ulrich Jurgens, and Thomas Malsch, "From 'Fordism' to 'Toyotism'? The Social Organization of the Labor Process in the Japanese Automobile Industry," *Politics and Society*, Vol. 14, No. 2, 1985; and Peter J. Turnbull, "The Limits of Japanisation—Just-In-Time, Labor Relations and the UK Automotive Industry," to be published Autumn 1988 in *New Technology, Work, and Employment*, Vol.3, No.2.

8. Monden, p.122.

9. "Testimony to the House of Representatives Committee, 1912" in Frederick Taylor, *Scientific Management*, New York and London, Harper and Brothers, 1917.

10. The actual NUMMI contract language on supervisors working is not that different from that in traditional contracts. Both reserve bargaining unit work for bargaining unit members. Both have exceptions and loopholes. Although the loopholes are bigger at NUMMI, the main difference is past practice and union enforcement. The result is that supervisors seldom work very long on bargaining unit jobs in traditional plants. When they do the union files a grievance and often a penalty is paid to union members. This policy was traditionally considered a point of union honor because it protects union jobs and gives workers some small power over management. It is common in MBS plants, however, to see supervisors and even higher management working the line, and to do so is even a matter of company pride.

11. Tetsuo Abo, "The Application of Japanese-Style Management Concepts in Japanese Automobile Plants in the U.S.A.," WZB Conference, Berlin, November 1987.

12. *Detroit Free Press*, January 25, 1988.

13. Jeff Stansbury, "NUMMI, A New Kind of Workplace," *UAW Solidarity*, August 1985.

14. John Junkerman, "Nissan, Tennessee," *The Progressive*, June 1987. Reprinted as Chapter 25 in this book. This expression or a variation is also used at the NUMMI and Mazda plants.

15. Sugimori, p.211.

16. See for example, *Agreement Between Chrysler Corporation and the United Auto Workers*, Production and Maintenance, Section 44, October 26, 1985.

17. *Agreement between New United Motors Manufacturing, Inc. and the UAW*, July 1, 1985, XXVII (1.2).

18. *Toyota Production System 2*, Toyota Motor Corporation, June 1984, p.52.

19. Monden. p.144.

20. Monden, p.145.

21. For international trends in outsourcing see Michael A. Cusumano, *The Japanese Automobile Industry: Technology & Management at Nissan & Toyota*, Cambridge, Harvard University Press, 1985, p.189.

22. David Kushma, "East Meets West on the Line," *Detroit Free Press,* November 2, 1986.

23. *Detroit Free Press*, December 30, 1986.
Also, Louise Kertesz, "More U.S. Hondas Due for Dealers," *Automotive News*, May 18, 1987.

24. Monden, p.124.

25. Wolfgang Reitzle, cited in Ulrich Jurgens, Knuth Dohse, Thomas Malsch, "New Production Concepts in West German Car Plants," WZB, Berlin, December 1984, p.5.

26. Sugimori, p.210.

27. John Krafcik, "Learning From NUMMI," Internal Working Paper, International Motor Vehicle Program, Massachusetts Institute of Technology, September 15, 1986.

28. *Manufacturing Week*, August 3, 1987.

29. L.S. Sklar and H. Anisman, "Stress and Coping Factors Influence Tumor Growth," *Science*, August 3, 1979, pp.513-515.

30. R. Sapolsky, "Glucocorticoids and Hippocampal Degeneration," *Abs.,* 69th Annual Meeting of the Endocrine Society, Indianapolis, June 1987, p.9.

31. Communications Workers of America, *Occupational Stress: The Hazard and the Challenge*, Instructor's Manual, 1986.
Also, National Institute for Occupational Safety and Health, U.S. Department of Health and Human Services, *Stress Management in Work Settings*, May 1987.

32. "Jobs Where Stress is Most Severe: Interview with Robert Karasek," *U.S. News and World Report*, September 5, 1983.
Also, Lee Schore, "Occupational Stress: A Union Based Approach," Institute for Labor and Mental Health, Oakland, California.
Also, John Holt, "Occupational Stress," in Leo Goldberger and Shlomo Breznitz, *Handbook of Stress*, New York, The Free Press, 1982.

33. *Psychology Today*, January 1979.

34. Monden, p.131.

35. Louise Kertesz, "Team Concept Makes Mazda Flat Rock a Different Plant," *Automotive News*, February 29, 1988, p.36.

4. A Workplace Designed for Workers

Words like "dignity" and "respect" lace the language of management at team concept plants. Indeed, one of the selling points of the team concept is the promise of management cooperating with—rather than commanding—labor.

A thesis of this book is that the substance of the team concept is quite different from these promises. But the union movement can take advantage of the fact that management has put these ideas on the agenda. We can begin a discussion of our own vision of a humanized workplace. What would the characteristics of a humanized workplace be? In this chapter, we describe some of the important elements of a workplace where human potential, dignity and respect are truly a priority.

This chapter will also evaluate how the team concept plants stack up against their own claims that they enhance dignity and respect and maximize human potential. We will draw heavily on comparisons between a humanized model and the NUMMI and Mazda plants, because those two plants employ the most advanced version of the team concept, management-by-stress (MBS). That system has become the model to which management aspires throughout the U.S. auto industry.

Our humanized model may seem unattainable today and indeed it is an ideal. Yet only ten years ago these issues were widely debated both inside and outside the labor movement as society tried to figure out how to beat the "blue-collar blues." Today unions are so preoccupied with defending themselves against concessions, layoffs, and plant closings that they have all but abandoned demands for a humanized workplace. It is a measure of the depth of the problems faced by workers today that this discussion has moved so far from labor's agenda.

But even if these goals are not on the bargaining table, there are several reasons why the labor movement needs to think about humanized work.

First, a list of features of humanized work is useful as a checklist in evaluating management's proposals for the team concept. A comparison between humanized work and the team concept disproves the corporations' claim that they intend to provide dignified and fulfilling working conditions. This can be seen particularly starkly when we look at the management-by-stress model for the team concept.

Secondly, management has couched the team concept in an appeal to workers' idealism. At the same time, unions are portrayed as concerned only with money or defending "special interests." The truth is that the labor movement has fought inspiring battles to win the gains we accept today as commonplace. Those inspiring battles still take place—witness the Watsonville cannery workers, the P-9 meatpackers, the Phelps Dodge steelworkers and the J.P. Stevens textile workers, not to mention the labor struggles in countries from South Africa to the Philippines. But with important exceptions, the U.S. labor movement today has failed to project its visions and ideals, leaving management with a clear field to win over those looking for such a vision.

Finally, the labor movement may not be able to win many of its goals right now, but if we can clearly identify them, we can try to move towards our goals, not away from them.

Two Views of Dignity

In the ideology of management-by-stress all effort is directed towards maximizing the success of the company. All employees, from the chairman of the board down to the workers on the line, are expected to measure their own success by the company's success and their failures by the company's failures. Those workers who make the company's goals of profitability and growth their own primary goals are honored and treated to favors…as long as the company actually has a use for them. In Japan, workers must retire between 55 and 60, so "valued workers" are not kept around after their value is gone.

In moments of doubt, management can fall back on a comforting rationale: "If we didn't have these standards, we wouldn't have any jobs at all. I feel bad having to fire Mary for poor attendance because her baby is sick, but I have to do it for the good of everyone else. If we can't maintain productivity and quality then none of us will have jobs."

As much as possible, management tries to maintain a workforce committed to the company's goals. If all the people in the workplace share the same philosophy, it is easier to believe that that system is the one which serves all of humanity. The hiring process is designed to select people with the "right" attitudes. On the job, the system generates peer pressure to force out those who do not share management's values.

Yet the trade-off of accepting management's world view in exchange for job security is badly flawed. No matter how selective the pre-employment screening, how inspirational the morale-building speeches or how frequent the shoulder-rubbing with management, for most workers long-term identification with the company's goals does not fit reality.

Few workers arrive on the NUMMI assembly

line out of a life-long ambition to put together a Toyota Corolla. They work because they need a job. They need to be paid decently so they can support their families, increase their pleasure during leisure, see that their children get a good education, participate in community activities, and so on. They "work to live" rather than "live to work." Within this context, workers want their jobs to be safe and to fill various personal needs. Some of those needs converge with the corporation's needs, some do not. At the point where the needs diverge, does the corporation encourage the worker's need for personal growth, or respect the worker's commitment to his or her family?

Sometimes workers' goals can mesh with company goals: the carrot can be more cost effective than the stick. Management generally accepts the notion that —where it does not cost too much—workers who experience job satisfaction and have happy, fulfilling lives outside work are more productive and do better quality work. For example, some corporations believe that providing computer program designers with the ideal conditions for creativity, flexibility, and individuality yields the highest profits. Many companies try to create cheap job satisfaction through Quality of Work Life or Employee Involvement programs. And some workers, because they see their future as becoming part of management, do adopt the company's goals as their own. That

should be their *right*, but it should not be a *requirement*.

Most of the time, however, the company's goals and the individual workers' goals do not entirely mesh, and then some clear choices have to be made. What takes priority? In the design of production systems do we make the choice that provides the most fulfilling, safest, most secure work for workers? Or do we choose what management believes would be the most profitable? We emphasize "believe" because the management fads of the past decades demonstrate that management's most strongly held beliefs may turn out to be myths backed by expensive PR.

The list that follows covers key elements of a humanized workplace. Doubtless there are others that could be added. We welcome discussion of what work should and could be like. Our assumption is that work should be designed to benefit workers. We believe that with the enormous increases in productivity brought about by technology and with so many plants lying idle, we can afford to be concerned about human beings, whether or not we achieve the maximum productivity or profitability.

The list that follows is in alphabetical order.

Attendance

Life is not fully predictable. People need time off work for illness and for psychological recharging. Par-

ents need to be home to care for sick children or to participate in some of their children's activities. Community involvement, education, and travel can require time which conflicts with work time. Not all activities can be planned in advance or fit into the neat periods allowed for vacations and holidays.

A humanized work design would allow for these outside demands by giving employees the right to flexible "personal" days. Personal days should be easy to schedule, and management's attitude should be to encourage time off for community activities and family commitments in the same way that the law and contracts provide time off for jury duty and National Guard duty. There may be some people who would abuse such allowances. But a humanized work system would establish ways to deal with the abuses without depriving the majority of the ability to participate in activities outside work.

For similar reasons, a humanized work system would address problems that are chronic causes of absence with appropriate solutions: on-site child care centers, special day care for sick children, medical clinics with convenient hours for shift workers, community-based after-school care, and company buses or vans to commute from residential areas.

The company policy toward personal absence has a lot to do with its policy for absentee replacement. If a reasonable amount of absenteeism were expected, the company would plan for this by employing additional relief workers.

MBS systems have a different philosophy. Absence even for the best of reasons is strongly discouraged, and the penalties for absence are severe. MBS systems consciously provide few absentee replacement workers so that the burden of absenteeism will fall directly on co-workers, and they in turn will apply peer pressure against the offender. Co-workers are given the responsibility of finding out why a fellow team member is absent and helping her overcome "her problem." But since they have no resources or authority to bend company rules, their interest and assistance become only another form of peer pressure.

Choice in Kind of Job

Luckily for the human race, people are different. They want different things from a job, and an individual worker will have different needs at different times in her or his life. For example, some auto workers prefer the variety and responsibility, even with the added stress, of utility jobs or parts supply jobs. Others prefer the clear cut expectations and relative stability of assembly line work. Some workers prefer muscular exertion while others seek to avoid it. Some need flexiblity to deal with child care. Some consider pay the top priority, while others want creativity.

Unions pursuing a humanizing model would seek to allow the widest possible range in kinds of jobs. It should be as easy as possible for workers to choose their jobs and to switch jobs in order to discover the one that is the "best fit." When they find that best fit, workers should be free from concern about being arbitrarily moved. Further, unions can attempt to ease the difficulty of moving between companies by bargaining for portability of pensions and benefits, training in generalized skills, and leaves of absence to try other jobs.

Management-by-stress systems seek to standardize and homogenize job content. They use policies that tie workers to corporations and limit their choice of job type. In traditional plants some jobs fit the humanized model more than others: skilled trades, repair, material handlers, metal finishers, inspectors, landscapers, and cleaners. These jobs include a degree of autonomy, flexibility, responsibility, creativity, or self-pacing. As we show in our description of the NUMMI plant, these are the jobs MBS seeks to get rid of entirely, or at least change in content so that they are more like assembly line jobs.

These "good" jobs are described by MBS management as NVA (non-value-added) or indirect labor. Part of the MBS operating principle is to find ways to reduce NVA jobs. This is the opposite of the humanization approach of Western European unions, which recognizes that the worst jobs are the "value-added" ones on the line. Their goal is to replace assembly line jobs through the use of technology and to increase the NVA jobs.[1]

Cleanliness of Plant

People feel better about work when the workplace is clean, well lit, and orderly. Not all work can be made clean. But where the work itself is necessarily dirty there can be careful attention to clean-up facilities, clean-up time, protective clothing, and work organization.

Visitors to MBS plants often remark on how clean and well organized they are. "A place for everything and everything in its place" is one of NUMMI's operating, if not original, slogans. Workers repeat stories—too many times be dismissed as public relations hype—of high management officials who stop and pick up a piece of litter. The MBS "visual indicator" system depends on the notion that anything out of place will be quickly corrected. In these days of super paint finishes and electronics which can be ruined by molecular-sized impurities, management's obsession with cleanliness may reflect concern about the product rather than the workers. But whatever the reason, a clean and orderly plant is greatly appreciated by the workforce.

Courtesy

Style can substitute for real respect. It is no coincidence that anti-union companies, ranging from Honda to IBM, make a big to-do about calling all employees associates, staffers, technicians, or some similar title. Yet the symbols of respect are not irrelevant. It is annoying when supervisors try to convey inferiority by addressing workers as "hey you" (or worse). It is a sign of respect when workers are addressed politely and with names or nicknames of their own choosing.

MBS companies are noted for maintaining the symbols of respect and formal courtesy.

Environmental Control

The work environment—heating, air conditioning, clean air, and noise control—make a world of difference to people who are working hard, day in and day out.

The record of MBS companies on plant environment is not clear. Extra expenditures for environmental controls seem to be driven primarily by what is good for the machinery or the processes, rather than human comfort. Neither the NUMMI plant nor the new Mazda plant is air-conditioned. In the Mazda plant, workers in the paint area are required to wear special nylon jump suits to protect the paint finish. Although these are uncomfortable in the heat, the area is not air-conditioned. Management has refused workers' requests to remove the suits when their jobs do not involve immediate contact with car bodies.

Ergonomics

"Ergonomics" means job design to fit human beings and is sometimes called "human factors engineering." Most people use the term in a more limited way to refer to the design of specific tools or working positions. Relatively simple and inexpensive adjustments such as changing the grip on a drill motor or the angle of a wrench handle, tilting a parts bin, or providing a platform or a stool can greatly reduce fatigue, stress, and various occupational injuries.[2]

MBS systems seem to be much stronger in this area than traditional plants. Training emphasizes proper lifting and holding techniques and basic tool design principles. Workers are encouraged to devise fixtures which can hold parts so that motions can be smoother and faster.

At the same time, MBS relies heavily on the concept of "standardized work procedures," where every motion is specified and measured and cannot be varied. The assumption is that the results will take care of themselves if the exact instructions are followed every single time. Few allowances are made for one worker being taller than another, being left-handed, or similar human variations.

While workers are encouraged to suggest changes—which management may or may not adopt— the procedures as well as the work pace in MBS plants make it difficult to experiment or try out alternatives. This is particularly true if the change only makes the job easier, as opposed to increasing speed.

Furthermore, attention to ergonomic design may ease a specific task, but management will no doubt rebalance the jobs and reassign tasks to absorb any benefits. The worker is likely to be working as hard and under conditions as difficult as before.

Under a humanized approach jobs would be designed to allow as much variation as possible to achieve specified results. Variations could include standing or sitting, right- or left-handed operation, and changes in sequence. Details of the way others do the job would be available, but workers would be encouraged to adapt the procedures to fit themselves and to improve the results. Time, information, tools, and materials would be available for experimentation.

Facilities

The quality and accessibility of locker rooms, showers, toilets, break areas, cafeterias, and parking rarely make someone's day. But a shortage of parking, a long walk to the restroom, or unpleasant eating facilities can become a daily irritant.

NUMMI and Mazda have improved personal facilities, including sports areas and exercise rooms, as do many new auto plants. At MBS plants management and workers use the same cafeterias, parking lots, and restrooms.

Learning New Skills

As we explain in Chapter 8, there is an important distinction between plant-specific and marketable skills. In this age of rapid technological and economic change there can be few guarantees that a job, company, or industry will exist ten years down the road. How many marketable skills workers learn on a job can make a big difference in determining how easy it is find another job.

MBS relies heavily on on-the-job training and emphasizes learning the operation of the specific machines and specific process. This is not to underestimate the skills learned in some versions of team training, including a range of problem-solving and organizational skills. But on the whole, the training under MBS is even more job-specific than in traditional plants.

Outside Contracting and Outsourcing

In the auto industry, "outside contracting" refers to the practice of hiring another firm to perform work on company property or on company materials, work that is usually or potentially done by members of the bargaining unit. "Outsourcing" means that the company buys a component or part that it could or has produced itself. Bringing in an outside firm to do electrical work or cleaning is outside contacting. Buying brake assemblies from another company is outsourcing.

Unions have approached outside contracting and outsourcing as job security issues, which they are. But even if job security were not at issue, outside contracting severely restricts the available job choices to workers within a company. It denies them the opportunity to develop new skills, or to find a job that "fits" better. These job options become especially important when it is very difficult or costly for workers to change companies.

MBS plants use outside contracting and outsourcing even more than traditional plants. The aim is

IN THE WORKPLACE OF THE FUTURE, BARRIERS BETWEEN UNION AND MANAGEMENT WILL DISAPPEAR...

WHY, WE'LL EVEN SHARE THE SAME CAFETERIA!

STRONG STEWARD SYSTEM

KONOPACKI
'85 HUCK KONOPACKI LABOR CARTOONS

to get the in-plant workforce, which is considered to be paid at premium rates, down to a minimum.

Pacing the Work

If you mount two tires on every car and the line runs at 60 an hour, you lift and place 900 tires and place and torque 3,600 lug nuts every eight-hour shift (figuring in breaks). In traditional factories, one way that workers cope with the repetition of the assembly line is to vary their work pace. Some will occasionally work faster (up the line) to create a little breathing room or break. The break can be extended by falling a little behind (in the hole) and working quickly to catch up. Varying the pace also allows use of muscles in slightly different ways to decrease muscle fatigue.

Humanized work design would increase the possibilities for workers to pace their own jobs. New technology creates some new possibilities we describe below. But on an assembly line individual pacing is only possible to the extent that buffers exist between work stations. Some analysts used to point to inclusion of buffers in the plants' assembly lines as a sign of the companies' concern for work design in the early team concept plants.[3]

A humanized workplace would design buffer areas into the production process. If a problem develops it can be repaired without the enormous pressure of shutting down all production. But even if there are no problems, buffers give workers some flexibility. Some have argued that buffers are particularly applicable in team situations. For example, one compressor plant is designed with a large buffer area between teams. If the team wants to have a meeting it works far enough ahead

to fill the downstream buffer so it can hold a meeting when it chooses.[4]

One of the basic principles of MBS is "just-in-time," which eliminates buffers. Any problem is immediately apparent, and pressure can be focussed on resolving it right away. Recent team concept plants pride themselves on their elimination of buffers.

Quality Work

When two people are introduced, one of the first questions they ask one another is: "What do you do?" Most people would like to be proud of the work they do. They do not want to be embarrassed when a neighbor or relative buys something they produce. Being allowed to do quality work is part of having a good job.

In MBS plants as well as traditional plants, despite all the quality campaigns, few workers have any control at all over the quality of their product. Quality is discussed in more detail in Chapter 10.

Resolving Grievances

Solutions to little problems may be simple, but when they get lost in a bureaucratic tangle, small problems magnify. This seems to be almost routine in traditional plants. Little gets settled without writing a grievance, and most grievances do not get resolved for weeks, months or years—when it is too late to actually change the offending practice. At best, from a worker's point of view, the grievance procedure seems to be a way to slap management's hand and "be made whole" for financial losses.

A humanized approach to work would find ways to separate out problems and deal with them in an appropriate amount of time at the appropriate level.

At the first step, MBS tends to trivialize problems. In the traditional grievance procedure, a worker's problem is considered important enough for the worker and steward to be allowed to discuss it quickly and on company time. At NUMMI, if the problem is not affecting production the worker and the union coordinator may not have an initial discussion about it until they can arrange to meet after work or on a break.

But one of the features of MBS systems that workers genuinely appreciate is that small problems are usually dealt with within a few days and the worker is involved in the solution. For example, a dispute between a worker and a supervisor may be settled at a meeting between the worker, the supervisor, a representative from the union, and a labor relations person. This is not necessarily out of concern for the worker, but because the smooth operation of the total system depends on quickly identifying problems and taking corrective action. That does not mean that problems will be resolved the way the worker wants, of course, and workers who file grievances because they are dissatisfied with the outcome of more informal procedures are considered uncooperative, sometimes by the union as well as the company.

MBS gets its reputation for efficiently resolving problems only in comparison to the black holes that the union and the company have allowed the grievance procedure to become in traditional plants.

Response to Problems

In any work situation problems appear, whether they are called variances, disturbances or glitches, and whether they are caused by acts of God, nature, designers, machines, outside contractors, maintenance, the previous department or the previous shift. Just-in-time makes any of these problems a lot worse because there are no cushions.

In a humanized work environment, problems such as a faulty batch of parts would be expected, and extra resources—machines, inventory, and people— would be kept in reserve to cushion the effect of the problem on the people involved. If inventory is cut, then the number of workers available to help out in a crisis would be increased.

MBS consciously cuts out the safety nets. Rather than provide relief in crisis, it is designed to focus attention on the problem and on the workers involved. This design leads to quicker solutions to problems, but also increases the level of stress.

Rights on the Job

In most plants, when workers walk through the gates they leave behind virtually all their rights as citizens, including free speech, free press, and freedom from unreasonable search and seizure. In fact, the only rights that workers do have are those derived from company procedures or the rights won by the union.

Unions in the U.S. have traditionally used seniority as the basis for various rights on the job. Though not a perfect system, seniority is the fairest way to counter arbitrary management action. Job rights also cover the right to transfer jobs or shifts at certain intervals, the right to refuse an unsafe job, the right to call for a union representative, and the right to get medical assistance immediately.

Having rights does not mean that one will exercise them at every opportunity. But it does mean that individuals can decide when to invoke their rights with the assurance that they will be honored even if it is not the most convenient timing for management.

In MBS systems, rights are severely cut back in the name of management flexibility. Eliminating classifications means taking away seniority rights to transfer. Taking away the right to speak to a union representative during work time takes away an important equalizer a worker has in dealing with a supervisor.

Task Size

There is increasing recognition that a larger job with more operations (in a greater time period) is often more satisfying. In some European plants, for example, workers build a complete assembly, such as a door, or even larger parts of the car. Working this way means a different method and technology than the assembly line.

MBS consciously attempts to break production down to small tasks for each worker. Typical *takt* time (length of a worker's involvement with each unit) at NUMMI is one minute. In this respect MBS is an intensification of assembly line systems.

Technology

Technology can be used to make jobs easier, safer, and more interesting. It can also be used to put workers out of jobs. Computers can be used to honor complex sets of preferences in assignments of jobs and hours and even to make some version of flex-time possible on complicated assembly operations. Or computers can be used by management as a weapon to tightly monitor every action a worker takes.

Consider, for example, the technology of automatic guided vehicles (AGVs). Each car can be assembled on its own individual carrier. Elaborate AGVs have the capability of holding the car at different heights or angles for different operations. The cars may follow signals in cables buried in the floor, or determine their position through radio or infra-red signals. The whole system is computer controlled to keep track of the location, contents, job requirements, and problems of each AGV.

Like all new technologies, countless technical hardware and software problems are a part of initial installation and use. Yet the technology can overcome major limitations of the assembly line. First, the cars do not have to stay in order. If one car requires more operations or if there is some difficulty, other cars can go around it on their AGVs. It is possible to reroute a carrier back to a previous station for rework on a particular job.

Second, the line can be reorganized easily for changes in production, usually just by reprogramming a computer. Even where a cable must be laid under the floor, the amount of work is tiny compared to the physical relocation of assembly lines.

Third, the system can usually keep better track of where every individual unit is, and which assembly steps have not been completed.

This flexibility can be used in different ways. AGVs can simply be substituted for the traditional assembly line, with each worker doing a very small part of the overall job on every unit, as in the first diagram. Used this way, AGVs can increase management control and allow management to keep the jobs balanced (i.e. every worker working all the time), even while allowing more options on cars and variations in production.

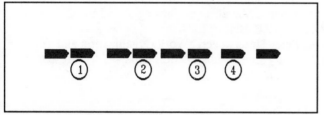

Automatic Guided Vehicles (carriers) allow management to have more flexibility in using basic assembly line machine pacing.

Used in a different way, AGVs can make breakthroughs in humanizing work. Several Swedish and German automobile firms with strong union involvement have experimented in this direction.[5] By organizing work in parallel lines of work stations it is possible for workers to have as large an operation as desired. Workers can have different sized operations. They can work at different overall speeds even on the same job, individually varying their pacing and even the methods they use.

MBS plants represent an attempt to perfect the assembly line method and there seems to be little interest in technology which provides more flexibility to the worker (see Chapter 8).

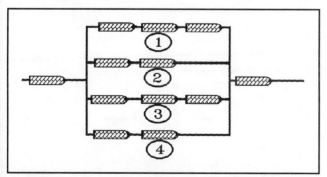

Automatic Guided Vehicles in parallel lines allow for the possibility of broadened jobs, different work times, and human pacing.

Trust

A humanized work environment is built on the trustworthiness of the overwhelming majority rather than on the dishonesty of a few. It is hard to feel respected when your lunchbox is searched going in and out of the plant, when you need a foreman's signature to get a tool from the crib, when your locker is searched, when you need a doctor's note to vouch for illness, when your urine is checked for signs of what you do on your time off, when you are presumed guilty unless you can prove you are innocent, and when the time clock determines the second you start and finish.

The record of NUMMI and Mazda in this area seems little different from traditional U.S. auto plants, where the implementation of security procedures periodically peaks and ebbs. Guards search packages. While formal time clocks do not exist, team leaders keep track of tardiness, and they are motivated to pressure a late worker because they must fill in until the worker arrives.

Voluntary Teamwork

Given the opportunity, most workers help each other willingly. If there is no time, of course, the help is decreased. The spirit of good will also tends to be restricted when the system rewards individual achievement. A humanized work design would encourage workers to help each other and would reward collective efforts at least as much as individual ones.

A humanized work environment would also allow time and provide facilities for workers to meet, talk to each other, talk to management, and solve problems. This does not necessarily require a formal team structure. In traditional plants, groups of tool and die makers or groups of maintenance workers cooperate as effective teams without a formal structure, indeed without ever using the word "team." The same thing tends to be true of production workers, especially where their jobs are more skilled. Teamwork is also a common way of functioning in many white collar jobs.

In some circumstances a formal team structure can be useful if its purpose is to enhance communication and coordination between peers, as opposed to functioning as a vehicle for management propaganda and control. Some of the questions that need to be asked about teams include: Are leaders selected by the group, responsible to the group, replaceable by the group? Can the real concerns of members of the group get on the agenda or is the agenda effectively controlled by management? Can meetings last long enough to deal with a substantive topic? Can the group discuss problems without the presence of management? Can the group get an unsatisfactory "advisor" (supervisor) replaced? Can the group get the resources and expertise it needs or is it dependent on what management supplies? Does the group have real authority or is it only advisory?

During start-up in MBS plants, before the line reaches full speed, the work is uneven—some workers face major problems while others have the time to help their co-workers. Voluntary cooperation is very much in evidence during these times, and many of the "good vibes" stories about MBS plants are generated from these experiences.

But once the line is at full speed there is little time to help someone else with a problem. And if a bit of time is created by difficulties in one part of the line, most workers would prefer to enjoy the breathing space rather than rush to get the line going again. Where assistance does take place, it is often forced cooperation—assigned by the team leader or group leader.

Similarly, once the lines are up to speed there is little real teamwork. At NUMMI and Mazda team leaders are appointed by management, the supervisor calls the meetings, and in most cases effectively controls the agenda.

Although the official ideology of MBS plants promotes teamwork, it is not clear that it actually rewards voluntary teamwork outside the official structure. Many NUMMI workers complain about favoritism. Given the relatively unrestricted power of supervisors to assign work, the system rewards good relations with your supervisor rather than good relations with your fellow workers. Where supervisors themselves highly value worker cooperation, it may be rewarded. Where supervisors value other traits such as blind obedience, voluntary cooperation falls by the wayside.

Notes

1. See Peter Unterweger, "Appropriate Automation: Thoughts on Swedish Examples of Socio-Technical Innovation," Industrial Relations Research Association, Spring 1985.

2. Dan McLeod, *Strains and Sprains: A Worker's Guide to Job Design*, Health and Safety Department, United Auto Workers, 1982.

3. Harry Katz, *Shifting Gears: Changing Labor Relations in the U.S. Automobile Industry*, Boston, M.I.T. Press, 1985, p.94.

4. Harvey F. Kolodney and Barbara Dresner, "Linking Arrangements and New Work Designs," *Organizational Dynamics*, Winter 1986, p.43.

5. Peter J. Mullins, "The Gang's All Here: Group Assembly, JIT and AGVs Rule Audi's New Body Shop," *Automotive Industries*, November 1987.
Also, Ben Dankbaar, "Teamwork in the West German Car Industry: Management Strategies and the Quality of Work," WZB, Berlin, 1987.
Also, Peter Unterweger, "Work Organization and Technology in Three Swedish Auto Plants," UAW Research Department, 1987.

5. What the Union Can Do

This is a tough time for unions. Corporations are emboldened and they are playing hardball. Richard Dauch, Chrysler's vice-president for manufacturing, explained how the company will deal with plants where the union is resistant to change:

> I will lead those that want to cooperate. Those who choose not to—there is no sense getting upset with them. We have too much capacity anyway.[1]

F. James MacDonald, past president of General Motors, put it even more bluntly:

> It's unfortunate there are still some in management, and some on the union side, who haven't quite got caught up with with the necessity for [a team concept] kind of operation. But I'll guarantee that those people are going to get run over.[2]

There are no easy answers for unions today. We are the first to admit that "just saying no" to team concept is neither simple nor, by itself, a long-term solution. Much bigger questions are at stake than can be solved at the level of the local union or the individual plant. But it is clear that team concept is not the answer to workers' needs either—for job security, for decent pay, for decent working conditions, for jobs which allow the exercise of human creativity. Management's version of the team concept is a union-busting strategy that hinders, not helps, the search for real solutions.

Many of those solutions require a stronger overall labor movement. A broader strategy is necessary to address the paramount issues of investment and whether people are to come before profits. We will not attempt to outline here such a strategy for the union movement, a strategy which could take on not only team concept but control over investment, the humane use of technology, guaranteed jobs, consumer-oriented production, racial and sexual equality, a firm social safety net, and all the other things a strong union movement would implement if it had political and economic power.

The first step, however, toward gaining that sort of power is to rebuild the labor movement at the very base of its power—on the shop floor. A political plan and a social vision for labor are necessary. But the most sophisticated political strategy in the world is worth little if the union is not organized at its base and does not have the participation and respect of the rank and file.

Shop floor power is more important now than ever, especially in industries where the shop floor is management's point of attack. Changes in technology, work organization and labor relations all require the union's attention at the level of detail, and its ability to mobilize at the level of the average member.

All too often in recent years unions' self-concep-

THE INTERNATIONAL LABOR MOVEMENT: STRATEGY AND CONVICTIONS CAN PAY OFF

The labor movement in the United States faces a difficult set of circumstances—but in many other countries the situation is equally bad or worse. In some of those countries—for example, South Africa, South Korea, Brazil, the Philippines, and Canada—the labor movement has actually gotten stronger in the last few years. Their experience shows that labor's weakness in the last decades of the twentieth century is not a given. Unions can organize despite difficult conditions, if they have a firm set of convictions and a strategy.

Canadian unions face similar conditions to their American neighbors, but they have followed a firmer and more unified policy against contract concessions than American unions. Union leaders and members are active in politics through the labor-based New Democratic Party (NDP). The Canadian labor movement has grown steadily to nearly 40 percent of the working population, in contrast to the U.S. labor movement which has shrunk to less than 17 percent. As of late 1987 the NDP was leading in the polls as the party favored to win the next election.

In the Third World, unions face not only difficult economic circumstances but often enjoy few legal rights. Their activists encounter jailing and physical repression, up to and including assassination, for exercising what would be everyday rights in the United States.

A good example is South Africa, where in 1985 most of the leading unions united in a giant federation, COSATU (Congress of South African Trade Unions). COSATU is seen more and more as the most important representative of working people in the fight against apartheid. COSATU affiliates have adopted the principle of "one union, one industry," so that workers in the same industry are not split up among competing unions. They have democratic structures which involve the rank and file and ensure that the leadership acts on their mandate. Principled policies such as these have allowed the union movement to become stronger under conditions that American unionists would regard as unthinkable.

tion has gotten blurred. Is the union's role to be a junior partner with management in beating the competition? Is it to help the companies improve profits through such chores as policing attendance or cheerleading for greater productivity? Does management really have any use for such a junior partner once the company has gotten what it wanted from the partnership?

Since their founding, the mission of unions has been to defend and advance workers' rights, humanize working conditions, increase wages and benefits, and protect jobs. Every time unions made an advance in these areas they were warned that they were demanding too much, that they would make unionized companies uncompetitive, and that jobs would be lost. In some cases union struggles did cause some jobs to shift. But overall, unions won more dignity, better working conditions and a higher standard of living, and these pulled up other workers' conditions and contributed to a booming economy.

The basic argument in favor of agreeing to management's team concept is "trickle down" economics: make the employer more profitable and that will save jobs. The fallacies in this argument have been well-proven by the plant closings of the last few years, the job-robbing technology management has introduced, and the shift of production overseas. But if a union and its members do choose to act on this theory, they might do better simply to hand back wages or benefits, or to let management raise production quotas. A union with its organization intact could presumably make a fight to win these back again in better times. The worst possible course is to give up the union's *power* in exchange for a few cents per hour, which is what usually happens with team concept.

Just Say No

By far the best way to deal with team concept is to keep it out of your shop altogether. A combination of determination by the local union and being in a good bargaining position can make it possible for the union to say no to the company and make it stick. Chapters 22 and 23 describe how two GM locals, at Pontiac Truck and Bus and Warren Hydra-Matic, used extensive membership education to fortify themselves against team concept. In October 1986 Chrysler Local 1700 in Sterling Heights, Michigan voted down a "Modern Operating Agreement" despite pressure from the International union. In September 1987 members of UAW Local 325 at Ford's St. Louis plant voted by a 62 percent margin to reject an agreement which would have empowered the bargaining committee to negotiate team concept. In the first case, the entire leadership was united in fighting team concept. In the other three locals, the elected leaders were divided, and it took a spirited political discussion within the membership to decide the issue.

In the auto industry the team concept has spread very fast, through management whipsawing and other forms of bullying. In other industries, however, the pro-

cess is not as advanced, and informed unions have a chance to fight the team concept before it achieves such a strong foothold. It is clear that the team concept in auto is not achieving the purposes the union hoped for —saving jobs, primarily, and worker involvement, secondarily. Unions both in auto and elsewhere which are just now being confronted with team concept can learn from this recent history.

The basic tools needed to keep team concept out are the same as those needed to fight any kind of concession: education, organization, communication, and an alternative.[3]

1. Educate

The information in the rest of this book, and in particular the "Myths About Team Concept" below, is your starting point. Use your photocopy machine, leaflets, and union newspaper liberally. Organize special classes on team concept, using the union's own "consultants" if necessary. Have the people who come to the classes pledge to pass on what they learned to ten other people each.

2. Organize

The union is in a much stronger position to say no to team concept if it is organized on the shop floor. This is the only way that members feel they have an alternative to the company's constant insistence on teams. The suggestions for organizing *under* team concept also hold true for organizing *against* or *instead of* team concept. The ideas in this chapter for establishing a long-range strategic plan, informal stewards and a "code of conduct" for union members will strengthen the union both in the fight to keep team concept out and afterwards.

3. Communicate

Since management often wins on the team concept by playing one local union against another, the best defense against it is a united front, to replace mutual

---

ON BROADER STRATEGIES

A new book, *An Injury to All*, explains what has happened to American labor and why. Author Kim Moody of *Labor Notes* draws on the experience of the many activists who are fighting to rebuild the labor movement, suggests strategies suited to the times, and outlines a new brand of aggressive unionism.

Among the ideas proposed to deal with multinational/conglomerate employers are corporate-wide stewards' councils, international grassroots worker networks, unionization of new service industries on an industry-wide (not piecemeal) basis, building racial and sexual unity, corporate campaigns, and solidarity campaigns that mobilize union members and allies. The book is published by Verso Press, London and New York, 1988. To get a copy, see the ad at the end of this book.

suspicion and competition with organization and cooperation.

Management hates to have its lies exposed. ("The Kalamazoo plant said they had no problem with team concept.") Establish regular contact with other locals in your product line, including at other companies (too often known as "the competition"). Invite their members to your union meetings and attend theirs. Exchange columns in your local newspapers. Send minutes of your bargaining sessions; get together to plan joint strategies ahead of time.

In 1982 a group of GM locals banded together against whipsawing. Soon after the national concessions contract was signed, locals in the union's Subcouncil 7A called a meeting to discuss the work rules concessions that management was demanding in local agreements. The locals held two meetings despite the International's warning that they were "unsanctioned," and took a "blood pact" not to go backwards on local practices.[4]

The blood pact worked for a while, but it was not enough. What the locals needed was an International union which would actively intervene to help them save their working conditions. It is the role of international unions to organize solidarity among locals. Whipsawing would not be possible if all locals as well as their International were committed to resisting blackmail.

4. Have an Alternative

A beleaguered local union may decide that it has to give in to management's desire for a speedup: its plant is too old, its location is unfavorable. But the local may be better off if it can convince management to just take the speedup straight out, without the team packaging. An activist from an East Coast assembly plant explained it this way:

> We've already lost our relief men and half of inspection even without teams. *If* we get a guarantee that our plant has a future, we're willing to talk about productivity increases—that is, concessions. But we feel it would be much better to just turn up the line speed and not get involved with teams. Before, there were kiss-asses but you could just ignore them. With team concept, all of a sudden he's your team leader.

A Strategy for Local Unions

The rest of this chapter is for locals which already have team concept. The question for them has become—how to live with it? The local does not have to throw in the towel. It can still fight to maintain union strength, membership rights, and worker dignity. The concerned local union can do four things:

1. Educate the membership about team concept.
2. Communicate with other locals.
3. Negotiate language which alleviates the worst aspects of team concept.
4. Strengthen the union's presence in the plant—and in the teams. Four points to strengthen the union will be elaborated:

-develop a long-range strategic plan.
-organize within the teams.
-establish a code of conduct becoming to a union member.
-begin a union involvement and action program.

Educate the Membership

The membership needs to know the big picture—the situation facing their industry and their union and what they can do about it. Once they know what management is up to overall, they can make an informed decision about the team concept. Later on in this chapter we give suggestions for such an educational program.

The immediate question, however, is how to respond to the team concept itself. Management in the auto industry is pushing through a version of team concept which has very little to do with popular notions of teams. The first step for the union is to break through the myths and misinformation that surround team concept. *The main point to get across is that their team concept is another name for speedup and union-busting.* For more detailed information to refute the following myths, see the chapters mentioned in parentheses.

Myth #1: **Team concept means job security.**

There can be no job security in a plant where all the less strenuous jobs such as sweeper and repair have been eliminated and where workers cannot keep up the pace as they grow older. Do you have job security if there is no job you can do if you get arthritis, tendonitis, or a bad back?

Neither are there any job guarantees in a system

"So long, partner!"

which is aggressively looking for ways to cut jobs at all times. A few team concept contracts say that the company will try to cut jobs through attrition (retirement, firing, or quitting), not layoffs. In fact attrition clauses are a rather weak kind of job protection.[5] When it cannot lay off, management has even more incentive to push people out the door as rapidly as possible. The trend is to make the jobs harder, in order to encourage workers to quit or take early retirement. Neither does management have any incentive to settle disciplinary cases. And, of course, in the long run eliminating jobs through attrition still eliminates jobs—maybe not yours, but will there be jobs for the next generation?

As team concept becomes the norm rather than the exception in auto plants, team concept plants lose whatever special status they *may* have had. Sometimes it seems that a plant has saved itself by capitulating, other times that a militant stance kept the plant open (see Chapter 16 on Local 645's struggle to keep GM Van Nuys open). UAW Local 2093 from GM Hydra-Matic in Three Rivers, Michigan tried to warn other locals about cooperation:

> Innovative Local Agreement—we've got it. Quality—we've got it. High Productivity—we've got it. Absentee Problems—NONE. Employee Involvement—we've got it. Teamwork—we've got it...
>
> At this plant the local parties did exactly what [the 1987 National Agreement] says all plants must now do...sit down jointly and determine ways to make their operations more effective and competitive to save existing jobs, enhance job security, and attract new work... From a lot of classifications [we went] to a few classifications (7 nonskilled). As a result...300 plus people are laid off on the street.[6]

Recent history has proven that the most important factors in whether corporate management chooses to keep a plant open include how well the plant's model is selling, the age of the plant, its geographic location, and state and local politics. Whether it has instituted the team concept does not override these factors.

Workers at GM's Leeds, Missouri plant—which opened in 1929—were told in 1986 that the team concept was their only hope of saving the plant. They voted yes, and less than a year later came the announcement: the plant's last remaining model was being moved to another plant. Leeds was indefinitely "idled." GM's Fiero plant in Pontiac, Michigan—one of the company's original star team concept plants—met the same fate in early 1988. Chrysler obtained team concept from four of its components plants in 1986 and 1987, but by the end of 1987 was actively seeking a buyer for its entire Acustar components division, including two of the team concept plants.

Besides, once management decides it no longer wants a particular plant, even a prior agreement to keep it open is not worth much. The GM-UAW 1987 National Agreement contains a three-year plant closing moratorium—and yet both Leeds and the Fiero plant were declared "idled" within five months of signing. ("Idled" means that a skeleton crew remains to do maintenance and that the company has not definitively said that the plant will never run again. But most industry observers believe that neither of these plants has a future.)

Myth #2: **Team concept boosts productivity.**

Although much has been made of the productivity of the Japanese-owned plants, the scanty evidence now available indicates that the team concept itself does not boost productivity (output per worker)—and it may even lower it. A study of 53 auto plants by prominent auto industry researchers Katz, Kochan and Keefe, who favor labor-management cooperation, found that "greater use of teams [has] either a negative or no asso-

---

CONCESSIONS HAVE NOT SAVED JOBS

Team concept should be viewed as just one more concession in the general concessionary trend which started in the auto industry in 1979. The trend began that year at Chrysler. In 1980, 1981, 1982, 1984 and 1987 the UAW made various concessions in national agreements with the Big Three, as well as hundreds of concessions in local contracts. These ranged from wage cuts to fewer holidays to fewer classifications to team concept.

Did those concessions save jobs? The record indicates that the answer is no. Since 1978, the peak pre-concessions year, the number of hourly jobs in the Big Three has fallen by nearly a third. And the number of jobs has been cut much more than the number of vehicles produced. Vehicle production by the Big Three fell by 19 percent between the peak year of 1978 and 1987—but the number of U.S. hourly workers fell by 32 percent.

Hourly Workers[7]

	Chrysler	Ford	GM	Total
1978	97,000	192,000	466,000	755,000
1987	59,000	102,000	351,000	512,000
% cut	-39%	-47%	-25%	-32%

Vehicle Production

	Chrysler	Ford	GM	Total
1978	1,613,000	3,790,000	6,807,000	12,210,000
1987	1,421,000	3,312,000	5,128,000	9,866,000
% cut	-12%	-13%	-25%	-19%

Concessions had no effect on the factors that determine the number of auto jobs in the U.S.—the state of the economy, car prices, customers' perceptions of quality, the level of imports, management's outsourcing decisions, the level of overtime. And some union concessions actually caused job loss themselves: for example, speedup and the giveback of Paid Personal Holidays in the 1982 contract.

ciation with labor productivity and product quality."[8] The researchers note that:

> ... the number of production worker job classifications consistently does not have a statistically significant association with either labor hours [per vehicle] or product quality. This result is particularly striking in the face of all the recent focus American management has put on reducing the number of job classifications.

On the other hand, the researchers found that a faster pace of work and greater management discretion on such issues as allocation of overtime, layoffs and transfers *did* increase productivity.

A study by Daniel Luria of the Industrial Technology Institute investigated the relationship of several plant practices to productivity. Luria found that a higher number of classifications, combined with other union restrictions on management, had a negative correlation with productivity. The factor which correlated much more strongly with productivity, however, was intense plant capacity utilization.[9]

In other words, plants with fewer classifications did tend to be more productive, other things being equal. But productivity had a much stronger relationship to having fewer plants and working them full-tilt— including the scheduling of lots of overtime. Luria also suggests that high capacity use increases productivity because it spreads indirect labor (supervision, maintenance, inspection) over more cars.

The first study suggests that where there are gains in productivity in team concept plants, it is likely the result of speedup or loss of worker rights on transfers, overtime allocation, etc. The second study suggests that management has increased productivity by cutting back plants and the workforce and distributing a greater workload to those remaining. This should not surprise union members. After all, increasing productivity *by definition* means getting the same production out of fewer workers (or more production out of the same number of workers). If productivity is increased, the only way not to end up with fewer workers is to increase output. In a saturated auto market as exists today, however, an increase in market share at one plant can only come at the expense of market share—and jobs—at another plant.

If unions promote management's productivity drive, that is what they are signing on to. There is no "soft" version of a productivity drive that achieves what management wants without workers paying the price.

Myth #3: Team concept means more control by workers.

Management-by-stress, now management's favorite team concept model, actually increases supervisors' strict control over how jobs are to be done, by specifying every motion in detail (see Chapter 9). The only "control by workers" that may be increased is this: sometimes a team gets to fine-tune jobs defined by management or help decide how to eliminate a job. In many ways team concept workers have less control over their jobs than the limited control in traditional plants, since they have fewer options to choose their job or to control the pace of their work (see Chapters 3 and 8). Team concept plants do not even pretend, of course, to give workers control over how *much* work is reasonable, let alone such basic decisions as production levels, technology, or product design.

Myth #4: Team concept means "working smarter, not harder."

All too often "working smarter" means that the company gets one person to figure out ways to make another person "work harder." At NUMMI, extra workers are placed on special *kaizen* teams which are assigned to observe their fellow workers on the line and figure out ways to boost their productivity.

Secondly, "working smarter" often does literally mean working harder. The company defines "working smarter" as passing on to management any methods you have devised to make your job easier on yourself. Management then uses your idea to "rebalance" your job (add more work onto it) so that you are left with even less breathing space than before.

Third, even in those cases where "working smarter" does not immediately mean working harder, it often eliminates jobs (which is why management thinks it's so smart). Many quality suggestions are in this category (see Chapter 10).

Myth #5: Team concept plants are looking for workers with skills and will upgrade skills with training.

In fact team concept plants are looking *not* for workers with skills or auto industry experience, but for workers with what management considers the right "attitude." The work itself is *de*skilled in two ways: production work is broken down to the tiniest tasks possible, so that tasks can easily be shifted from job to job and worker to worker. The idea is to reduce the proficiency necessary for each job so that workers will be thoroughly interchangeable. A worker who is trained to do six of these thoroughly deskilled jobs is no more skilled in any real sense than she was before. It is no slip of the tongue that the theoreticians of NUMMI's production system say that automation should be used for "foolproofing."[10]

The number of skilled trades workers at NUMMI and Mazda, the model team concept plants, is far below that in Chrysler and GM plants. In addition, the more challenging skilled trades work is contracted out (see Chapters 8 and 11).

The strong emphasis on cutting jobs at such plants means that there is little room for advancement. Production workers cannot move into the skilled trades or even into the more highly skilled production jobs when those jobs no longer exist.

Myth #6: Team concept is the way to deal with foreign competition.

Management can use teams anywhere—and is.

The auto multinationals are using or pushing teams in Mexico, Brazil, Britain, Spain, and Belgium, among others, besides the U.S., Canada and Japan. In fact, use of the team concept here could even *help* management shift work to other countries, because more and more of the intimate knowledge of how production works has been transferred away from the workforce and into the hands of management (see Chapter 3). Ford used technical and management personnel from its U.S. plants and from its partner, Mazda, to start up its Mexican assembly plant (see Chapter 24). Every multinational company has specific procedures to discover the techniques that work well in one plant and then spread them to others. The techniques even spread from company to company, when managers skip from one firm to another, at trade shows, and when plant managers give their competition friendly tours.

Even the zealous speedup possible under team concept is not enough to make American workers as inexpensive as Mexican workers, who make less than $10

CHOOSING SIDES

When you hear the word "teams" you think of competition. When it comes to the team concept, just who is "the other side"?

When the corporations and the UAW International first began advocating team concept, the competition was Japan. Soon the conception of "our" opponent had to be expanded, to include the Japanese-owned plants in the U.S., whether unionized or not. All the talk of "the competition" neglected to mention that many of those competitive Japanese transplants were partially owned by the Big Three themselves.

Very quickly auto workers at one Big Three company came to see other Big Three workers as their rivals. And corporate whipsawing soon brought the enemy even closer to home: workers who made similar vehicles within the same company. The plant that used to be your "sister plant" became "the competition." Union members who called each other brothers and sisters at union conventions did not want to share information about the company's plans at their respective plants, for fear that "the competition" was trying to steal their work.

The members of your team had changed. From labor vs. management, it had become GM Janesville vs. GM Pontiac. The competition and the bad blood became overt.

For example, some union officials at Chrysler's Newark, Delaware plant, where team concept had been voted in, gloated when they heard that Chrysler might shut a St. Louis assembly plant that did not have team concept.

Now the team logic is being carried to the next step: "business teams" (see Chapter 23). With a business team set-up, each department in the plant seeks to achieve a better "bottom line" by shifting costs or blame to the workers in the business teams upstream or downstream from them.

"JUST-IN-TIME" CAN GIVE THE UNION POWER

The February 1988 strike by British unions against Ford Motor Co. has management thinking twice about "just-in-time" and the methods that go with it.

The strike lasted only nine days, but it cost the company $927.5 million in lost production—which is why it was willing to settle.

Here's what the *Wall Street Journal* had to say about the strike even before it ended:

[The] walkout underscores how modern factories increase labor's power. The costly strike against Ford Motor Co. in Britain is driving home a sober lesson to manufacturers throughout Europe: New factory techniques, far from weakening the region's restive unions, are enhancing labor's power to disrupt production and slow the badly needed modernization of European industry.

In recent years, Ford stood out in Europe as an advocate of cost-cutting manufacturing methods used in Japan. It computerized factories, slashed inventories and boosted productivity. The big U.S. auto maker linked diverse European factories into one giant car- and truck-making machine. Ford Sierras, assembled in Belgium, ran on French-made transmissions powered by British engines. Ford's market share grew, particularly in the United Kingdom's highly competitive market.

"The downside [of this modernization] is what we're seeing now," a spokesman for Ford's U.K. unit acknowledged.

Production Halted

Ford's European juggernaut stalled within hours of a walkout Monday by 32,500 British workers. Without U.K. parts, some Ford production lines in Belgium have shut down, with 2,500 workers laid off yesterday at one plant and 100 more at another... Analysts expect closures to spread quickly to other countries. Each day that Ford loses production of 2,930 vehicles, it sacrifices at least $34.1 million in retail sales.

The auto maker's troubles are sending a shudder throughout the board rooms of Europe's leading manufacturers. To many executives, the Ford dispute dramatizes the one great risk of the new manufacturing techniques: a strike.

Walkouts "will grind operations to a halt far more quickly" than usual, said [a consultant]. The new methods cut costly inventories, and without big stockpiles of parts, strikes immediately close assembly lines.[13]

---

per day. As team concept and other speedup measures are implemented in other countries as well, American workers lose whatever "advantage" they might have gained from giving up work rules. One study showed that skill levels were no barrier to producing in the Third World: it took only three to six months longer to get an engine plant up to speed in Mexico than in the United States.[11]

Myth #7: **Team concept and cooperation make the union stronger.**

Team concept means a weaker official shop floor organization. At NUMMI, Mazda and Chrysler, team concept contracts reduce the number of union representatives allowed (see Chapter 13).

Team concept means that union representatives are confused or disoriented about their role: are they to stop filing grievances? How are they different from their "management counterparts" (a favorite team concept expression)? Many members complain that the union doesn't act like a union once team concept comes in (see Chapters 11, 12, 20 and 21).

In Japan, where the team concept is most developed, a study conducted by the labor federation Sohyo revealed that only seven percent of workers surveyed turned to their union steward when they had a problem at work; they were more likely to talk to the boss.[12]

The team concept gives up contractual protections and past practices in exchange for management flexibility. Seniority in particular is undermined. The union has much less basis for challenging management favoritism (see Chapters 11 and 16).

Team concept breaks down solidarity between workers. In effect team concept breaks down the philosophy of trade unionism, replacing it with a vague—and unfulfilled—"jointness."

Myth #8: **Team concept brings the feeling of teamwork on the shop floor.**

In fact the overloaded jobs under team concept serve to prevent workers from helping each other. Team concept tries to break down the solidarity and teamwork of natural work groups that develop on the shop floor, by trying—usually unsuccessfully—to channel that sentiment into formal, highly controlled, company-designed team structures.

Management says it wants to build "worker loyalty," but top managers themselves are loyal only to their careers, not their companies. When workers join management's "team" to beat the competition, they too often find that management has become a free agent and sold itself to a higher bidder. Dennis Pawley left one of GM's early team concept plants, the Fiero plant in Pontiac, Michigan, to become plant manager at Mazda—and then left Mazda for Otis Elevator.

Myth #9: **Under team concept the union has no power.**

This is really a question of the union's attitude almost as much as what's written on the paper of the contract. A crucial thing to remember is that in many plants *"just-in-time" delivery has made the union potentially more powerful than ever* (see Chapter 3). The lack of buffer stocks makes quickie stoppages or slowdowns in support of an immediate demand extremely effective.

Action by even a few members has the power to disrupt production drastically.

In addition, in these times of changing technology the company needs cooperation to install and debug its new machines. It is not profitable for a company to let its expensive technology sit idle. This also makes it possible for the union to bring immediate pressure to bear.

However, the union has to be willing to *use* this power and able to *organize* it. All too often unions are reluctant to use the power they do have, for fear of hurting the company too much. Decisive action by the UAW in early 1988 showed that the union can still back management down if it is willing to take some risks.

In January 1988 word leaked out that Chrysler was seeking a buyer for its components division, Acustar. The UAW had received no advance notification, although President Owen Bieber sits on Chrysler's board of directors. More than 11,000 UAW members would have been affected by such a sale.

The Acustar locals and the union's Chrysler Department reacted swiftly and angrily. Local unions throughout the corporation were told to prepare strike packages over outstanding health and safety grievances (strikable during the contract). The union "suspended" its cooperation in joint programs, including the Product Quality Improvement Partnership. It even suspended the team concept "Modern Operating Agreements" already signed at six plants, including two Acustar plants. A thousand workers demonstrated outside Chrysler headquarters, tying up traffic for two hours.

Within a week, as the *Detroit Free Press* put it, "Chrysler blinked." The corporation agreed not to sell the Acustar division, although four plants would be sold or closed, employing 2,100 hourly and salaried workers. The confrontation was seen as an unaccustomed flexing of the UAW's muscle and a victory for the union.

Nowadays it is common to hear union leaders or members argue that striking does not work for unions any more—"it hurts us more than it does the company, because of (pick one or more) technology, scabs, overcapacity, the need to fight imports." The UAW's victory through the mere threat of strikes was an indication that there is still life in the the old-fashioned tactic, if unions will only dare to use it. If the union had gone further perhaps it could have taken on the outsourcing and plant closings that also plague Chrysler workers.

A final demonstration of the fact that unions still have power is the victories that have been won using "insider strategies"—i.e., letting the contract expire, staying on the job, collecting dues by hand, and engaging in innumerable small and large daily confrontations with the company.[14] Two well known examples are the UAW's "run-the-plant-backwards" campaigns at Moog Automotive in St. Louis and at LTV in Dallas. There is no union tactic which requires an organized and active rank and file more than the insider strategy. Local unions which have used this tactic have been successful

when they got their members thoroughly involved, when the union was a living, breathing presence in the plant once again. Their victories have shown that a well-organized union can be successful even in the face of a determined company attack.

The rest of this chapter is about how to organize the union's dormant power.

Communicate with Other Local Unions

Even after team concept, regular contact with sister locals is important. Knowing what your company is up to at other plants will keep you prepared for what to expect at your own. Use the suggestions made earlier in this chapter to maintain regular contact.

Just as the company sometimes sends workers to visit vendors or customers, the union should send representatives, including rank and filers, to visit the plants upstream or downstream from them. Let each other know what advances you've made in curbing team concept in your respective plants. Plan together for the next round of bargaining. The best step may be to move to division-wide or company-wide agreements on work rules instead of local ones, to stop whipsawing. Then the lowest can be brought up to the highest, not vice versa.

The lessons are also transferable from industry to industry. A concerned local union could call a seminar, brainstorming session or conference of all the different unions in its town that are curious about team concept. This might be organized through the Central Labor Council or more informally.

Language for a Team Concept Contract

The union should bargain over both the changes caused by team concept itself and the other changes management is probably implementing at the same time.

Some of the demands we suggest here may seem unobtainable at this stage of the game, since it seldom happens that a union makes substantial gains at the same time that it is making substantial concessions like the team concept. Such demands do, however, demonstrate which side—union or management—is *really* for job security, "working smarter," worker participation and quality. They can thus be part of a strategy of opposing team concept. In any case they educate the membership and help the union to sharpen its pro-worker vision and its long term goals.

This section will suggest language which deals with the team concept itself, and the following section will deal with related issues. Where the language appears in an existing contract, this is noted.

1. Absentee Replacement

One of the biggest differences between a thoroughly management-by-stress plant and other team concept plants is the existence of absentee replacement operators (AROs). At NUMMI, for example, workers blame each other for missing work instead of blaming management for not providing enough help. At plants with AROs such peer pressure is minimal.

If possible, negotiate a contractual number of AROs—x number per team (depending on team size), or x percentage of the workforce. Preferably, AROs should be attached to a particular team, not functioning department- or plant-wide and thus loaned out all over.

2. Rights of Teams

(Where noted, some of the following are modifications of provisions in the UAW-GM contract at Shreveport. Exact language is at the end of Chapter 12.)

• The team may ask the foreman to leave the team meeting. (Shreveport) This is important on two occasions: 1) when an individual member is making life difficult for others or there is a personality problem that needs to be worked out; and 2) when the team needs to conduct union business, such as election of its steward (described below) or discussion of action against management's latest ploy.

• The team may call a meeting in addition to regularly scheduled ones if circumstances arise, or lengthen the regular meeting. (Shreveport) The team cannot be expected to discuss problems seriously in a half hour per week.

• Team meetings will not be unilaterally cancelled or adjourned by management. (Shreveport)

• Team meetings will not be held on breaks or lunchtime unless the team chooses. Meetings held on breaks or before or after the workday will be paid at overtime rates.

• Decisions made at a team meeting will not be overturned by management unless management follows a specific procedure, including notification of the team, in writing, of its reasons for doing so. (In other words, there must be exceptional circumstances for management to overturn a team decision.)

• The team may request a union representative (committeeperson or other) to be present at its meeting. Union representatives may also attend any team meeting on their own initiative. A team decision may be superseded by a union decision that the team decision is contrary to union policy.

• Teams may call joint meetings with other teams or send representatives to other teams' meetings.

• Teams set their own rules of functioning, as long as they do not conflict with the contract. Violation of team rules will not be subject to management discipline.

• The company will honor a team's request for a new supervisor or "advisor."

(Under a special project agreement which included teams, the Maintenance and Construction unit of UAW Local 600 at Ford's Dearborn plant got management to agree in advance that if the construction team felt a supervisor was not cooperating properly, he could be removed. The union exercised this right and a supervisor was transferred.)

3. Choosing the Team Coordinator

There are several possibilities for deciding which team member becomes team coordinator or team leader: election by the team, rotation among team members, appointment by management, and seniority. Appointment by management should be avoided, for obvious reasons. Each of the other options has some points in its favor.

Letting all team members rotate through the job would help maintain equality among members. The drawback, of course, is that not all members will want to be coordinator.

The more traditional union response would be to favor seniority. Going by seniority reduces the chance that team coordinators will be the types who see themselves as junior management. And it provides high seniority workers the chance for what some consider a better job. Under this system the team coordinator position will be much like the old "utility operator" classification.

On the other hand, election by the team could also have benefits. If the team is alert to the need to organize itself, the election method makes it possible to choose a union-conscious natural leader as team coordinator.

If team coordinators are elected they should have a relatively short term of office, and they should be re-electable. Members should also have the right to recall them if they are dissatisfied with their performance. Some local leaders have been concerned that this right could lead to "instability." But the right of recall is one way teams can exert some *group* power over their daily work lives—an experience the union should be encouraging.

The team coordinator should have the right to resign at any time and return to his or her previous job. The team should also decide on a mechanism for deciding what job the team coordinator will take when a new coordinator is chosen. This could be based on seniority or could be a swap with the person who becomes coordinator.

4. Rights of Individuals

• Attendance at team meetings is voluntary. With this clause in place, members can organize a boycott of team meetings as a pressure tactic when a particular issue is hot.

• If the plant has a pay-for-knowledge system, no individual should be required to participate in it. Once he has entered the pay-for-knowledge system, he should have the option to leave it and return to being paid for knowing only one job. He should be able to move back and forth between the two options at reasonable intervals (say three months). UAW Local 1999 in Oklahoma City has language that says a worker may withdraw from the "Voluntary Input" program four times a year, on the first Monday in January, April, July and October, and may enter it at any time. UAW Local 5960 in Orion, Michigan allows workers to switch every six months.

5. Size of Teams

Often management decides on team size because of a preconceived notion—often handed down from above. (The latest preference within GM, for example, is for small teams a la NUMMI.) For workers there are more advantages to large teams. Large teams can make daily life on the job more bearable, because there is a greater variety of jobs within the team. Also, if one day there is a problem with production or one member is not feeling up to snuff, the problem can more easily be absorbed. A 15-member team that controls a larger chunk of the production process gives its members more power in dealing with management; it cannot be as easily isolated as a four-member team. It is also easier for the union to keep in contact with.

However, the union which is successful in negotiating large teams should make sure that there is a sufficient number of team coordinators and Absentee Replacement Operators per team.

6. Union Independence

Avoid language which prevents union officials from doing their jobs, such as NUMMI's clause which can be read to say that workers cannot talk to their union rep before taking a complaint to their team leader or group leader. Also avoid language requiring union and company reps to act together to solve grievances.

In particular, avoid language that commits the union to making the plant "competitive." Do not commit the union or the individual worker to *kaizen* ("seek continual improvement") or to "assist the company in meeting production goals and schedules"[15] (see box on The Team Concept and the Law).

7. Classifications

It is difficult to maintain classifications under the team concept, since getting rid of classifications is one of management's main objectives. Nonetheless, General Motors' Orion assembly plant has 25 production classifications, although they are not used for transferring (see Chapter 21). Chrysler's Sterling Heights, Michigan assembly plant (not a team concept plant) opened in 1984 with only three production classifications, but the union

---

THE TEAM CONCEPT AND THE LAW

By Ellis Boal

From a legal standpoint, the team concept presents several unusual issues.[1] Labor-management cooperation and work teams were discredited ideas when the National Labor Relations Act (NLRA) was passed in 1935 and amended in 1947. The law conceived the interests of workers and management as fundamentally different and opposed. The drafters did not imagine that such plans would revive or that unions would ever endorse them. But team concept is here, so the law will deal with it.

A team can be described as a quality circle with an added twist. That is, workers are formed into groups and ordered to brainstorm productivity schemes for the company's benefit. The teams also deal and bargain with management on topics of traditional union interest. So although contract or grievable issues are theoretically not to be discussed, the agenda commonly includes items on working conditions, safety, comfort, ventilation, sanitation, work assignments, transfers, vacation time, and job stress. And the teams are established and dominated by the company.

The added twist is that the contracts which set them up also enable the company to harass the workforce when things aren't going well.

Thus, in the NUMMI contract the union agreed that both it and the employees must "promote *kaizen*."[2] *Kaizen* is not defined in the contract, though presumably it refers to seeking constant improvement. Whatever that means, if the employer thinks someone is not doing it, he or she can be disciplined or fired. And if employees collectively fail to "promote *kaizen*," the company can sue the union.[3]

To make the team concept more attractive, companies commonly offer the union two benefits with it which they legally don't have to give. The first is a prediction that the plant will stay open or get more work. Of course, a prediction is not an enforceable promise and there may not be any benefit.

The second is union access to management information. For instance, introduction of technology is legally considered a "management prerogative" which management need not discuss in advance with the union. Playing off the idea of cooperation, management now invites the union to review information of this nature. Theoretically the union can then use its skill to influence important company decisions before they happen.

However, the union gets no right to strike over or arbitrate disputes on these matters.[4] And if the union did get a measure of co-equal power, it would open itself to litigation if workers were hurt by it. Suits have been filed in the past where a union committee failed to assure a safe workplace,[5] or where the union had vital information and failed to inform the membership.[6] The same theories could be applied if the union helped design a job that later caused injury.

With all of these problems it might seem that the team concept would not survive legal challenge. This turns out to be correct—where it is used by non union companies.

Without a union, the NLRB's traditional view

Ellis Boal is a lawyer in Detroit and a contributor to Labor Notes. *He has handled many cases involving the UAW. He is the author of* Teamster Rank and File Legal Rights Handbook.

was able to bargain for nine in its first local agreement.

From workers' point of view the important thing about classifications is not differentiation for differentiation's sake. Many local unions have decided that technology and other changes have made some of their classifications obsolete. Traditionally, classifications have served two purposes: to provide for transfer rights (see Chapter 7), and to keep the company from adding different types of work to one job, thus preserving more jobs. (They have also been used to differentiate pay levels.) The union should figure out for itself what classifications it needs and bargain from there. Even if you cannot maintain many classifications, you should try to retain as many of the *rights* that went with classifications as possible. The next point below discusses transfer rights in more detail.

Even in traditional plants a production worker does not usually have the right to refuse work which is outside of her classification. In most plants you must do whatever work is assigned to you no matter what your classification, and you will be paid the higher rate if it is higher paid work. But the existence of classifications at least gives you the basis for a grievance when management assigns you to do jobs from two classifications at the same time. When team concept comes in the union should try to negotiate a contractual provision that a worker has the right to refuse a job for which he doesn't feel qualified or cannot do safely.

8. Transferring

Transfer rights are one of the biggest losses experienced by workers in team concept plants. When classifications are eliminated, the right to transfer to another classification is, of course, eliminated too. And the loss of many of the "good jobs" means that there's less reason to transfer.

In many plants the question of who should have first crack at an open job is already controversial, even without team concept. Should those within the depart-

---

THE TEAM CONCEPT AND THE LAW, continued

would be that teams are illegal. In most cases they are not really just work teams, as employees are told. Teams also deal with management on behalf of workers about working conditions and other topics of importance to unions the NLRB would look at them as tiny "labor organizations" or unions. Under NLRA Section 8(a)(2), a company may not "dominate" any labor organization by funding it or choosing its officers. Workers should be free to formulate their own views on working conditions in a labor organization. The law recognizes the interests of a labor organization and management as "inherently adverse."[7] Illegal teams must be disestablished if they are challenged.[8] The present members of the NLRB may not like this state of the law, but it is on the books, and so far it has been enforced.[9]

The legality of the team concept is different in a unionized plant. The NLRB reasons that if a union agrees to it—for any reason—that is a choice the union is free to make. But the union can also reject the team concept. A company may not establish it unilaterally, because otherwise it would undercut the union's ability to function.[10]

If the union does accept the team concept, it stays only as long as the union allows it.

Several points should be kept in mind, though. As with any other written contract in the UAW (or most other unions in which contracts are subject to membership approval), the members must be allowed to vote on it. If a contract which omits mention of a particular past practice is ratified, and later the past practice is changed and reduced to writing, the members are entitled to vote again.[11] The union could get around this by putting language in the voted contract

referring past practices to a designated committee.[12] But the current UAW team concept contracts don't do this.

Secondly, to maintain its legality, the plan must in practice have real input from the union in its official capacity. If not, and the union in effect abandons its bargaining and grieving responsibilities to the teams, the situation would be the same as in the non-union sector.[13] The teams could be disestablished as illegally dominated labor organizations.[14] And the union could be liable for failure to represent its members.[15]

Thirdly, team leaders could be held to be supervisors and excluded from the bargaining unit under certain circumstances. If they are appointed by management and feel responsible to management, rather than being elected as spokespersons for the team, this would weigh heavily in the NLRB's view.[16] If a case arose where a union officer was found to be a supervisor by virtue of being a team leader, the company could ask the NLRB to decertify the union.[17]

Fourthly, if a team member gets fellow team members to join in pressing for real improvements in working conditions through the team, and then is harassed because of that, the retaliation would be illegal.[18]

Finally, to the extent that the International union encourages its members or its locals to compete against each other to get the team concept, it is violating the spirit of the National Labor Relations Act. The International union is not supposed to be about creating "winners" and "losers." The union's most important legal obligation is to represent all workers and locals together.

ment, or classification, or supervisor's group, have more rights to transfer to a job they're presumably more familiar with, or should strict plant-wide seniority govern?

The principle should be that whatever the procedure, everybody understands it and it is strictly enforced. If before the team concept your plant gave first transfer rights within the department, it is probably better to stick with what members have become accustomed to. In general, however, it is best to opt for the widest possible application of seniority. Avoid the system that exists at GM's Orion and Shreveport plants (see Chapters 12 and 21), which always gives first pick of an opening in a team to members of that same team. Such provisions weaken broader seniority rights and encourage team isolation (management would call it "building team cohesion"). At Shreveport some teams even assign jobs by "team seniority"—how long you've been in that particular team!

At GM's Van Nuys plant, the committeepeople were determined to see open jobs go to the top seniority person, wherever he or she came from. They went beyond the contract to negotiate informal agreements to this effect on the department level. Management found that since the *amount* of transferring was cut down under team concept, it was not such a big burden to have an orderly system—i.e., seniority—for regulating the transfers that did occur.

In any case, the union should negotiate the maximum number of choices possible for the individual worker: transfers from team to team and transfers from department to department, as well as shift preference by seniority. Other recommendations are the same as the union would try to get in a traditional plant: no limit on the number of applications a worker can have on file, and a short or no waiting period before an application is valid.

9. Rotation

At most plants regular rotation has become voluntary in practice; only a small minority actually rotate. Whatever the contract language says, workers usually stay on a particular job most of the time, even if they are paid for knowing more jobs. Management prefers this as long as they have the flexibility to move someone if they want to and if workers remain adept at all the jobs they're being paid to know.

Language guaranteeing that workers can remain on their regular jobs should be as strong as possible (while still allowing those who choose to do so to rotate). A sample (adapted from UAW Local 1700's agreement with Chrysler's Sterling Heights Assembly Plant):

Management acknowledges that continuity is desirable and therefore will assign employees to specific jobs. It is understood that an employee may be assigned to a different job from time to time when it is necessary to train other employees on his or her job. In the event that it becomes necessary to temporarily reassign an employee, management will inform the employee of the reason for and duration of the temporary assignment. Management will not permit reassignment of employees for the purpose of harassment or as a punitive measure.

If the union believes an employee's assignment has been changed for such reasons, it shall immediately take the matter up with the departmental superintendent. If not satisfactorily disposed of, the matter shall be immediately taken up with the Labor Relations Manager.

Possible additional language:

Employees who are proficient at each other's jobs may switch jobs on an hourly, daily or weekly basis. Any problems arising from such rotation will be taken up by the team.

10. Involvement in Design of Jobs

If the union is strong enough, team say over job design could give members some real control over their daily lives in the plant. It could mean some freedom for team members to sort out the assigned tasks in a way that was most agreeable to everyone. Teams could see that the jobs were more or less equally loaded, if this were their preference, or they could create a few lighter jobs for high seniority people or for all team members to rotate through.

However, worker involvement in job design is more often an attempt by management to get team members blaming each other for extra work which management adds. At some team concept plants, such as GM's Shreveport plant, where management tries to involve teams in dividing up their assigned work, this "right" causes more grief than it's worth. In practice at Shreveport, "worker participation" means that the team gets to decide who will take on an added task, or how to eliminate a job from the team. Each team elects a "planner" who works with engineers, especially at model change time, to figure out the reorganization of the jobs. Some Shreveport workers say that the planner job is now a figleaf, with everything decided in advance by the engineers. There are also complaints that the planner is likely to be much more zealous in keeping additional work off his own job than off the jobs of other team members. This is an indication that "worker involvement" is only a benefit when it includes "union involvement."

If the union decides to get involved in job design, overseeing the process in each team should be a prime responsibility of the team steward (described below), together with the committeeperson. The union should demand the following:

• Team members have the right to union-run training in the company's time-study methods so that members can be informed as to what goes into designing a job, what is contractually allowed, and what is prohibited.

• Any proposed changes in job content or production levels must be approved by the team and the union. (A compromise might be to demand that the team could reject additional work for 30 days, to allow time to find a better solution.)

• Where two or more teams do essentially similar work (e.g., on different shifts or parallel lines), one team shall not be used as the sole standard for setting production level or job content. Such teams shall meet together to discuss such level or content.

• This provision also applies if similar work is done at more than one company location. The company will allow lost time for union conferences to establish standards. (This is an anti-whipsawing provision.)

11. Training and Education

The contract at GM's Fort Wayne, Indiana truck plant provides for an automatic 2.7 hours of training per month for each team member, and the team is given some flexibility in how those hours can be used. The company will always try to pressure to have this training fill immediate needs. For a contract provision such as this to work the union has to make alternative kinds of training known to the team, perhaps through an "Education and Training Fair." The choices should be as broad-ranging as possible, including training which is not of immediate use on the worker's particular job if that is what he or she desires.

12. Team Concept Training

It is not enough for the union to have a veto over a company-designed team concept training program, or for the shop committee to have the right to add a few words to management's presentation. The courses should not consist of management training slightly warmed over for team use ("imagine you are a department superintendent... "). The union should be able to hire its own consultants to work over or design team training from scratch. Union facilitators and trainers should be appointed by, recallable by, and responsible to the local union.

Demand that management's consultants and training designers demonstrate knowledge of and commitment to unions—no consultants who double as union-busters.

13. Dignity and Respect

Most team concept contracts contain language which commits management to the idea that worker dignity is an important goal. Chapter 4 takes up many illustrations of what a workplace which truly offered respect to workers would be like. It could be used as a checklist to determine how close your local agreement comes to this goal.

Here are some examples:

• No requirement for doctor's notes. An employee is to be taken at his or her word. (Yes, there will be "abuses" of this right. But it makes no sense to deny the rights of the majority in order to weed out those few who misuse a right.)

• Management may not send a worker home on a disciplinary layoff in the middle of the shift.

• "Innocent until proven guilty" is the rule on discipline.

• Automatic granting of unpaid personal and educational leaves.

• Automatic granting of contractual personal days (Paid Absence Allowance days in the auto industry).

• Two weeks' advance notice of layoff; when recalled, worker has up to two weeks to return to work.

14. No "Living Agreement"

Retain as much previous contract language, in writing, as possible. Experience has shown that there is no advantage in getting rid of it in favor of verbiage about "mutual trust." Make changes in plant operation subject to formal negotiation with the union and membership ratification.

15. "Working Smarter"

If management wants to involve the teams or individual workers in thinking of ways to "work smarter," it should not expect workers to pay the price for the improvements.

• The teams should have nothing to do with "problem-solving" when it is really disguised speedup.

• All team suggestions will be evaluated, with union involvement, for any possible impact on the number of jobs. Any decrease in jobs caused by a team suggestion must be compensated for through:

a) Creation of new jobs. These could come from improvements in the physical plant, expanding the products or services available from the company, or expanding the quality program, for example.

b) Reduction of work time, distributed among all workers. More break time or a shorter day, vacation or personal days off, sabbaticals, or time off to attend classes.

There are some "working smarter" cases that can be genuine "win-win" situations. These are the issues the union should address.

For example, in one company over the years the two sides had developed an elaborate procedure for allowing workers to exercise weekly preference for the specific machines they would operate, taking into account seniority and ability. Management complained that the procedure was so complicated that sometimes jobs would not get assigned or were assigned improperly, causing confusion as well as grievances. Management proposed to get rid of the preference bidding and give itself the flexibility to assign jobs. The union came back with a proposal for a computer program to handle the assignment process. The result was that workers still got to exercise their preferences, with fewer foul-ups than before, and management got all the jobs assigned in an orderly manner.

Language on General Issues

When management achieves ratification of the team concept in a plant, it is usually hungry for other changes as well. Implementation of a complete management-by-stress system involves many aspects which have little to do with teams themselves. These include just-in-time parts delivery, outside contracting, outsourcing, and the use of technology. The union should be prepared to put forward its own program on these.

1. Effects of Just-in-Time

Buffers—banks of parts—should be negotiated so that workers can pace their own work to some extent. In addition, the union should demand "flying squads" of workers to deal with emergencies that arise, rather than having the burden fall on the individual worker and his or her teammates.

2. Contracting Out

Some plants, such as GM's Buick Reatta and Warren Hydra-Matic, have paint technicians employed by suppliers or "rent-a-techs" (temporary agencies) who work full-time in the plant, because management claims no workers have the proper skills. Since management projects its long-term needs, it is not too much to ask that they also plan ahead by sending employees to school or to supplier companies for training to fill any jobs they plan to create.

The union should demand that no work be contracted out, except that the company may contract out for jobs that require special training as long as a bargaining unit person goes into training to take over that job within a reasonable time.

In addition, the company will not use any contractor which is non-union.

3. Technology

The union needs provisions so that technology does not become a tool of tight control over union members. In many plants assembly line workers now have to inspect their own work and punch into a computer whether they did it right or wrong. Even more insidious is the new monitoring technology. Simply by installing inexpensive communications hardware and software, individual machines are now being connected to central computers in supervisors' offices. Supervisors thus gain the capability to continuously monitor any action of any employee and to do a continuous time-study. The union should negotiate language barring any monitoring that is not union-supervised and barring the results of computer monitoring from being used for discipline.

The union should negotiate the conditions under which visual display systems, such as *andon*, will signal management that there is a problem. For example, in Germany one union insisted that signal lights come on only when the worker had exceeded the average time to do the job. Since by definition the average is exceeded roughly half the time, this meant that the lights were flashing continuously, making them essentially meaningless for monitoring an individual. The only thing the lights could indicate well was when the whole workforce was behind.[16]

The union should also demand "technology stewards" who are trained in computer techniques. These stewards should have access to terminals to examine programs and settings in all computer automation to see that they comply with the contract.

All functions created by new technology should become bargaining unit jobs, including programming and maintenance. If in-depth training is required, workers should be given that training.

4. Outsourcing

In some companies outsourcing is the biggest threat to jobs that workers face, with plans to spin off everything from components production to stamping to entire car lines. The union should demand a ban on all new outsourcing. In addition, the company will not source from a non-union supplier.

5. Rate-busters

Management often uses new employees as temporaries, who then have an incentive to become rate-busters in hopes of impressing management enough to keep them on. The union should demand that new employees have callback rights after 30 days of work for the company. They may be dismissed only for cause. By giving them automatic callback rights, the incentive to impress mangement is greatly reduced.

6. Skilled Trades

Protecting the skilled trades—both their numbers and the content of their jobs—helps both the trades and production workers. There should be no outside contracting and no hiring of new skilled tradespersons off the street. All openings, including "temporary" jobs, should be filled by promoting production workers through the apprenticeship program. Thus every skilled job defended becomes an opening for a production worker, and every new tradesperson on the rolls improves the choices for the tradespeople higher on the seniority list.

The Printed Word

Language is not everything; unless it is enforced it means nothing. How even team concept language gets interpreted depends partly on how the union acts, day to

---

THE UNION CHAIN OF COMMAND: WHO'S IN CHARGE HERE?

There are two obstacles to getting team stewards in the contract. First, management won't want them. Team stewards have been included in only two contracts, NUMMI's and Mazda's. Second, many committeepersons will not be comfortable with the idea. They may fear 1) that active team stewards would usurp their authority with management and the membership, and 2) that they could become a political threat come election time.

The first fear is not justified. A good committeeperson already has such a system informally—people they can count on in each area. Committeepeople who have organization on the shop floor have *more* authority with management, not less. A committeeperson with a network behind her can count on her constituents to back her up when she tells management that such and such an issue is something she's got to have.

If you were management, which would you rather face: an isolated committeeperson you can keep tied up 90 percent of the time, or a committeeperson backed by a dozen "junior committeepersons" keeping the membership informed and ready to beef in a united fashion?

As to authority with the membership: who has more authority and popularity with the rank and file —someone who tries to do it all himself (which we know is impossible), or someone who shows he cares enough to organize a network on the members' behalf?

There is no getting around the second fear: a good team steward could become popular and could run against a committeeperson who was falling down on the job. But since when are elections uncontested in any case? There will always be competition for committee positions, and the creation of team stewards just means there might be more candidates in the race.

Committeepeople who fear team stewards will have to ask themselves the following question: which would you rather be a part of, a weak union where the incumbents can keep their jobs because most members are too apathetic to run for office, or an organization with some life in it? In every organization there will be some who prefer the former. The Catch-22 for them is that they are likely to get voted out anyway.

A system similar to team stewards was tried by UAW Local 600 at Ford's Dearborn assembly plant. The plant does not have teams, but "sections" (groups of about 20 workers) each chose a representative to receive special union training. Those representatives made up the plant's "solidarity committee." The plan was for them to act as informal stewards. Unfortunately, the committeepeople were not required to attend the training sessions and ended up feeling alienated from the program and jealous of the solidarity committee. The program foundered.

Local 600's experience shows that a team steward program will have to have the backing, participation, and understanding of the shop floor union reps if it is to succeed. Such a program is best initiated around a specific campaign—such as responding to team concept—rather than in the abstract.

day, in its implementation. And many times certain procedures become "rules" simply because the union acts as if they were written in stone and they become "past practice." The worst team contract language need not be followed to the letter if the union can get away with not following it, or with enforcing a better version.

That brings us to our final point, strengthening the union so it can have such enforcement power.

A Stronger Union

Letting the team concept in the door does not have to mean that the union withers away on the shop floor. This is, however, the most likely result if the union does not take aggressive action to prevent it. The demoralization of having team concept pushed down your throat under company threats is bad enough; the loss of language that used to be integral to the contract, such as classifications, doesn't help either. The only way the local union can maintain its health after team concept is to take conscious, assertive steps to change complacent habits it may have fallen into. Some old ways of functioning—in particular being nonchalant about rank and file apathy—will have to go.

1. Develop a Long-Range Strategic Plan

The union must cease being only a "reactor" to management's initiatives and become an "actor." It must figure out what it is trying to accomplish and define its mission. What is the basis of this local's power within the company? What are management's weak points and strengths? How can the union's leverage be increased? What are the union's weaknesses and how can they be corrected? Who are potential allies (such as unions in other plants in its division, other unions, community groups, church groups, etc.)? Where can the union get technical and research help?

The union should put forward a positive program, not just a defense against the worst aspects of team concept but a vision of what it would like to

achieve for its members. It would do well to get its own "consultants"—outfits such as Labor Notes, the Midwest Center for Labor Research, the American Labor Education Center, and Corporate Campaign, Inc.[17] University labor education centers might also provide useful advice.

2. Organize within the Teams

It is not the union's job to "make the teams work" (by management's definition), but to protect the membership from the bad effects of teams. The following ideas are to help the union use the team structure for its own objectives.

In many ways the existence of teams would seem to be ideal for union purposes. Workers come together to discuss problems in natural groups—and they're even paid for attending! Given the low level of attendance at most union meetings, this is an opportunity for the majority of union members who aren't active to get together in an organized way. The team meetings are, of course, organized by the company. This doesn't mean the union can't have a hand in them.

Most auto workers in the plants today do not remember when the UAW had tangible shop floor power. Over the years the union gave up much of that ability to influence how the work day went. Instead it bargained for income protection and a rather complicated set of rules governing workers' rights (see Chapter 7). Now team concept is stripping away those contractual protections. It is up to the union to try to rebuild shop floor organization so that worker rights can be enforced in a more informal way. A union that functions this way has to be much more aware of the hundreds of daily power confrontations with management. Less can be sloughed off on the grievance procedure, since there are fewer rights to grieve about. This means rebuilding the shop steward system.

Until 1958 the UAW had "blue button" or line stewards at Chrysler, one for every foreman or about every 25 workers. (That is why still today the lowest level union reps at Chrysler are called "chief stewards"—there used to be stewards under them.) Although not recognized in the contract, these stewards engaged in informal bargaining with the immediate supervisor. The 1939 constitution of Local 3 at the huge Dodge Main plant said:

> The Chief Shop Steward may appoint or elect, if the group wishes, as many deputy stewards as may be necessary to aid in his or her duties. There shall be at least one deputy steward for a group of 20 or less.[18]

It was no coincidence when, in 1958, the union gave up blue button stewards at the same time that it gave management much more authority to unilaterally set production standards.

The blue button stewards kept workers informed of what was going on throughout the plant and organized them, when necessary, to resist the latest management offensive. From day to day, their activities could

---

WHAT'S WRONG WITH TEAMWORK?

There is nothing wrong with teams or teamwork per se. On the contrary, many people have had some of the best experiences of their lives on basketball teams or volleyball teams—that feeling of working together in harmony, with everyone contributing and everyone sharing in the glory (or the pain), cannot be beat. It's even possible to get that feeling in the plant, when the whole crew decides to pitch in and get production out early, and the machines don't break down. In general, any set-up which breaks down isolation and encourages people to work together is *positive* for unions.

It is not teams themselves which are harmful to workers and unions, but the particular way the team concept has been defined and put into practice by management.

range from interceding for a worker who was getting harassed to organizing an overtime ban. Their constituencies were small enough that they could keep in daily touch with every member. A foreman could not pull some trick and hope that his people would be too apathetic to let the union know. The higher level officers had eyes and ears on the shop floor.

Ironically, a pale semblance of the blue button system has been resurrected at NUMMI, one of the worst team concept plants in terms of speedup and erosion of worker rights. The NUMMI contract calls for one "union coordinator" to be elected for every 20-30 workers (see Chapter 11). He or she gets two hours' extra pay per week, for handling problems that arise day to day. Usually the union coordinators do this during breaks or lunch, although, depending on the group leader, they may get relieved by the team leader to investigate a problem.

In the discussion that follows we'll call these first-level shop floor reps "team stewards" to avoid confusing them with team coordinators.

If teams are small it is better to elect one steward for every two or three teams. "A steward for every foreman" is probably a good guideline. Representing more members also gives each individual steward more clout. The teams should elect their stewards in the regular team meeting (joint meetings, if necessary) to set the precedent that the teams can discuss union matters. If this proves to be impossible, team members can stay after for 15 minutes to vote.

As soon as they are elected, the union should set up classes in contract enforcement for the new team stewards. It would be best if all members were encouraged to sign up for these as well; explain that living under the new team concept system, people will need to be more aware of their rights than ever before. The union can also set up classes in group dynamics, similar to those the company often uses in team concept training. Yes, these can be used to the union's advantage too —if you take out the pro-company assumptions and exercises.[19] The nearest college labor education program might come in handy for team steward training, especially if there is someone who can talk about the history of the union on the shop floor. Better yet, find some retirees who can remember when action on the shop floor was the norm, not the exception.

The stewards in each committeeperson's district should work as a "team" with him or her. They should meet together frequently and should report to the committeeperson on what is going on in the district. They are the committeeperson's best avenue for two-way communication with the members.

Even if the union cannot convince management to officially include team stewards in the contract, there is nothing to stop the union from setting up an informal system. Management is not likely to want to deal with these informal stewards. How effective they are will depend on how seriously the union takes them and how aggressive they are. Each supervisor should discover that the team members are more cooperative with him when he is cooperative with their team steward.

What can team stewards do? They should have the right to get off the job to handle problems during working hours and they should be able to write grievances. (Many members do not know that they already have the right to write grievances themselves.) They should not hesitate to call in the committeeperson when it looks like an issue needs someone with more experience. If the member is not satisfied with the team steward's functioning he should be able to call the committeeperson.

Perhaps most important, they should go directly to the foreman with problems even if they are not contractual. Members often will not bother to call the committeeperson because they feel their gripe is too individual or too small, or that by the time it gets solved it won't matter any more. If a union rep is always on the scene, problems like lack of gloves or the height of a work table are more likely to be addressed. A team stew-

IF YOU HAVE A TEAM
(to the tune of "Young at Heart")

Fairy tales can come true
it can happen to you
if you have a team

An adversarial mind
changes quickly you'll find
when you're on a team

Though the line speed's extreme
you never do scream
Jobs designed by your team
aren't as hard as they seem

And though you're working faster
every passing day,
the company is in your heart—
work feels like play

Don't you know it is worth
all the unions on earth
just to have a team?

The boss is your friend
as long as you bend
on a flexible team

And if you can survive
till you're 55
think of all they'll derive
cause you've eaten this jive

But here is the main bite
they'll shut your plant tight
unless you go along and
vote to have a team.

ard, who is presumably familiar with the daily conflicts that go on, could also act as a mediator in clashes between employees.

Plant-wide, the team stewards along with the committeepeople should form a stewards council that meets regularly—at least every two weeks—to compare notes about what is going on on the shop floor. These meetings are a vital forum for disseminating information from the officers, finding out what the membership is thinking, and planning plant-wide strategies.

Members should be encouraged to be active in the teams *in a union direction*. They can take management at its word and make suggestions for improvements in working conditions. It is legally "protected activity" to speak up in team meetings. The union should let members know that they will be backed up if they are harassed by the company as retribution.

On the other hand, boycotts of team meetings can be organized over a specific issue or when management is misusing the meetings. (Very often they become simple rah-rah sessions for attendance or productivity or beating "the competition.") If 90 percent of the members exercise their contractual right to refuse to attend the meeting, it is a "visual indicator" (in the management-by-stress terminology) of the depth of their feeling about the issue at hand.

3. Establish a Code of Conduct Becoming to a Union Member

The union should renew the idea that there are certain standards of behavior as a worker and a union member. Many members say that once team concept sets in it becomes much more socially acceptable to be buddy-buddy with management than ever before. The local union should take the attitude that just because the national contract mandates union cooperation, it doesn't follow that union members give up their independence and identity.

The union should not allow the company to confuse the members about the fact that they still have an adversarial relationship. When union members see a videotape of the union president embracing the plant manager at his retirement, they find it difficult to believe when the union says it is going to get tough. Union officers should refuse to sign statements declaring that union and management are "partners" in anything. They should not appear in company video tapes (which can be dubbed with different voice-overs), use union newsletters to promote company programs such as attendance control, or attend "offsite" meetings at fancy resorts. When joint actions or statements are necessary, they should be treated as contracts and limited to the specifics.

In the early days of unionism, before there were complex contracts, unions often included a code of ethics and on-the-job conduct in their local by-laws or in a "union rule book." The rule book was written and passed solely by union members, not negotiated with the employer. It gave guidelines for who should do what

work and how union members should relate to bosses and to each other. These guidelines were enforced by social pressure or, if necessary, by union action. The team concept tries to reproduce the situation of no written language governing classifications and other working conditions. Under these circumstances a union rule book seems relevant once again.

Such a rule book, backed up by the committeepeople and team stewards, should make it clear that certain behaviors and attitudes are part of being a good union member:

• passing on all relevant information—about production, problems, rumors, management violations of the contract—immediately to the union.

• spreading the union position on issues when they come up. For example, if the union meeting votes to oppose concessions which the company says might save a particular department, active members should explain to others both within and outside of the plant what the position is and why the union took it.

• safety and health always come first.

• it is more important to protect jobs than to show how smart you are.

Likewise there are certain actions which are outside the boundaries of "conduct becoming to a union member":

• volunteering for more work on a job—especially if you are on it temporarily.

• working unsafely because management is in a hurry.

• rate-busting on a job on which another member has filed a work standards grievance.

• complaining to management that a fellow worker is not working hard enough. A member's behavior that causes more work for others should be taken up with the individual, the union, or the team, without management present.

• making suggestions that eliminate jobs.

• sexual harassment or discrimination.

• racial harassment or discrimination.

• discussing union business with members of management.

• snitching to management.

• committeepeople being buddy-buddy with members of management.

• union officers applying for management positions. The union can pass a bylaw prohibiting such conflicts of interest. The NLRB has held that the employer must furnish the union with the names of officers and stewards who have applied for such positions.

4. Begin a Union Involvement and Action Program

• Encourage union reps to write grievances where appropriate. Management now claims that writing grievances is "uncooperative"—inappropriate under the team concept. But the grievance procedure was instituted precisely to provide an orderly way to solve problems. If the grievance procedure is now viewed as uncooperative, how are workers to get their problems resolved? Management may try to channel all "problems" to the teams—but usually the teams are management's turf. A union which refuses to write grievances could also be liable for failure of its "duty of fair representation."

Under contracts which allow the union to strike over certain kinds of grievances (such as health and safety, or production standards), having such grievances on file is the only way the union can be prepared when it needs to threaten strike action (as the UAW did to Chrysler over the sale of Acustar).

• Begin a union education program with ongoing classes. It should discuss technology and economic trends as they affect both the industry and workers themselves. (It is ironic that just when the union needs its own information and strategy most, UAW local leaders are being encouraged to participate in leadership education programs such as the UAW-Ford and UAW-GM Paid Educational Leave (PEL) program where the company polices the course content and training.) It should include information about labor movements in other countries which are using aggressive strategies despite the companies' worldwide whipsawing.

If the union can afford it, it is very effective to call members out of the plant 30 or so at a time for such classes on union lost time (see Chapter 22). This way the information will reach more than just the regulars. Again, a university labor education program may be helpful.

• Use the union newspaper. The same information disseminated in classes can be gotten out through the union newspaper. Distribute the paper in the plant, not just through the mail. The members need a chance to discuss the ideas with each other. Add such features as "question of the month" interviews, with members' pictures.

• Make the union meetings interesting and worthwhile.

a) The meeting announcement should tell members what is going to come up—not just list "old business, new business," etc.

b) There should be a time on the agenda at an early enough point for members to bring problems to the union leadership. These should be recorded and a report made at the next meeting.

c) Even if there is no quorum, the officers should stay at the meeting to talk with and help the people who did attend.

d) Schedule outside speakers on a variety of topics (not just candidates). When possible these should include speakers from other countries too often viewed as "the competition."

e) Provide childcare, of high quality and without charge.

• Actively recruit volunteers for union committees and give them leeway to function creatively.

• Establish a solidarity committee whose job it is to seek out and support other locals who are on strike or planning for a strike. This includes locals of other unions. These efforts will be repaid when your own local needs morale-building. Don't neglect unorganized workers. The best way to enforce a "no scab suppliers" rule is to help organize the suppliers yourselves.

When the UAW won a union election at Injex, a low-wage supplier to the NUMMI plant, the company still refused to recognize the union. UAW Local 2244 at NUMMI urged its members to

keep a very close eye on every part. The slightest discrepancy should be brought to your Team Leader and Group Leader's attention. Don't correct an Injex mistake. Point it out. Make them fix their mistakes.[20]

In Canada, Canadian Auto Workers Local 1973 helped workers at one of their supplier plants to get their first contract. A textile plant in North Carolina supplied material to GM's Windsor, Ontario trim plant. When the North Carolina workers voted to join the Amalgamated Clothing and Textile Workers Union (ACTWU), Local 1973 had ACTWU delegates tour the trim plant and describe their bargaining situation directly to CAW members. The CAW national leadership also put pressure on management both in Windsor and in North Carolina. The solidarity, wrote ACTWU, was instrumental in achieving a union contract.[21]

Both solidarity on the shop floor in each plant and solidarity between plants will be needed before the team concept is stopped. In particular, local unions need the backing of their international unions to organize and even enforce a united front. In the meantime, local unions can use the steps outlined in this chapter to preserve their strength for the battles ahead.

Notes on What the Union Can Do_____

1. Marjorie Sorge, "Better Listen to the Bell: Chrysler exec warns plants must be productive or close," *Detroit News*, January 15, 1988.

2. *Automotive News*, May 1987.

3. These are described in detail in Jane Slaughter, *Concessions and How To Beat Them*, Detroit, Labor Notes, 1983. The ten-step list for fighting concessions includes: don't reopen the contract, research your employer, demand information, use financial information, educate the membership, put forward an alternative, develop joint strategies, encourage labor movement and community support, strike (or be prepared to), and take legal action.

4. Jane Slaughter, "GM's Grab for Givebacks Is Creating Militants," *Labor Notes* #40, May 26, 1982, p.1. *Also*, "General Motors: 'U.S. Workers Too Expensive, We'll Outsource the Whole Car,'" *Labor Notes* #41, June 24, 1982, p.10.

5. The job security programs in the UAW's National Agreements with Ford and GM recognize this fact by re-

quiring the company to replace one out of every two jobs lost to attrition.

6. From a leaflet distributed at the National Jobs Program Conference in Washington, D.C., January 19, 1988, and signed by the Local 2093 president, bargaining chairman and membership.

7. Figures for numbers of workers come from the UAW. Figures for vehicle production (cars and trucks) come from *Ward's Automotive Report,* January 15, 1979 and January 18, 1988. These figures show that the Big Three have cut jobs drastically since 1978. They also give a rough idea how much more efficient the companies *have* become since then. It would be more precise to compare efficiency, however, by using "hours worked per year" rather than "number of workers," to take overtime into account.

8. Harry C. Katz, Thomas A. Kochan and Jeffrey H. Keefe, "The Impact of Industrial Relations on Productivity: Evidence from the Automobile Industry," paper presented at the Brookings Microeconomic Conference, Washington, D.C., December 3-4, 1987, forthcoming in *Brookings Papers on Economic Activity,* Special Issue. Although the researchers do not say, it can be deduced that the company studied was General Motors.

9. Daniel Luria, "The Relations Between Work Rules, Plant Performance, and Costs in Vehicle Assembly Plants and Parts Production," paper prepared for "The Future of Work in the Automobile Industry," WZB Conference, Berlin, November 1987.

10. Yasuhiro Monden, *Toyota Production System: Practical Approach to Production Management,* Industrial Management and Engineering Press, 1983, p.145.

11. Harley Shaiken and Stephen Herzenberg, *Automation and Global Production,* Center for U.S.-Mexican Studies, University of California, San Diego, 1987.

12. "Consciousness of the People," [Kokumin Ishiki Chosa], March 1986. Study commissioned by the Japanese labor federation, Sohyo.

13. Richard L. Hudson, "Strike at Ford shows problems of new methods," *Wall Street Journal,* February 10, 1988.

14. The AFL-CIO has an excellent manual for let-the-contract-expire in-plant campaigns. *The Inside Game* is free from the AFL-CIO Industrial Department, 815 16th St. NW, Washington, DC 20006.
Labor Research Review has also published a number of excellent articles on tactics which the labor movement can use. See in particular Issue #1 "Labor-Community Unity: the Morse Strike Against Disinvestment and Concessions," Issue #7 "New Tactics for Labor" which includes "insider strategies," Issue #8 "Organize!," which contains an article on one-on-one organizing on the shop floor, and Issue #9 (the section on labor-community coalitions). Send $4 for each issue to 3411 W. Diversey, Chicago, IL 60647.

15. *Agreement Between New United Motor Manufactur-*

ing Inc. and the United Auto Workers, July 1, 1985, II 1.6.

16. Ben Dankbaar, "New Technologies, Management Strategies and the Quality of Work," WZB, Publication Series of the International Institute for Comparative Social Research/Labor Policy, November 1986, p.11.

17. Labor Notes, 7435 Michigan Ave., Detroit, MI 48210. 313 / 842-6262. Midwest Center for Labor Research, 3411 W. Diversey, Chicago, IL 60647. 312 / 278-5418. American Labor Education Center, 1810 Kilbourne Place NW, Washington, DC 20010. 202 / 387-6780. Corporate Campaign, Inc., 989 6th Ave., 8th floor, New York, NY 10018. 212 / 967-3180.

18. Steve Jefferys, *Management and Managed: Fifty Years of Crisis at Chrysler,* Cambridge, Cambridge University Press, 1986, p. 82. See also pages 70-75, 84, 140-145.

19. See Mike Parker, *Inside the Circle: A Union Guide to QWL,* Detroit, Labor Notes/South End Press, 1985, Chapter 10, for information on how to use this type of training for union goals.

20. *Labor News,* UAW Local 2244, special edition, October 1987.

21. "U.S. Textile Workers Praise CAW Solidarity," *CAW Contact,* Vol. 18, No. 5, February 5, 1988, p.2.

Notes on Team Concept and the Law_____

1. Several of the same issues are examined in greater detail in Ellis Boal, "Legal Challenges to QWL" in Mike Parker, *Inside the Circle: A Union Guide to QWL,* Detroit, Labor Notes/South End Press, 1985, pp.95-100.

2. NUMMI Contract, Article 2, Sections 1.3, 1.5, 1.6.

3. *Complete Auto Transit v Reis,* 451 US 401, 101 S Ct 1836, 107 LRRM 2145 (1981).

4. The NUMMI contract does establish a separate grievance procedure to address some of these problems, but it contains no provision for the union to try to enforce its position. NUMMI Contract, Article 28.

5. *Hechler v IBEW,* _____ US _____, 107 S Ct 2161 (1987), on remand _____ F2d _____, 127 LRRM 2135 (CA11, 1987); *Helton v Hake,* 564 SW2d 313, 98 LRRM 2905 (Mo Ct App, 1978); *Dunbar v Steelworkers,* 602 P2d 21, 103 LRRM 2434 (Idaho, 1979).

6. *Teamsters Local 860 v NLRB,* 652 F2d 1052, 107 LRRM 2174 (CADC, 1981).

7. *NLRB v US Postal Service,* _____ F2d _____, 127 LRRM 2807, 2811, (CA6, 1988); *Metropolitan Edison v NLRB,* 460 US 693, 704, 103 S Ct 1467, 112 LRRM 3265 (1983).

8. See e.g. *Ona Corporation,* 285 NLRB #77 (1987).

9. The Supreme Court has unanimously upheld liability in every Section 8(a)(2) case to come before it. See e.g. *Garment Workers v NLRB (Bernhard-Altmann Texas*

Corp., 366 US 731, 81 S Ct 1603, 48 LRRM 2251 (1961). The courts of appeal have sometimes interpreted the law less strictly. See e.g. *NLRB v Streamway Division of Scott and Fetzer Co*, 691 F2d 288, 111 LRRM 2673 (CA6, 1982). The Labor Department is currently looking at the possibility of reinterpreting and weakening the NLRA on this point. US DOL: *US Labor Law and the Future of Labor-Management Cooperation, First Interim Report* (February 1987) and *Second Interim Report* (October 1987).

10. *Jafco*, 284 NLRB #139, 126 LRRM 1038 (1987).

11. *Frenza v Sheet Metal Workers*, 567 F Supp 580, 113 LRRM 2619 (ED Mich, 1983).

12. This is done in Teamster contracts where the subject concerns seniority rights in a plant closing or merger.

13. The 1987 General Motors local agreement in Shreveport may be vulnerable for this reason. Section 7(c) of a memorandum of understanding provides that team decisions are "final and binding and will not be changed by the Union or Management unless the change is due to a sound business purpose or the decision is contrary to the National or Local agreement."

14. *Cabot Carbon Co*, 117 NLRB #211, 40 LRRM 1058 (1957), aff'd 360 US 203, 79 C St 1015, 44 LRRM 2204 (1959).

15. US DOL: *US Labor Law and the Future of Labor-Management Cooperation, Second Interim Report* 62 (October 1987); *Branch 6000 Letter Carriers v NLRB*, 595 F2d 808 (CADC, 1979).

16. *Anamag*, 284 NLRB #72, 125 LRRM 1287 (1987). *Anamag* is the only NLRB case to specifically discuss the team concept.

17. *Sierra Vista Hospital*, 241 NLRB #107, 100 LRRM 1590 (1979); *College of Osteopathic Medicine*, 265 NLRB #37, 111 LRRM 1523 (1982).

18. *Hancor Inc*, 278 NLRB #30, 121 LRRM 1311 (1986).

6. The Japanese at Work: Illusions of the Ideal

By Pamela Briggs

Many people have an image of the Japanese at work which comes close to a utopian vision. This image is particularly prevalent in recent advertising: workers are seen as secure in their jobs, protected by the paternalistic attitudes of their employers; management and shop-floor workers dress in similar style, and both make valuable contributions to the running of the company; the workers strive for the same goals as the management, having adopted the values of the company wholesale. Contentment reigns—apparent from the workers' dedication and their reluctance to take industrial action. All this is seen as a function of a style of management which is rapidly becoming more widespread.

Without an appreciation of the explicit mechanisms through which Japanese organizations operate, and an understanding of the culture which lies behind these facets of organizational behavior, it is easy to be taken in by these images of ideal working practice. The purpose of this paper is to break these misguided utopian images into five prevalent "illusions," described below, and to remind us of the need to understand the Japanese system in terms of the real demands placed upon employees. Only in this way can we assess the desirability of Japanese management techniques for British industry.

1. A Job for Life

While much is made of the paternalistic attitude of Japanese companies which provide their workers with lifetime employment, there is a growing awareness that this security is offered to a minority of the workforce. The *nenko* system, as it is called, is operated only by large firms, who take on less than one-third of the workforce.[1] Of the rest, 35 percent are employed by small firms of less than 50 employees. The trappings of a secure life are therefore the exception rather than the rule: most of the Japanese workforce live without the aid of company housing schemes; recreational facilities; and, more importantly, company welfare schemes. This

Pamela Briggs is a social psychologist at the University of Sheffield in Sheffield, England. This chapter first appeared as an article in a special issue of the Industrial Relations Journal, *titled "The Japanisation of British Industry," Vol. 19 Nol. 1, Spring 1988 (Basil Blackwell, Oxford). The guest editors, Barry Wilkinson and Nick Oliver, have edited a book of the same title (to be published by Basil Blackwell in August 1988).*

rift within the working population exists even within the confines of the large organizations; many of whom employ large numbers of temporary employees who are not entitled to membership in the company union, nor to any of the other benefits extended permanent employees.[2]

The situation for these temporary workers is made difficult by the inadequacies of the Japanese welfare system, where there exists little commitment to individual welfare outside of the mass of private company-operated schemes. The government-operated scheme is a late arrival on this scene, and is clearly viewed as a last resort. Within the company these temporary workers are clearly viewed as second class citizens, although life is perhaps more unpleasant for the subcontractors: second-tier companies brought in to do the dirty work.

Women, out of all the Japanese workers, suffer most from the system, facing discrimination in almost all areas of employment.[3] Despite the fact that women are recruited from the same sources as men, often with similar qualifications, companies almost always expect women to retire upon marriage, and those women who fail to find a husband within a "suitable" period following graduation will find few companies willing to consider offering promotion. Even within occupations such as kindergarten and primary school teaching, considered traditional for women, employment contracts are often offered on a yearly basis, and can be terminated without notice.

Lifetime employment, then, is clearly not every Japanese worker's due. As a result, the Japanese feel pressure, even as children, to compete for the "favored" jobs. One of the more infamous aspects of Japanese life involves the *kyoiku mama's*[4] attempts to guide her children through the "right" educational institutions in order to secure employment within a major company. For those embraced by the major corporations, security is theirs, and its value is clearly understood. However, the cost is dear, since the Japanese company holds formidable power over the average employee.

2. I Love My Company

Although the Japanese are often fiercely patriotic, their relationship with their company is seldom forged in the same manner. The ties that bind are made from sterner stuff: Japanese employees are explicitly rewarded for "desirable" behavior, and ostracized should they display attitudes not in keeping with the company philosophy. A number of factors ensure that this system works. The first has already been raised: permanent employment within a large organization is an achievement for a minority of Japanese; none of whom would be given a second chance at any rival company. They have only one bed to lie in, hence all of the workers understand the need for loyalty and obedience to the firm. Secondly, it is widely known that as much as a third of the Japanese worker's salary is often paid in the form of a bonus. While this bonus is sometimes tied to an individual worker's rate of production, more commonly it is tied explicitly to the company profits, thus ensuring that the success of the company matters to each individual. Finally, the very advantages the large organizations offer their workers can become chains in themselves. This situation is described by Kamata in his vivid portrayal of life within the Toyota company. Talking of the loan system operated to help employees buy their own houses, Kamata states:

> Approximately 4,000 workers have supposedly bought houses built with the help of these two types of loans, and in a very real sense these young married men are tied to the company—that is, to the assembly line—by their loan payments until the day they die.[5]

Being tied to the company, the individual is left with little choice but to conform to the mores and standards expected of him, and standards are often exacting. Thus we find, in Kamata's account, that the company punishes those employees found taking girls into their rooms, and demands that employees wearing the company uniform are not seen smoking in the streets. In addition, employees are under pressure to offer political support to a candidate of the company's choice. While Kamata's book is sometimes seen as rather dated, my own experience in Japan—a friend lost his job within a major company because he showed the wrong attitude in marrying a "foreigner" (an American)—indicates that little has changed. Certainly it is still vital to show the right "attitude" by working evenings and weekends, and taking less than your holiday entitlement; just as it is important to the company that you marry at the right time, and to the right woman.

Ted Rall

These displays of company loyalty are often taken as indices of strong organizational commitment by the Japanese; and yet impartial measures of organizational commitment have shown that the Japanese rate lower than Americans.[6] These authors felt their result to be surprising, but it simply betrays the fact that the low turnover rate in large Japanese organizations cannot be explained by the Japanese worker's love of his company. Japanese loyalty may best be viewed as an economic, rather than a spiritual, matter.

3. The Happy Worker

Incorporated within the popular understanding of "the miracle of Japanese management" is the notion that Japanese management practice has succeeded in creating particularly happy or contented workers; yet research has done little to support this view.[7] Indeed, studies of job satisfaction have shown time and time again that Japanese workers do not compare favorably with Western workers in this respect.[8]

It seems that the Japanese often feel nervous or tense at work,[9] which may help to account for the incredible amount of alcohol they consume each evening (alcoholism is a major problem in Japan, but it is a culturally accepted means of relieving stress, and drinking with one's colleagues after work is a pasttime encouraged by most companies). While absenteeism is usually low, when it does occur it is often attributed to stress: a 1985 Ministry of Labor survey showed that, of all workers absent for more than one week, 47 percent were suffering from stress-related illness. Still worse is the incidence of suicide resulting from pressure at work: a recent newspaper article[10] revealed that suicide accounted for three times as many deaths as road accidents last year—a particularly bad year because of *endaka*, the sharp appreciation of the yen.

Nevertheless, if we take hours of unpaid work as an index, it is true that the Japanese are a nation of workaholics. Taylor quotes a 1978 Japanese Ministry of Labor estimate which had the average Japanese outworking the average American by 212 hours, stating:

> I suspect this is an understatement... Twelve hour workdays are not unusual for low-level office workers, and if need be, they will cheerfully work around the clock.[11]

While the need to show the right "attitude" by putting in overtime has already been discussed, there remains a mystery as to why the workers put up with the long hours and intense company demands. The answer lies in the Japanese notion of *gaman* or endurance. In Britain we've recently been entertained by Clive James showing television clips from a Japanese game show of the same name. The sight of teams of Japanese youth (all men) being immersed in a vat of worms is comical to the Japanese, as it is to us, but the source of our humor is incredulity, whereas for the Japanese the humor lies in the parody of such a highly valued and respected national characteristic.

The concept of endurance is fundamental to the Japanese, and owes much to their notion of *bushido* or the way of the warrior. To follow in the footsteps of their illustrious ancestors (most Japanese, if asked, will claim descendance from a noble samurai family), the Japanese must be exponents of *seishinshugi*—the victory of spirit over material things. Ian Buruma, in his book *A Japanese Mirror: Heroes and Villains of Japanese Culture* writes:

> *Seishinshugi* or *konjo* often involves a Zen-like suppression of reason and personal feelings, a blind devotion to direct action and an infinite capacity for hardship and pain.[12]

While most Japanese only aspire to *seishinshugi* (which may be more suited to the battlefield than the factory), they are all masters of *gaman*, the modern equivalent, which involves the resigned acceptance of hardship without complaint. Complaint is an anathema to the Japanese: not only does it show the wrong spirit, but it also involves the kind of blunt communication they prefer to avoid. "If you didn't like it, don't complain, just don't go again" was the advice given to me following a disastrous meal in a restaurant. To the workers of Japan, this advice is reduced to "endure it," a phrase which sounds uncomfortable in English, but which fits snugly into the Japanese vocabulary.

4. Group Success

Still writing on the subject of *seishinshugi*, Buruma continues:

> But the real issue is... how to reconcile self-efface-ment and Zen with self-aggrandizement and the sword. If one takes away Zen and the sword, neither of which plays much of a role in modern Japanese life, one is still left with a paradox every Japanese adolescent has to face: how to be an achiever, which is expected, particularly by one's family, and a self-effacing conformist at the same time? Or, to put it another way, how to be a winner in a society that discourages individual assertion?[13]

The Japanese in school, business and industry have long known the answer to this one: compete as a member of a group, rather than as an individual. With an unfailing eye for the main chance, large organizations have been swift to harness this Japanese proclivity for group identity, one obvious example being the quality circle.

Quality circles do seem to be successful: the Toyota circle program, started in 1964, involved over 4,000 workers, most of whom were blue collar. While a healthy number of suggestions had been previously voiced by individuals, the increase resulting from the circle program was a staggering 1,086 percent.[14] It is difficult for the British to understand the effort which seems to underlie this phenomenal suggestion rate, given that individual workers are not explicitly rewarded for their suggestions. True, money is sometimes given as a prize for the better suggestions; but the amounts are

fairly insignificant.[15] Indeed, it is not uncommon for ideas to be passed on to immediate superiors who will then pass them on as their own. Perhaps the key to understanding the Japanese system lies in the fact that they recognize a currency of indebtedness, one worker to another. A senior member of staff who attains promotion will not forget the junior member whose contribution was so valuable. It is seldom that a favor will go unacknowledged, but this is an implicit rather than explicit understanding between colleagues.

To understand this, we must understand something of the Japanese sense of duty. Ruth Benedict, in her classic portrayal of the Japanese "shame culture,"[16] describes Japanese indebtedness (*on*); and two types of repayment: *gimu* and *giri*. Each of these can be broken down into a number of obligations. Of those she describes, the following are of interest here: duty to one's work; duty to one's superiors; duties to non-related persons, due to *on* received, e.g. from other members of a work party; and one's duty to oneself—to admit no (professional) failure or ignorance. Thus the Japanese worker feels a strong sense of obligation, not only to other members of his team, but also to his immediate supervisor. In turn the supervisor's debt to his workers develops as a result of their contribution to his success.

This system clearly helps to bind a working team together, so much so that it is often assumed that Japanese workers are exceptional in the extent to which they develop close personal ties with their colleagues. In fact research does not support this viewpoint: a study of 522 employees of Japanese-owned firms in the United States by Lincoln, Hanada and Olsen found that native Japanese workers did not differ from either Americans nor Japanese-Americans in terms of the extent to which they developed personal ties with their co-workers. Far from being a force capable of uniting colleagues in a personal sense, *giri* is a debt to one's co-workers which must be paid back exactly, and is commonly considered the duty "hardest to bear."[17]

To return to the quality circle: this is also seen as a burden by many workers. Cole, cited in Munchus, feels that established quality circles are viewed more as an instrument of management than as an opportunity for employees to initiate improvements. Certainly this is the impression which is conveyed by Kamata in his description of life at Toyota. There he describes the weekly postings of each employee's suggestion rate. One can speculate that the shame for each individual was considerable should they fail to make the requisite number of suggestions. How much more, then, was this exacerbated by the introduction of group pressure, in the form of quality circles, and the consequent danger of letting one's colleagues down (i.e., failing to repay *giri*)? The data (cited above) would suggest 1,086 percent more.

5. The Humble Manager

One of the most poorly understood symbols of the Japanese method is that of the manager, dressed in company overalls, working shoulder to shoulder with his blue-collar employees. While it is recognized that Japanese companies operate a rigidly hierarchical system, it is nevertheless a common claim that it is egalitarian.[18] This claim seems to rest upon the absence of an explicit class system within Japanese industry. White and Trevor, for example, point to the absence of class markers (uniforms, different dining rooms, etc.) within the Japanese workplace as an illustration of the egalitarian nature of the Japanese management system. The absence of these class markers is misleading, however, since status is so clearly signalled in other ways.

Most notably, the Japanese language is such that the relative status of any two speakers is signalled immediately. Declension verbs are dependent not only upon tense, but also upon the status of the listener, with five levels of politeness in common parlance. Not only verbs, but also adjectives and personal pronouns take these different status inflections. As a result, the finely graded hierarchy which exists within the Japanese organization is explicitly mirrored in the language, and is thus apparent to all. In addition, while the status markers we employ in Britain can be cast off at the end of the day, this would be impossible in Japan: it has been my misfortune to be an unwilling eavesdropper upon many a conversation held between colleagues in Tokyo bars. In work or play, drunk or sober, the divisions between members of the different hierarchies hold. Indeed one can often hear them widen as the evening progresses—a behavior described in English as "creeping."

Language is not the only means by which the Japanese signal status. Consider the following account of a formal call made upon a Japanese corporation:

> We take our seats on opposite sides of the coffee table, as our hosts instinctively arrange themselves according to rank: senior man farthest from the door, junior man closest to it. The receptionist brings us each a cup of green tea. Naturally she serves us in rank order. Protocol requires that Saito and their senior man do most of the talking. We probably won't hear a single word from their most junior man, and my comments should be brief... Our goodbyes are punctuated by a little dance of stiff bows from the waist. We carefully match the depth of our bows to the rank of our partner. Our hosts see us to the elevator, where there are more bows. Then we are off.[19]

Unless we are conversant with Japanese language and customs, it is easy for us to miss these signals. The sight of a manager in overalls, eating at the same table as his blue-collar workers, may be enough to impress us with his humility and readiness to work in close cooperation with his workforce, but the workers themselves may not value his presence: Japanese rate low on their desire for a good working relationship with their managers.[20]

In keeping with the image of the humble manager is the view that managerial practice in Japan is more human-centered than that in the West, i.e. more reliant upon collective decisions, made with the interests of the worker uppermost. While there is evidence that decision-making is more diffuse within the Japanese company,[21] there is little reason to suppose that the managers themselves are more human-centered in their outlook. Indeed, a number of studies have shown the opposite: with Japanese managers emerging as more task-centered than their Western counterparts.[22] In addition, despite their adherence to the complex *ringi* system of decision-making, there is evidence to suggest that Japanese managers are more likely to ignore group decisions.[23] While these results should not carry too much weight, given that the groups involved were newly formed, they nevertheless reinforce the point that the Japanese hierarchy is a formidable mechanism.

One final point: Japanese companies are sometimes viewed as egalitarian because of the potential for upward movement through the company: the barriers between blue and white collar workers are not synonymous with class, as in Britain. However, success within the Japanese firm is much more heavily dependent upon a university education, and most of the universities in Japan are private, and very costly. True, the very able will secure their places in the national universities, and may subsequently achieve company status, but then this is also true of Britain. The inequalities of the British system are simply more obvious.

Conclusion

Undoubtedly the Japanese system as it stands is effective in economic terms. In human terms it is acceptable to the Japanese because it is consistent with their own cultural values, but the cost to the workforce in terms of quality of working life is dear. Are we in Britain hoping to take the entire Japanese package on board, despite the vast cultural differences which exist between the two nations? It seems not. White and Trevor describe the Japanization of British industry in terms of the adoption of only a small subset of the management practices common in Japan. The lifetime employment, company unions, seniority-based payment systems, lifelong training schemes and elaborate group decision processes are not considered exportable commodities. Given the cultural differences described above, this cautious approach is probably very sensible. However, British industry does seem keen to experiment with the *kanban* method of production which forms the basis of the Japanese success story.[24] This method, sometimes described as "just in time" or "module production,"[25] involves a finely tuned scheduling system, where stocks are supplied only when needed, and work in progress is closely controlled. The system also encourages a modular organization of work, where members of a team are responsible for the completion of any one stage in the production process.

One of the reasons for the popularity of the *kanban* method is that it seems the most readily exportable of the Japanese techniques, i.e. least dependent upon culturally specific attributes of the Japanese people. Yet once again we may not be fully aware of just what it is we intend to import. In a recent study of Lucas Engineering (LE), an organization currently experimenting with the *kanban* method, Peter Turnbull noted that:

> The success of module production is dependent on a social organization of the production process intended to make workers feel "obliged" to contribute to the economic performance of the enterprise and to identify with its competitive success.[26]

While the Japanese are masters at fostering this sense of obligation, the British are not; nor do we necessarily want to foster it, if it means the adoption of some of the more coercive elements of the Japanese method, discussed above. In particular, we should note Turnbull's warning that: "... it is precisely these elements which appear (initially at least) to be more prevalent at LE."

The current economic climate is such that we may not feel able to ignore the Japanese methods, be they coercive or cooperative. If industry advocates the adoption of Japanese techniques, then the workers in turn may have no alternative but to adapt, or be made redundant [laid off] (as at Lucas). Under these circumstances we must be fully aware of the true nature of the Japanese system, and suffer no illusions concerning the pressures and demands placed upon the workforce.

Notes

1. T.K. Oh, "Japanese Management: A Critical Review," *Academy of Management Review*, 1978, 1, p.14-25.

2. H. Collick, "A Different Society" in *Inside Japan*, ed. H. Smith, London, British Broadcasting Corporation, 1981.

3. J. Taylor, *Shadows of the Rising Sun: A Critical View of the "Japanese Miracle,"* Tokyo, Charles E. Tuttle, 1983.

4. *Kyoiku mama*: a mother who pushes her child to do well at school. This often involves additional lessons in the evenings, even for kindergarten children.

5. S. Kamata, *Japan in the Fast Lane: An Insider's Account of Life in a Japanese Auto Factory*, London, Allen and Unwin, 1983.

6. F. Luthens, H.S. McCaul, and N.G. Dodd, "Organizational Commitment: A Comparison of American, Japanese and Korean Employees," *Academy of Management Journal*, 1985, 28, 1, pp.213-219.

7. M. White and M. Trevor, *Under Japanese Management: The Experience of British Workers*, London, Heinemann, 1983.

8. K. Azumi and C.J. McMillan, "Worker Sentiment in the Japanese Factory: Its Organizational Determinants," in *Japan: The Paradox of Progress*, ed. L. Austin, New Haven, Yale University Press, 1976.
Also, R.E. Cole, *Work, Mobility and Participation: A Cooperative Study of Japanese and American Industry*, Los Angeles, University of California Press, 1979.
Also, J.R. Lincoln, M. Hanada and J. Olsen, "Cultural Orientations and Individual Reactions to Organizations: A Study of Employees of Japanese Owned Firms," *Administrative Science Quarterly*, 1981, 28, pp.93-115.

9. G. Hofstede, *Culture's Consequences: International Differences in Work Related Values*, Beverly Hills, CA, Sage, 1980.

10. *The Guardian*, August 18, 1987.

11. Taylor, p.175.

12. Ian Buruma, *A Japanese Mirror: Heroes and Villains of Japanese Culture*, Penguin Books Ltd, 1985, p.139.

13. Buruma, *p.140.*

14. G. Munchus, "Employer-Employee Based Quality Circles in Japan: Human Resource Policy Implications for American Firms," *Academy of Management Review*, 1983, 8(2), pp.255-261.

15. Munchus.

16. Ruth Benedict, *The Chrysanthemum and the Sword*, Tokyo, Charles E. Tuttle, 1946.

17. Benedict.

18. R.P. Dore, *British Factory, Japanese Factory*, London, Allen and Unwin, 1973.
Also, White and Trevor.

19. Taylor, p.161.

20. Hofstede.

21. R.T. Pascale, "Communication and Decision-Making Across Cultures: Japanese and American Comparisons," *Administrative Science Quarterly*, 1978, 23, pp.91-109.

22. B.H. Bass and P.C. Burger, *Assessment of Managers: An International Comparison*, New York, Free Press, 1979.
Also, Hofstede.
Also, White and Trevor.

23. R. Klauss and B. M. Bass, "Group Influence on Individual Behavior Across Cultures," *Journal of Cross-Cultural Psychology*, 1974, 5, pp.236-246.

24. R.H. Hayes, "Why Japanese Factories Work," *Harvard Business Review*, 1981, 59(4), pp.56-66.
Also, Wheelwright, S.C., "Japan—Where Operations Really Are Strategic," *Harvard Business Review*, 1981, 59(4), pp.67-74.
Also, White and Trevor.

25. Peter Turnbull, "The Japanization of Production and Industrial Relations at Lucas Electrical," *Industrial Relations Journal*, 1986, 17, pp.193-206.

26. Turnbull, p.203.

7. The Union's Early Days: Shop Stewards and Seniority Rights

By Nelson Lichtenstein

Much of the debate that is now going on about how to make auto work more humane and efficient takes place as if no one had ever thought about these issues before. Or if they had, as if the problems workers confronted in 1914, 1937 or 1946 were irrelevant to the crisis American workers are facing today. We hear references to "antiquated" work rules, "confrontational" styles of union leadership, and "traditional" job classifications. It's as if these were relics of a bygone age, best swept aside as we rethink how auto factories should be run in the 1990's.

A lot has changed, of course, and history never repeats itself exactly. But a closer look at the last half century in the auto industry shows that many of the issues which seem so fresh today have had a long and troubled history. The meaning of employee participation, managerial flexibility, and workers' rights has been the subject of a protracted struggle. Today industry spokespeople are promoting an ideology of labor-management cooperation, a "we're all in this together" credo, which actually echoes personnel practices and corporate propaganda from the years just after World War I.

As we will see, two of the most controversial management innovations of the 1980's—team production and the effort to eliminate job classifications, work rules and other obstacles to "flexible" organization—are strikingly similar to some of the labor control techniques that bedeviled auto workers in the industry's early, non-union years. The role played by contemporary "team leaders" bears an uncanny resemblance to that of the old "straw bosses" which the UAW largely banished when it organized the auto shops in the late 1930's and early 1940's.

Likewise, the effort to break down the system of job classifications and in-plant seniority rights may well return auto workers to the days when foremen had an unimpeded right to assign jobs, offer promotions and make transfers. Early union activists were determined to curb this power in order to bring security and fairness to daily work life.

Unfortunately, the struggle is being re-fought today, but under the lash of global competition and in the interest of a still vaguely formulated program of shop floor cooperation and participation. Many in the union movement are actually promoting some of these same management practices an earlier generation of unionists were determined to eliminate.

Under the Workman's Cap

In the 19th century factory management as we know it hardly existed. The craft worker stood at the center of the production process. The employers might own the workplace and the machinery, but "the manager's brains under the workman's cap" (an old Wobbly phrase) enabled these skilled machinists, cigar makers, woodworkers and blacksmiths to "legislate" their work rules, not through negotiations with the employer, but by mutual agreement among themselves.

Craft workers usually selected their own crew members, assigned men and boys to tasks at their own discretion, and transferred them among one another's teams as they saw fit. Throughout heavy industry this characteristic sense of workplace autonomy lent substance to an ethical code that emphasized a "manly bearing" toward the boss, solidarity with one's co-workers and an abiding belief in the dignity of labor.[1]

In some industries the union assumed many tasks that would later seem to be obvious managerial functions. For example, in the coal industry three-person pit committees supervised the checkweightman, distributed empty coal cars on an equitable basis, made periodic safety checks, and repaired weakened mine structures. Their power was the living embodiment of the miners' cohesiveness. In fact, at the turn of the century it was widely believed that the United Mine Workers could "run coal" better than the capitalists.

Of course modern managers saw the craft practices and social values of the late 19th century workplace as an intolerable constraint on the property rights of ownership and the necessary flexibility of management. Where skilled workers had established a well defined set of production techniques and output norms, supervisors who believed in the new scientific management saw only pigheadedness and retrograde inefficiency.

Direct managerial assaults on the power and ethic of these craftsmen often sparked some of the most famous strikes of the late 19th century, such as those at Homestead and Pullman. Relying on the armed might of the state, capitalists won these battles, but the success of scientific management never rested on sheer brute force. Instead, the new theories looked to a reorganization of production technology, a new system of shop governance, and a transformation of the work culture to marginalize skilled workers and the values they championed.

Nelson Lichtenstein teaches history at the Catholic University of America and is the author of Labor's War at Home: The CIO in World War II.

Frederick Taylor has often been caricatured as a man obsessed with time and motion studies, a petty tyrant who armed management with the "scientific" tools necessary to speed up work and discipline workers. Taylor did use a stopwatch and clipboard, but his system involved far more than the micromanagement of a workers' time. In fact, Taylor considered time and motion studies a very small part of his contribution to modern management, and in his later years roundly denounced those of his followers who peddled such techniques as a total solution to factory efficiency problems.

The Human Product

The Taylorites are best understood as one wing of the early 20th century Progressive Movement, which sought to reform cities, factories and governments so as to ameliorate social conflict and make their operation more efficient and humane. For industry this meant finding some way to make workers see their interests as parallel to those of management. Thus Taylor's many experiments with piecework and incentive pay were premised on the idea that just as managers were interested in maximizing profits, so too must workers desire an increased pay packet. His psychology proved crude, and would be modified by his disciples, but Taylorism's core set of ideas remains central to virtually all managerially inspired efforts to recast the workplace environment: to build a more efficient and profitable company, managers must transform the consciousness of their workers as much as the machinery of production.[2]

The most famous work reform inspired by Taylor remains the assembly line pioneered by Henry Ford just before World War I. The assembly line would never have succeeded without a reasonably cooperative, easily trained, and interchangeable workforce. One way to do this was to make production jobs as unskilled as possible. Another was to pay the then unheard of wage of $5 a day, which guaranteed that there would always be lots of willing workers outside the factory gates.

Finally, corporations took steps to insure that workers had the right attitude. Managers sought to teach a new set of "skills" that emphasized punctuality, reliability, and orderliness. Ford set up a "sociological department" that initially served as a combination personnel department and social work office for the company's tens of thousands of workers. The department investigated the home life of Ford employees, including their sleeping arrangements and bathing facilities, noted their politics, and organized language classes for the heavily immigrant workforce. English classes held on company property mixed elementary language instruction with a large dose of "Americanism." Those who failed to attend found their job security and promotion prospects sharply diminished. A Ford official asserted: "As we adapt the machinery in the shop to turning out the kind of automobile we have in mind, so we have constructed our educational system to producing the human product we have in mind."[3]

For a while in the 1920's and 1930's managers thought that another "progressive" innovation, incentive pay schemes, would convince workers that their interests were the same as those of the company. Group piecework plans in particular seemed to hold out the possibility that the men themselves might not only internalize the production goals of the company, but take steps to enforce those goals on their workmates. The psychology of the scheme had some remarkable similarities to contemporary "team production" work. UAW pioneer Tracy Doll remembered:

> If one man slowed down he was slowing down the livelihood of all the people. So the other guys went over and jumped onto him and said 'hurry up, get moving.' This was the idea. Now they got the men stretched out to where they could not stretch any longer and we have got the fast men carrying the slow men and all of them getting wages based on a percentage of their day rates.

If one person was consistently unable to keep up the pace, co-workers might ask the foreman to shift him to another department. There were even instances of workers fighting outside the plant, faster workers beating up slower ones to persuade them to pick up the pace and keep pay rates high.[4]

Job Classifications

Ford and other modern manufacturing firms also set up elaborate job classification systems in which pay was linked not to the worker, but to the skill and experience necessary to perform the task. There were two reasons for this innovation.

First, although much production work was being deskilled, there were still plenty of jobs which required a certain level of experience and aptitude. Moreover, factory bosses and their new handmaidens, the personnel managers, recognized that a well developed job hierarchy might reduce shop floor discontent by giving workers a ladder of social mobility within the factory.

For example, Ford's 1913 skill classification system gave a worker an automatic wage boost as soon as he moved on to the next skill grade or reached a specific standard of efficiency. Before, the worker who was denied a pay increase usually "knocked" (complained) about the foreman, but now, claimed Ford's new personnel department, the worker could only blame himself when he failed to maximize his earnings. Thus the new system sought to internalize within each worker discipline and efficiency.[5]

By the early 1930's, Ford's wage classification scheme had more than 540 distinct occupations—Bullard Machine Operator, Core Maker, Drill Press Operator, Metal Finisher—further subdivided according to a skill classification system which paid a few cents more or less according to one's proficiency, seniority and ability to stay on the right side of the foreman. By this time, of course, the entire scheme was a source of great resentment because management favoritism and petty corruption had generated thousands of different wage brackets, which meant that workers doing the same work might well be paid at different rates for no apparent reason.[6]

The evolution of factory seniority systems proved an additional reason for the elaboration of a detailed job classification system. Seniority was thought to develop company loyalty and insure a workforce thoroughly familiar with a particular factory's production technique. Of course, managers made their own modifications to the system. Married men and a special group of "all-round" workers were given advantageous treatment, while "troublemakers and malcontents" were struck from the list. As a result of the proliferation of personnel departments that were established during the labor shortage of World War I and of the pressures generated by workers and reformers in the early New Deal years, most automakers had begun to rely on a seniority schedule to determine layoffs during annual model changeovers or periodic industry slumps.[7]

But managers also wanted to minimize the disruptive impact of layoff by seniority: rather than having a plant or department-wide seniority list, most managers insisted on narrowly defined seniority groups, in some cases amounting to operators of a specific kind of ma-chine. At Ford there were hundreds of such seniority classifications, which generated a large number of extremely short seniority lists. This meant that when layoffs took place there would be less "bumping" of high seniority workers into the jobs left vacant by those with fewer years at work.[8]

Straw Bosses and Tin Gods

Of course, the scientific management of these early auto factories never succeeded in molding workers into the willingly responsive workforce they sought. Immigrants resisted the crude efforts to "Americanize" their native cultures, and production workers failed to offer the loyalty managers expected. Underground unionization efforts and slowdowns persisted even in the boom era of World War I and the 1920's. Within just a few years after Ford had declared the $5 day a solution to the problems of modern industry, his company's paternalism had degenerated into a harsh regime that used factory spies, community vigilante groups and stepped up supervision to root out those not sufficiently patriotic or productive. After World War I, when a brief surge of radical unionism and a deep recession threatened heavy industry, most corporations were forced to aug-

ment scientific management with more direct systems of control, including close supervision and heavy-handed discipline.[9]

One of the most notable features of this repressive era was the rapid increase in the proportion of foremen to production workers. Between 1910 and 1930 the ratio increased by more than 50 percent, and in automobile factories probably grew even more rapidly. In the 1920's, an era of social quiescence and rapid technological change not dissimilar to our own, there was much managerial talk of the new foreman's "leadership by example," "teamwork," and even "cooperation." But companies were still extremely reluctant to deprive foremen of their traditional disciplinary tools. Foremen could still fire workers; they had the unfettered right to assign jobs of varying levels of pay, difficulty and pleasantness; and their opinions went far in determining promotions or transfers.[10]

On the assembly line, a foreman's authority was further advanced through the intermediators he chose from among the workers. Variously named set-up man, crew chief, lead man, pusher, gang boss or straw boss, these intermediators, in contrast to the foreman, spent most of their time in actual production. Set-up men were experienced or clever workers who made the initial adjustment when a machine was installed or its work load altered. Paid a nickel or so more than production workers, they were also responsible for determining, in consultation with the foreman, the pace or quota of the new machine operation. Pushers and lead men, also paid a few cents extra, were selected because of their loyalty and propensity to hard work. They were placed in strategic locations in the production process, such as the first person on a subassembly crew, where their work rhythm could automatically set the pace for the rest of the work gang.[11]

Finally, the straw boss, or working leader, played a key role. "What we call a straw boss," reported a Ford worker in 1934, "is a man who is not officially recognized as a foreman... but is usually appointed by the foreman himself to look after particular gangs." Although straw bosses were hourly workers often of the same ethnic or language group of those they supervised, they were hated by most auto workers because of the way they combined an intimate knowledge of the task at hand with the disciplinary power delegated to them.

Frank Marquart, who would later conduct labor education classes for many of the big Detroit-area UAW loals, remembered the night he got fired from the Chevrolet Gear and Axle plant. "One night I had machine trouble and fell behind in production. The straw boss, a sub-human pusher who had the authority to hire and fire, bellowed like a bull. When I tried to explain that I had machine trouble, he roared: 'I don't give a damn what you had, you get out production or you get fired—that's the rule around here, and no goddamn excuses!' "[12]

When the Ford Motor Company was struggling out of the postwar recession in 1922, management doubled the number of straw bosses to intensify the work pace. Straw bosses assigned daily tasks, enforced work quotas and recommended favored workers for minor promotions or wage advances. Even where seniority systems existed, their power to assign a worker to a particular seniority group enabled them to play a crucial role in determining how long a worker would retain his or her job during a layoff.[13] Although the power of both foreman and straw boss was sometimes contested by the plant personnel department, these first line supervisors presided over a kind of shop floor "empire."

"Before organization came into the plant," reported the UAW, "foremen were little tin gods in their own departments. They were accustomed to having orders accepted with no questions asked. They expected workers to enter into servile competition for their favors."[14]

When the UAW won recognition at most of the big auto companies, the union was determined to draw a sharp line between workers and management. The first thing the union did, therefore, was to strip foremen of the lead men, pushers and straw bosses who had provided them with so much of their power to intimidate their underlings or speed up the work pace among those they supervised. The UAW insisted that anybody who worked on production had to be a union member and subject to its discipline. Straw bosses were eliminated outright, while other quasi-supervisory workers like lead men and pushers were enrolled in the union. In the River Rouge Foundry some 90 straw bosses were eliminated in one day. Forty-two were upgraded to foreman status and the rest returned to the production worker roll.[15]

Win for the Union

The establishment of a strong shop steward system was perhaps the most important way the UAW sought to assert its power. Union activists demanded a steward for every foreman, or about one for every 25 workers. In a 1941 stewards' handbook, "How to Win for the Union," the UAW declared its vigorous system of shop stewards and committeemen a "weapon of democracy" that would overthrow the foreman's "small-time dictatorship" and restore a "democratic system of shop government." To the steward it announced: "Your relationship with the foreman should be that of equals seeking a solution to a common problem. But don't forget: the stronger the organization behind you, the more powerful your argument." Stewards were reminded that their task was one of continuous education and leadership. "... forces hostile to labor inside and outside the plant are at all times seeking to win influence over his men," announced this guide for UAW activists. "Unless the steward gives positive leadership in behalf of CIO principles, he will find his men pulled away from him."[16]

For a few years in the late 1930's and 1940's UAW shop stewards played a direct role in determining the pace and assignment of work in many organized auto plants. At Chrysler a bitter, two-month strike in the fall of 1939 won semi-official recognition for several hundred "blue button" stewards, who were then able to jointly set production goals and reorganize seniority lines.[17]

At Studebaker it became standard practice for shop stewards to meet every morning to plan their approach to the day's work and to monitor the composition of work groups. They exercised effective control over the company's piece rate pay system and, as a consequence, recalled a local union officer, the foremen were "just clerks."[18] At the Ford Rouge plant a supervisor wishing to change a worker's classification always informed a committeeman first. (They could put the change through without union approval, but then a grievance automatically followed.)[19]

Even at General Motors, where the company successfully fought formal recognition of a shop steward system, "consistent work by the stewards" for a time "brought the foremen around to effective bargaining with the unofficial approval of top management."[20]

In addition to building up the shop floor authority of the steward, the early UAW sought to extend and codify the seniority principle, initially to protect union activists from corporate discrimination during layoffs, but also to establish the principle that workers with long service had earned the moral right to keep their job or move up to a better one in their department or skill classification.[21] Few American workers were so radical as to think that their union should actually run the auto factories, but a large majority were convinced that their tenure gave them a kind of "property right" in the job at which they labored, a right which must be policed by their shop steward and defended by the whole might of the UAW. Thus, in the March 1937 UAW-GM agreement seniority provisions took up fully 35 percent of the four-page text.

In general, newly organized auto workers wanted to broaden seniority classifications to a department or plant-wide basis while managers favored the narrowest possible seniority groupings, which in non-union or weakly organized plants often amounted to those employees who worked on a particular machine or process. Companies found that a series of short seniority lists eliminated in-plant "bumping" from job to job, but from the workers' point of view, the proliferation of seniority classifications opened the system to the usual sort of anti-union discrimination or personal favoritism. Of course, most white male workers hardly wanted this principle to apply to women, who were usually given their own seniority classifications, or to Blacks, still mainly segregated in foundry and janitorial groups, also with separate seniority.[22]

In the late 1930's, workers in Chevy's South Unit Trim Department at Flint tried to reduce from 24 to six the number of seniority groups into which management had divided their department. They argued that such in-clusive seniority rights would not only be more equitable, but

> that in order to promote efficient and economical operations... and provide flexibility in the working group at any production level it is necessary that all employees be familiar with, and experienced in, as many operations as possible. To accomplish this it is agreed that employees can be interchanged upon operations to gain necessary experience, and that no resultant loss in production will occur."[23]

We don't know if the South Unit Trim workers ever won departmental seniority, but their announcement that they favored job trading and flexibility in the work group may well have reflected the self-confidence and the shop power that the UAW wielded in its early years. Where the shop stewards were strong, as at GM in the very early years and at Chrysler, Ford, Studebaker and Hudson through most of the 1940's, unionists were able to negotiate directly and advantageously with the foreman over work assignments and skill classifications. But where the shop floor union presence grew weak, the UAW had to try to protect workers through a more elaborate set of contractual guidelines that defined jobs more precisely and allocated job bidding rights strictly in accordance with an employee's seniority. This would divide up a limited number of good jobs on a fair basis and offer workers a partial shield against company discrimination or a foreman's threats. Such work rules were no substitute for an aggressive local union, and in fact they were often the product of militant local bargaining. But once they were imbedded in the structure of plant governance, they might well outlast the generation of unionists who first understood their importance. They embodied a legacy of fairness and order handed down from one generation of auto workers to the next.

No Middle Ground

GM's successful effort to replace the dense steward system of the union's early years with a weaker committeeman setup coincided almost precisely with the growing interest that UAW locals took in workers' transfer and promotion rights at GM. Before 1940, UAW contracts at GM contained no discussion or guidelines that might cover such movement of workers from one job to another. But in the next decade, Paragraph 63, the section of the UAW-GM contract that set out the guidelines covering such transfers and promotions, was fought over again and again in every contract negotiation and in numerous special conferences and arbitrations.

In the early war years GM argued that if seniority determined who got higher paying or more pleasant jobs as they came open, management would lose the "flexibility" needed to run the shop. GM wanted to make seniority distinctly secondary to its judgment of the "merit, ability or capacity" of an employee. The company asserted that it would try to accommodate an employee's wishes in the administration of its promotion and transfer policy, but in terms of management's pre-rogative to assign work, "when the chips are down in a given situation, one of the parties either has a right or does not have it. There is no middle ground."[24]

But unionists were equally convinced that all of GM's talk about the need for individual initiative and flexibility was just a cover for the company's determination to restore the foreman's pre-union power to intimidate the work crew and reward pro-company workers with the best job assignments. The 1940 GM-UAW agreement asserted that in promoting and transferring employees "seniority will be secondary to other qualifications but will be given reasonable consideration." Unionists found this a license for favoritism, and they sought to strengthen the contract language when a government mediation board practically wrote the next GM contract in 1941.

A new paragraph, number 63, now stated that "the transferring of employees is the sole responsibility of Management," but in the case of permanent promotions to new, usually higher paid jobs, "when ability,

merit and capacity are equal, employees with the longest seniority will be given preference."[25] For most of the war this language was frozen into the contract, and remains the basis of Paragraph 63 to this day, but the union and the company wrangled over the meaning of merit, ability and seniority and when and where these criteria might be applied.

Although the issues sometimes sound like a debate over semantics, what was at stake here was nothing less than the union's effort to shield workers from intimidation by defining as a quasi-legal "right" the distribution of job openings according to a system that most workers considered fair and orderly.

During World War II General Motors tried to reduce the weight given to seniority in promotions and transfers in the interests of efficient and timely war production. The company complained that union committeemen filed a grievance any time a worker was promoted to a higher classification out of line of seniority. GM argued that new jobs could be filled by new workers without regard to Paragraph 63, and management re-

---

THE "MY JOB AND WHY I LIKE IT" CONTEST

By Ronda Hauben

In 1947 General Motors sponsored a contest for its employees called "My Job and Why I Like It."[1] Two hundred thousand entries were submitted by hourly workers.

According to management consultant Peter Drucker,[2] this contest was dreamed up by GM Chief Executive Officer Charles E. Wilson. Wilson was dissatisfied with the union-management relations prevalent in the auto industry and wanted to make some changes. He wanted to create a "responsible worker" with "managerial aptitude," but he felt more information about the workforce was needed. A contest would find out where workers saw "opportunities for improvement in what we now call 'the quality of working life' and where they felt themselves competent to take on responsibility for job and performance." There would be outside judges, many small prizes, and some big ones, including a Cadillac.

Wilson and Drucker felt the contest entries were "a veritable gold mine of information, the richest source of information ever about workers, their needs and capabilities." With this information Wilson "was all set to start...'Work Improvement Programs.') He had even picked out the GM divisions where the program would first be started and tested out."

And then the whole program was hastily dropped. Indeed, even work on the entries of the contest was stopped and its findings suppressed. (They have never been published.) The main reason was violent opposition to the contest, its find-

ings and especially to anything like a work improvement program, on the part of GM's union, the UAW. To the UAW anything that would establish cooperation between company and workers was a direct attack on the union.[3]

Even though assurance was given that the union would be involved in the process, the UAW, according to Drucker, took a strong stand against instituting any such activity.

There was also strong vocal opposition among the rank and file of UAW locals, such as 659 in Flint, to the "My Job" contest and the kind of "new" labor relations it was introducing. The headline of Local 659's newspaper, the *Searchlight*, on September 25, 1947 declared, "My Job—Why Do I Like It: Some Letters By They Who Remember." For several issues, the newspaper carried articles, letters and poems presenting the response of the grassroots.

One such poem was called "My Job Contest: And Why I Like It or Can Lump It."

They ask me why I like my job
And offer several prizes.
Some household things, some odds and ends
And cars of different sizes.

They all look good from where I sit
Say! Maybe I could lie
And tell 'em how I love my job
And give 'em reasons why.

For instance, I like my job
Because the boss is kind.
(He reprimands me from in front
And kicks me from behind.)

sisted all union efforts to limit the foreman's authority to transfer workers from one job to another within the same department or classification. But GM Department Director Walter Reuther, who would soon become president of the UAW, insisted that GM's effort to limit seniority in promotions and transfers really amounted to

> returning to the old setup where the local foreman... can get back into playing the old game of favoritism.
> And if you take away the protection we have, you will merely resort back to the setup where you get ahead if you play golf with the boss on Sunday, or if you have a good relationship with him, and you get the business if you fight for the things you think are right inside the plant.
> I mean we haven't gone through our period of struggle for nothing. We know that unless you have rules to govern the relationship of people, both Labor and Management, on the lower levels in the Agreement, unless these rules are explicit, you will revert back to where they pick this guy, not because he has potential... [but because he or she most readily accommodates to the foreman's wishes.][26]

The War Labor Board, which sought to codify a system of shop floor jurisprudence, tilted toward the union in 1945 when it divided Paragraph 63 into two sections: "Part A" covered the advancement of employees to higher paid jobs and made seniority the determining factor when all other qualifications were constant. In practice, arbitrators ruled that only if one worker were "head and shoulders" above his peers could he or she be promoted to a new classification out of line of seniority. "Part B," however, which covered transfers to new positions or vacancies within a department, proved much less satisfactory to the UAW and also more controversial with the company. The labor board announced that the "temporary" transfer of employees remained the "sole responsibility of Management," but that rules for "permanent transfers between occupational groups" must be negotiated locally and worked out in the local seniority agreement. Not unexpectedly, union efforts to work out a systematic procedure that would have allowed employees to maintain their job transfer rights proved fruitless: a revision of Paragraph 63b held up settlement of the great 1945-46 GM strike for more than a month. A new and still ambiguous version of the para-

---

JOB CONTEST continued

> Or else I like my job because
> My wages here are greater
> (I have bologna once a week
> And with it, boiled potater).
>
> I like my job because they keep
> The plant so clean and purty.
> (The flies don't come in anymore,
> The dining room's too dirty.)
>
> They look out for my comfort, too.
> At least that's how I feel
> (In summertime I slowly melt,
> In winter I congeal.)
>
> And, gentlemen, I quite forgot
> (While we're in sweet communion),
> To thank you for your dirty work
> Which helped to build our union.
>
> Your mail will surely bulge with notes
> That praise you to the skies,
> Delude yourself how much you may
> You'll know it's simply lies.
>
> And guys like that should stop and think,
> They'd see the whole thing's funny,
> For Judas did the same damn thing
> For a hell of A LOT LESS MONEY!
> —R.E. McDonald
> (Ruby "Hoss Buster" McDonald)

Another entry insisted that good labor relations were only possible when workers had the protection of a strong union:

Dear Sir:

I like my job because it used to be, when I first worked here in 1927, the foreman would come in in the morning sometimes with a bad feeling. He would say, "You have got to get more production. If you don't get more production there are men at the office who want your 'job.'"

In 1936, a guy named Travis told me "to join the CIO and the foreman can't act like this."...I joined the CIO in 1936. In 1937, the union steward told me we would shut the plant down and sit down and not work until the foreman stopped being so mean and promised not to fire me because he was mad at his wife or other silly reason (such as needing a job for his brother-in-law). We sat down and I liked it as it was the first time I ever sat down in Chevrolet.

Kermit Johnson and Gib Rose told me to help keep the scabs out....Tom Klasey got hit on the head by one of your watchmen. Maybe this was a mistake as we are a big happy family.

However, the company said we could have seniority. This seniority business is darn good. It means the foreman can't fire me because he is mad at his wife or his brother-in-law wants my job. So I like my job because the CIO told the boss about seniority, and the committeeman has been telling him about it ever since.

Yours for more seniority and the pension plan, John

P.S. If the CIO gets the pension plan, I will write another letter because I will like my job better.

graph was finally slipped into the contract at 2:25 a.m., just hours before negotiators announced a settlement.[27]

One of the key issues here was what constituted a transfer. GM argued that transfers only referred to those changes which involved the movement of an employee from one department, wage classification or seniority group to another and which were evidenced by a change in job title, seniority listing or clock number. The union, on the other hand, argued that a transfer covered any basic change in an employee's job assignment, and that under Paragraph 63b employees could apply not only for vacancies in other wage classifications or departments, but also for vacancies on specific machines or operations in their own classification.

This distinction would prove important because under the contract a worker had job bidding rights if the change of work involved a transfer, but if he or she merely sought a change of job assignment within an already established classification, then they confronted the company's determination to maintain the foreman's unfettered authority to make daily work assignments within his work area.

In early 1947 an important series of arbitration rulings confirmed that workers could rely on their seniority if they sought a permanent transfer or promotion to an entirely new job classification, but that the foreman's authority governed transfers to a new job assignment within a classification.[28] Since the UAW could win no further substantial modification of Paragraph 63, this arbitration ruling set in motion a long-term process in which the union welcomed an expansion of the number of job classifications that would be subject to job bidding based on seniority. Once the union had won plant-wide seniority for layoffs, it no longer had any reason to oppose a proliferation of classifications. More classifications actually gave the individual worker more transfer opportunities, more flexibility in choosing the kind of job he or she would like. By the early 1960's there were more than 100 classifications for production workers alone.

Therefore, the corporations' recent efforts to combine and eliminate job classifications represent an effort to restore to lower level management much of the shop authority they were forced to relinquish when the UAW won bargaining rights in the late 1930's.

What lessons can contemporary auto workers learn from this history? Although a lot has changed in the last three-quarters of a century, much of the terrain is still remarkably familiar. Managers in the auto industry, as elsewhere, want a cooperative and willing workforce, the freedom to respond quickly and flexibly to the competition, and low cost production. The slogans, techniques, and management styles associated with these long-term goals have come in and gone out of fashion, but an essentially Taylorite world view remains largely in place. The needs and aspirations of auto workers haven't changed that much either. They want their own version of freedom and security, which has made them skeptical of each wave of management innovation.

The UAW has fought, not always successfully, to replace the petty and manipulative tyranny that has so often characterized the factory work regime with its own vision of an orderly and just shop society. The UAW has been in existence for more than 50 years—that's a quarter of the life of the American republic—and its efforts to extend to the workplace a kind of constitutional government of quasi-legal rights and procedures have been among its proudest achievements. Times change and things certainly don't have to remain the same, but auto workers should look long and hard before they discard these safeguards for an untested promise of cooperation between those who own and those who work in America's auto factories.

Notes

1. David Montgomery, *The Fall of the House of Labor: The Workplace, the State and American Labor Activism, 1865-1925*, New York, Cambridge University Press, 1987, pp.9-57, 336.

2. Daniel Nelson, *Frederick Taylor and the Rise of Scientific Management*, Madison, University of Wisconsin Press, 1980, pp.168-174, 198-202.

3. Stephen Meyer, *The Five-Dollar Day: Labor-Management at the Ford Motor Company, 1908-1921*, Albany, State University of New York Press, 1981, pp.156-157.

4. Joyce Shaw Peterson, *American Automobile Workers, 1900-1933*, Albany, State University of New York, 1987, p.49.

5. Stephen Meyer, *The Five-Dollar Day*, pp.102-104.

6. Ford Motor Company, "Labor Rate Comparison by Classes," 1933, "Number of Men on Each Occupation," 1935, in box 196, Accession 157, Henry Ford Museum, Dearborn, Michigan. Also, author's interview with Walter Dorach, former UAW Local 600 President, August 12, 1982, Dearborn, Michigan.

7. Sanford Jacoby, *Employing Bureaucracy: Managers, Unions, and the Transformation of Work in American Industry, 1900-1945*, New York, Columbia University Press, 1985, pp.193-99.

8. Author's interview with Walter Dorach.

9. Meyer, pp.169-194.

10. M. J. Kane, *The Relation of the Foreman to the Personnel Department*, New York, American Management Association, 1926, p.4.

11. W. Ellison Chalmers, "Labor in the Automobile Industry: A Study of Personnel Policies, Worker's Attitudes and Attempts at Unionism," Ph.D. Thesis, University of Wisconsin, 1932, pp.171-2.

12. Frank Marquart, *An Auto Worker's Journal: The UAW from Crusade to One-Party Union*, University Park,

Pennsylvania State University Press, 1975, pp.30-31.

13. Nelson Lichtenstein, " 'The Man in the Middle': A Social History of Automobile Industry Foremen," in *On the Line: Essays in the History of Auto Work*, edited by Lichtenstein and Stephen Meyer, Urbana, University of Illinois Press, 1988.

14. International Education Department, UAW-CIO, *How to Win for the Union: A Discussion for UAW Stewards and Committeemen*, Detroit, 1941, p.8.

15. Author's interview with Shelton Tappes, Rouge committeeman, October 7, 1982.
Also, Harry Shulman, "Elimination of Semi-Supervisor Job (Yardmaster)," Opinion A-220, April 8, 1946, in *UAW-Ford Arbitration Awards*, Detroit, UAW, 1947.

16. UAW-CIO, *How to Win for the Union*, pp.8-9, 19-20.

17. Steve Jefferys, "Matters of Mutual Interest: The Unionization Process at Dodge Main, 1933-1939," in *On the Line*, ed. Lichtenstein and Meyer.

18. Steven Amberg, "The Triumph of Industrial Orthodoxy: The Failure of Studebaker Corporation," in *On the Line*, ed. Lichtenstein and Meyer.

19. Harry Shulman, "Opinion A-17" in *Opinions of the Umpire, UAW-Ford*, Detroit, UAW, 1946.

20. UAW-CIO, *How to Win for the Union*, p.18.

21. Carl Gersuny, "Origins of Seniority Provisions in Collective Bargaining," *Labor Law Journal*, No. 33, August 1982, pp.518-524.

22. Carl Gersuny and Gladis Kaufman, "Seniority and the Moral Economy of U.S. Automobile Workers, 1934-1946," *Journal of Social History*, No. 18, Spring 1985, p.467.

23. "Proposed Seniority Plan, South Unit Trim Department," January 5, 1939, in Everett Francis Papers, Archives of Labor History, Wayne State University.

24. 1955 Negotiations with the UAW, GM Presentation on Paragraph 63, in Vertical File, General Motors Institute, Flint, Michigan.

25. Ralph Seward, *Decisions of the Impartial Umpire Under the March 19, 1946 Agreement Between GM and the UAW*, Detroit, UAW, 1950, p.93-94.

26. Transcript, National War Labor Board, January 4, 1944 in Record Group 202, National Archives. *Also*, UAW vs. GM, Case No. 111-4665-D, pp.291-292.

27. Ralph Seward, *Decisions of the Umpire*, p.93-94.

28. Author's interview with Irving Bluestone, former UAW Vice-President, October 25, 1987, Detroit, Michigan.

Notes on My Job Contest

1. This box is excerpted from a longer article titled "The 'New' Labor Relations: The 'My Job Contest' for 1947-48." It was published in UAW Local 659's "Searchlight Special Edition," February 11, 1988 to mark the 51st Anniversary of the Flint Sit-Down Strike. For a copy of the original article, including more contributions by Local 659 members, send $2 to Ronda Hauben, P.O. Box 4344, Dearborn, MI 48126. Hauben has done considerable research on the story of the UAW that is told in early local union newspapers.

2. Peter Drucker, *Concept of a Corporation*, New York, 1946. The quotes are from the Epilogue, which was written in 1983 and appeared in the most recent edition.

3. The story of the rejection of the "quality circles" comes from *Concept of a Corporation* and *Adventures of a Bystander* (New York, 1979) by Peter Drucker, pp.256-293.

[More information on the "My Job Contest" is available in Alan Raucher, "Employee Relations at General Motors: The 'My Job Contest,' 1947," *Labor History*, Spring 1987, Vol.28, No.2, pp.221-232.]

8. Work Rules and Classifications: The Balance of Power

The auto companies and other employers have worked hard to spread the notion that U.S. industry is uncompetitive because of outmoded, irrational and restrictive work rules, defended only by some old fogies in the union who are afraid of change. Unfortunately, many union leaders who should be defending work rules do not do so, either because they have accepted management's view that being competitive requires getting rid of work rules, or because they find work rules are the easiest concessions to make.

Yet, as historian Nelson Lichtenstein explains in the previous chapter, work rules were a key element in the UAW's struggle to win dignity and rights in the auto industry. Today's discussion about work rules may seem to be nit-picking, but the real issue is the balance of power between management and workers on the shop floor.

Unions have accomplished a lot, but U.S. auto plants remain authoritarian systems. Once workers enter the plant gates they lose virtually all the rights enjoyed by citizens of a democratic society. When management talks about getting rid of work rules, it means eliminating what few rights workers do have. Management wants to abolish those rules which give workers some control and some flexibility, so as to further tip the balance of power toward management.

Workers' Rights

In a society many laws ("rules") are the result of a political struggle. The National Labor Relations Act of 1935 was passed because of the growing industrial upheaval by American workers. The NLRA established union rights that workers could draw on for years to come. The Taft-Hartley Act of 1947, on the other hand, was an employers' victory and put new restrictions on unions, such as outlawing secondary boycotts.

In the same way, some work rules allow management to restrict workers, while other rules establish workers' rights. Since management still controls the fundamental decisions, any worker rights gained through work rules—important as they are—are at best a limited protection against arbitrary and capricious acts of management.

Many of management's arguments about how work rules limit flexibility are the same arguments that we hear about other democratic rights. Isn't it "inefficient" to require police to have a search warrant before they break into your house? Isn't it "inefficient" that a government official has to go through an eminent domain procedure before seizing your house? In society

we strike a balance between the rights of government—supposedly representing all the people—and the individual. In the workplace, the rules that workers have won over the years may make plant functioning slightly more "inefficient" in some sense, but they are important in protecting workers from management abuse of power.

The other type of rule—the kind which gives power to supervisors—is not on management's list for repeal. Just the opposite: in team concept plants, at least the management-by-stress variety, management's rules are made stricter than ever.

NUMMI and Mazda, both management-by-stress plants, have uncompromising rules about absenteeism, tardiness, and what workers can and cannot do. One rule simply says no food or drink is permitted except in break areas. The rule is not flexible—for example, "workers can bring coffee to their work areas as long as they keep the area clean," or even "workers may have cold drinks at their work stations on days when the temperature exceeds 80 degrees." At Mazda workers must wear assigned uniforms. A worker who adds pockets to the nylon jumpsuit to carry tools is breaking the rule. (See Chapter 11 for excerpts from NUMMI's rules of conduct.)

The rights that workers have won sometimes function ambiguously. Using seniority as the basis for fair treatment, for example, is not a perfect system. It tends to perpetuate the past injustices done to minorities and women in the plants. There are also times when a worker who has learned a job resents it going to someone else who may lack the skill but has more seniority.

Despite the problems, seniority has proven fairer than "merit" systems, which promise to reward hard work and skill, but end up rewarding those who know how to curry favor. Union old-timers recall that before the union, keeping or improving your job frequently depended on doing outside jobs for the supervisor.

Although many work rule disputes seem extremely technical to outsiders, they make a big difference to the people who work in the plants. Work rules may determine, for example, whether a worker will be able to transfer to an easier job when she gets older or will have to work wherever management puts her from day to day. They also give individual workers and unions leverage in dealing with abusive supervisors. While it is true that many work rules have been carried over from bygone periods and the original conditions generating a particular work rule are long gone, the rule may have come to serve a different but still important function.

Here we will examine just what is at stake in the

proposals to change work rules and abolish classifications to achieve the flexibility that management longs for.

Five Kinds of Work Rules

Several very different types of practices are often lumped together under the heading of "work rules." Some are specific provisions in national or local union contracts; these tend to establish workers' rights, e.g., to choose shift preference by seniority. Others are rules invented and enforced by management (often called "shop rules"). Still others are unwritten rules established through past practice, which management, the union, or individual workers enforce through informal pressure. Whatever their form, work rules can be divided into five types according to their content.[1] Note that classifications are not work rules themselves but are meaningful insofar they are used to apply work rules.

1. Division of labor among workers. These rules determine which workers can do which jobs. Classifications often play an important role here. The rules may say, for example, that management may not assign a worker to do work from two classifications at the same time.

2. Division of labor between management and labor. In the auto industry these types of rules are usually part of the contract. They limit the conditions under which a member of management may do work normally assigned to a member of the bargaining unit. They also limit the kinds of typically management tasks such as job assignment or paperwork that can be required of an hourly worker. Classifications usually require definitions of hourly jobs, and these definitions then serve as the boundaries for what constitutes bargaining unit work.

This type of rule can be a two-edged sword: it keeps management from infringing on the bargaining unit, but on the other hand it can keep bargaining unit members from moving into new types of work brought about by new technology.

3. How workers move through the organization. These are the rules governing layoff and recall, transferring between jobs, and advancing to better jobs. How these rules operate is greatly affected by how they interact with classifications and seniority rights. For example, if seniority gives workers the right to transfer between classifications, then the more classifications there are, the more options workers have. If seniority is the rule for layoffs but the layoff unit is the classification rather than the department or the whole plant, then the power of seniority is lessened.

4. Production standards. In many plants there are standards specifying just how much work each employee is to do, the size of crews, the speed of the line, and the methods and equipment to be used. In most cases these are established by management. Under traditional UAW contracts, the company must notify the union if it would like to change production standards, and do any time-study under restrictive conditions. The union can

grieve work standards and strike over them if necessary. We discuss work standards in more detail in the next chapter.

5. Behavior rules. In most plants management has established a series of rules to govern behavior. These include prohibitions against fighting or threatening a supervisor, penalties for absenteeism, where one can eat, when one can stand in line at the time clock, how early one can arrive at the plant before work, bulletin board posting, and the use of safety equipment.

Classifications

Classifications, while not work rules themselves, are often the underpinning which allow the rules to function. A good example is the rule allowing workers to apply for a transfer between classifications by seniority. This interconnection between classifications and work rules is the main reason that management is now trying to eliminate classifications.

Many contracts restrict management's flexibility to move workers between classifications. If all workers are in a single classification, such restrictions are wiped away. So are rules that keep supervisors from assigning a person to do work from two classifications simultaneously. Getting rid of classifications means that management can now assign one person to do both a sweeper's and an assembler's jobs, for example.

In theory, the right to move from job to job could be maintained without classifications. Workers could "own" and transfer to individual jobs rather than to classifications. But this is not the type of alternative management has in mind when it demands to eliminate classifications.

Balance of Power

Rules which institutionalize workers' rights give them additional bargaining power with management. In plants where work rules have developed over a long period of time, it is extremely difficult to maintain normal operations—and virtually impossible to meet abnormal situations—without violating one of the many work rules. Normally, workers voluntarily stretch the rules—including those that protect them—in order to get production out. Examples: a production worker will move a bin of parts even though it is technically a material handler's job; an electrician will remove a metal guard without waiting for a millwright in order to get access to an electrical panel; workers will step on a moving conveyor to cross it rather than go the long way around to a safety walk.

This arrangement of convenience gives individual workers some informal bargaining power with management. Since cooperation is voluntary, if a worker feels that supervision is "messing" with her, she can withdraw the cooperation and become a stickler for the rules. And on a larger scale, if the union as a whole feels that management is overstepping its bounds, the union can organize a "work-to-rule" campaign on the shop floor.

For example, production workers may normally do some minimal maintenance work to keep production running, such as resetting tripped electrical circuit breakers. When management tries to raise output quotas, they can protest by refusing to reset the breakers unless specifically ordered. But if the work rules are changed so that resetting circuit breakers becomes an official part of the job, the workers have lost their means of protest.

Workers *could* use these kinds of rules to slow production down all the time. But this little bit of power only works if it is exercised as an exception. If you never bend the rules you can't punish a bad supervisor by "working-to-rule." Thus the normal state is voluntary cooperation with management. But it is not genuine cooperation when one side makes the rules and the other side has no choice but to obey. Management's demand for flexibility is the demand that workers do, on command, those things over which they have had some degree of voluntary choice, or at least have had the contractual basis to protest. Genuine cooperation can exist only when workers have the right to choose not to cooperate.

Management, too, enforces its rules selectively. Many rules are conveniently ignored except when the supervisor is looking for some way to harass someone. For example, Jim often forgets to put his safety glasses back on after break. Normally, the supervisor will just remind him. But when he wants to be tough (perhaps because Jim was exercising one of *his* rights), the supervisor will write him up for petty violations.

Although both sides enforce their rules selectively, the system does not make both sides equal. One management rule is that a worker must always obey a direct order from a supervisor (unless the worker can prove it is a life-threatening situation). A worker who fails to follow a direct order will be disciplined even if the order was directly contrary to the contract. The worker's recourse is to call for union representation and initiate a grievance. It may take from hours to years before the worker's right is enforced—or, more likely, paid for—

and during this time the worker is carrying out the supervisor's command.

On the other hand, the union has yet to win "innocent until proven guilty" as a general principle. If a supervisor believes a worker has violated a management rule the worker can be immediately disciplined or removed until the worker can prove otherwise.

Going from a strict set of rules to a more flexible situation benefits whichever side is more powerful. Thus, where a union has strong shop floor organization and can enforce its conception of how things should be done, a more "flexible" environment can actually benefit the union. As Nelson Lichtenstein shows in the previous chapter, in the days when unions had shop floor strength they were not particularly interested in most formal work rules. Work rules actually developed as a substitute for the more informal exercise of union power, which was only possible with an active rank and file.

In Britain, unions have exercised active rank and file power on the shop floor without contractual rules because they have a strong steward system. To counteract this informal and flexible power, note two researchers, many British companies today are

> trying to impose a system of formal rules not unlike that now being abandoned in the U.S. These formal rules are designed to reduce advantages that unions gained previously through shop-floor bargaining and a system of flexible, discretionary work rules.[2]

In the last few years some local unions in the U.S. have found that they can use the absence of rules to their advantage. This is what happens when the union lets the contract expire, stays on the job, and embarks on a "running the plant backwards" campaign. With no rules, the union runs some risks, but it is also free to take creative job actions it may have felt constrained from doing before. Such "inside strategies" can be very effective in dealing with an employer who is trying to break a union. They depend, however, on workers being extremely well organized and involved.[3]

Such situations are the exceptions, and there is no question which side usually benefits from flexibility

'85 HUCK/ KONOPACKI LABOR CARTOONS
KONOPACKI

today. The companies are demanding changes in work rules from a position of strength, in order to further enhance their position.

Measuring the Value of Work Rules

One reason management is so interested in work rule changes is that it believes that work rule changes can go deeper and last longer than monetary concessions. Two academic researchers, Peter Cappelli and Robert McKersie, point out that although wage and benefit cuts immediately show up on management's bottom line, this visibility also puts a limit on how much can be cut without provoking resistance from the union. Work rule changes, on the other hand, do not seem to affect a worker's immediate standard of living.[4]

How much are work rules worth to management? You would expect that management would attempt to measure various work rule changes in order to know which ones truly have an effect on the bottom line. But auto industry researcher Daniel Luria searched the literature and could find only one attempt to put a dollar value on work rule changes: in 1982 *Business Week* quoted a GM source who estimated that changes in some local agreements could cut hourly labor costs by $4.50.[5]

Why does management avoid putting a dollar value on work rule changes?

For one thing, it would be bad strategy vis-a-vis the union. To announce beforehand that such and such a work rule change will save X number of dollars by laying off Y number of workers would likely provoke union resistance.

Secondly, work rule changes often produce no *immediate* benefit to management's bottom line. To save money, management must take advantage of its new flexibility to either reduce the workforce while maintaining the same production, or increase production with the same workforce. In most cases the market will not support the latter alternative. Especially if the union contract contains restrictions, management may wait for other events such as model changes or introduction of

technology to lay workers off, or simply wait for attrition to take its course. For example, when one classification is merged into another, management will often agree to "red circle" the disappearing classification (allow those presently in it to remain there until they retire).

Thirdly, often a change in work rules doesn't save money itself, but makes it easier for management to do something else that saves money: enforce a speedup, or force less productive workers to retire.

Fourthly, many of the changes that management wants simply affect the shop atmosphere and thus the overall balance of power on the shop floor. It is hard to quantify what management gains, for example, from the workforce's generalized feeling that the union is feeble. At GM's Shreveport, Louisiana truck plant, one team passed a rule that no calls for the committeeman could be made while pay-for-knowledge training was going on (because the team coordinator would be tied up). Management clearly gains when the principle is established that access to union representation can be restricted (especially when union members write the rule themselves). But it is difficult to put a number on that gain.

A favorite saying in management circles, particularly in the campaigns for quality, is: "What can be measured gets the attention." The focus on work rules flies in the face of this saying. Not only do management efforts to measure the cost of specific work rules seem to be lacking, there is barely concern for differentiating between kinds of work rules and determining which make sense and which are most costly under which circumstances. The effect of various rules on quality, safety, turnover, or worker skill are not evaluated. Luria notes with surprise that in not a single one of over 40 interviews did a manager support the need for flexible work organization by referring to the needs of new flexible technology.[6] Management simply "knows" that work rules seem to reduce the proportion of time that workers spend working.[7]

Thus management's campaign for flexibility has become a general principle which no longer requires

justification or evaluation. Management correctly understands that in bargaining with the union, the work rule issue is really about power. It does not know specifically how it will use that power in the next week or the next year. Once the corporation gets the flexibility, then individual managers can decide when and how to apply it. With unions on the defensive, now is the time for management to grab power.

Job Flexibility and Rotation

One of the most widespread myths about the team concept is that team members have the "privilege" of rotating jobs, that is, to regularly exchange jobs on an hourly, daily or weekly basis. According to enthusiasts in the media, few of whom have ever worked in a factory, workers benefit from swapping jobs instead of being stuck on the same one all the time.

In fact workers have a wide variety of opinions on this subject. Some workers do favor flexibility and/or rotation. They cite the following reasons:

1. Repetitive work is boring and learning new jobs is a break in a dull routine.

2. Rotation is the only access to the better or easier jobs.

3. A worker who learns many different jobs can apply for the utility or relief jobs (if they still exsist), which usually pay more and may be more interesting because the work is constantly changing.

4. If the plant has a pay-for-knowledge system, workers can earn more by learning new jobs. At Chrysler, for example, one can typically earn up to 40 cents per hour more.

5. Learning as many jobs as possible is part of the path into management.

However, even though work in an auto plant is usually hard, repetitive, and boring, given a choice, many workers prefer not to make themselves available for multiple assignments or to rotate. The following reasons are offered:

1. Whatever the abstract appeal of changing jobs, few workers wish to give management more leeway to jerk them around.

2. Where jobs are distinctly unequal, those who hold the better jobs would prefer to keep them every day.

3. Even where jobs are roughly equal, each demands different skills, effort and mental processes. Workers develop distinct preferences for certain jobs and dislikes for others. Some prefer the variation, responsibility, mobility, and self-pacing of material handling, making sure that each position on the assembly line has the required components. Others do not like the stress involved and prefer a line job where you know exactly what is expected and can develop a rhythm.

4. When working one job for a long time, a person develops techniques and shortcuts that can make the job easier. When only the regular worker on the job knows these, management cannot load additional work

onto it because a relief person or a vacation replacement would not be able to keep up. In a traditional plant, if the engineers come to time-study the job, the worker can simply go back to doing the job exactly as she was told.

5. Some workers feel a sense of ownership and pride about perfecting a job and doing it really well. Others develop an attachment to their specific machine and take pride in tuning it up, keeping it in good condition and making it operate smoothly. Many craftspeople prefer using their own tools because they know exactly how the tools will respond. Machine operators often feel the same way.

6. Some find that switching between three or four boring jobs is no better than doing just one. The advantage of doing one is that you can settle into a routine and allow your mind to be elsewhere. The day becomes intolerably boring when the job is altered not enough to make it interesting, but just enough so that you must think about it. It's like driving a car. On a familiar road, the driver can engage in conversation or enjoy music. But change that to an unfamiliar route or a rainy night, and the driver must pay full attention and feels considerably more stress.

7. Factories are dangerous places. When a person works one job regularly he gets to learn both the hazards of the job itself and the hazards of the immediate environment.

Many workers have mixed feelings about switching jobs. One NUMMI inspector, Arlene Diamond, described her reaction when other members of her team pressed for rotation:

> It was about a year and a half before we started rotation. At first I was leery of rotation. It takes a lot of experience to do inspection jobs. I was concerned that someone else on my job without as much experience would miss defects that I would catch.
>
> But since we did start rotating, I guess [missed defects] do occur. But I psyched myself into not worrying about it and doing my best on all the jobs I do....
>
> Now I am really glad we rotate....It breaks the monotony, expands your knowledge, makes you more versatile and gives you more things to have an opinion on.

But for others, once they learn all the jobs on a team, the excitement of learning something new disappears and the disadvantages become more evident. As another NUMMI worker describes it, "At first I really liked rotating, but after a while I found all the jobs boring."

Management's Attitude

Given the choices in today's plants, most workers prefer a steady job. Unfortunately, how workers feel is of secondary concern to management, which has its own reasons for being ambivalent about rotation.

In practice, despite the media myths, there is little rotation in team concept plants. At NUMMI, for example, despite management's stated desire that every worker should ideally learn every job in the plant, under pressure to get production out many supervisors and teams try to avoid the extra time and effort required for rotation. In several cases, rotation only became a reality when team members pressed for it. It is difficult to rotate outside a supervisor's group except for teams which have been specifically paired. And in other team concept plants there is even less rotation than at NUMMI. Asked how much job rotation goes on in their plants, union officials and workers usually answer, "None."

Instead of rotation, what does exist is management flexibility to move workers around from task to task without facing a grievance, because the workers have been required or paid extra to learn more than one job.This flexibility offers management a number of advantages, such as:

1. An absent worker can be easily replaced without worrying about classifications, qualifications, or worker resistance.

2. It is easier to redistribute the elements of different jobs among team members—say if one job in a team is eliminated—if all the team members are already trained on all the jobs. The speed of the line can be varied more easily while still maintaining high productivity.

3. Knowing jobs plant-wide will supposedly make workers identify with the entire plant and its product. Once workers see how it all goes together they will appreciate management's problems and will offer broader suggestions.

4. Once a worker knows different jobs she can serve as an unofficial inspector for the work done on those jobs. Management can hold workers responsible for catching defects in previous jobs in addition to their own.

5. Job flexibility increases the possibility for management to pit worker against worker. It makes writing grievances about work standards more difficult, because there are more people who at least from time to time do exactly the same job. No matter how much work is loaded onto the job, management can likely find one person who can and will keep up.

At the same there are strong reasons why management needs to limit the amount of training and movement that a full-scale organized rotation would imply.

1. Workers with regular experience on a job do higher quality work and know better how to respond to exceptional circumstances.

2. The cost of training is high. Even when training is entirely on-the-job, there must be another worker, team leader, or trainer present during the learning process—one job done for the cost of two. There is also the cost of correcting the mistakes of an inexperienced worker. Add to this the costs of any off-job training required. If every person is trained for five jobs, training costs are five times the total if everyone were trained for just one job. And if everyone were trained for every job in the plant, training costs would be astronomical.

3. To get any benefit out of teaching employees many jobs, their qualifications must be kept up. Much of the ability gained through training or experience on a particular job is lost when the worker does not do that job for a while. This is especially true of those techniques which apply only to a particular job ("job-specific skills"). For example, one study of team production in Germany found cases where team members practiced certain operations involved in adjusting robots so infrequently that they did not feel capable of doing them, and the operations had to be given back to skilled maintenance workers.[8]

4. If job movement is through a regular rotation schedule, it is more difficult for management to use job assignments as rewards and punishments. It also makes it harder for management to isolate workers regarded as troublemakers to a remote corner of the plant.

Thus, management wants workers to learn several jobs and to accept flexible assignments in order to readily shift people around or rebalance jobs. But it needs to keep a strict limit on the amount of movement in order to keep up quality and productivity and keep down training costs. When the pressure builds, as several researchers have noted, management tends to cut back on rotation.[9] At GM's Poletown plant, management initially required workers to learn 20 jobs and ro-

TWO KINDS OF SKILL

Two kinds of skills can be distinguished: job-specific and marketable. Job-specific skills are those gained from experience on a particular job, such as knowing which adjustment on a particular machine successfully compensates for a variation in a specific brand of raw materials, knowing where to find a scarce part, knowing who to contact to take care of a certain task. As valuable as job-specific skills may be to the employer, they are of limited value when looking for a job in the labor market (except for the recommendation from the previous company that the individual "works hard and learns quickly").

Marketable skills, by comparison, are those which are of value to many companies and usually translate into higher wages or an easier time finding a job. Besides those trades officially classified as "skilled" in the auto industry, jobs which have marketability include metal finisher, paint sprayer, and certain machine operators. Training for marketability means more emphasis on the theory behind the process. For metal finishers, it means teaching metallurgy and the characteristics of different metals besides the specific ones the metal finisher deals with every day. For paint sprayers, it means chemistry and paint mixing. It means more use of formal classroom training and more exposure to different processes.

tate; later management called a halt to rotation to try to remedy quality problems.

Worker movement in the form of transfers can be even more limited in team concept plants than in traditional ones. At Mazda, management has let it be known that for the first five years, until quality is up, transfers between departments will be strictly limited. The result is that people who were initially randomly assigned to the tough departments, such as the body shop, have little chance to transfer to openings in more desirable departments—which go to new-hires.

Multiskilling

It is possible to design factory jobs to require a broad range of worker skills. One example is the utility person in a traditional plant, who can do all the jobs in an area.

But the "multiskilling" which is part of the team concept is not the same as making every worker a utility person, precisely because becoming a competent utility person does require a fair amount of training and experience. Management's desire for flexibility requires that all team members be capable of doing any task. But accomplishing this without extensive and expensive training requires that each job have as little skill content as possible. The less training and skill required, the greater the interchangeability without increasing costs. Multiskilling every worker means deskilling every job.

Training in team concept plants typically emphasizes learning team procedures, the company's particular version of standardized work, and motivation, so that workers can quickly learn and precisely carry out the detailed step-by-step job directions on their standardized work sheets. To the degree that the company can focus on "plant-specific" training, it further ties the worker to the company and does not increase the ability of the worker to get a better job elsewhere.[10]

This attitude toward skills is usually reflected in hiring policy. A human relations manager from TRW, an auto components and defense contractor, put it this way:

> Tightly controlled employee selection and hiring practices are also commonly cited as critical in fostering work force flexibility and employee involvement. Companies often use extensive prescreening processes, including technical training programs and multiple

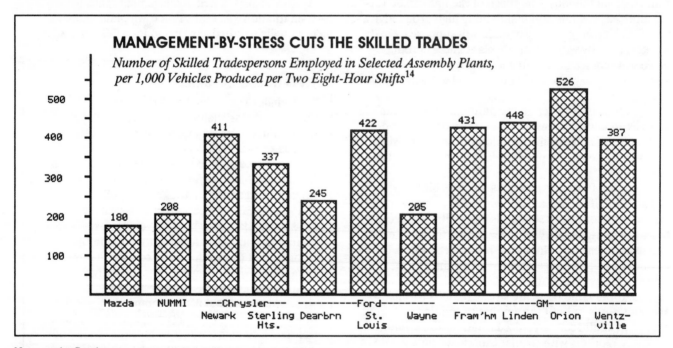

MANAGEMENT-BY-STRESS CUTS THE SKILLED TRADES

Number of Skilled Tradespersons Employed in Selected Assembly Plants, per 1,000 Vehicles Produced per Two Eight-Hour Shifts[14]

Notes on the Graph:

Since different plants produce different numbers of vehicles and operate different numbers of hours, it was necessary to standardize these figures so plants could be compared with each other. Thus we divided the actual number of skilled trades workers in each plant by the number of vehicles that would be produced if the plant ran two full eight-hour shifts and multiplied that figure by 1,000 (to get a whole number in the range of typical assembly plant daily production). The results are the figures in the graph.

Some of the variation shown in the chart results from differences in the complexity of the vehicles built. Ford's Wayne assembly plant produces a smaller car (the Escort) than the others, for example, and the Ford St. Louis plant assembles vans, which may explain at least part of the wide variation for the Ford plants.

Different plants follow different procedures for laying off or hiring when they change output levels. Thus since the figures in the graph are extrapolations, they could vary slightly from the actual number of skilled trades workers employed if the plant should change to the output levels shown here.

It would be more accurate to compare "number of skilled trades hours worked" averaged over a year or two rather than "number of skilled tradespersons" but these figures were not available. Some of the variation in the graph may occur because plants vary in their use of "normal" skilled trades overtime.

Unlike the other plants, both of the management-by-stress plants (NUMMI and Mazda) include stamping operations. Thus the NUMMI and Mazda diemakers who work exclusively in stamping have been subtracted, to partially correct for this difference. (Dies are the mating forms mounted in stamping presses which, when forced together, cut and shape the sheet steel.)

interviews, to identify candidates best suited for the organization's culture and practices. Often these organizations hire individuals who have not had similar past work experience, thereby enabling them to mold employee attitudes, expectations, and skills. This practice also minimizes the need to unlearn bad habits.[11]

The "new labor relations" sounds much like the engineer on the Ford Model T assembly line explaining why the company had "no use for experience":

It desires and prefers machine-tool operators who have nothing to unlearn, who have no theories of correct surface speeds for metal finishing, and will simply do what they are told, over and over again from belltime to bell-time.[12]

Where management has a production job that does require significant skill, it tries to protect that job from being subject to worker turnover. One way is by assigning the skilled portions of the job to management employees or at least to the team leader. Another way is by relying on outside contracting.

Still another way is by creating a "non-interchangeable" classification or getting some special contractual arrangement to build a fence around these special workers. (This is one instance where management *wants* a narrow classification.) At GM's Shreveport, Louisiana team concept plant a technicality in the new union contract opened up some desirable and skilled production jobs—mixing paint—so that higher seniority workers had the right to transfer in and bump the incumbents off those jobs. Management complained that it would take six months to train new paint mixers, and prevailed on the shop committee to waive the seniority rights. Learning new skills is supposed to be one of the main attractions of the team concept. But when a job actually required serious training, management used that as the reason why the skill could not be spread to more workers.

Cutting the Skilled Trades

It is logical to predict that the increasing use of robots and other new technologies in assembly plants would result in a sharp reduction in the number of production workers per vehicle produced. But one might also expect that the installation and maintenance of this same automation would increase or at least maintain the number of skilled trades jobs.

Yet the management-by-stress plants now used as the model of team concept have sharply cut the number of skilled trades workers. For management this seems to be a point of pride. One Mazda executive "contrasted GM's Fiero plant where there are 400 skilled trades workers with Flat Rock [Mazda] where there are just 189."[13] While Ford has already cut its skilled trades workforce as part of an overall squeeze, it is looking for further cuts through the team concept. At the Wayne, Michigan assembly plant, for example, where the ratio of skilled workers to cars produced is already one of the lowest in the industry (see graph), top management is

trying to use a reorganization of the plant connected to a recent team concept agreement to cut the trades population by another 33 percent. According to Jimmy McWilliams, skilled trades chairperson at the plant, this proposal has even middle managers wondering how they will be able to run the plant.

The fight over cutting the skilled trades is of vital importance to production workers. Most current tradespeople can expect to keep their jobs over the long run while attrition slowly whittles the trades. The big losers from cuts in the trades are those production workers who could have looked to the trades for learning marketable skills, job security, increased wages and a better job. The most cheated are minorities and women, who have only recently gained access to many trades and now may not have a chance to increase their foothold.

One of management's stated goals in team concept plants is to reduce the amount of "non-value-added" (NVA) labor as much as possible. NVA labor is any which does not directly produce vehicles, and the work of skilled tradespeople is usually its largest component.

Even the term "non-value-added" shows management's bias and direction. It certainly sounds rational to get rid of workers who aren't adding any value! But such work is also called "indirect" (as opposed to "direct") labor—terms which would indicate a different attitude about how to increase productivity.

In Sweden, for example, because of union pressure, management has adopted a policy of using *more* indirect labor and less direct labor, through automation. More automation means that the number of indirect labor jobs increases, to build, maintain, and support the new technology (although not as much as the direct labor jobs decrease). The union feels that this strategy (which would not be feasible without Sweden's strong social safety net) makes for more staisfying jobs as well as increasing productivity.

According to Luria, 24 percent of the automotive workforce in Swedish Saab plants is skilled trades, as compared to 19 percent in the U.S. and 15 percent in Japan.[15] Thus the companies which are trying to apply the "anti-NVA" Japanese system here in the U.S. want very deep cuts in skilled trades.

The sharp reduction in tradespeople is possible not because management has found a more efficient way to do the work. It is possible because management has been able to shift entire areas of skilled work away from the skilled trades. There are several devices for doing this:

1. Outside contracting. NUMMI and Mazda attempt to limit their own tradespeople to machine tending and basic maintenance. Construction jobs and major maintenance jobs are contracted out along with such jobs as carpenter, painter, and glazier. The purchase of extended warranties on production equipment means that that equipment will be serviced by the vendors rather than in-house.

Even more outside contracting can be accomplished by the design of the machines. One such feature is easily removable electronic or mechanical modules that can be sent out for replacement, allowing outside firms to do most of the repair work.

2. Shifting skilled work to production workers. Virtually every recent team concept agreement specifically requires production workers to do "minor maintenance" on machinery. The point is not the small amount of work involved (at first); it is that once the clear line between skilled and production is breached, management then presses for production workers to take over more and more skilled work.

3. Using technology to transfer skills to management. We do not wish to enter the ongoing debate over whether new technology itself tends to skill or deskill the workforce.[16]

Either way, the technology offers new possibilities for shifting the skilled components of jobs. For example, one of the new areas of work and corresponding skill acquired by electricians in the past decade has been troubleshooting and programming devices called "programmable controllers"—specialized computers which control the operation of individual machines and sections of assembly lines. The technology which now allows electronic communication between these programmable controllers and central computers also allows management or non-union personnel to take over from floor electricians the job of troubleshooting and programming. Computer Aided Design/Computer Aided Manufacturing (CAD/CAM) and Direct Numerical Control (DNC) allow management personnel to take over from skilled diemakers or machinists the job of programming computerized numerical control (CNC) machines.

The job-cutting effect of new technology on skilled trades is usually not obvious at first. The introduction and debugging of new technology usually requires *more* skilled tradespersons. Layoffs will come later, when management cashes in its gains.

Besides shifting work away from the skilled trades, management also reduces their numbers by breaking down lines of demarcation between trades and through "multiskilling," described below.

In principle none of these ways of cutting skilled trades requires the team concept. As the figures for the non-team concept Ford plants in the graph show, it is possible to cut trades without formally getting rid of classifications. But most of these management policies go along with the team concept, either explicitly or through the back door. Management gets unions to consent to such policies using the same scare tactics which it uses to push the team concept.

Multiskilling the Skilled Trades

Not only are skilled trades reduced in number under the team concept, but those who remain find that instead of deepening their skills in their central trade, they are "cross-trained" to superficial skills in other areas.

Which is better for factory maintenance: a team of eight skilled tradespersons each of whom is a specialist in his or her area (say two of each electricians, pipefitters, millwrights, and machinists) or a team of four persons trained in general maintenance? The management mind immediately chooses the general maintenance option. When you have specialists around there is usually some kind of imbalance. One day there may be a lot of work for the electricians and none for the pipefitters; the next day it could be the other way around. So you always seem to have some tradespeople sitting around reading the newspaper, refusing work management wants done because it is "out of their classification." With general maintenance you can tell anyone to do anything.

There is little data available to show just how much cross-training is worth to management. One study of an engine block line in a plant with nine maintenance classifications found that "waiting for maintenance [workers] to arrive" amounted to just over one-fifth of maintenance-related lost production or about nine percent of total lost production.[17] Management would like to claim that all the wasted time is the fault of lines of demarcation or because it is not allowed to assign maintenance work to production workers. But communications problems and the need to find the person who actually knows how to make certain repairs undoubtedly contribute to the figure. One solution would be for management to discover which trades were more frequently in short supply and increase their number. (In the case of the block line study it appeared that much waiting time could have been eliminated by assigning a millwright and a pipefitter to the area.[18]) Of course this kind of solution—having enough support during emergencies —would tend to increase idle time during non-emergency periods.

But in a modern factory, the fact that some maintenance workers are idle some of the time should not be the only consideration. In deciding whether a team of specialists or generalists is better, a rational analysis would take into account many factors. The fact that management and unions weigh the following points differently demonstrates that different interests are involved.

1. Safety. Skilled trades work is dangerous. Maintenance work does not usually take place under normal circumstances. Often the machine must be worked on when it is operational but not behaving predictably.

The tradesperson's work also determines the safety of others in the area of the machine. Under pressure to get production started, it is common for repair people to temporarily "jumper out" safety or quality monitors which might be prohibiting production. The less a person knows about the trade the less likely he is to find the problem in a short time, and is therefore subject to greater pressure to take such shortcuts.

2. *Uptime of production machinery*. When millions of dollars of equipment goes down, which system will get it running most quickly? And even more important, which will fix it so that it is least likely to break down again? The relevant figure is not percentage of lost production due to "waiting for maintenance." If that figure doubles, but at the same time *total* lost production is reduced to one-quarter because of high quality work, the amount of production is increased.

3. *Tolerances and quality*. As important as getting the machine running is getting it running to close tolerances so that product quality is maintained.

4. *Suggestions*. Who will be in the better position to make suggestions for improvements?

5. *New technology*. Who will most quickly adapt to changing technology in the field?

6. *Benefits to trades*. Which system benefits the tradesperson more?

7. *Parts*. Which system requires stocking more spare parts?

8. *External support*. Which system requires more external support from vendors, outside contractors or management experts?

9. *Training*. Which requires more training?

There are undoubtedly instances, especially in the short run, where general maintenance workers would be more efficient from any point of view. But on most of the above considerations a team of specialists is more efficient—even from management's point of view. Most outsiders do not understand the degree of difficulty and responsibility involved in skilled maintenance work, however, so management complaints about the skilled trades make good press copy.

Under a traditional system it is common for tradespeople to teach each other aspects of their respective trades. Generally speaking, skilled tradespeople like to learn other work and often feel great satisfaction when they can do an entire job. The issue here is choice for the workers versus the company's policy for how work should be generally organized.

We have seen no attempts by management to study or prove its case that teams of generalists are more efficient. It is simply assumed that management will do better with interchangeable workers. Presumably, when GM Chairman Roger Smith needs surgery, he demands to be operated on by a team of general practitioners.

In fact, in this age of technology there needs to be more specialization, not less. The techniques of an electrician who troubleshoots low power analog circuits are different from those of an electrician who troubleshoots digital logic or computer electronics. These are different still from the skills of an electrician who specializes in high current semi-conductor drives, which are different from those required in high voltage power distribution. In diemaking, the trend to use fewer presses in a stamping line means much more complicated dies. The wide range of new materials used, entirely new techniques such as laser cutting or laser interferometers

(measuring devices), and the closer tolerances required all make it impossible for skilled workers to know even their own field fully, let alone everyone else's field.

The move to "multiskill" the skilled trades goes in the opposite direction. Instead of providing more specialty courses in the skilled trades apprentice programs to cope with new technology, the move at NUMMI is to create a general maintenance apprenticeship. Even while technology is changing rapidly, rather than updating and deepening skills in core trades the companies are using valuable training time to "cross-train" so that tradespeople can do the more superficial work of all trades.

Not all skill comes from training; as much or more is gained through experience. When management transfers work away from skilled workers as described above, the chance to develop skills on the job is taken away. An electrician who only replaces motors or swaps circuit boards according to step-by-step instructions is not learning much on the job. Few electricians at NUMMI or Mazda use an oscilloscope or learn to troubleshoot circuit boards to the component level.

When the Mazda plant opened, the company hired experienced diemakers who had been trained elsewhere. One Mazda diemaker comments:

> Management is constantly amazed at our skills when some crisis takes place. We told them we could fix a broken die in a few days and they didn't believe it.... We didn't have the right tools and materials—we had to use contacts at Ford to do it....
>
> But I pity the guys who are going to learn diemaking here. We don't do any construction and we hardly do any re-engineering on dies. We are just chunkers and chewers [welding and grinding on die surfaces—regular upkeep operations to compensate for wear as dies are used].

> **"Better to be proficient in one art than a smatterer in a hundred."**
> — Japanese proverb[20]

An electrician at Ford's Rouge Steel plant writes:

> [Under the 1987 team concept contract] electricians are now responsible for their own lifts [lifting and moving heavy units with a crane]...and were given a 15-minute presentation by riggers on equipment. [Rigger is a skilled trades classification management wants to eliminate which specializes in moving heavy equipment.] A few days later the electricians got the pleasure and the responsibility for doing all the lifts to take apart our Bottom Mill Motor which has an armature weighing about 40 tons and which requires great care not only because of its size but its expense. During the repair more than a dozen steel cables and about ten fabric slings were broken....
>
> Electricians will also receive welding responsibili-

ties starting next year. I would hope that we will receive more than 15 minutes instruction on equipment before our welding skills are tested with someone's life.[19]

Who Does the Skilled Work?

The truth is that management understands full well that specialization is necessary. Within management's own ranks, engineers are becoming more specialized; there are no proposals for accountants to rotate jobs with designers or for corporate lawyers to rotate with marketing managers.

Only a minor part of everyday skilled trades work requires in-depth skills. A major part can actually be done by people with relatively little training (although the in-depth skills are always important in knowing when the more skilled work is required and in maintaining safe conditions).

Skilled trades workers have tried through their union to keep these two parts of the job together, to force management to provide full training for more people and allow more people to gain skills. Management's strategy is to try to separate the everyday skilled work from the smaller amount of more difficult skilled work. But if management generally reduces the skill level of the trades, where does it get the specialists it needs to handle those problems which do require more skill?

One alternative is to train people to be general experts on specific machines. But given training costs, this is only cost effective if the worker can be tied to the machine—that is, by limiting transfer rights and turning the skilled worker into a glorified machine tender. Ironically, this limits management flexibility when the need arises to use different types of machines. As a result, training under this approach rarely develops the specialist skills needed. Specialists with solid backgrounds in their fields are still needed when difficult or unusual problems arise.

Another management answer is to rely on outside contracting for the more complex work, as described earlier. Russ Leone, chair of UAW Local 600's Tool and Die Unit at the Ford Rouge, points out that there is a strong connection between deskilling, outside contracting, and management flexibility:

> They try to get away without training you, and then they tell you they need to contract out because you can't do the job. Of course, once they get to contract out you never will get trained. Or only one or two tradespeople are trained and then they say that they have to bypass seniority so they can get the job done. We've taken a position that there is no bypassing seniority and no outside contracting. That's our hammer that makes them take care of training.

When you are firm with management on outside

SPECIALIZATION REQUIRES MORE TEAMWORK

Being a specialized skilled trades worker does not mean isolation from other trades and other knowledge. On the contrary, as technology becomes more integrated there is a vital need for tradespeople to learn portions of related trades which cross classification lines. True teamwork becomes more necessary and team members need to be able to speak each other's language.

Take the case of an electrician servicing a computerized numerical control milling machine. The machine operates under extremely close tolerances. A variation of .0001 inch may be unacceptable. It moves along several axes simultaneously, and may have several sources of feedback for each axis. A sophisticated machine may have a tachometer for speed feedback, an encoder or resolver to precisely measure position, and a Hall-effect device for current feedback. In addition, the control itself may have compensation for pitch-error in the ball screw which converts the rotary motor motion to the linear motion of the table or cutter. Further, all of the axes may have internal corrections to compensate for each other or for the spindle.

The cause of a problem is difficult to track down. Because control is maintained through a circular control loop (the end result is fed back as an input and then compensated for), the problem seems to appear almost everywhere in the circuit. The problem

could be a slipping mechanical drive coupling, a problem in a gear box, a slipping encoder coupling, a dirty tachometer armature, a defective resolver, a bad ground condition, loss of power supply filtering, a problem in the computer program, a problem in the setting of machine parameters, or an operator error.

The machine operates as a system. While a general maintenance person will lack the training to understand any part of the problem, an electrician who knows nothing about mechanical devices or how that particular machine is supposed to operate will also have difficulty analyzing it. The same is true for a machine repairman who knows nothing of electronic feedback devices. There is a clear need for teamwork between production and skilled workers and for cooperation and communication between specialists. The first thing a good maintenance electrician will do is talk to the operator to learn the machine's normal operation, its history and any symptoms the operator has observed. Where the problem appears to be mechanical, the electrician will work with a machine repairperson to understand the most efficient way to break the control loop or isolate the defective mechanical component.

Cross-training which is designed to improve communication and cooperation between specialists —rather than eliminate specialization—is a vital part of a skilled trades response to new technology.

contracting, seniority, and bargaining unit work, Leone adds, management suddenly becomes interested in classifications. Ford management is discussing with the Tool and Die unit a separate classification for new computerized five-axis tracing mills. These machines, which convert the shapes of large complicated models into computer instructions and then mill the shape, require extensive training to operate and to modify their programming.

Another management answer is to shift highly skilled work to management employees. Sometimes this shift can be disguised by invoking the complexities of new technology, but often it means the relaxation of work rules which restrict management from doing work normally done by union members. At least for the short run, one auto manufacturer was able to use mainly inexperienced "multiskilled" tradespeople at a Mexican plant by delegating decision making to experienced salaried employees brought in from the U.S.[21]

Still another management answer is to allow the trades to specialize to some extent, as long as management can ignore classifications and seniority in making assignments. Then management has the best of both worlds. It has its specialists for the occasions when they are necessary, but can assign workers for any reason that it wishes and does not have to train for any more than its immediate needs.

At Mazda, management attempts all four approaches. There is extensive outside contracting and supervisors regularly work on jobs. Although there is only one classification for all skilled workers, management keeps people with diemaker backgrounds together in a die maintenance group which does not rotate with the "mutricians" or "bicraftuals," as some skilled maintenance workers call themselves. Mazda also limits transfers between departments so that training can be focused on machine-specific knowledge.

These strategies may well backfire in the long run. Management may be creating a future shortage of workers with in-depth skills. This has happened before: management's attempts to deskill the metal-working trades through over-specialization in the 1920's resulted in a shortage of skilled workers in the 1930's.[22] A shortage of skilled trades workers will increase the power of both those who work in the plants and those who work for outside contractors.

Pay-For-Knowledge

Pay-for-knowledge (PFK) plans (also called knowledge-based pay, multiskill compensation, or ability rate progression) were among the hottest fads in auto industry labor relations from about 1984 to 1986. Despite the dignified name, pay-for-knowledge is not about workers acquiring more knowledge. A metal finisher who goes to school to study metallurgy gets no pay increase under this system. Nor does a carburetor assembler who goes to the library to better understand the principles of carburetion. Workers get additional pay

for giving management the right to assign them flexibly, not for what they know.

Under the traditional pay systems a worker was paid for doing a specific job. If the job changed or the worker moved to a new job, the worker was paid according to the rate for the new job. Under pay-for-knowledge the worker is paid not for what job she is doing at any particular time, but for which and how many jobs she is *capable* of doing.

Here is an example of how PFK is to work at Chrysler's Jefferson assembly plant: a new-hire is initially trained to do one assembly job, is classified as Technician II, and paid a base wage. When she learns and is declared qualified on five jobs in the same team, she receives a 14 cent increase. If she learns all the jobs in her team she will receive another ten cents. If she then learns all the jobs on two teams she will earn an additional eight cents. A Technician III (including janitors and material handlers) starts at a lower base and can receive up to a 38 cent increase. The highest paid production classification, Technician I (metal finishers and repair), can get an increase of up to 42 cents. (See the case studies of the Shreveport and Orion plants for descriptions of other pay-for-knowledge plans.)

Sticky Problems

PFK plans are attractive, but a closer look reveals some sticky problems. How does a worker get trained on new jobs? Who decides who gets trained in what? What happens if a worker does not want to be trained in a particular job? Who decides whether a worker is qualified and entitled to the additional pay? What happens if a worker is ready for more training but there is no training available? It becomes clear that PFK has meaning only as part of a bigger system.

Many claims have been made about the effect of pay-for-knowledge on productivity and worker morale. But as a study published by the U.S. Department of Labor in 1986 points out, "Systematic evidence for supporting these claims about pay-for-knowledge are rare." The report warns:

> Little is known about how well these plans work, the conditions under which they are most likely to succeed, the possible unanticipated consequences of such plans, and the impact of such plans on workers, on management, and on management-labor relationships, both in the short and in the long run. Until these issues are addressed, it is somewhat precipitous to urge the widespread use of these plans.[23]

The main study contained within the DOL report covers 20 firms only one of which was under a union contract. There has been little research about what happens with PFK in unionized plants.

Experience with pay-for-knowledge at several General Motors plants shows that it can become divisive. Since it involves a wage increase, workers are motivated to get "qualified" as quickly as possible. But if teams determine who is qualified, sometimes cliques develop whose members vote for qualifying each other. If, on the other hand, it is management who determines training assignments and who is qualified, then the union has handed the supervisor considerable power over team members and a financial motivation for them to curry favor with the supervisor. In effect this is a return to the old "merit pay" system that the union fought for so many years.

A problem can also arise for management when the teams have the say over who is qualified. Many teams simply vote to qualify everyone, since "it's not coming out of my pocket," as a Shreveport worker says. This solves the divisiveness problem by quickly getting everyone into the top-paying category.

This "topping out" creates another problem for management. Once a worker has moved through all the steps in a PFK system, then what? After a few months or more, most workers who want to participate have reached the top of the pay scale. If management has been depending on PFK to provide motivation for learning more jobs, or as a perk for supervisors to hand out, these disappear once workers are drawing top pay. Another problem for management is that the pay incentive causes workers to push for training on different jobs even when management finds such shifting around inconvenient.

An additional problem with PFK for both management and the union is the hassle of keeping track of the system and dealing with disputes over it. One result has been a tendency to resolve conflicts or hold-ups in the system by simply awarding the pay increment (see Chapter 19). This has had the effect of shortening the time until the system "tops out."

There are two generally acknowledged results of pay-for-knowledge. First, PFK does provide management with more flexibility by making workers capable of multiple job assignments. The second result is a wage increase. Thus PFK essentially becomes the deal whereby the union sells work rules back to the company for a modest pay raise. Some workers call it "pay for scabbing." It can act as a sweetener in the transition to team concept, although the pay raises offered by PFK are small. At Chrysler's Sterling Heights assembly plant, for example, which turned down a team concept contract in 1986, the major argument put forward by members of the shop committee in support of the contract was that PFK would mean more money.

In the auto industry, management's enthusiasm for pay-for-knowledge is definitely on the decline. Full-fledged management-by-stress plants, including all the Japanese transplants, do not use the system.[24] Although the Chrysler team concept contracts all include PFK, many of the newer GM team concept arrangements (Tarrytown, Fairfax, Van Nuys) do not. If, as it appears, the main value of PFK to management is as a buyout of the seniority/classification system, why not skip the bureaucratic complications and just give the sweetener straight out?

Notes

1. Peter Cappelli and Robert McKersie, "Management Strategy and the Redesign of Workrules," *Journal of Management Studies*, September 1987. The first four categories parallel the typology used by Cappelli and McKersie. They include "employee misconduct" under production standards.

2. Cappelli and Mckersie, p.458.

3. Jack Metzgar, " 'Running the Plant Backwards' in UAW Region 5," *Labor Research Review*, Fall 1985. AFL-CIO Industrial Union Department, *The Inside Game*, 1986.

4. Cappelli and McKersie, p.445.

5. Daniel Luria, "Work Organization and Manufacturing Performance in the U.S. Automotive Sector, 1982-1992," WZB Conference, Berlin, November 1987. Using regression analysis on the inadequate data available, Luria estimates that if GM assembly plants had work rules similar to NUMMI's it would save $70-$100 per car at the assembly plant level, all other things remaining equal (p.19).

6. Luria, "Work Organization and..." p.16.

7. Stephen Herzenberg, "But Does the Union Get the Management It Deserves?" presented to MIT U.S.-Italy Conference, February 22-24, 1987, p.31.

8. Ben Dankbaar, "Teamwork in the West German Car Industry: Management Strategies and the Quality of Work," WZB Conference, Berlin, 1987.

9. Committee on the Effective Implementation of Advanced Manufacturing Technology, *Human Resource Practices for Implementing Advanced Manufacturing Technology*, Washington, DC, National Research Council, 1986, p.45.
Also Harley Shaiken and Stephen Herzenberg, *Automation and Global Production: Automobile Engine Production in Mexico, the United States, and Canada*, Monograph Series, 26, Center for U.S.-Mexican Studies, University of California, San Diego, 1987, p.63.

10. Michael J. Piore and Charles F. Sabel, *The Second Industrial Divide*, New York, Basic Books, 1984, p.273. Piore and Sabel recognize that the training costs of multiskilling encourage employers to teach mainly plant-specific skills. They say that if workers are to get broader, more marketable skills such training will likely have to come from sources outside the company.

11. Ian V. Ziskin, "Knowledge-Based Pay: A Strategic Analysis," *ILR Report*, Fall 1986.

12. David Montgomery, *Workers' Control in America*, Cambridge University Press, 1979, p.119.

13. Richard Child Hill, Michael Indergaard, and Kuniko Fujita, "Flat Rock, Home of Mazda: The Social Impact of a Japanese Company on an American Community," Paper for 8th Annual International Automo-

tive Conference, University of Michigan, March 22-23, 1988, p.20.

14. The following are the raw figures from which the data in the graph were obtained. LS = line speed (vehicles per hour); WT = actual time the line is moving in an 8-hour day (e.g. 7.23 when there is 46 minutes break time); SK = skilled trades population.

Mazda: planned LS = 67 (company prediction is "65 to 70"), WT = 7.5, planned SK = 180 (plus 20-24 diemakers in stamping). (During orientation company spokespeople said that 180 skilled trades workers were planned; knowledgeable insiders say 180-210; number of diemakers supplied by a Mazda diemaker.)

NUMMI: top LS currently planned = 64, WT = 7.5, SK =200 (plus 25 diemakers in stamping). (Supplied by NUMMI spokesperson February 1988; number of diemakers supplied by a NUMMI diemaker.)

Chrysler Sterling Heights Assembly: LS = 65, WT= 7.23, SK = 390 (February 1988).

Chrysler Newark: LS = 69.1, WT = 7.23, SK = 336 (December 1987 when running full production).

Ford Dearborn: LS = 51, WT = 7.23, SK = 181 (February 1988). The plant has been regularly working 10-hour shifts.

Ford Wayne: LS = 70, WT = 8 (tag relief), SK = 230 (February 1988). Plant regularly working 10-hour shifts.

Ford St. Louis Van: LS = 48, WT = 8 (tag relief), SK = 324 (March 1988).

GM Framingham: LS = 45, WT = 7.23, SK = 283 (plus 8 powerhouse). Figures for when plant last ran two full shifts, November 1987.

GM Linden: LS = 70, WT = 7.1, SK = 445 (March 1988).

GM Orion: LS = 66, WT = 7.23, SK = 502 (March 1988).

GM Wentzville: LS = 75, WT = 7.23, SK = 420 (January 1988 before line speed reduced due to slow sales).

15. Luria, p.27. However, overall productivity (vehicles produced per worker) is very high in Sweden, close to

Japanese levels. The ratio of Swedish skilled trades workers to the number of vehicles produced (the measure used in the bar graph) is probably roughly comparable to the ratio in the U.S.

16. See David Noble, *Forces of Production*, New York, Alfred A. Knopf, 1984; Harley Shaiken, *Work Transformed: Automation and Labor in the Computer Age*, New York, Holt, Rinehart, and Winston, 1985; Paul Adler, "Technology and Us," *Socialist Review*, January-February 1986; Bryn Jones and Stephen Wood, "Tacit Skills, Division of Labour and New Technology," Department of Industrial Relations, London School of Economics, 1985.

17. Shaiken and Herzenberg, p.115.

18. Shaiken and Herzenberg, p.95.

19. Letter to *Labor Notes*, unpublished.

20. Chapter lead in Herman Holtz, *How to Succeed as an Independent Consultant*, New York, Wiley, 1983.

21. Shaiken and Herzenberg, p.10.

22. Steve Babson, "Class, Craft, and Culture: Tool and Die Makers and the Organization of the UAW," *Michigan Historical Review*, Spring 1988.

23. Nina Gupta, G. Douglas Jenkins, Jr., William P. Currington, Christine Clements, D. Harold Doty, Timothy Schweitzer, and Connie H. Teutsch, *Exploratory Investigations of Pay-For-Knowledge Systems*, U.S. Department of Labor, Bureau of Labor-Management Relations, BLMR 108, 1986, p.3. A TRW human relations manager also notes that "little empirical evidence exists to substantiate or refute claims regarding the advantages and disadvantages [of PFK]." Ian V. Ziskin, *ILR Report*, Fall 1986.

24. At NUMMI the skilled maintenance workers turned down a pay-for-knowledge scheme. Instead the whole maintenance classification gets a pay increment as management judges the workers in it to be sufficiently cross-trained. Tool and diemakers who qualify for the die try-out classification make 40 cents additional.

9. Standardized Work: Time-Study with a Vengeance

In evaluating the team concept, and especially management-by-stress, it is easy to look at the frills instead of the essence. Management may address workers as respected partners or as something less than human. Workers may or may not get to park and eat alongside their supervisors. Team meetings may be stimulating sessions or they may be organized coffee breaks or a transmission belt for management propaganda. All of these things can affect how workers feel about their jobs and themselves.

But team meetings last only a half hour a week. Ultimately the team concept must be judged on what workers actually do during the eight to 10 hours per day, five to seven days per week, that they spend working.

In traditional auto plants most production workers are paced by machines. The assembly line is the clearest example, but increasingly automation determines the pace of all kinds of machines and their human operators. Management time-study experts analyze each job and instruct the operator on what actions to take. Management is constantly looking for ways to improve motions or the physical arrangement of the machines to require less operator time, resulting in either the operator doing more jobs or the same number of jobs at a faster pace. The time-study approach is commonly identified with Frederick Taylor and "scientific management." When it is combined with mass production and machine pacing many refer to it as "Fordism."

A big misconception about team concept in the U.S. auto industry is that it represents an alternative to telling workers every move to make.[1] The media image is that management relinquishes control to workers, who plan their own jobs, either individually or with other team members. By getting rid of narrow classifications and using job rotation, work is organized around workers' brains, we are told, rather than their arms and legs. Workers can now utilize their "creative and managerial skills," according to GM advertisements. Workers now consider their labor a craft.[2]

Some of these misconceptions arise from management propaganda. The team experiments in Western Europe and theories about what team production might be have also given rise to misunderstandings of the reality in the U.S. auto industry.

If we look at the two team concept plants now being used as the model for the rest of the domestic auto industry, NUMMI and Mazda, we find no repudiation of Taylorism or Fordism. Instead there is an intensification of both. In fact, the specific methods used under management-by-stress are not new. What is new is that management is now getting unions to cooperate in the use of old methods. The labor movement's long history of fighting Taylorism and Fordism seems to have been forgotten.

The procedures for standardizing work in the various plants are very similar. In this chapter we will describe the methods used at NUMMI, Mazda and the new General Motors Fairfax II plant in Kansas City, Kansas. NUMMI and Mazda use Japanese terms for various problems and processes. Fairfax relies on U.S. industrial engineering jargon.

Standardized Work

In all three plants the end result is a "standardized work sheet." The job functions are broken down into "transferable work components," as they are called at Fairfax. Such a component is defined as the smallest practical combination of acts that can be transferred from one worker to another.

ACT BREAKDOWN

Study File No. A469   Date 7-29
Oper. Name-Equip. Description Gas Tank Solder Machine Auto Apply Solder
Tools Used   Solder Pot Brush
Standard Time   .80 Min. (48 Sec.)
Analysis By   Mike Gonz

Step No.	LEFT HAND DESCRIPTION	OBJECT	ACT	PRO	ACT	OBJECT	RIGHT HAND DESCRIPTION
1	From Bench	Tank	G		G	Tank	From Bench
2	To Fixture	Tank	P		P	Tank	To Fixture
3		Fuel Tubes	G		G	Tank	
4	Bend Tubes For Clearance	Tubes	P			Tank	Hold
5		Palm Button	G		G	Palm Button	
6		Palm Button	P	X	P	Palm Button	
7	Wait				G	Solder Pot	
8	From Pot	Brush	G		P	Pot	Toward L. Hand
9	To Tube	Solder	P			Pot	Hold
10	To Pot	Brush	P			Pot	Hold
11	Wait				P	Pot	To Holder
12	From Bench	2nd Tank	G		G	2nd Tank	From Bench
13	To Fixture	Tank	P		P	Tank	To Fixture
14		Fuel Tube	G		G	Tank	
15	Bend Tubes For Clearance	Fuel Tube	P			Tank	Hold
16		Palm Button	G		G	Palm Button	
17		Palm Button	P	X	P	Palm Button	
18	Wait				G	Solder Pot	
19	From Pot	Brush	G		P	Pot	Toward L. Hand
20	To Tube	Solder	P			Pot	Hold
21	To Pot	Brush	P			Pot	Hold
22	Wait				P	Pot	To Holder
23	From Fixture	First Tank	G		G	First Tank	From Fixture
24	To Finish Bench	Tank	P		P	Tank	To Finish Bench

"Act Breakdown Analysis" sheet from GM Fairfax II. This is part of a training example describing how to eliminate waiting periods.[3]

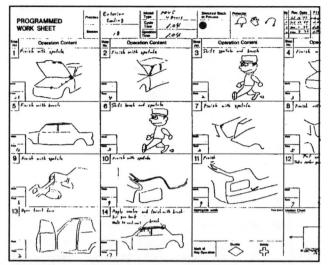

"Programmed Work" sheet from Mazda. The sheet defines one person's job, made up of several "transferable work components" (called "details" at Mazda). Note that the time (1.04 minutes) the operations take to perform is exactly the same as the time available to work on each car (cycle time).[4]

For example, installing a piece of trim would be a transferable work component. It might include three acts: getting the trim, applying the glue, and pressing the trim into place. It would probably not make sense to assign these three acts to different people. But the whole task of installing the trim could readily be shifted from one worker to another. For each worker, two, three or four "transferable work components" would make up the total job.

Line Balancing

One of the reasons management wants to specify every motion and operation is to make it easy to rearrange job assignments, or rebalance the line. If the line speed is cut because sales are slow, it becomes possible to remove one worker and shift her operations to the remaining operators. If ways are found to cut out specific operations, the remaining operations can be shifted around so that a worker is eliminated. The philosophy of MBS plants is explicit. The goal is *not* to ensure that work is evenly distributed among all workers at all times. Rather it is to try to organize the work so that as many operators as possible are working every second of the *takt* time (time that the car is at each operator's sta-

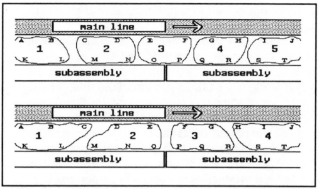

Subassembly jobs mixed with line jobs. Each letter represents one transferable work component and each circled area represents one operator's total job. Instead of speeding up the line, work can be sped up by withdrawing one of the workers in the top diagram and redistributing the work components to those remaining, as illustrated in the bottom diagram.

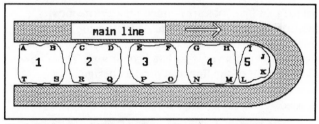

U-shaped assembly operations allow easier rebalancing.

tion). If this leaves one operator with little to do temporarily, that is okay, because the obvious idle time will serve as a motivation to eliminate her job altogether.

The ability to shift operations around in this manner requires both a "multifunctional" workforce and a physical arrangement which puts jobs very near each other. One approach is mixing off-line subassembly operations with assembly line jobs.

A similar approach is to use U-shaped lines, as illustrated above.

Just-in-time applied to machining operations requires reducing the time that parts spend waiting for their next operation. Consider a situation where an engine part requires work by four different machines, say a cutter, a rough grinder, a boring machine, and a finish grinder. Assume each worker, being "multifunctional," can operate all four machines. There are four of each machine. A traditional layout would assign a different

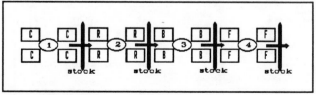

In a traditional layout, each operator operates only one type of machine.

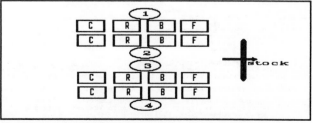

In the preferred MBS layout, each operator operates four different machines plus possibly jobs in the adjoining area.

worker to operate all four cutters or all four grinders, etc.

But such a layout would not allow management to vary the number of parts produced without causing idle time. If the production quota is cut 25 percent, then all four workers are idle 25 percent of the time (or additional work of some sort must be found for them).

A more ideal layout from the MBS vantage point would be where four operators each operate four different machines. One advantage is that there is no accumulation of parts between stations—a definite just-in-time plus. Also, if production is reduced by 25 percent, it is a simple matter to remove worker A while keeping the others working with no idle time. If the reduction is by ten percent, then it is only necessary to find additional tasks for one of the workers, rather than all four.

Who Designs the Jobs?

One of the most prevalent myths about team concept plants is that team members get to design their own jobs. In fact, jobs are defined long before most operators are assigned to them. At Fairfax jobs are designed by the group leaders and team leaders, who themselves work within very restricted conditions. The technology, layout of the line, and product design have already been determined. And additional conditions are imposed:

> The primary task presented to Group and Team Leaders is that given various job functions and a predetermined amount of manpower to complete these functions, [to] assign jobs to operators in such a way as to create a balanced and efficient operation.[5]

The initial "transferable job components" and the standard time allotted to each are not even devised at the plant itself but come from corporate headquarters. The times attached may be modified by the local industrial engineer or the group leader, however.

The group and team leaders write up initial job descriptions. They run these through a computer to check for balance. The leaders then fill out several reports, draw up flow diagrams of each job, create transparencies for use in instructing the operators, and assign the operators.

Supervisors Create Standardized Work

At each Toyota plant, the worksite supervisor is in charge of establishing a standard work sequence for every worksite.

Toyota manual used at NUMMI makes it clear who has the authority to design the jobs.[9]

Only then do the operators get involved:

> When the Group and Team Leaders have decided on a final operation layout and all operator assignments appear to be functioning properly, each operator should then complete a manual describing his operation in detail. This is done so that any worker previously unfamiliar with the operator's particular assignment would gain a relatively good understanding of the work assignment by reading the manual.[7]

At NUMMI Production Control establishes a target time for each operation. The procedure is in the union contract: "Team Leaders and Group Leaders discuss and develop each suggested standardized work. The Manager approves the suggested standardized work."[8]

Fine-Tuning the System

Once the basic system has been put in place and is operating, workers are encouraged to make suggestions to improve the system. Here is where management-by-stress differs from Taylorism. For Taylor, it was the job of the industrial engineer to continue studying time and methods to make work more efficient and reduce required labor time. Management-by-stress, on the other hand, shifts *responsibility* for this kind of industrial engineering work to the group leader, the level of management closest to the production process, although he or she does not have formal training in it. Management-by-stress also includes both inducements and pressures to get workers to help time-study themselves. (See Chapter 3.)

```
                GM ASSEMBLY DIVISION INDUSTRIAL ENGINEERING LINE BALANCE EVALUATOR          FAIRFAX PLANT   1988 MODEL YEAR
PROGRAM:  W522CI      STATION NO. 19-01-34  SUB-SECTION        NO. OPERATORS  1- 1    NO. TEAMS  0   LINE SPEED  75.0 JPH    SCHEDULE WCAR
                              CYCLE TIME  .80 MIN.           FLOAT SPACE  .0          DATE RUN 09/23/86              PAGE   1
*** EXPANDED LISTING ***                    STATION NAME - DECK SEAL          RT                                    TIME 11:52

   REQ S CH WS    ENGR        M C B      D E S C R I P T I O N      RL  CAR    M O D E L S      # W BGUS      STD.    JPH   MPH    MNPWR
   NO.  A CO CD REFERENCE             ACCESSORY CONDITION       N8  LINE              L CODE X *D   MIN.
        EL NO.              E L E M E N T  D E S C R I P T I O N          CO  SDF   CV TIME

E21790   C 17  W3340806  STK D/L OR F/COMPT W/STR TO JOB        N  W-CAR   ALL MODELS                          .17   78.00  12.75   .2125
         020.0  GET D/L OR F/COMPT W/STR FR HOOK*S/J,24IN; 0-2LBS, 24VO    A  05011A   V  .03
         030.0  WALK TO RR OF BODY*4P                                     A  05019O   V  .04
         040.0  TOSS W/X ACROSS RR COMPT PNL OR POSN TO FRT COMPT* CT      A  10307A   V  .06
         060.0  RTB*4P                                                    A  05019O   V  .04

E22080   C 17  W3340806  INST D/L W/STR                         R  W-CAR   ALL MODELS                          .36   75.00  27.00   .4500
         001.0  ENGAGE W/STRIP TO F/WELD FLANGE OF BDY OPNG*CL,64IN       A  10308A   C  .36

400330    19  W3340806  ROLL D/LID W/STRIP TO SEAT              R  W-CAR   PONT MODELS                         .20   75.00  15.00   .2500
         002.0  GET W/STRIP INST 9T TL FRM APRON*                         A                     V  .02
         004.0  ROLL PERIPHERY OF W/STRIP TO SEAT*RO,128IN;31R            A  10308O   C  .16
         006.0  PLC SEAT TOOL TO APRON*                                   A                     V  .02
```

Checking the job assignments by computer at Fairfax II.[6]

The Fairfax manual explains:

> Once a team's operation is well under way and functioning, it still is subject to review and testing... Constant improvement in team operations is the direct responsibility of Group and Team Leaders. They should encourage suggestions from Team Members to enlist better and more efficient production practices.[10]

Involving workers in self time-study can generate many suggestions valuable to the company. At least at the beginning, it also helps give workers the illusion that they have some say over their jobs. The idea is that they will then offer less resistance when the leaders continually rebalance the lines.The Fairfax manual explains:

> Once a team's operation is well under way and functioning, it still is subject to review and testing... Constant improvement in team operations is the direct responsibility of Group and Team Leaders. They should encourage suggestions from Team Members to enlist better and more efficient production practices.[10]

But workers' involvement is only in the form of suggestions. The decisions are to be made by the group leader. A worker is never to simply try a slightly different way of doing things to make work more comfortable, or move an item to make work more efficient. All the manuals stress this. A Mazda training manual explains:

> For all work we perform in the workshop, a work procedure sheet has been provided... If the operator changes the work procedure at his discretion, he may put the processes before and after that process in jeopardy, or increase the cost though the quality is improved. Therefore the operator should always observe the specified work procedure sheet faithfully. If you have any doubts, you may propose a change to the team leader and should never change the work procedure at your discretion.[11]

Another Mazda manual is quite specific: "Team members do not on their own judgment decide on different locations for parts other than the counts and locations already established."[12]

At NUMMI standardized work charts are supposed to be posted at each work site "so that the supervisors can regularly check the actual work against the standardized work."[13] Note that here the supervisor is not checking to see that the *results* are as specified. The supervisor is policing to make sure that the job is being performed exactly the same as the written instructions.

There is some worker resistance to such an inflexible system, as there is on every rigid assembly line. Even the most elementary preferences can put a worker at odds with the system: someone with a sore shoulder might prefer to take more steps and have less distance to reach, for example. And most would like to find ways to shave their operations to create more breathing space. The degree to which workers can get away with varying from the standardized work sheet depends in part on whether the team leader identifies with management and whether the union will back the worker.

Mazda teaches "Therblig Analysis" to identify and eliminate unnecessary movements. Work is broken down into 17 basic types of motions.[14]

Time and Motion Study

The time-study techniques used in management-by-stress plants are not new; the only thing new is how little resistance the union is putting up. Management teaches workers time-study, including the use of the stop watch and various recording techniques. Mazda video tapes workers as they work so that they can analyze their own motions.

One of the key questions in time-study is how to establish a standard time for an operation, since people differ in how they do things and in their natural pace of work. The UAW-Ford contract specifies that:

> Such production standards shall be fair and equitable and shall be set on the basis of normal working conditions, the quality of workmanship, and the normal working capacities of normal experienced operators, with due consideration to fatigue and the need for "personal" time.[15]

Compare this to the assumptions used at the Fairfax plant: "Operator performance is always 100 percent. No learning or fatigue effects are considered."[16]

But what about the problem of determining who is the "normal" operator? The Fairfax plant uses GM's usual method: in order to set the standard for how long the job must take to complete, the time-studier multiplies the actual time he measures as he observes the worker by another figure—an "operator performance rating" which can range from zero to one hundred percent. In other words, the expert judges how much effort the operator is putting out as compared to some "standard" worker in the time-studier's mind. The expertise to arrive at this percentage is, we are told, "accomplished after years of experience in time-study... [and is] a very subjective process because the analyst must judge the operator's speed."[17]

Thus the supposed science of time-study is reduced to one management-paid expert's judgment of how fast someone else should be working. This is one of the reasons that unions have long fought to put restrictions on time-study.

NUMMI establishes work standards by choosing as the "normal" operator an experienced worker who likely aspires to management. Again, this is written into the contract:

Time-study on a pilot vehicle: Group Leader and Team Leader evaluate each suggested standardized work [suggested by Production Control] by having a Team Leader who does not always work on the actual operation try it out.[18]

Time-study training shows how management

Time-study requires a standard pace to be kept in mind, as the Mazda manual illustrates.[19]

uses numbers to give the appearance of science to what is actually the time-study "expert's" subjective judgment about what is a reasonable amount of work. The Fairfax training, for example, includes precise details on the operation of the stopwatch to record the smallest work elements to the nearest hundredth of a minute. The manual goes on to explain how to make this measurement even more accurate by averaging it out over many operations.

Mazda provides video tapes of what management considers a normal, fast, and slow work pace for use as standards. Workers training in time-study watch the video tapes and record their own ratings. They then compare their ratings of the taped workers to management's (called the "actual ratings"). Workers practice with the video tapes until their ratings approximate the "actual."

So this is science. How can anyone object to it? Picture yourself as the scientific worker studying another worker. You time a job very carefully, taking many samples under many different conditions. You average them out and come up with the precise figure of .55 minute for the time it takes to complete the job. Then you need an "operator performance rating." You say to yourself:

Let's see, when I was training with the video tapes I was always rating too high. I'd better put down something on the low side. Shall I give him a 50 percent rating or an 80 percent? Let's split it down the middle and give him a 65 percent.

So you multiply your very precise .55 by your thoroughly subjective .65, and come up with a "scientific" .35 minutes (or 21 seconds) as the standard time for this job.

Although the standard work time includes a large component of subjective judgment, it is difficult to challenge it. The group leader is the lowest level of management with authority to adjust a standard. Since both the group leaders and the team leaders participated in establishing the standard they are likely to try to defend it. Since workers are "multifunctional" and many can be assigned to any particular job, it is likely that manage-

---

"THE THREE EVIL M's"

Muda: Waste. The Mazda manual gives some examples:

"Waiting *muda*: if you are standing in front of your machine doing nothing, you yourself are not gaining respect as a human being. And, moreover, because this results in higher costs of the car, the customer will not buy the car."

"Operational *muda*: If you are walking around looking for a component or tool, time is being wasted."

"Conveyance *muda*: If you move components from a large pallet to a small pallet, and then from that to the workbench, this piling and re-piling is eventually becoming an increase in costs."

Other forms of *muda* include inferior goods production, overproduction, and too much inventory.

Mura: "Irregular or inconsistent use of a person or a machine in such a way as to cause inconsistent results. For example, making two trips carrying two boxes the first time and four boxes the second, not doing the job continuously the same way."

Muri: "Working a person, machine, or tool beyond capacity."[21]

ment can find a worker who will do the job (at whatever the cost to his popularity with his fellow workers).

Management's desire for interchangeable workers does limit the top pace that can be established as "standard." The work standard has to be "do-able" by most of the workers who might be assigned to a particular job. Taking this into account, the end result is still a very fast pace (see Chapter 11 for examples). Those who can't keep up with the pace use their break time to catch up, or they are forced to quit.

In traditional Big Three plants, disputes over work standards, including the pace of the line and the number of operations required of an operator, can be taken to the grievance procedure. Since they are not covered by arbitration, these issues are also strikable during the term of the contract.

At NUMMI, on the other hand, "problems" with standardized work are taken through their own special procedure and are not strikable. Each step in the procedure is ruled upon by a joint company/union committee, presumably operating by consensus. While the contract language is vague, it would appear that unless a higher level of management were willing to reverse a lower level's decision, that lower level's specifications for what is "standard" would hold. (Details of the UAW/NUMMI appeals procedure are in the appendix to Chapter 11.)

Tips For Efficient Work

All the training programs contain many tips for making work easier and faster. The idea is to eliminate all forms of "waste," which is broadly defined to include anything that lowers productivity (see box "The Three Evil M's" on the previous page).

One tip from Mazda management is to reduce the number of hand motions by using the feet. An example is foot-operated electrical switches to start the machine moving. "Not that you must constantly use

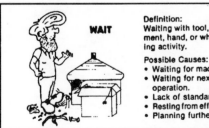

WAIT

Definition:
Waiting with tool, part, piece of equipment, hand, or whole body, for following activity.

Possible Causes:
• Waiting for machine to finish cycle.
• Waiting for next operator or operation.
• Lack of standardization or training.
• Resting from effects of previous work.
• Planning further activity.

HOLD

Definition:
A temporary halt of active muscular movements in order to maintain a definite relationship between two or more objects.

Possible Causes:
• Poor fixture design.
• Unbalance of hand activity.
• Lack of operator training.
• Clamping device absent.

"Ineffective Worker Movements" from the Fairfax training manual.[22]

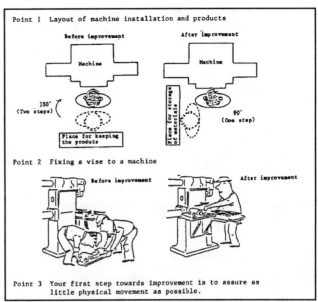

Point 1 Layout of machine installation and products

Before improvement   After improvement

Machine   Machine

180°
(Two steps)   90°
                            (One step)

Place for keeping the produts

Place for storage of materials

Point 2 Fixing a vise to a machine

Before improvement   After improvement

Point 3 Your first step towards improvement is to assure as little physical movement as possible.

"Principles Underlying Motion Improvement" from the Mazda training manual.[23]

your feet, but it is worthwhile to consider if you can freely use your feet."[24]

Building a special fixture to hold the parts may make an assembly operation quicker. Redesigning a tool or hanging a tool from overhead with a counterweight may make a job easier. Rearranging the work may reduce walking by five steps per operation. Five steps per operation, of the size specified at Fairfax of 2.5 feet/step, add up to more than a mile per day. Management encourages ideas like these. But again, we need to remember the context:

1. Once lines are up to full speed there is normally no time during regular work to engage in even the most minor experiments.

2. Whatever ideas an operator may have are supposed to be approved by a supervisor before they are tried out, and approved again before they are adopted.

3. Standardized work is just that. In theory there is no room for operators on different shifts doing the same job to do it slightly differently from the standard or from each other.

4. While it may be called "working smarter, not harder" to eliminate five walking steps from an operation, the savings do not go to the operator in the form of some breathing space. Management will fill up the time saved by providing the operator with another operation. For management, the question whether this productive operation is harder on the worker than walking the five steps is not an issue.

Notes

1. See, for example, the editorial in *Business Week*, August 31, 1987.

2. Advertisement in *Business Week*, April 20, 1987.

3. *Fairfax Industrial Engineering Training Program: Team Leader/Group Leader Edition*, General Motors Fairfax Kansas plant, no date (about 1986), Chapter 4, p.14.

4. *Kaizen Simulation*, Mazda Motor Manufacturing (USA) Corporation, no date (about 1986), pp.17-18.

5. *Fairfax...Training Program,* Chapter 10, p.1.

6. *Fairfax II Industrial Engineering Planning Guide: Team Leader/Group Leader Edition*, General Motors Fairfax plant, October 1986, p.15.

7. *Fairfax...Training Program,* Chapter 10, p.3.

8. *Agreement Between New United Motor Manufacturing, Inc. and the UAW*, July 1, 1985, Appendix C.

9. *Toyota Production System 2*, Toyota Motor Corporation, manual used in NUMMI training, June 1984, p.3.

10. *Fairfax ...Training Program,* Chapter 10, p.3.

11. *Quality Control In Which All Employees Will Participate In and Help Advance*, Mazda Motor Manufacturing (USA) Corporation, 1986, p.20.

12. *MMUC Production System: Concept and Outline,* Mazda Motor Manufacturing (USA) Corp., 1986, p.17.

13. *Toyota Production System 2*, p.35.

14. *Kaizen Simulation*, p.9.

15. *Agreements Between the UAW and Ford Motor Company, Volume 1*, 1987, p.18.

16. *Fairfax...Training Program,* Chapter 8, p.1.

17. *Fairfax...Training Program,* Chapter 6, p.7.

18. *Agreement Between New United Motor Manufacturing, Inc. and the UAW*, July 1, 1985, Appendix C.

19. *Kaizen Simulation*, p. VII-2.

20. *Kaizen Simulation*, p. VI-2.

21. *Kaizen Simulation*, p. VI-2. (Illustration from same source.)

22. *Fairfax ...Training Program,* Chapter 3, pp.4-5.

23. *Kaizen Simulation*, p. V-14.

24. *Kaizen Simulation*, p. V-12.

10. Their Quality and Ours

Less than 25 years ago "made in Japan" was a synonym for shoddy materials and poor construction. By the mid-1980's the public's perception had reversed; automobile buyers in the U.S. were willing to pay higher-than-sticker prices to get Japanese quality. Even Chrysler, whose top management is most vocal about "buy American," sold its import models by headlining that they were "From the Master Car Builders of Japan."[1]

Management's drive for the team concept often begins with the following propositions:

The buying public is highly conscious of quality. Only a quality product will sell. Only a quality product will maintain jobs. Only a quality product will make profits.

The training workers receive when team concept is introduced emphasizes finding answers that benefit everyone involved—"win-win" solutions. Surely, we are taught, quality is win-win. Workers keep jobs, management makes profits, the customer is happy. Add to this the fact that workers take pride in doing quality work, and there seems to be every reason that workers and their unions should join wholeheartedly in company quality efforts.

The United Auto Workers has signed on to a number of joint programs with the corporations to pursue quality. These include the Product Quality Improvement Partnership[2] at Chrysler, the Quality Network at GM, and the "Best-in-Class" Quality Program at Ford. Teams are often told that quality is their prime mandate.

But it is precisely because quality ranks with baseball, hot dogs and apple pie that management has been able to shift both its definition of quality and these joint quality programs themselves to include much more than what is commonly understood by "quality." In addition to some benefits for workers and unions, the quality programs also contain a number of traps.

Quality = Waste Reduction

The term "quality" is used with two meanings. The everyday, common sense definition is found in the dictionary: "The degree of excellence which a thing possesses; hence excellence; superiority."[3]

But consider a very different usage, implicit in the following exercise similar to those used in team training (although not similar to what teams do in real life):

There is poor quality on the knuckle line. Normal production is about 200,000 knuckles per year. But about ten percent (or 20,000) have to be rejected because their holes do not line up properly.

The company estimates that each rejected knuckle costs $4.00, of which the cost of raw materials equals $1. This totals $80,000 per year, of which $20,000 is raw material cost.

In the exercise, a team of workers attacks this problem and cleverly solves it in a way that involves no cost to the company. What are the results? The workers have achieved "zero defects," the company saves money, quality goes up.

But let's look more closely at what has happened. Quality? There is no increase in quality for the consumer. The consumer never had to put up with defective knuckles in the past. Inspectors caught them and they were scrapped. The quality of the knuckles the consumer sees is the same as before.

The company, however, has saved $80,000 because it no longer has to pay for the knuckles previously scrapped. Of this $80,000, $20,000 is the savings in raw materials.

Where does the other $60,000 savings come from? Previously the company had to produce 200,000 parts to get 180,000 good ones. Now it only needs to produce 180,000. The $60,000 savings comes from not having to pay anyone to produce the extra 20,000, and possibly the costs of inspection. The savings to the company is a reduction in paid work time, perhaps reducing the number of people on the knuckle job from ten to nine. Thus the "quality" improvement is really a productivity improvement.

Quality defined as reduction of waste usually means job loss.

This is not to say that unions should favor wasted time or the production of faulty parts in order to maintain production and inspector jobs. But a recognition that these sorts of "quality" achievements come at least in part at the expense of workers is a critical first step to a union strategy for dealing with worker suggestions. For example, it would be reasonable to refuse to make scrap-reduction suggestions unless there are guarantees that workers will benefit through the creation of other jobs or shorter work time. See Chapter 5 for some specific ideas.

Quality = Customer Satisfaction

The commonly accepted use of the term "quality" would involve improving value for the consumer. Often *this* kind of quality improvement can only be achieved by putting on additional jobs. For example, a reduction in the number of defective parts shipped may require increasing the number of inspections. Adding an extra operation to improve a product (like an additional coat of rust inhibitor), adding an additional feature as standard (like anti-lock brakes), or providing greater service to the customer (like immediate and full investigation of complaints) all require more labor.

Not every improvement in quality creates jobs. Sometimes a suggestion for a simpler technique or a different application of technology can increase quality to the consumer but also reduce the labor required. The union must be vigilant in this area too.

Quality which is passed on to consumers can create jobs.

Quality = Conformance to Requirements

Management's definition of quality is an attempt to direct efforts toward the waste reduction view and away from concern for the value to the consumer. Most training in quality control, whether part of team concept training or in a formally separate joint quality program, begins by having workers discuss the meaning of the word "quality." The instructor then explains why the common sense definitions are not workable. How do you measure excellence or superiority? Isn't one person's view going to be different from another's?

The solution, we are told, is to define quality as "conformance to requirements" or "conformance to specifications."

One of the leading proponents of this view is Philip B. Crosby, former vice-president and director of quality for ITT. General Motors owns part of Crosby's Quality College in Florida. Chrysler and Ford have also adopted many of Crosby's methods and materials for their quality programs.

It is easy to see why Crosby is so popular with management. First, Crosby's prescriptions are comfortable for the bureaucrat. Many quality specialists, such as W. Edwards Deming, the American pioneer in quality statistics whose methods are widely used in Japan, place the blame for poor quality on management and call for a management shake-up. Not Crosby. According to his manual, management need only carefully execute each of his 14 steps and quality will be the result. Second, according to Crosby, quality doesn't cost anything—in fact, he titled his book *Quality Is Free.*[4] Actually, quality is better than free. Whatever minor costs a quality program entails are far outweighed by the expense of doing things wrong, including scrap and rework.

In theory, it works this way. Only the customer can know his or her exact requirements for a new car. The assembly plant must meet the car buyer's requirements. To do this it must make these requirements its own and pass them on to its parts suppliers, which in turn must pass them on to their suppliers. If everybody conforms to the specifications of the next stage, in the end the customer will have what he or she wants.

Abstractly it sounds plausible, but the auto industry does not work this way, and neither do very many other industries. Cars are not made to individual customers' specifications. Instead, auto companies do re-

search to try to guess which features combined at which prices are most likely to sell three to five years from now. They then design those cars using "simultaneous engineering" or "design for manufacture" (where the design takes into account the cheapest ways to manufacture), and the company builds them. The company also decides on market and pricing strategies, targets specific consumers, and attempts to convince them to buy.

In a later stage of the game, quality is defined as "conformance to requirements"—and those requirements are dictated by management's chosen design. "Conformance to requirements" means produce what management wants and do it the way management wants it done. "Quality" becomes the justification for the rigid system of standardized work, discussed in the previous chapter, which specifies how the worker is to perform every motion of every operation.

"Conformance to requirements" means do it exactly the way management wants it done.

Consider a hypothetical example: a component determines how smoothly a car door will close. If the piece is exactly three inches long the door operates very smoothly. To the extent that the piece is slightly longer or shorter than three inches the door closing will be a little rougher. The further off, the rougher the closing will be. Since nothing can be manufactured perfectly, management decides on a permissible amount of variation from three inches—say plus or minus .01 inch. In other words, management decides that even when the part is 2.99 inches or 3.01 inches, the roughness in door closing is acceptable.

A worker is assigned to adjust the machine that makes the part, and gets the machine to produce just within tolerance—all the parts vary in length between 2.99 and 3.01 inches. At this point "getting control of the process"—a favorite management expression— means that the worker must stop adjusting and go on to some other work. The machine operator may know, through experience, that with a little more time to work on adjustment, the machine will work with a variation of less than a hundredth of an inch. The result would be more cars with smoother door operation—higher quality in the common sense definition. But management, using its definition of quality—"conformance to specifications"—would consider this extra time to be waste.

"Getting control of the process" does not mean human beings mastering a tool or a manufacturing procedure. It means that management has complete control over what goes on. One of the characters in Crosby's book, *Quality Is Free*, describes an incident in which management loses control:

> We were running behind in the machine shop, and we took some parts we had been making for years

and put the raw materials plus the paperwork in a box and sent it out to a very good machine shop. You know what? They couldn't make them. If you did it just like the print it didn't compute. No way. All kinds of little variations were involved. And none of them were written down. We found that we had several very proud craftspeople in our shops who know how to shave a little here and there in order to make the product come out usable in spite of faulty specifications.

Do you know how horrible that was? The company management didn't control the place anymore.[5]

Horrible? The consumer was getting quality and the workers had some protection against outsourcing. The horror was the lack of management control. From management's point of view it would have been better for the craftspeople to produce the parts to the specifications that didn't work, so that management could discover that its specifications were wrong—and maintain control.

Internal Customers

Another version of this approach is the idea of the "internal customer." A document for the General Motors Production System explains: "While the ultimate customer is the purchaser of the product, each production process along the line is the 'customer' of the preceding process and must be treated as such."[6] If your department subassembles dashboard panels, then your "customer" is the department which installs them in the car.

A Mazda quality manual explains

If the process concerned thinks of the following process as the consumer, and requests and reacts to quality feedback, customer satisfaction "within" the company will be achieved.

For example, the Body Plant is the producer for the Assembly Plant and consumer for the Press Plant, the previous process. Therefore the Body Plant is responsible for manufacturing products of high enough quality to satisfy the Assembly Plant, the following process.[7]

While this idea contains a grain of truth, it denies the fundamental structure of the corporation. No auto company is a big free enterprise marketplace where every machine operator or assembler works out the best combination of product, service and cost with his or her suppliers and customers. Nor do departments work this

Internal customer illustrated in Mazda's quality manual.

way. An auto company is a top-down economic system with overall planning. Someone decides what products will be offered for sale. The car is designed as a whole, and specific operations are assigned to specific departments.

Workers can fine-tune management's plan and make it more efficient and profitable. But this effort has nothing to do with behaving like "suppliers" or "customers." It also has nothing to do with whether they are meeting the desires of the ultimate customer, the buyer.

Quality ≠ Job Security

Up to now we have used hypothetical examples to illustrate the significance of the two definitions of quality. The real life story of General Motors' two-seater Pontiac Fiero demonstrates the importance of these distinctions.

One day in February 1985, Plant Manager Dennis Pawley and UAW Shop Chairman Bob Farley hosted a free lunch for the Fiero plant's 2,400 workers. They were celebrating the highest weekly quality rating in GM's history—138 out of 145.[8] The Fiero included many technological innovations, including a plastic body bolted to a "bird cage" type metal frame. Many of the car's production methods broke new ground in the auto industry.

The plant was an early team concept experiment: the union agreed to break up a plant-wide contract, cut classifications, allowed supervisors to work on the line, and reduced the number of grievances to a trickle. Through 1985 the plant was one of GM's featured models for other team concept plants.

Sales of the Fiero plunged from nearly 100,000 in 1983, its first full year, to less than 50,000 three years later. In March 1988, GM announced it was discontinuing the model and "idling" the plant. (Although GM President Robert Stempel admitted that the plant was closed permanently,[9] to officially call the action a "closing" would have violated the terms of the 1987 GM-UAW contract.)

Why were the Fiero workers out of a job? It could not have been poor quality. The high quality audit figures showed that workers were producing in "conformance to requirements"—they built the car exactly as it was designed and as they were told. "We did everything they asked us to do to improve quality and productivity and to cut costs," said one UAW official. "And we still couldn't keep the plant open."[10]

So why did the Fiero die? GM claims that the main reason was a shift in customer preferences away from two-seaters. Another reason was the well-publicized recalls because of engine fires and a high failure rate of engine connecting rods; the entire 1984 model year was recalled. The problems, according to GM, were the fault of the owners or their mechanics: operating temperatures were set too high or hoses and wiring were connected improperly.[11]

Most analysts believe that the car was misdesigned from the beginning. While it was marketed as a sports car, it was underpowered. In 1983 the *Detroit Free Press* reported that "car enthusiasts appeared to be disappointed in the sluggish performance of the new Fiero two-seat sports car (it is equipped with a rather mundane X-car engine)."[12]

The choice of an X-car (Chevrolet Citation) engine to power the Fiero was not an accident; it was part of GM management's overall strategy. The *Free Press* quoted a Massachusetts Institute of Technology auto industry expert:

> By using an X-car engine and transmission on the Fiero, according to [Martin] Anderson, GM has avoided the costs of developing a new powertrain for the car... "What they are doing there is an extremely important part of GM's long range strategy," says Anderson. "GM is looking at its high-volume componentry and using it to build low-volume cars in new ways."[13]

In other words, GM was more concerned with using a particular engine that it wanted to produce in high volume than it was with choosing an engine suitable for the Fiero's special niche.

Workers had no control over the design of the car, the choice of engine, how to market the car, or GM's high-volume components strategy. Nor did workers have control over the design of engine connecting rods or the placement of the hoses which GM claimed were being misconnected by customers or mechanics. Workers may have made suggestions through the teams about how to meet management's design with less scrap or fewer workers. But it was always up to management to decide. The workers just continued to produce in "conformance to requirements" set by management.

In the meantime, the team concept atmosphere had declined. As in many other team concept plants, when production first started, workers were encouraged to shut the line down if there were problems. But once production was established, management's main goal changed to productivity. One worker explains:

> They told us if there's some problem, shut the line down. [But now] if we shut the line down we get in trouble.... They got everyone to jump on the bandwagon, and everyone got on but management.[14]

Yet workers believe that management had made them a promise. As one put it:

> We built the best quality in the corporation for four years. Why are we being laid off? All we've heard since we came to this plant, is that if you build good quality you won't get laid off.[15]

Unfortunately, Fiero is only one of many examples where quality has not protected jobs. GM's Fremont, California plant (later reopened as NUMMI) produced a pickup truck which tied for first place in GM quality ratings in the early 1980's. But the truck line was the first to go when management began the process of closing the plant. Committeeperson Shelley Kessler recalls that on the day that the end of the truck was announced a QWL group met in a room with a giant banner that read "Quality = Job Security."

Using Quality Programs Against the Union

Often quality training becomes a vehicle for the company's attempts to get workers to adopt a pro-management perspective. Much quality training is very similar to team concept training, where workers are told "we're all in this together." (See the description of GM Wentzville team training in Chapter 18.) The interchangeability of the two types of training was demonstrated at GM's Windsor, Ontario Hydra-Matic plant in 1984: when the union voted to end a pro-company QWL program, management simply transferred that same QWL training to its quality program, under the guise of statistical process control.[16]

The quality programs typically involve the appointment of many union members to full-time positions. In some cases these are nothing more than patronage jobs. At times, some potentially very good union leaders take the positions, but because of the lack of a union perspective on quality, they get more and more drawn into the way of thinking of their management "counterparts" with whom they spend most of their time. At the Willow Run Hydra-Matic plant in Michigan, for example, the statistical process control trainers have been enthusiastically pushing for adopting the team concept.

Unions and Quality

Quality is a union issue. Workers do take pride in producing quality work. They like to be identified with a company and a product that their friends and neighbors see as high caliber. As with much else in the team concept, management has taken workers' concerns and twisted their meaning.

Unions need to be the champions of quality in the sense of consumer satisfaction. One reason is that unions need allies. Part of today's political attack on unions is to isolate them as "narrow special interests" who are not concerned about the general public. Unions need to reestablish that within the corporation, it is they who stand for the public concern. Walter Reuther, for example, was one of the early (unheeded) advocates of fuel efficient cars.

When management cuts back on quality, the union should directly inform the public. The union can also publicize specific examples in all companies where its members have taken the initiative to improve the quality the consumer receives.

The other reason for unions to champion quality is that union members are consumers too. Few workers can afford to trade in their cars for a new one every year or support the care and feeding of a lemon. Once the union rejects the idea that quality equals "conformance to requirements," the demand for quality can strengthen the natural alliance between the union and the community.

Notes_____

1. *Detroit Free Press*, May 1982.

2. Renamed from Product Quality Improvement Program in January 1988.

3. Webster, *New World Dictionary*.

4. Philip B. Crosby, *Quality is Free: The Art of Making Quality Certain,* New York, Mentor Paperback Edition, 1980.

5. Crosby, p.40.

6. R.M. Donnelly, "GMPS Report #1" to General Motors Operating Group Vice-Presidents, June 18, 1987.

7. *Quality Control in which All Employees will Participate in and Help Advance*, Mazda Motor Manufacturing (USA) Corporation, 1986, p.25.

8. Helen Fogel, "Blueprint for Saturn: Union, Company Work in Harmony at Fiero Factory," *Detroit Free Press*, February 17, 1985.

9. John Lippert and Paul Lienert, "How Pontiac's Fiero Met Its End," *Detroit Free Press*, March 20, 1988. Stempel's internal memo told other GM officials, "We see no future use for the plant... Don't raise false hopes for our people."

10. Lippert and Lienert, "How Pontiac's Fiero..."

11. John Lippert, "GM Recalls All of Its '84 Fieros," *Detroit Free Press*, November 26, 1987.

12. James Risen, "Assembly-Line Innovations," *Detroit Free Press*, September 18, 1983.

13. James Risen, "Assembly..."

14. John Lippert, "GM to Idle Fiero Plant, Kill Model," *Detroit Free Press*, March 2, 1988.

15. Lippert, "GM to Idle..."

16. For more information on the bias inherent in such training and on how the companies use the joint program staffs (trainers and facilitators) to undermine the union, see Mike Parker, *Inside the Circle: A Union Guide to QWL*, Detroit, Labor Notes/South End Press, 1985, Chapters 2-6.

11. NUMMI: A Model of Management-by-Stress

Tatsuro Toyoda, president of New United Motors Manufacturing Inc. and grandson of the founder of the Toyota Corporation, addressed 1,200 production workers at the dedication of the NUMMI plant on April 4, 1985. During his ten-minute speech, Toyoda was interrupted seven times by loud applause, cheers, and shouts of "*Itchi bon!*"—Japanese for "We're number one!"[1]

New United Motors Manufacturing Inc. (NUMMI) is a joint venture of General Motors and Toyota. The new corporation operates an assembly plant in Fremont, California which was shut down by GM in 1982. GM claimed that the Fremont plant was unprofitable, but it was reopened two years later employing many of the former Fremont workers and using much of the old GM layout and track.

In its first two years of operation NUMMI achieved such high productivity and quality figures that the plant became the model for the rest of the U.S. auto industry. In Chapter 3 we described the operating principles of management-by-stress, the production system used by NUMMI. Here we take a closer look at the operation of the plant.

The NUMMI plant is strikingly clean. No coffee cups, newspapers, cigarette butts, or fast food wrappers litter the floor. In fact, no smoking, eating, drinking, or reading are allowed except in specified break areas. All workers keep their areas clean through practice of "the four S's":

Seiri—Clearing; removal of unnecessary material and equipment

Seiton—Arrangement; a place for everything and everything in its place

Seiso—Cleaning the equipment and area

Seiketsu—Overall cleaning, including the previous three S's.

"Just-in-time" (JIT) parts delivery adds to the feeling of spaciousness. Only the parts needed for a few hours are stacked by the line. Mostly these require small cartons rather than the large storage bins that clutter traditional plants.

- *New United Motors Manufacturing Inc. (NUMMI)*
- *Location: Fremont, California*
- *Employment: 2,100 hourly, 300 salaried on two shifts*
- *Product: Chevrolet Nova, Toyota Corolla FX16*
- *Production began: 1984*
- *Team Concept began: 1984*
- *UAW Local 2244*
  Address: 45201 Fremont Boulevard, Fremont, CA 94538
  Phone: 415 / 657-0800

Hourly and salaried workers and top management all use the same cafeterias and parking lots. All workers and supervisors are issued a uniform of gray pants and blue shirts; about two-thirds wear it.

The number of robots in the plant—about 170 during the first stages—is more than in many older assembly plants, but short of the 300 to 400 in newer plants. NUMMI has also built a 200,000 square foot stamping plant with five press lines to directly feed the assembly line with major body panels and selected small stampings.

NUMMI takes a conservative approach to technology. It is modern, but it is not the cutting edge of technology. There are no automatic guided vehicles (AGV's); the just-in-time inventory system relies primarily on paper cards called *kanbans* rather than on bar code readers and computer terminals. Almost all the automation was designed and tested by Toyota in Japan and then shipped to the U.S. for installation. The plant sports Komatsu stamping presses, Hitachi robots, and Toyopuc programmable controllers (computers which control the lines and other automation).

The job security provisions at NUMMI have attracted much attention, although the contract stops short of providing job guarantees. It states:

> The Company agrees that it will not lay off employees unless compelled to do so by severe economic conditions that threaten the long term financial viability of the Company.
>
> The Company will take affirmative measures before laying off any employees, including such measures as, the reduction of salaries of its officers and management, assigning previously subcontracted work to bargaining unit employees capable of performing this work, seeking voluntary layoffs, and other cost savings measures.[2]

Just how secure NUMMI workers' jobs are will depend on how the loopholes are interpreted. Contract language aside, many workers believe that NUMMI made a commitment to a policy of no layoffs.

Productivity and Quality

As the first unionized Japanese-managed auto plant in the U.S., NUMMI has attracted much interest. This interest has been magnified by the high productivity and quality ratings the plant has achieved in only two years of operation.

NUMMI's productivity statistics are indeed impressive. A 1986 GM internal report shows that NUMMI's Nova required 21.2 hours of direct and indirect labor per car, compared to an average of 37 hours at the three GM J-body (Cavalier) assembly plants.[4] The raw figures would give NUMMI a 90 percent productivity advantage, but this figure should be reduced to account for differences in the car and in the manufacturing method. The report also broke the production process down into departments, giving the highest ranking for each department to the plant that used the least labor. NUMMI ranked first in all areas except inspection, where it ranked 14th out of 20.

A study conducted at the Massachusetts Institute of Technology compared the NUMMI plant to the GM Framingham plant, which builds the Celebrity and the Ciera. This study attempted to adjust for factors such as automation, number of welds, contractual relief time, and the size and complexity of the car. The study concluded that NUMMI has about a 50 percent productivity advantage—operations on a car that take 20 hours at NUMMI would take slightly more than 31 at Framingham. The same study found that labor productivity at NUMMI is only slightly less than at the Toyota plant in Takoara, Japan.[5]

One reason for NUMMI's high productivity is its extensive outsourcing and outside contracting. Seat cushions, for example, are made by an outside firm and delivered to the plant only hours before installation. (There are also some jobs at NUMMI which, until recently, have not been part of traditional assembly plants. For example, NUMMI does major stampings in its own highly efficient press room.)

Outside contracting substitutes for much of the indirect labor needed in the plant. NUMMI's policy is to use skilled trades workers only for preventive and minor maintenance and to contract out all major maintenance and construction. NUMMI also contracts out truck driving, landscaping, cleaning, accounting, data processing, and security. While these show as reduced labor costs for NUMMI, no figures are available to show how much this outside contracting actually reduces bottom line costs.

NUMMI has consistently achieved high quality ratings. According to the MIT study, NUMMI rated 135-140 out of a perfect 145 compared to Framingham's 125-130. On an owner satisfaction survey scaled 0-100, NUMMI scored 91-94, compared to Framingham's 85-88.

The just-in-time system contributes to quality because there are no long pipelines full of bad parts. While there are repair areas in the plant, there are very few specialized repair workers. NUMMI's technology and training are designed so that inspection is ongoing, and as many problems as possible are caught immediately. If a defect is found, it is corrected by someone from the area that did the job originally; the team leader or a team member will either follow the car down the line or go to the repair area.

NUMMI workers feel genuine pride in producing a high quality product. One NUMMI worker said, "It's nice to be at a party and know you won't be embarrassed when someone says they own a Nova."[6] Workers also hope that quality translates to job security.

In fact, NUMMI workers' concern for quality is one of the sources of their criticisms of management. Once production reached full speed and the pressure was on, many workers felt harassed when they stopped the line, as they had been instructed to do if there was a problem. More defects began to get through. Similarly, when there was a breakdown in parts supply management was less inclined to stop the line, instead tagging the cars to have the part installed later. Around the end of 1986 normally unused areas of the plant were filled with assembled cars waiting for missing parts.

Ultimately the defect is repaired or the missing part is installed, but both management and workers understand that when this happens, quality suffers. When a

A NUMMI CHRONOLOGY

March 1982—General Motors closes the Fremont assembly plant.

February 17, 1983—Toyota and General Motors announce a plan for a joint venture.

September 21, 1983—Letter of intent signed with United Auto Workers, specifying that a "blending of American and Japanese production methods" will be used in the plant and that a majority of workers will be laid-off Fremont workers. Agreement effectively makes the UAW the bargaining agent.

February 1984—New United Motors Manufacturing Inc. (NUMMI) officially formed.

March 30, 1984—Former Fremont workers invited to start application process.

April 11, 1984—After anti-trust investigation, Federal Trade Commission approves the joint venture. Because of industry objections—Chrysler the most vehement—the FTC limits GM's participation in management to eight years.[3]

December 10, 1984—First Chevrolet Nova rolls off the production line.

June 25, 1985—Three-year collective bargaining agreement signed with UAW. Wages equal or exceed those in U.S. auto industry, no changes in the way production is organized.

December 1985—Second shift in operation, plant now fully staffed. Approximately 2,200 employees represented by the UAW.

April 1986—Line at full speed.

September 1986—A second model of same basic car, marketed as Toyota Corolla FX16, begins production.

January 1987—Stories in media about problems at NUMMI.

May 1987—Following reduced sales, line speed cut.

December 1987—Continued Nova sales slump. Line speed cut to a low of 45 per hour.

job is done "in station," the right tools apply the proper torque to fasteners, and already installed parts do not have to be removed or forced aside. While workers insist that during this period NUMMI maintained high quality by careful inspection and repair, management was clearly back-sliding from "doing the job right the first time." The fact that management tried to maintain full production with missing parts and unsolved problems was a symbol that perhaps NUMMI was not so different from traditional U.S. auto plants after all, where "making production" justifies anything.

Management Structure

GM describes NUMMI as having three levels of management (with managers and assistant managers counted as one level). The lowest level supervisor, the group leader, is in charge of two to six teams, collective-ly called a "group." A team consists of four to eight workers plus an hourly team leader. Group leaders report directly to assistant managers of sections or departments (stamping plant, body shop, assembly, etc.). The section managers report to the general manager of manufacturing or his assistants.

While group leaders are responsible for disciplining workers, many of the other responsibilities of traditional first-level supervision are delegated to team leaders. The group leaders do much of the work of industrial engineers in traditional plants, such as enforcing and changing the work methods and work standards. Group leaders have veto rights in hiring new workers for their teams, and the group leader's assessment during probation usually determines the outcome.

Approximately 40 team meeting rooms are scattered around the plant. Each ceilingless room contains desks for the group leaders and team leaders, bulletin boards, blackboards, and tables for team meetings. Outside of the room is a bulletin board with production charts, quality charts, and absentee records.

Team Leaders

Team leaders are key to the functioning of the NUMMI system. They are members of the union, but they have a number of critical supervisory responsibilities. They are carefully selected by the company. The first team leaders were chosen from hourly applicants and given an extensive orientation. They were sent to Japan for up to three weeks to learn methods there.

During this evaluation period some were screened out for having the wrong attitude. One was a black worker with 20 years and a good record at GM who was enthusiastic about the NUMMI system, but had been an active unionist and expressed doubts that U.S. workers would be willing to work as fast as their Japanese brethren.[9]

Now that the plant has reached stable operation, openings for team leaders are posted. Since one of the qualifications for the position is to be able to do all jobs on the team, applicants usually come from the team or at least the group which has the opening. Applicants must attend, on their own time, three-hour classes, two nights a week, for five to six weeks. The classes emphasize communication skills and use role playing for problem solving. For example, "John always comes to work with alcohol on his breath. As his team leader, what do you do?" It is common for management "assessors" to come to the classroom and observe the applicants.

The instructor's evaluation, an in-plant test on problem solving, and the group leader's evaluation determine which applicants get the team leader positions.

The team leader is paid an additional 50 cents an hour and has a range of responsibilities:

-Filling in on the line for workers who are absent, tardy, seeking medical attention, or on bathroom breaks

-Training new workers in their jobs

TOYOTA IS IN CHARGE

The initial capital investment in NUMMI, estimated at $300 to $400 million, was split evenly between GM and Toyota. The $120 million value of the old Fremont plant was included as part of GM's share.[7] NUMMI's eight-person board of directors is evenly divided between Toyota and GM.

But the participation and interest of each of the corporate partners is very different. GM gets the right to study the plant and rotate a few managers through it. Toyota runs the plant. Under the terms of the Federal Trade Commission's approval of the joint venture, GM will be out of the management by 1992.

Initially, General Motors assigned 16 management people to NUMMI for a three-year rotation. In 1985 two of these were on the general manager level. Already several of these NUMMI-trained managers have been distributed over the GM system to help "diffuse the process," including at the Van Nuys, California plant, the Saturn project, and the Ellesmere Port, England Vauxhall plant. GM has also established a "Technical Liaison Office" which coordinates GM contacts with NUMMI. This office has produced video tapes, training materials, and a computer database on NUMMI methods, all available to managers throughout the GM system.

The GM employees who are section managers work under a "double management system" with a "coordinator" from Toyota, who "assures that the manager's decisions fall within the guidelines of the Toyota Production system."[8]

Toyota is experimenting with NUMMI, using it to learn how to deal with American suppliers, legal structures, and workers. Many of the managers from Toyota are being trained for future Toyota operations planned for Kentucky and Ontario.

-Assisting workers who are having difficulty

-Keeping attendance, tardiness, and off-the-job records

-Assigning work when the line stops

-Minor maintenance and housekeeping

-Assessment of new team members

-Leading *kaizen* (improvement) or quality circle sessions

-Organizing social events outside the workplace.

Many NUMMI workers say they would never want the team leader job because there are too many demands and the team leader always gets caught in the middle. As workers describe it, some team leaders serve as buffers between the workers and unreasonable management pressure. Others see the team leaders as management's spies who, in addition to gathering vital production information, are emotional gauges to assess how far the workers can be pushed. Most workers we interviewed felt that the personality and role of the team leader was the single most important factor in determining how bearable work is. As one put it; "If he's good, it'll be okay. If he's bad, you're f____." For example, in a team that rotates regularly, a "bad" team leader will cover for an absence by taking the softest job on the team, rather than the job vacated by the absent worker.

The recruitment and training of new team leaders has become an important vehicle for management to convince a key section of the workforce to adopt its goals and implement its programs. Not only do all applicants go through the management-designed training course, they must also attempt to prove their abilities while they are still team members. According to one study, 900 workers have been through the team leader training program.[10] There is no official union input into the selection or training process.

There are usually many applicants for each team leader opening. While the company was hiring and the need for team leaders was expanding, significant numbers of workers could reasonably believe that they had a chance for advancement. But once the workforce stabilized, that hopefulness was replaced by frustration and resentment as people realized they might never achieve team leader. Many workers, including strong advocates of the team concept, expressed the view that the selection process is subject to favoritism (and in some cases union deals)—"just like it was at GM"—rather than merit. Further, as management stabilized, the team leader job became less attractive because advancement to group leader was harder.

Team Functioning

Team meetings are of two kinds. Team leaders hold very brief meetings at the work location just as the line is starting up to make announcements, distribute work gloves, or survey for overtime. These are similar to daily preparations in many traditional plants.

The group leader usually schedules a more formal team meeting during lunch, before work, or after work. The group leader is usually present during the meeting and turns in members' time cards for overtime pay for the length of the meeting. Occasionally, a group leader may call a team or group meeting when the line is down.

The frequency of formal meetings varies considerably. Some teams meet weekly for an hour or more. Some meet monthly, and some less than that, or on an "as needed" basis. Meetings occur more frequently when there are production problems to be worked out, as the line was being brought up to speed, for example, or when production of the Corolla FX16 began. Once the lines were running smoothly and the jobs were balanced, group leaders were less inclined to call meetings.

In addition, teams are encouraged to hold team building activities after work, such as sports and parties. NUMMI's conception of teams explicitly involves building a web of personal relations among team members, the group leader, and the team leader. "P.T." (for "personal touch") guidelines are specified for team and group leaders. One management handout lists "Facts a Group Leader Must Know" about team members:

-Is the member married?

-Does the member have children? What ages?

-Birthday

-Anniversary

-Hobbies

-Work experience
-Other interests.[11]

Team members are encouraged to help each other deal with personal problems.[12]

Every six months, the company provides each group with P.T. funding—$15 per member—for use in whatever after-work activity the group chooses (subject to group leader approval). Common activities are pizza and beer parties or Mexican dinners.

Job Rotation

Management's stated desire is for each worker to learn every job in the plant. The most obvious advantage for management is that it can then easily shift workers in response to production problems, or to handle changes in production quantities and mix. Management claims other benefits from rotation as well. First, rotation allows workers to have a thorough understanding of the whole plant, to see how their job fits with other operations and how a mistake in one place can affect a job elsewhere. Also, by knowing many operations a worker will more likely notice defects in other jobs and call attention to them.

Furthermore, rotation is supposed to be the antidote to alienation. One group leader explained:

> Now we are multifunctional—we no longer feel like robots doing the same thing over and over again. We do many things... fixing our own machinery, quality of the car, working out problems between team members. Now we do everything as a team.[13]

The amount of actual job rotation varies considerably from team to team. When the line started up, management seemed to favor a six-month rotation so that the job would not always be done by a novice. Management clearly wants every worker to be able to do all the jobs in the team and, if possible, the group. Management does not seem to favor any more rotation than necessary to accomplish this.

Decisions about rotation are generally left to the group leader, although some teams have successfully exerted pressure to change the rotation time period. Most teams rotate jobs on a monthly or weekly basis. A few teams rotate within a shift. In one case—installing seats—the team rotates every two hours because the job is so physically wearing.

Management expects all production workers to be "multifunctional." There is no pay-for-knowledge. Under the 1985 contract, after 18 months all production workers make a base rate of $13.28 per hour plus cost of living and shift premiums. This is 10 to 30 cents higher than assembler wages at traditional GM plants and roughly the same as GM's other team concept plants.

Standardized Work on a Fast Line

When a new model is introduced at NUMMI, group leaders and team leaders break tasks down to the smallest possible units and enter them on "standardized work" charts. The charting is refined when production starts, and suggestions from team members are considered. When the line is up to speed, it is "balanced" so that every worker is fully utilized. If there are eight workers on a team and each has about 15 percent idle time, one worker can be removed and the tasks divided among the remaining seven. But the system depends on workers' being "multifunctional" or "interchangeable" so that tasks can be shifted without causing problems in production. Standardized work procedures are described in Chapter 9. The NUMMI contract language on the procedures for establishing work standards and for addressing workers' complaints are in the appendix to this chapter.

One result of standardized work is that NUMMI has eliminated virtually every job that production workers traditionally have regarded as easy, good or preferred. Because job balancing often mixes both on-line and off-line work, there are few specialized jobs. Many jobs considered highly desirable, like landscaping, are contracted out.

Custodial jobs in other auto plants are usually considered desirable. Although they pay slightly less than other jobs, there is less pressure, and workers can pace themselves. Many workers bid for cleaning jobs as they grow older or if they develop physical difficulties. NUMMI has eliminated custodial jobs as a category. Some cleaning tasks are done by production workers when the line has stopped. Others are done by outside contractors which pay their workers several dollars per hour less than NUMMI.

In most plants, material handling is a desirable job because it is not paced by the assembly line. But at NUMMI, just-in-time has changed that. Steve Bera, a production control supervisor, explained the change from a management perspective:

> The best job used to be material handling. Because what did you do when you walked in in the morning. The first thing you do... is stop at the newspaper stand and pick up a paper, right? Then you get on your truck and you scout the line and you look for a place to stack material. And you put on eight hours, 16 hours, if you could put on 16 *days* of material you would do it— because what's the next thing you do when you stack the line? You went to the satellite area, got a coffee, and you read your newspaper and you didn't have to do anything anymore.
> What does this plant do? Every 60 minutes we are stocking the line. The people who are in material handling now—they are working eight hours a day.[14]

A good job in stamping plants is metal finishing, which entails repairing imperfections, dents and dings in parts that will go on the outside of the car. At NUMMI, metal finishing is added to the many duties of a press operator. The list includes:
-Inspecting quality of finished parts
-Doing minor maintenance
-Housekeeping the area
-Participating in changing dies
-Ordering of dies and blanks

-Metal finishing of defective panels

-Keeping production records.

In most traditional plants inspection jobs are highly desirable, but at NUMMI the workload for inspectors has increased dramatically. Arlene Diamond explained:

We work hard, we sweat, it's very physical. We are not lifting anything except for our pens, but there is a lot of bending, a lot of pulling, a lot of testing, a lot of reclining [testing seat backs] and then sit-ups.

It's not easy any more; it's not what it used to be. When we were starting up, people would put in requests for transfer to inspection. They would come down and watch us work, and they would withdraw their transfer request. They thought they could get something easy, and it's just not.... Now there are very few transfers to get into our department.

In 59 seconds, inspector Richard Aguilar has to get in and out of the car and check to make sure each contains the items specified on a form for that particular car. Each item is also checked to see that it operates correctly. The list includes:

-Headlights

-High beam

-Turn signals

-Back lights

-Side marker lights

-Parking lights

-Radio

-Speakers

-Heater

-Air conditioner

-Dome lights

-Air ducts

-Steering wheel

-Console

-Dash

-Shift lever

-Check upholstery for color, cleanliness, tightness, damage

-Check headliner for tightness and damage

-Check garnishes (moldings which cover joints).

It is possible to do these jobs. They may not even look difficult to the touring visitor who has never worked in a factory. But keeping up this kind of job, car after car, day after day, takes its toll when you are at your best, let alone when you are feeling slightly ill or worried or have missed a good night's sleep. One worker says that a cold requiring him to blow his nose regularly puts him too far behind to catch up.

Because most assembly line jobs are so demanding in traditional auto plants, workers look to the off-line "desirable" jobs as a form of job security. If they cannot keep up the pace when they get older, they can hope that they will have enough seniority to select a job that matches their capabilities. At NUMMI, these jobs do not exist. Because the jobs are so difficult and require so much stamina, many NUMMI workers wonder how they will make it when they grow older.

Absenteeism

One of the reasons that NUMMI achieves such high productivity is the heavy pressure on workers to be punctual and to achieve perfect attendance. In traditional plants, workers are expected to be on the job at starting time, but the job may be five minutes away from the time clock. A worker who is occasionally late to the job but has punched in on time usually is not penalized financially, although the supervisor will not be pleased. At NUMMI there is no need for time clocks. At starting time, workers are expected to be at their work stations, in work clothes, optional exercises completed, ready for the line to start. The team leader keeps lateness and absence records.

In many traditional plants, at the end of the day workers line up at the time clock, waiting to punch out. At NUMMI, there is no clean-up time. The line runs until the last minute. If a worker is in the middle of a job when the line stops, the job must be finished.

GM claimed that one of the problems in its Fremont plant was that during lunch, particularly on payday, workers would go out to their cars or to local bars or decide to celebrate a nice day. They would return late or not at all. NUMMI has solved this problem by paying workers for an extra half-hour for their lunch period. Workers are permitted to leave the plant at lunch time, but if they do, even to go to the parking lot, they lose the extra pay. In addition, the gates closest to the parking lot are locked so that anyone who leaves has to go the long way around through the guarded main gate.

Applicants at NUMMI are carefully screened for poor attendance records. Although they had access to GM's records, NUMMI required all applicants to fill out forms explaining their absences while working at GM.

If a worker is late or leaves early, the group leader talks to him or her and gives a written warning (which does not go on the record). If this happens three times in 45 days it constitutes an offense on the worker's company record. Four such offenses in one year, and the worker is fired.

NUMMI has what it likes to call a "no-fault" absence policy—all absences except those contractually "allowable" (bereavement, military, jury duty, vacation, and approved leaves) are counted in the disciplinary procedure. Personal illness or illness in the family is not an allowable reason for absence. Normally a three-day absence counts as three separate absences, but if the company accepts the employee's doctor's note, it is only counted as one. Approved leaves may be granted for extended illnesses. Three absences in a 90-day period equal an "offense." Four offenses in one year result in firing.

There are additional offenses related to absence. These include failure to report an absence at least 60 minutes before the start of the shift (twice in 90 days equals an offense) and failure to report an absence before start of the shift (one offense each time). Any com-

bination of four tardy or absence offenses also results in firing. A GM official estimates that two to four NUMMI workers are discharged for absenteeism each month.[15]

A worker who has more than ten days of unallowable absences in a year forfeits 20 percent of vacation time. A year's perfect attendance yields one bonus vacation day.

Team and group leaders have considerable discretion in dealing with both tardiness and absenteeism. Team leaders fill in for tardy workers. If a favored worker arrives late, the team leader, who also keeps the time records, need say nothing. Similarly, while the "no-fault" absentee policy is usually strictly enforced, the system allows the group leader the flexibility to grant retroactive leaves. This flexibility can be extremely powerful given the heavy emphasis that upper management places on absenteeism and tardiness. Many workers complain of favoritism.

To generate peer pressure against absenteeism, management has waged an intensive ideological campaign about how fellow team members are hurt by it. Absence records are displayed prominently on the bulletin board outside each team room: yellow for vacation, orange for emergency, and red for no excuse. A worker

must fill out a special explanation form for every absence, with copies to the group leader's and department manager's files. Explanations for absenteeism may be discussed at team meetings. The union has participated in maintaining peer pressure; issues of the union newspaper have devoted one-fourth of their space to recognition of those with perfect attendance, complete with pictures.

But the most effective pressure against absence is the way the jobs are structured. There are no regular absentee replacement workers, so the team leader usually fills in for an absent worker. But the team leader is supposed to be responsible for other relief and assistance, so one person's absence makes all team members' lives more difficult—because management has organized it that way.

All of these factors—the hiring process, strict enforcement of rules, public visibility of any absence, and peer pressure—have reduced NUMMI's absenteeism to exceptionally low levels. In 1985 management claimed to have only 1.5 percent absenteeism.[16] This figure is remarkably low. It means that workers miss on the average only three days per year due to illness or any other "unallowed" reason. More recently management used a figure of about two percent.

One might think that with such a low rate, absenteeism would hardly affect working conditions. But because management runs the system so tightly, even a few absentees produce enormous pressure. The absentee replacement policy has become a major issue; many workers want it changed. In February and March 1986 more than a thousand workers signed a petition:

We, as concerned New United Motors Team Members, are requesting to Human Resources and the UAW to help us solve the absentee problem we are currently experiencing.

If it means that we must redesign our attendance policy in order to effectively resolve this problem, and assure quality and job security, let's not hesitate to do so. The burden placed on our teams, due to absenteeism, is an unnecessary one.

Workers who circulated and signed the petition believed that they were politely asking for management to provide replacement workers, at least for long term absences. Instead, the company and the union established an hourly Attendance Coordinator who mainly counsels absentees on overcoming *their* problems.

When the line speed was decreased in the summer of 1986, the pressure caused by absenteeism declined. A decrease in line speed and a cut in the number of workers on the line should not affect how hard each individual's job is, since "rebalancing" will increase the number of tasks each worker must do. But it can make a difference in the overall pressure level. First, there is still one team leader per team. If the size of the team is reduced, then the relief and assistance provided by the leader for each member is increased. Secondly, since there are now "excess" workers, management may be more willing to use them as replacements for those on leaves of absence.

In the fall of 1986 the pressure built again because of higher line speeds, compounded by the introduction of a new model, parts delivery problems and quality problems. The company refused to hire additional people, instead relying on overtime and using team and even group leaders to work the line. Some team leaders worked line jobs continuously for weeks at a time to substitute for workers on personal leaves.

In the spring of 1987 poor sales of the Nova caused management to drop the line speed again. The sales slump continued throughout that year, and line speed was eventually reduced to about 45 per hour. While the no-layoff policy was maintained, management also refused to allow reduction of workloads. Instead teams were rebalanced and the "excess" workers were assigned to training programs (one-day training in problem solving) and to special project *kaizen* teams. Some *kaizen* teams prepared for the 1989 model. Others were assigned to observe and *kaizen* their fellow workers still working on the line. Still others appeared to be doing nothing but wandering around the plant. Needless to say, those still working at full production pace felt some resentment towards those who got the soft jobs.

Skilled Trades

NUMMI has two skilled trades classifications: about 200 workers are "general maintenance" and about 25 are "tool and die," who work mainly in the stamping area. Those tool and die tradespeople who qualify as "die try-out" receive an additional 40 cents per hour.

General maintenance workers are supposed to be able to do all jobs, but they are often known and assigned by their "strong points," that is, as electricians, pipefitters, millwrights, etc. Roughly every six weeks maintenance workers go for a two-week, two hours per day cross-training course to learn another trade. Gradually the "strong points" shift; a tradesperson will be considered an electrician, for example, when he or she understands and can adjust the Toyopuc programmable controllers used on most of the automation. Maintenance forces are kept small and busy. In the entire assembly area, the maintenance group on one shift consists of 22 tradespeople, three team leaders, a group leader and a clerk dispatcher (a salaried clerk-typist job). Lights on a master console keep track of the six main lines. When a light indicates a problem, such as a stopped assembly line, the clerk or a leader dispatches a maintenance team immediately. The first defense against breakdowns is two mobile maintenance vehicles, each staffed by one electrician and one pipefitter or millwright. The clerk can call the maintenance shop for additional help if required.

The organization of maintenance is one area that poses contradictions for the NUMMI system. Management tries to eliminate idle time by assigning maintenance workers to preventive maintenance (PM) programs. But management's aversion to idle time can be counterproductive. When a major breakdown occurs, maintenance workers may not be immediately available. Large numbers of production workers stand idle, and the problem is compounded by just-in-time. The pressure to get the line started up again is enormous.

NUMMI also wants maintenance workers to take initiative "above and beyond" to get things moving. Often speedy repairs or efficient maintenance require a tradesperson to work through a scheduled break. But if the worker tries to make up the break during a non-scheduled time, a supervisor—trained to see red at any idle time—may try to assign other work or initiate disciplinary action.

As a result management vacillates between regularizing preventive maintenance and finding ways to have maintenance people available at the first instance of trouble—without, of course, increasing the number of skilled workers. The very slow production during 1987 and into 1988 provided a temporary solution: assign all preventive maintenance to the graveyard shift and absorb idle time during other shifts with special projects. But the dilemma will resurface once production returns to capacity. The same problem exists in traditional plants, but it is intensified at NUMMI because of just-in-time and management's zealous ethic about idle time.

NUMMI management is trying to get tighter control over maintenance by keeping track of how long jobs take. The time that the line stops and starts is automatically logged on chart recorders, and the time that maintenance workers are dispatched is noted. Some maintenance teams have posted charts indicating the measures taken and the length of time to correct each breakdown.

Many NUMMI maintenance workers, particularly those who did not previously work for GM, like the single classification system. "If your field is a wide field you just learn more," one said. Some point to the satisfaction of being able to complete an entire job. Those who worked at GM are most critical of this system and believe that their crafts are being destroyed—"Jack of all trades, master of none."

Through cross-training, NUMMI maintenance workers are definitely learning skills that they would not have the opportunity to learn in a traditional classification system. At the same time, the range and depth of skills within particular trades is more limited. Few tradespeople get experience in major construction or major repairs since these jobs are contracted out. Repair of most electronic equipment is taught at the level of "board swapping." Training barely touches on board repair or circuit analysis. Few skilled maintenance workers know how to use an oscilloscope.

Union Structure

The contract provides for an in-plant union structure with a full-time chairperson, five district committeepersons on the day shift, and three to five on the night shift. There is no separate skilled trades representative. Four hourly employees appointed by the International union are assigned to the company Human Resources Department to work in health and safety, benefits, employee assistance, and apprentice/cross-training. In 1986 the union and company also established the union attendance coordinator.

The "union coordinator" is the first level of union representation in the plant. The contract specifies one coordinator for every two groups (each group consisting of those teams under a group leader), but the practice seems to be one coordinator for each group leader.

Union coordinators are elected in in-plant elections every three years. They work full-time at production jobs and get an additional two hours pay per week from the company. At most auto plants, union representatives deal with problems during regular working

---

RULES AND CORRECTIONS

Listed below is a summary of our rules. Violation of these rules results in the corrective action noted. Obviously, we cannot list rules to cover every situation, therefore, violations of company rules are not restricted to the following list. These rules will be periodically reviewed and upgraded as the need arises.

PENALTIES OF VIOLATIONS

		First Offense	Second Offense	Third Offense	Fourth Offense	Fifth Offense
(R1)	Not being ready to start work at the starting signal or preparing to leave work before quitting time	Written Correction Notice	Written Correction Notice	One Day Corrective Suspension	Three Day Corrective Suspension	Forfeiture of Employment as Team Member at New United Motor
(R2)	Wasting time, idling, loitering or leaving assigned work area, except for authorized breaks, without permission during working hours	Written Correction Notice	Written Correction Notice	One Day Corrective Suspension	Three Day Corrective Suspension	Forfeiture of employment as Team Member at New United Motor
(R3)	Failure to maintain satisfactory production levels based upon Company performance standards.	Written Correction Notice	Written Correction Notice	One Day Corrective Suspension	Three Day Corrective Suspension	Forfeiture of Employment as Team Member at New United Motor
(R4)	Carelessness causing loss, waste or breakage or failure to maintain established quality levels and\or failure to follow operating procedures, standards, practices, or specifications.	Written Correction Notice	Written Correction Notice	One Day Corrective Suspension	Three Day Corrective Suspension	Forfeiture of Employment as Team Member at New United Motor

The flexibility in NUMMI's conduct rules is that management can add more, as this excerpt from NUMMI Standards of Conduct and Good Attendance *illustrates. There are a total of 40 conduct rules and six attendance rules.*

hours, but NUMMI's union coordinators are expected to handle all union business on lunch time, breaks, or before and after work. If the union coordinator has rapport with the group leader, or if an issue is tense, or if there is a lot of pressure from the workers, a coordinator may be permitted to handle union business during work time. But this is the exception because there is usually no one available to take the coordinator's place on the line.

Grievance Procedure

The word "grievance" is not used in the NUMMI contract. There are only "problems." The very language represents a subtle but important shift. A "grievance" implies that the worker finds fault with the system or its implementation. But to say the worker has a "problem" suggests there is something the worker needs to correct. The four-step "problem resolution procedure" is as follows (see also the appendix to this chapter):

1. The employee must discuss any problem with the team leader or group leader. The contract says:

> If the problem is not settled to the satisfaction of the employee, he may discuss the problem with the union coordinator during the period when there is clearly no interference with their job duties such as lunch, break period, etc.[17]

Some group leaders have used this clause as the basis for objecting to workers even talking to coordinators before approaching the group leader. In fact, as some observers describe it, the union coordinator "does not assume an active role in workshop affairs until discussion with the group leader reaches an impasse."[18] Thus, usually a worker with "a problem" must take the first step in dealing with management by him or herself.

If the problem is not resolved after discussion among the worker, union coordinator and group leader, the union's district committeeperson and the company's human resources representative will be called in. They share the same office and usually work together to investigate and solve problems.

2. If the matter is unresolved the committeeperson can submit the problem to the Labor Relations Department on a "Problem Notice Form," which most workers refer to as a grievance. The union chairman and the manager of Labor Relations attempt to resolve the issue at this step.

3. At the third step different forms are used and the problem goes to the Joint Union/Management Committee. The union is represented by the International representative, the president, and the chairman. The company members are the general manager of Human Resources, the manager of Labor Relations, and a general manager related to the problem. If this committee cannot resolve the problem, then the company makes the decision.

4. The union can appeal the company's decision by taking the issue to arbitration. In the standard UAW/

Big Three contracts, health and safety, work standards, and outside contracting are strikable between contracts and do not go to arbitration. There are no strikable issues in the NUMMI contract. Work standards are resolved through a separate, but similar, problem solving procedure (see chapter appendix).

In practice, at least in the initial period, the system seems to solve small problems fairly successfully. When asked how the NUMMI problem solving procedure compared to GM's grievance procedure, none of the workers we interviewed wanted to go back to GM's procedure. At GM, they said, once the grievance was written, you never heard again...the grievance took forever...it just got kicked upstairs...general supervisors would always back the foremen...you never won...if you won it was too late to do any good.

At NUMMI the rank and file worker participates more in the process. Often the solutions are not in favor of one side or the other, but involve some compromise or third option, which the worker might be involved in formulating. Although the approach is patience and letting things cool down, many problems are solved within a few days. In fact, management truly seems to practice the idea that it is better to solve small issues quickly and at the bottom than to let them fester and build up. To give an example: management agreed to pay a worker whose street clothes were ruined by grease where there should not have been any. NUMMI's style is to avoid public rebuke and humiliation. When a department manager overrules a group leader or rules against a worker, it is usually done with a few days consideration and then presented as a solution to a problem rather than as one side winning and the other losing.

Richard Aguilar, who is the union coordinator for his group, points out that the patient approach is fine until you get to something that has to be solved quickly—where working for two or three more days under the same circumstances imposes hardship.

One of the reasons that NUMMI management can afford to be more flexible than traditional management about small issues at the lower level is that it starts from a position where it has more authority and workers have many fewer specified rights. There are not many issues that a worker has a chance of winning if pushed to a formal complaint. Workers who are upset about favoritism in the assignment to *kaizen* groups find that their complaints don't go anywhere. As one put it:

> When the good jobs were bid by seniority at least you knew where you stood. Now when they give the good jobs by favoritism you call the committeeman and he says there is no grievance here, nothing he can do because there is nothing in the contract against it.

On the other hand, the contract does give management language it can use. Individual workers and the union are contractually obligated to "promote *kaizen*," achieve quality goals, support the team concept, and "assist the Company in meeting production goals and scheduling." Workers who fail to meet these vague requirements are subject to management discipline.

Also, since the contract is clear that anything settled at the first step has no significance as precedent or "past practice," any concession made by management does not limit its future flexibility.

Even where a worker does have a right, he or she may decide not to pursue it very far. Because the supervisor has so much authority to determine whether one's work day is comfortable or unbearable, it may not be worthwhile to challenge a supervisor who takes losing badly.

The atmosphere of cooperation tends to discourage workers from asserting their rights. The story of one skilled tradesperson illustrates this: J had some problems with his supervisor so he put in for a transfer to another department. For family reasons he needed to work days and had the seniority to hold days. But the manager of the department said he would only accept J's transfer if J worked graveyard shift for six months. Co-workers told him the company couldn't do that and that he should take it to the union. J's response:

> I already have one group leader pissed at me. If [the department manager] wants to do this to me and I fight him, I am no better off there than I am here. I am not going to bother the union to force me into a department.

Role of the Union

There is no consensus among workers on what the role of the union should be at NUMMI. The union leadership is sharply divided.[19] The leadership of the opposition People's Caucus, Financial Secretary Bob Fernandez and Committeeperson Bob Silva, are careful to point out that they support the team concept. The issue, Fernandez and Silva say, is whether workers get representation and respect through their union in dealing with the real problems in the plant.

The union does not seem to have much of a presence in the plant. One indication is the fact that a thousand people signed the very cautiously worded petition on absenteeism, which was directed to both the company and the union. In most traditional plants, workers would think first of going to the union and getting the union to take action. Few workers we interviewed mentioned the union unless asked. Most spoke about the union as the officers, and saw the union as a continuation from the GM operation, since most of the current officers are the same as when GM closed the plant. Many noted a change in the union's attitude. Some charge that the union is in bed with the company and that the officers "back management more than they back the people."

On the other side, some workers dismiss "complainers" as being "just hard core union." One said:

> Those people were always the ones who wanted to do less for more. They don't believe in helping other people if it's not their job…. The union used to

protect the wrong people. Now it is not like that; [the company] gives people the benefit of the doubt but if they don't work, they are out the door.

Many workers view the union coordinator as a traditional steward whose job it is to represent the worker in dealing with management. They complain about coordinators who try to act as mediators between the worker and management or even "act like supervision." One said:

> He tells me that other people can do this job— why not me? I say I can do it, but I shouldn't have to run. He says that with my attitude the place will close again.

But others think that union coordinators should try to look at issues from the overall company view as well as the worker's. Although their official name is *union* coordinators, many workers refer to them as *team* coordinators. In several instances, team leaders are also union coordinators. NUMMI management is proud of this fact,[20] and most workers do not see anything wrong with it in principle. Even many who are critical of the union as too cozy with management do not object to the practice.

The problem solving procedure at step two and above is not used as much as the grievance procedure is in other plants. During the first year and a half of the contract at NUMMI fewer than 100 problems reached this stage. There are several possible explanations: 1) problems are solved at step one; 2) workers don't expect anything to come of pushing things to a higher level so why bother? or 3) the union actively discourages filing problem notices. The opposition People's Caucus believes the last explanation is the most important one. Supporters of the union leadership seem to share the company's aversion to grievance writing—one gave as evidence for labeling Committeeperson Bob Silva a militant that "he writes grievances."

No one accuses the present leadership majority of being too militant. The most common defense of the leadership is that it is "realistic…they have learned from the GM experience that if you push the company to the wall you lose." As another worker put it: "If I got involved [in the union] I would be with the Administration [majority leadership] Caucus because I am for the company."

Dan Simons strongly approves of the NUMMI philosophy and also considers himself a good union person. Yet, he says, "It feels like when I worked in a nonunion place. The union just isn't there." After showing up three times for monthly membership meetings which could not get a quorum, Simons gave up. In fact many workers have given up. There was not a quorum for a membership meeting in almost two years.

A Vision and Job Security

The vision that NUMMI tries to project is one of cooperation, participation, harmony, respect, fulfill-

ment, and job security. Many workers started at
NUMMI with high hopes.

Dan Simons described his initial feelings:

> At my old job, if the boss didn't take a liking to
> you, you had a problem. When I came to work for
> New United Motors I sighed with thanks—"At last I
> finally have a home."

But some of the promises are wearing thin. Simons, like many others, is concerned that "old ways are
creeping back here," particularly among some of the
first line supervisors. Others point to the constant pressure, the job overloading, the feeling of being pushed to
the breaking point on the line. "It turns out that this is
like every other plant—they want production and if
something gets in the way, too bad." Despite all the talk
of equality, there are clear differences between bosses
and workers even on small issues not immediately connected to production roles. One worker, for example,
considers it degrading that he may not post anything on
a bulletin board without his group leader's permission.

Whatever the criticisms, nobody says they want
to return to the days when GM ran the plant. Most
workers see the core of the problem in the way the system has been implemented. Bad apples, individual self-
ishness, and "thinking the old way" are commonly cited.
Most workers seem to have high respect for the top management and focus the blame on group leaders—the
lowest level of management—or union leaders. When
you have a problem, according to skilled tradesman
Mike Condon, it is because

> the top Japanese who know how the program should
> be run are not involved. I'm dealing with ex-GM su-
> pervisors who don't play the game...don't follow
> [team concept] and don't understand it.[21]

In its management training video, "This is
NUMMI," management stresses that NUMMI is a system where everything fits together. However, few workers link the problems in the plant to the NUMMI Production System (what is generally referred to as the
team concept or what we call management-by-stress).

When problems come up they are often dismissed as bad communication. Teddy Holman, a standardized work trainer, wrote in the local union newspaper:

> We not only don't hold enough Team, Group,
> and Section meetings with each other, we don't com-
> municate between shifts when we do standardized
> work and strive on each shift for constant improve-
> ments...
> We also hear that there are places in the plant
> that we don't have a say in the way standardized work
> is set up and/or carried out...
> We hear talk of the old GM and Ford ways and
> how they are on their way back.... Yes, it is easy to fall
> back into the old ways, and we really need to get a
> handle on it, and we can do this through better com-
> munication and proper use of our system. Believe me,
> it does work, all we have to do is get involved.[22]

Why do workers see the team concept as a good

system marred by individuals who fail to carry it out
properly, rather than as a system with fundamental defects?

First, working for General Motors was no picnic
either. NUMMI workers very much want to hold on to
management's promises of job security and dignity and
respect as long as they have the slightest credibility.

Second, the two years between the closing of GM-
Fremont and hiring at NUMMI was for most workers
truly a "significant emotional event" (GM Vice-President Al Warren's phrase for a condition that gets workers to accept major concessions). When unemployment
compensation and Supplemental Unemployment Benefits began to run out, workers were forced to choose between moving to plants in Kansas or Oklahoma or being
dropped from "safety net" programs. High-paid industrial jobs on the West Coast were disappearing. The former GM workers were faced with the prospect of a vastly
reduced standard of living. When the letter from
NUMMI arrived in the mailbox inviting them to apply
for a job, it was the miracle hand reaching from the sky
just when they were going down. It is understandable
that the former Fremont employees are born-again
workers who see NUMMI as a second chance for life.

Everything else, at least for a while, is reduced to
this one issue. Bert Wright, a production worker, said:

> I've had as many problems in the plant as any of
> you guys. But we have production; we have quality
> and we have jobs. Under the old system they didn't
> have production, they didn't have quality, and we even-
> tually lost the jobs. If anything else needs to be said
> you better think about that first.[23]

Despite the formal job security provisions in the
contract, the atmosphere is one of insecurity. Every discussion almost always returns to the same theme. Describing the role of the committeeperson in the problem
solving procedure, Cheryl Franklin concludes:

> They do not have time and we do not have time
> for the little petty stuff. The main thing we are con-
> cerned with is keeping our jobs.[24]

Third and most important, NUMMI's is a sophisticated and complicated system. Criticizing the system
and finding alternatives to it requires leadership, resources and organization—normally roles of the union.
But well before the plant opened, most of the respected
local union leaders from GM-Fremont were brought
into line by the company, which methodically convinced
these people to commit themselves to the NUMMI system in exchange for maintaining the union structure.
Perks, such as trips to Japan, buttressed the argument
and promises. When the plant opened, union leaders
were in place who saw their main responsibility as making the NUMMI system work.

It takes time to convert vague discomfort and
gripes into realistic alternatives. It is especially difficult
when everyone—from the media to your union leadership—tells you the only alternatives are far worse. One

worker summed up the hope, frustration, and fear which all exist at the same time:

> The team concept is a great idea—the problem is that some group leaders are taking advantage of it. But sometimes, deep down, I get this feeling that it is a form of union busting.

But the pressures are building that will lead workers to again look to their union. Although the sluggish Chevrolet Nova sales at the end of 1987 have not yet produced any layoffs, analysts and the UAW International are warning that "no job security agreement can offer an ironclad guarantee."[25] Many workers are now looking to the union to negotiate safety net programs for layoffs when the current agreement expires in June 1988.[26] Another source of insecurity is uncertainty about what will happen when the joint venture expires. The assumption had been that Toyota would buy GM out and continue running the plant. But now Toyota is building two other plants in North America, so NUMMI workers are not so confident about their future.

Most likely the new model scheduled for 1988 will again bring NUMMI up to full production, and there will be no layoffs. But while that may quell fears about job security, running at full capacity will again force workers to question whether they can maintain the pace of work until retirement. Issues such as the absentee replacement policy will resurface. Sometimes the NUMMI production system seems to be able to get way with anything in the name of job security. Whether workers are willing to challenge that system will be affected not only by events in the plant but also by the state of the economy and whether workers get direction and backing from the rest of the UAW.

Notes

1. Described in speech by Dennis Cuneo, NUMMI management representative, May 1, 1985, San Francisco, California.

2. *Agreement Between New United Motor Manufacturing, Inc. and the UAW*, July 1, 1985, Section III.

3. Many documents and testimony relevant to the joint venture are contained in *Future of the Automobile Industry*, Hearings Before the Subcommittee on Commerce, Industry, and Tourism, February 1984, Serial 98-117.

4. General Motors, *D-150 Labor Performance Report— Passenger Assembly*, week ending May 11, 1986, No.36.

5. John Krafcik, "Learning From NUMMI," Internal Working Paper for the International Motor Vehicle Program at Massachusetts Institute of Technology, September 15, 1986. Krafcik is a former NUMMI quality control engineer.

6. Note on sources—Unless otherwise specified, quotations are from our interviews. Many of the NUMMI workers we interviewed did not wish to be identified. In

a few instances, situations have been slightly disguised to honor those wishes. Other interviews are contained in Neil Chethik's series in the *San Jose Mercury News* included in the appendix of this chapter.
Also, KQED Television, *Express,* program of interviews and discussion with NUMMI workers, March 4, 1987.
Also, Tim Wise, "Life on the Fast Line," *Dollars and Sense,* April and May 1987.

7. *Automotive Industries,* May 1983.

8. General Motors Technical Liaison Office, "This is NUMMI," videotape for GM managers, 1985.

9. *Oakland Enterprise*, February 13, 1985.

10. Tetsuo Abo, "The Application of Japanese-Style Management Concepts in Japanese Automobile Plants in the USA," WZB Conference, Berlin, November 1987, p.6.

11. General Motors Technical Liaison Office, "Team Concept," November 26, 1984, description of NUMMI.

12. See, for example, Jeff Stansbury, "NUMMI: A New Kind of Workplace," *UAW Solidarity*, August 1985.

13. "This is NUMMI."

14. "This is NUMMI."

15. *Detroit Free Press*, January 25, 1988.

16. "This is NUMMI."

17. *Agreement Between New United Motor Manufacturing, Inc. and the UAW, July 1, 1985*, Section X.2.1.

18. Abo, p.7.

19. Wise, "Life on the Fast..."

20. "This is NUMMI."

21. Videotape interviews, January 21, 1988.

22. *Local 2244 Labor News*, August 1987.

23. KQED Television, *Express*, March 4, 1987.

24. Videotape interviews, January 21, 1988.

25. *UAW Solidarity,* November 1987.

26. Neil Chethik, "NUMMI Struggles to Boost Sales," *San Jose Mercury News*, January 3, 1988.

Appendix

The contract language reprinted below is excerpted from the 1985 Local Agreement between NUMMI and UAW Local 2244.

I. Introduction

1.1 This Agreement is made and entered into this 1st day of July 1985 by and between New United Motor Manufacturing, Inc., hereinafter referred to as the COMPANY, and the International Union, United Automobile, Aerospace and Agricultural Implement Workers of America, UAW and its affiliated Local Union 2244, hereinafter referred to as the UNION.

The Parties recognize that this is an historic endeavor and that progress for the Company and the members of the Union is to a large extent interdependent and therefore together we are committed to building and maintaining the most innovative and harmonious labor-management relationship in America.

1.2 In the Administration of this Agreement, and in our day to day relationship, we will exhibit mutual trust, understanding and sincerity, and, to the fullest extent possible, will avoid confrontational tactics.

Should differences or misunderstandings occur they will be resolved through full and open communication. The manufacturing environment will be based on team work, mutual trust and respect that gives recognition to the axiom that people are the most important resource of the Company. We are cognizant that if this endeavor is to be a success, labor and management must work together as members of the same team.

II. Commitments and Responsibilities

1.1 The Company's primary objective is to grow and prosper. Since the catalyst for its progress is its employees, it recognizes its obligation to keep them employed and improve their wages and working conditions. It accepts Union organizing and collective bargaining as an essential and constructive force in our democratic society.

1.2 The Union's primary objective is to improve the quality of life for its members and their families by assuring that they will be treated with dignity and provided with economic security. In addition, it is essential to the Union's purpose to assure that workers are afforded the opportunity to master their work environment; to achieve not only improvement in their economic status but, of equal importance, to gain from their labors a greater measure of dignity, self-fulfillment and self-worth.

It recognizes, however, the necessity of increasing productivity as a factor in its role in contributing to the development of the Company which is the source of its members' employment and income.

1.3 To achieve the common goal of maintaining and improving the quality of life for employees and their families through Company growth the Parties are committed to:

- Maintain a prosperous business operation necessary to maintain fair wages and benefits that will assure a satisfactory standard of living and to provide secure jobs with the opportunity for advancement;
- Provide workers a voice in their own destiny in decisions that affect their lives before such decisions are made;
- Provide that the plant is operated under methods which will promote, to the fullest extent possible, economy of operation, quality and quantity of output, cleanliness of the plant, and protection of property;
- Work together as a team;
- Build the highest quality automobile in the world at the lowest possible cost to the consumer;
- Promote full communication over the established policies and procedures;
- Cooperate with established standards of conduct and promote fair and equitable treatment;
- Maintain a safe work place utilizing new and innovative programs that could be a model for use throughout the entire industry;
- Resolve employee concerns through procedures using problem solving and non-adversarial techniques that are based on consensus instead of confrontation;
- Recognize the full worth and dignity of all employees, both bargaining unit and non-bargaining unit, and to treat each other with respect;
- Constantly seek improvement in quality, efficiency and work environment through *kaizen*, QC circles, and suggestion programs; and
- Recognize and respect each other's rights and perform all responsibilities sincerely.

1.4 Management Responsibilities

In carrying out the above commitments, the Company has the exclusive responsibility, except as specifically relinquished in this Agreement, to plan, direct, and control Company operations, including items such as products to be manufactured; method of manufacturing, including tools and equipment, schedules of production, and processes of manufacturing or assembling; establishment of standardized work; purchase or making of products or services to be incorporated into the products manufactured or processed; establish standards of conduct, including discipline or discharge for good and just cause; hiring, laying off, assigning, transferring, promoting, training and communication with all employees. In performing these responsibilities, the Company will inform the Union about the following matters:

- The inauguration or retirement of top management;
- Annual Company objectives;
- Major organizational changes;
- Semi-annual business plans;
- Company's long-range plans and policies;
- Establishment of quarterly production schedules;
- Contemplated insourcing or outsourcing decisions;
- Technological changes that will impact the bargaining unit; and
- Other major events.

Additionally, the Company will meet and confer and make its best efforts to reach a consensus with the Union prior to initiating or changing Company policies relating to terms and conditions of employment. The Company shall make no change in Company policies contrary to the terms of this Agreement except as by mutual agreement of the Parties.

1.5 Union Responsibilities

The Union has the exclusive responsibility of representing its membership regarding all terms and conditions of employment and to ensure that they are treated consistent with the terms of this Agreement and that they receive fair and equitable wages and benefits.

The Union accepts the responsibility to promote the common objectives and to cooperate with the Company in administering, on a fair and equitable basis, standards of conduct; attendance plans and Problem Resolution; to promote constant improvements in quality and productivity; and to cooperate with the Company in dealing with governmental entities.

1.6 Employee Responsibilities

The Company and the Union recognize and accept their responsibility to strive to create and maintain a positive work environment. To accomplish the same for the present and the future, all employees shall have the following responsibilities:

- Support the performance of the total team and actively support other members of the team;
- Meet reasonable team goals and participate in setting of team goals;
- Work within reasonable Company guidelines and philosophy;
- Respect the individual rights of others;
- Support and abide by reasonable standards of conduct and attendance policies;
- Promote good housekeeping and maintain a safe work environment;
- Promote *kaizen* by continually looking for opportunities to make the Company more efficient;
- Achieve quality goals and improve quality standards;
- Support the team concept; and
- Assist the Company in meeting production goals and schedules.

III. Job Security

New United Motor Manufacturing, Inc. recognizes that job security is essential to an employee's well being and acknowledges that it has a responsibility, with the cooperation of the Union, to provide stable employment to its workers. The Union's commitments in Article II of this Agreement are a significant step towards the realization of stable employment. Hence, the Company agrees that it will not lay off employees unless compelled to do so by severe economic conditions that threaten the long term financial viability of the Company.

The Company will take affirmative measures before laying off any employees, including such measures as the reduction of salaries of its officers and management, assigning previously subcontracted work to bargaining unit employees capable of performing this work, seeking voluntary layoffs, and other cost saving measures.

In summary, the Parties to this Agreement recognize that job security for bargaining unit employees will help to ensure the Company's growth and that the Company's growth will ensure job security.

VIII. Representation

For the purposes of representing the employees relative to the terms and conditions of this Collective Bargaining Agreement and to carry out the mutual commitments and responsibilities set forth in Article II, the Union shall have the following representation structure:

1. Local Union President

1.1 The Local Union President, who is elected from the employees of the Company, will be responsible for representing the Union in a variety of functions in, as well as out of, the plant. He shall perform functions as defined in the Problem Resolution Procedure, Article X, and such other Articles as may be applicable.

1.2 He shall have such other duties and responsibilities as shall be determined by the parties, such as coordination and assistance in the areas of safety, training, education, orientation, and Joint Company/Union Programs.

2. Chairperson of the Bargaining Committee

2.1 The Chairperson of the Bargaining Committee, who is elected from among the employees of the Company, shall represent the entire bargaining unit. He shall be responsible at the Local Union level for the overall administration of the Collective Bargaining Agreement. He shall perform functions as defined in the Problem Resolution Procedure, Article X, and such other Articles as may be applicable. He shall make assignments to members of the Bargaining Committee consistent with the terms of this Agreement.

2.2 One of the key mutual goals of the parties is to resolve problems at the earliest possible stage. The Chairperson of the Bargaining Committee will meet with the Manager of Labor Relations on a day to day basis to discuss how best to carry out that goal, and how best to meet the mutual commitments of the parties as set forth in Article II.

3. Acting Chairperson of the Bargaining Committee

The Chairperson of the Bargaining Committee shall designate any member of the Committee as Acting Chairperson, who will perform the duties of the Chairperson in his absence.

4. The Bargaining Committee

The Bargaining Committee shall consist of the Chairperson, three (3) Bargaining Committeepersons, and the President of the Local Union. The Bargaining Committee shall have the responsibility, in conjunction with the International Union, of negotiating a new Collective Bargaining Agreement to replace the present agreement or make modifications thereto. The three (3) Bargaining Committeepersons will also function as District Committeepersons as defined in Section 5, below.

5. District Committeepersons

5.1 For the purpose of representation, the Chairperson of the Bargaining Committee and the Manager of Labor Relations, shall by mutual agreement, establish Districts in the plant. There shall be five (5) Districts on the Day Shift and five (5) Districts on the Night Shift (2nd shift). There shall be five (5) District Committeepersons assigned to the Day Shift. There shall be at least three (3) but no more than five (5) District Committeepersons assigned to the Night Shift as shall be determined by mutual agreement of the parties. Three (3) District Committeepersons on the Night Shift shall be designated by the Union as District Shop Committeepersons. Whenever possible, District Shop Committeepersons shall be selected from among employees in the Districts that they represent.

5.2 Where there is an overlap period between shifts where employees are working outside of the normal two (2) shifts, the Chairperson of the Bargaining Committee shall assign the responsibility of representing those employees to one or more of the above District Committeepersons.

6. Duties of District Committeepersons

Each District Committeeperson shall have responsibilities relating to proper administration of this Agreement with the Company. These duties include:

- Meeting with Company representative to resolve complaints under the Problem Resolution Procedure;
- Participating with the Company in Standards of Conduct and Attendance Counseling Committees;
- Joint investigations with the Company in potential suspension/discharge cases;
- Represent an employee(s) (if requested by the employee(s)) in disciplinary action that may result in suspension or discharge;
- Implementing this Agreement and cooperating with the Company in implementing Labor Relations Policies such as attendance control, vacation scheduling, safety records, call-in duties, lost time accident reports, and leaves of absence.

7. Alternate District Committeeperson

There shall be one (1) Alternate District Committeeperson per shift who shall be designated by the Union. In cases where a District Committeeperson is absent for an entire day, the Alternate District Committeeperson may function in his place. However, the Alternate shall not be paid for performing representational duties when the Committeeperson is absent and being paid by the Company for his representational duties.

8. General Representatives

8.1 Two (2) representatives, appointed by the International Union, will be assigned to positions in the Safety and Employee Benefits Sections of the Human Resources Department. The General Representatives will have regular full-time duties, determined by the Company and the Union.

8.2 Two (2) additional representatives shall be appointed by the International Union in the areas of Employee Assistance and Apprenticeship/Skilled/Cross Training if the parties agree they are needed.

They will function according to the need in those areas of activity. They shall become full-time when agreed to by the parties.

9. Rate of Pay

The Local Union President, the Chairperson of the Bargaining Committee, the District Committeepersons and the General Representatives shall be paid according to the mutual agreement of the parties for time spent in representational duties at the plant. In addition, the President of the Local Union shall be paid for up to sixteen (16) hours per week and the Chairperson shall be paid for up to sixteen (16) hours per week according to the mutual agreement of the parties for time spent on representational duties off the plant premises. Before leaving plant premises, arrangements must be made with the Manager of Labor Relations. Normally Committeepersons will not perform representational duties off premises but they may, when given permission by the Manager of Labor Relations. Requests for permission to perform off premises representational duties must come from a representative of the International.

10. Union Coordinator

10.1 There shall be one (1) Union Coordinator designated by the Union for every two Groups in the Plant. The Groups will be combined by the Manager of Labor Relations and the Chairperson of the Bargaining Committee. He shall be selected from among the employees in the Group that he represents. The Union Coordinator will perform a full-time job in the Plant.

10.2 The function of the Union Coordinator, in part, is to provide representation and assistance in the solution of problems and potential problems within the Groups that he works. It is the intent of the Parties, in the spirit of true teamwork, that all best efforts be made by the affected employee(s), Union Coordinator and Group Leader to quickly resolve problems arising within the Group, in an informal atmosphere and on a nonprecedent setting basis. The Union Coordinator will perform functions as defined in the Problem Resolution Procedure, Article X, and other activities as agreed to by the parties, including but not limited to, Group Meetings.

10.3 Meetings with the Union Coordinator for problem handling shall be arranged during the periods in which there is clearly no interference with the job duties of both the Coordinator and Employee, such as lunch or break time. Union Coordinators will be paid two (2) hours pay per week at their straight-time hourly rate for performing their representational duties. This two (2) hours pay shall not be included for purposes of computing overtime.

11. General Provisions

11.1 Upon entering a Section to perform representational responsibilities and in order to facilitate communication and create a positive atmosphere, all Union representatives shall notify the Manager or Group Leader (or Team Leader in the absence of the Group Leader) of that area of their presence and purpose.

11.2 The names of all Union Officers, Committeepersons and Union Coordinators shall be given to the Human Resources Department in writing by the President of the Local Union, the Chairperson of the Bargaining Committee, or an International Representative. No person shall be allowed to function in these positions until forty-eight (48) hours after such notice.

11.3 Upon the request of the President or Chairperson of the Bargaining Committee of the Local Union, or an International Representative, the Company shall excuse an employee without pay for all or part of a shift, unless such excuse would substantially interfere with production, for the purpose of conducting Union business of such nature as attendance at the UAW Convention, attendance at Board Meetings of the Local Union, and summer programs conducted by the UAW, etc. The Manager of Labor Relations shall receive a written absence notification from the Local Union President, Chairperson of the Bargaining Committee or an International Representative as far in advance as possible, but in no event less than twenty-four (24) hours before the absence.

IX. Joint Conference

1. Purpose

The Company and the Union will have periodic Joint conferences to allow both parties full understanding of situations within and surrounding the Company and the Union. The purpose of these Joint Conferences is to facilitate joint efforts in establishing a work environment and relationship characterized by mutual respect and trust.

2. Level/Composition

2.1 Joint Conferences shall be held at the Company Level (Executive Joint Conference), and sectional level within the bargaining unit (Section Joint Conference).

2.2 Executive Joint Conferences shall be composed of the President, Executive Vice President, Vice President Manufacturing, General Manager Human Resources, and other designated management personnel relating to the issues to be discussed, and the International Representative, President of the Local Union, Bargaining Committee Chairperson, and Committeepersons.

2.3 Section Joint Conferences shall be composed of Section Manager, Assistant Manager, if any, and designated personnel related to the issues, the Committeepersons and Union Coordinators within the Sections.

3. Agenda

An agenda shall be determined by mutual agreement and shall not include problems defined in Article X or negotiation matters. Each party shall furnish the other with an agenda which they wish to discuss as far in advance of the meeting as possible.

4. Meeting Hours

Executive Joint conferences shall be held at a mutually agreeable time. Section Joint conferences shall be held at a mutually agreeable time after working hours.

X. Problem Resolution Procedure

1. Scope of Problem

1.1 In the event any employee has a "problem" concerning the interpretation or application of any terms of this Agreement, or any other work-related problem, such matters shall be adjusted according to procedures in this Article except where the Agreement specifically states that a certain matter shall not be subject to this Problem Resolution Procedure or where a certain matter is subject to other resolution procedures.

1.2 The Union agrees that this procedure shall be the exclusive procedure for any problem resolution and it further agrees to discourage any employee to appeal to any court or other government agency any resolution rendered through this procedure.

2. First Step

Informal Discussion—Team Effort for Resolving Problem

2.1 The Company and the Union shall encourage all employees to attempt to resolve problems within the Group using problem-solving methods. Any employee with a problem shall first discuss the problem with his immediate Team Leader and Group Leader. If the problem is not settled to the satisfaction of the employee, he may discuss the problem with the Union Coordinator during the period in which there is clearly no interference with their job duties such as lunch, break period, etc.

2.2 Because of the value and importance of full discussion in clearing up misunderstandings and preserving harmonious relations, every reasonable effort shall be made to resolve problems promptly at this point through discussion. The resolution of an employee problem at this stage shall not set a precedent or a binding past practice on either party.

2.3 The Group Leader shall answer the problem within three (3) working days from the date on which the problem is made known to him. The Group Leader's answer shall state the basis for his position. If the problem is not resolved through discussion with the employee(s)' immediate Group Leader, and/or the Union Coordinator, the Union Coordinator or the employee(s) may request the Group Leader to call the District Committeeperson. The Human Resources Representative shall be notified by the District Committeeperson within five (5) working days after the Group Leader answers the problem.

2.4 Investigation of Problem

The Committeeperson and Human Resources Representative shall jointly complete the investigation of the circumstances of the problem within three (3) working days from the notification to the Human Resources Representative. Thereafter, they shall discuss the problem with the Section Manager and others concerned in order to resolve it.

3. Second Step

3.1 If the matter remains unresolved, within five (5) working days after completion of the investigation, the Committeeperson may present the problem to the Manager of Labor Relations on a Problem Notice Form supplied by the Company and agreed to by the Union.

3.2 The Problem Notice Form shall state the nature of the problem and the pertinent facts, the date on which the act or conduct forming the basis for the problem occurred, the contract provision or provisions alleged to have been violated, the nature of the problem and the remedy requested, and be signed by the grieving employee and/or the Union. All employees involved in a group problem shall be identified on the form. The form shall also be signed and dated by the Committeeperson.

3.3 The Chairperson of the Bargaining Committee and Manager

of Labor Relations shall meet within seven (7) working days from the time that the written problem is presented. They shall review the investigation made at the First Step and shall seek to resolve the problem. If they are not able to resolve the problem, the Manager of Labor Relations shall give the Chairperson of the Bargaining Committee a written Second Step answer to the problem within seven (7) working days after the Second Step meeting, stating the reasons for his position.

9. Time Limits

9.1 A written problem shall be filed within fifteen (15) working days after occurrence of the event giving rise to the problem unless the circumstances of the case make it impossible for the employee or the Union to know that there were grounds for the claim prior to that date. If a written problem is not filed within the time limit, the problem is not valid under this Problem Resolution Procedure.

9.2 Any problem not appealed within the time limits shall be considered settled on the basis of the last decision and not subject to further appeal or to arbitration. However, an employee who does not appeal a problem from one step to another shall be given one automatic two (2) day extension of time to properly perfect his appeal. An employee or Union who uses this extension shall have no further extension at any step of the problem solving procedure. If the Company does not answer a problem within the time period specified, the problem shall be deemed denied and may be taken to the next step of the Problem Resolution Procedure.

9.3 The time limits provided for in this Article may be extended by written agreement of the parties. The party requesting the extension shall initiate the request in writing.

9.4 Prior to the hearing by the Arbitrator, the parties may agree to refer a problem back to the preceding step of the Problem Resolution Procedure for the purpose of further discussion or investigation including new evidence not set forth in the prior written record.

9.5 At any step prior to the hearing by the Arbitrator, the Union representative(s) and Company representative(s) designated for that step shall have the authority to resolve a problem, provided that the problem settlement does not supersede or conflict with any provisions of this Agreement.

9.6 During or after the hearing by the Arbitrator, a problem may be withdrawn by agreement of the parties.

10. Effect of Resolution

10.1 Any claim against the Company shall not be valid for the period prior to the date the written problem was first filed, except that:

a) For a back wage claim based on a non-continuing violation, the claim should be valid for a period of not more than fifteen (15) days prior to the date the written problem was first filed;

b) For a back wage claim based on a continuing violation, the claim shall be limited retroactively to a thirty (30) day period prior to the date the claim was first filed in writing, if the circumstances of the case made it impossible for the employee or the Union to know that there were grounds for the claim prior to that date.

10.2 Amount of Back Wage

The claim for back wages shall not exceed the amount of wages the employee would otherwise have earned at his regular rate, including overtime, less:

a) any unemployment or worker's compensation he received, or was entitled to, or,

b) any compensation for personal services received or earned during the period covered by the problem that he would not have earned if he had been working.

11. Discipline and Discharge

11.1 If an employee is called to the Human Resources Department or to a meeting with his supervisor concerning discipline, he may request the presence of his Committeeperson to represent him during the interview.

11.2 In the case of potential suspension or discharge, a Review Committee, comprised of the Manager of Labor Relations, a Section Manager, President of Local Union and Chairperson of Bargaining Committee, will review any unusual or mitigating conditions and circumstances relevant to the potential suspension or discharge. This review will take place prior to a final decision on the suspension or discharge except for acts of violence or other situations which require prompt removal from the premises. If the Review Committee finds unusual or mitigating circumstances, its recommendations will be forwarded to the General Manager Human Resources for further consideration.

11.3 Immediately after any corrective suspension or issuance of second and any subsequent written corrective notice for violation of the Standards of Conduct or Good Attendance program, the Good Conduct and Attendance Counseling Committee shall confer with the employee. The Committee will discuss all relevant facts and circumstances to assist the employee in improving his conduct or attendance. In addition, the committee shall impress upon the employee the importance of Good Conduct and Attendance.

11.4 The Good Conduct and Attendance Counseling Committee shall consist of a Group Leader, Team Leader, Human Resources Representative and Committeeperson.

11.5 A written corrective notice is not subject to the Problem Resolution Procedure in this Article, provided, however, that if a problem involving a suspension or discharge is appealed to arbitration, all written corrective notices preceding the suspension or discharge also may be contested during the arbitration.

11.6 Any problem regarding suspension and discharges shall be filed to the Third Step provided in Section 4 of the Problem Resolution Procedure, within three (3) working days from the disciplinary action taken. If a problem regarding discharge is not resolved in the Problem Resolution Procedure, it shall be expedited to the Arbitration Step taking precedent over all other problems and the Arbitration shall be held within two (2) weeks where possible.

11.7 The employee and the Union will be provided a copy of any written corrective notice, suspension or discharge entered in his personnel file.

XII. Transfers

1. Definitions

Transfer means an employee moving from one Group or Section to another. A regular transfer is a transfer for more than three (3) months. A temporary transfer is for no more than three (3) months.

2. Regular Transfer

The Company may transfer employees. If efficiency and production needs permit, the Company will give priority to employees who have made application for a regular transfer as set forth below.

3. Application for Transfer

3.1 An employee may file an application to be transferred to an open job in another Section or Group, if he has worked in a Section or Group for at least twelve (12) months. The application shall be filed with the Human Resources Department, and shall include:

    a) employee's current job and all previous jobs held in the Company;

    b) employee's plant and division seniority dates;

    c) job for which a transfer is sought; and

    d) experience, qualifications, and knowledge the employee has for the job.

3.2 Each employee may have two (2) applications on file at any one time. An employee who is transferred cancels automatically any other applications, and is not eligible to apply for another transfer until after twelve (12) months from the effective date of the transfer.

3.3 All open applications for transfer will be voided at the end of the calendar year. Applications filed during the months of November and December will be deemed valid for the following calendar year.

4. Selection

4.1 When an open job is to be filled, the Company will review those applications on file for the job. Production needs permitting, the Company will select for transfer the employee or employees it believes have the capability and knowledge to perform the job. For Division I, where two or more employees have relatively equal capability, and production needs permit the selection of any one of them, the employee with the greatest seniority will be transferred. For Division II, where two or more employees have relatively equal capability and knowledge, and production needs permit the selection of any one of them, the employee with the greatest seniority will be transferred. If no employee makes application for the job and the production needs permit, the Company will transfer volunteer(s) or the least seniority employee(s) among those who are qualified for the job in the Group from which transfers are required. Current employees who have made application for transfer will be given preference over new hires for permanent openings.

4.2 For transfers between Groups, any opening created by a transfer may be filled at the discretion of the Company. This provision shall not apply to transfers between Sections.

4.3 If an employee files a transfer application based on health reasons, the Company will make a decision whether or not to transfer after consultation with the Company Medical Officer.

5. Temporary Transfer

5.1 The Company may temporarily transfer employee(s) for a maximum period of three (3) months per transfer, without regard to the other provisions of this Article. Where practical, the Company will transfer a volunteer or applicant. If there is none, the employee having

the least seniority among those who are capable of doing the required job in the team from which the transfer is required will be transferred.

5.2 An employee temporarily transferred from Division II to Division I shall be paid at his regular Division II rate. An employee who is temporarily transferred to Division II will receive the rate of pay for the job being performed for all hours worked.

6. Notification

6.1 Except in emergency cases, the Company shall give prior notice to the employee who is to be transferred.

6.2 For transfers from one shift to another, the Company will give one (1) week notice where possible.

6.3 Management will furnish the Chairperson of the Bargaining Committee a list of such permanent openings as far in advance as possible of such transfers.

XIII. Shift Assignment

1.1 The parties recognize that it is necessary, from time to time, to re-assign employees to different shifts to maintain quality, efficiency of production among shifts, to train other employees, or to accommodate employee's desires. It is also recognized that employees who desire to change shift should be given shift preference based on seniority and qualifications. During the initial evaluation period, the new employee will be assigned to an appropriate shift decided by the Company for training purposes, for up to the first ninety (90) days of employment.

1.2 Assignment from one shift to another shall be in the following manner:

    a) Once every six months a team member may make a written application to his Group Leader for reassignment to corresponding Group on another shift.

    b) An applicant who is eligible under the terms of the Agreement, shall have his shift changed as soon as possible, but not later than the first Monday following ten (10) working days from the date the application is filed. This reassignment shall be made in accordance with seniority in the respective Division, subject to his qualification to perform the required work and the ability of the employees on his former shift to perform the remaining work. An employee who is displaced as a result of a greater seniority employee exercising his right under this Article will be reassigned to the corresponding Group on the other shift.

1.3 When the Company believes it is necessary to reassign an employee(s) from one shift to another to maintain quality, efficiency or for training, these reassignments shall be made first from qualified volunteers who can be released from their current shift assignment. If there are no such volunteers, reassignments shall be made from the least seniority employees who are qualified to perform the work. Such reassignment shall not normally exceed three (3) months except where to do so would adversely effect the Company's operation.

1.4 When the Company implements a new shift(s), the Company may assign the lowest seniority qualified employee from the present shift to the new shift to maintain quality and efficiency of production. Employees who have made a written applications for the new shift will be given preference. Employees who have been reassigned may make application to be reassigned to another shift after three (3) months, in accordance with this Article.

1.5 In the event of the addition of a Production shift, there will be no shift preference for ninety (90) days. In cases of model changeover which require more than one week shutdown, there will be no shift preference for thirty (30) days.

XIV. Team Concept

1.1 The parties agree that the Company will utilize a team concept, whereby employees will be organized into teams of approximately 5-10 members. All members of a team share responsibility for the work performed by the team, and for participation in Quality/productivity improvement programs such as QC Circles and *kaizen*. Generally, and as practical, team members are expected to rotate jobs within the team.

1.2 Each team will have a Team Leader selected in accordance with Article XVI in this Agreement. Team Leaders shall be members of the bargaining unit.

XV. Bargaining Unit Work

1.1 Salaried employees or other non-bargaining unit employees will not be used as substitutes for hourly employees nor will they deprive bargaining unit employees of available work.

1.2 The principal function of the Group Leader is to direct the activities of workers in his particular area. The Parties recognize, however, that it may be necessary for the Group Leader or other non-

bargaining unit employees, including employees of Toyota Motor Corporation, to perform the work that is normally performed by bargaining unit employees for the following reasons:
- Assisting in engineering or break downs;
- *kaizen* and training employees;
- Performing work of an experimental nature; and
- Unexpected circumstances requiring immediate attention to avoid interruption of work.

XVI. Team Leader Selection Procedure

1.1 The Parties seek to attract, retain and motivate individuals who contribute to the mutual growth and success of the total team. An objective of the Parties is to identify the most capable individual for team leader positions within the Company. In so doing, the Company tries to provide growth opportunities for employees and to assist them in developing to their full potential.

1.2 The Company will establish selection criteria and promote employees from those qualified who are most capable for the team leader position. Where two or more candidates are considered most capable, the employee with the greater seniority will be selected. In identifying qualified candidates for promotion to team leader, the following guidelines will be utilized: experience, ability, capacity to perform the team leader job, etc.

XVII. Wage

2. Team Leader Premium

Team Leaders shall be paid a premium of fifty cents ($.50) per hour effective the date of promotion or after completion of evaluation period, whichever is later.

XIX. Working Hours

1.2 The Company shall provide a thirty (30) minute paid lunch as contained in Appendix "A," and two (2) fifteen (15) minute rest periods per shift. One rest period shall be scheduled during the first half of the shift and the other during the last half. Rest periods during overtime shall be provided as follows:
- One hour overtime scheduled. Seven (7) minutes.
- Two hours overtime scheduled. Fourteen (14) minutes.
- Breaks to be taken at the beginning of scheduled overtime hours.

XX. Overtime

[Summary: A special procedure is established for a worker to refuse "voluntary" overtime. He or she must file a form (usually on the Wednesday before the overtime is scheduled). Voluntary overtime includes: that over 10 hours per day; the third Saturday in a row if no days during that week are missed; Sundays if no days during the week are missed. These restrictions on mandatory overtime do not apply in certain situations determined by management, including necessary maintenance work, critical operations, build-out of old models, start-up of new models until the line reaches scheduled production, or emergencies.]

XXV. Safety

1.1 The Company recognizes its obligation and responsibilities to provide a safe and healthful working environment for its employees. The Parties recognize their obligation to cooperate in maintaining and improving a safe and healthful working environment, and to use all their best efforts jointly to achieve these objectives.

1.2 Therefore, it is agreed by the parties that a Joint Safety Committee be established which will have the overall responsibility and authority to establish, maintain and supervise a complete, total and comprehensive Health and Safety Program in the plant that will meet the objectives noted above.

2. Joint Safety Committee

2.1 The Joint Safety Committee shall consist of three (3) Representatives of each party:

The Union Representative will be:
President of the Local Union or his designee;
The UAW General Representative in the Safety Section; and
One (1) Bargaining Unit Employee, who will serve for one year—rotating term, appointed by the Union, and shall not be a Committeeperson.

The Company Representative will be:
The General Manager of the Plant, or his designee;
The Manager of Safety; and
The Manager of Labor Relations.

2.2 President of the Local Union and the Manager of Safety shall serve as Co-Chairpersons of the Joint Safety Committee.

3. Problem Resolution

The ultimate resolution of disputes related to health and safety matters may be referred to a Committee consisting of the Vice President Manufacturing (or his designee), General Manager of Human Resources, the International Representative of the UAW and the Chairperson of the Bargaining Committee. Either party may call upon the UAW Regional Director and William J. Usery for final resolution of the problem.

XXVI. Bulletin Boards

1.1 The Company will furnish four (4) bulletin boards to be used by the Union for posting of notices of meetings, elections, recreational events, and similar notices. Bulletin boards shall be glass enclosed and lockable. Notices referring to controversial matters shall not be posted. The bulletin boards shall be placed in conspicuous places on the Company's property, as agreed by both parties. Additional informational areas shall be provided for by mutual agreement.

1.2 All notices must be signed by the President or Chairperson of the Bargaining Committee prior to posting.

XXVIII. Standardized Work

1. Description and Objective

1.1 For some time prior to the execution of this Agreement, the Company has been utilizing a procedure for establishing and changing Standardized Work. Under this procedure, described in Appendix "C" and based on Toyota Production Methods, employees are encouraged and expected to participate with their Team Leaders and Group Leaders in designing and establishing Standardized Work. The objective of the Standardized Work procedure is to insure that employees work at a safe and reasonable pace, in the most efficient and safe manner, while maintaining quality standards. In the interest of safety, efficiency, best quality and other production needs, the Company may establish and change Standardized Work by continuing this procedure. The Standardized Work includes items such as required manpower, *Takt* time, model mix, operation arrangements, tools, operation methods, and required times for performing operations.

1.2 As part of the New United Motor's production system, employees are expected to use their best efforts in performing the job within the *Takt* time and to alert their Group/Team Leader of production or quality problems. If the problem in production or quality is such that they cannot complete their tasks in the proper manner, they are expected, without being subject to discipline, to pull the cord or push the button to sound the alarm, and ultimately stop the line, alerting a Group/Team Leader of the problem. If the problem is of a recurring nature, the employees will work together to *kaizen* the operation according to the procedure set forth in Appendix "C."

1.3 The Company will explain and discuss monthly production schedules with the Union for mutual understanding. This meeting will be held monthly for discussion of production related matters, including three month production forecast, manpower balance between sections, assembly line *Takt* time, model mix, and estimated scheduled overtime.

2. Procedure for Review of Standardized Work Problems

2.1 Problems relating to Standardized Work or production standards shall be subject to the procedures set forth in this Article.

2.2 The purpose of this procedure is to establish a method consistent with our philosophy of mutual trust and respect whereby the Union and Company jointly assess Standardized Work concerns which are not resolved through reasonable and best team effort.

2.3 An employee who has a problem with Standardized Work can utilize this procedure to resolve the problem.

2.4 If the Standardized Work problem is not resolved between the Group Leader and the employee(s) within five (5) working days from the date the employee(s) has addressed the complaint to the Group Leader, the Union Coordinator may submit the problem to the Standardized Work Committee (SWC). The SWC shall consist of a Production Manager or Coordinator, a Human Resources Representative, the Chairperson of the Bargaining Committee or his designee, and the respective District Committeeperson.

2.5 When a written Standardized Work problem is filed with the SWC, the SWC shall meet and conduct an immediate fact-finding investigation. This investigation will include but not be limited to the following:

a) Discussion with the affected Group Leader, Team Leader and Team Members to determine the exact nature of the problem;

b) Review of Standardized Work charts, manning, and current *kaizen* efforts (if any) to improve work process/sequence;

c) Assessment of physical capabilities of employee(s) to perform the operation;

d) Nature and extent of training received by the employee(s);
e) Tooling and process; and
f) Quality and location of stock.

2.6 Upon completion of the investigation, the SWC will determine the specific nature of the problem and make recommendations for correction to the affected Section.

2.7 If, within five (5) working days from completion of the investigation, the problem is not resolved by the SWC, it will be submitted to a Standardized Work Board (SWB) consisting of the Vice President Manufacturing (or his designee), the General Manager of Human Resources, the International Representative of the UAW, and the Chairperson of the Bargaining Committee of the Local Union for resolution. Either party may call upon the UAW Regional Director and W.J. Usery for final resolution of the problem.

2.8 Both parties agree to utilize this procedure in the event that problems arise. This procedure shall be the exclusive remedy for any problem on Standardized Work or work standards.

Appendix "C" Standardized Work

1. Planning (Designing)
   A. Elements to be considered:
   • Past data (actual required time on each operation).
   • Required time for each factor of operation; not factor of movement. For instance, a clamping bolt needs two (2) seconds.
   • Target time established by Production Control.
   • Conditions of equipment, tools, layout of parts and other technical information provided by Engineering Staff.
   B. Activities:
   • Team Leaders and Group Leaders discuss and develop each suggested standardized work.
   • The Manager approves the suggested standardized work.
   • Engineering Staff advises Group Leader and Team of technical

matters and provides them with necessary engineering information.

2. Try-out and Check
   A. Time study on pilot vehicle:
   • Group Leader and Team Leader evaluate each suggested standardized work by having a Team Leader who does not always work on the actual operation, try it out. This evaluation should accumulate actual time data on each factor of an operation.
   B. Amendment and *Kaizen*:
   • Standardized Work is changed through a time data evaluation by the Team Leader and Group Leader. *Kaizen* is performed to reduce the required time for accomplishment of the target.

3. Pilot Assembling and Training
   • To find out the difficulty and easiness on each standardized work through repeated training, employees will assemble and disassemble pilot vehicle on a pilot line.
   • All employees ("all employees" as used in the Appendix C means bargaining unit and non-bargaining unit employees) do *kaizen* to achieve the target.

4. Commencement of Mass Production
   A. If employees find difficulties in doing actual work at a specified work pace, they are expected to pull the cord or push the button to sound the alarm and ultimately stop the line, alerting a Team/Group Leader of the problem.
   B. All employees do *kaizen* (repeated as required) to attempt to achieve target. If necessary, training will be provided to employees and work assignment will be adjusted.
   C. As a result of *kaizen* by all employees or reassignment of work, standardized work will be approved by the Manager and changed.

5. Repeating above process.
   • New problems are resolved through the same process mentioned in #4 above.

The Intercultural Honeymoon Ends.

Reprinted with permission from the San Jose Mercury News, Sunday, February 8, 1987.

By Neil Chethik
Mercury News Staff Writer

Autoworker Bill Stevens came up with a better way to do his job. The bolts he used to build brakes on the Chevrolet Nova kept falling off the end of his drill, so he suggested his company put a magnet there.

For his idea, Stevens earned 20 "points" in the company suggestion program—enough to swap for a pocketknife, a bath towel or a pair of socks.

It was a typical Japanese reward. And Stevens had a typical American response: He stopped offering suggestions.

It has been more than two years since American workers began building cars under Japanese management at New United Motor Manufacturing Inc. in Fremont. But the two cultures are still groping for a middle ground.

Top officials at NUMMI, led by about 30 Toyota managers, are pushing an almost purely Japanese approach. Using Japanese terms, they seek uniformity, loyalty and constant improvement in speed and quality.

But many of those who work on the factory floor are resisting. They say the Japanese approach sometimes ignores the basic nature of American workers, who generally are more individualistic and demanding than their Japanese counterparts.

In recent months, the friction has worn the luster off the GM-Toyota joint venture, according to interviews with more than two dozen workers, managers and union leaders at NUMMI. And as production pressures have increased, so too has the threat to the plant's most precious commodity—the quality of its product.

"When you try to blend two cultures together, it's never easy," said Gus Billy, vice president of United Auto Workers Local 2244 at NUMMI. "But there's one thing we know: The old ways (of building cars) didn't work. The jury's still out on this deal."

Merits not an issue

The merits of the Japanese system were not an issue among most NUMMI workers when the first cream-colored Nova rolled off the assembly line in December 1984.

Instead, workers shared a sense of excitement and commitment. Nearly all had been laid off when General Motors shut down its Fremont plant in 1982, and they were willing to trust almost any system that promised them a steady job for premium pay. The "NUMMI Team Member Handbook" introduced them to the Japanese policies and philosophies.

"At NUMMI, you will be treated fairly," the handbook said. "You will find open lines of communication. And you will have an active role in determining how best to do your job and improve the working environ-

INSIDE NUMMI
TROUBLES IN TRANSLATION

ment."

It added a Toyota adage: "Good thinking. Good products."

Intensive training

In intensive orientation and training programs, the workers learned the basics of the Toyota production method:

- Constant improvement. They would practice *kaizen*, the Japanese term for seeking ways to make their jobs more efficient.
- Standardized jobs. They would do each assembly line job the same way every time.
- Quality first. They would put the priority on quality, stopping the assembly line if necessary to ensure that defective cars would not reach the customers.
- Teamwork. They would work in teams of five or six, helping their fellow workers when they got behind and filling in for them when they were sick or on vacation.
- Trust. They would work out their problems in peace, often in group meetings designed to air employee differences.

Strict attention

With the assembly line starting slowly, production ran relatively smoothly in the early months. Most workers started their days with calisthenics, rotated jobs and paid strict attention to the quality of the work they performed.

Their product reflected it. In a fall 1985 audit of 20 Novas at the plant, three cars were found to have no defects—a performance unequaled by any other GM plant in history, according to the UAW.

"I'm proud to say I work for NUMMI," assembly line worker Shannon Cook said at the time. "We were all frustrated auto-

workers before. We were looking for a place to go to work where they cared. And we found it."

But soon after, the honeymoon ended, employees say. The turning point came early last year, after company officials finished hiring the plant's 2,500 employees, split the work force into two shifts and began steadily speeding up the assembly line.

Over the first five months of 1986, production doubled to about 900 cars per day. In the process, the basics of the Japanese system began slipping away, many managers and workers agree. The first principle to suffer was teamwork. Under the higher production pressures, most workers found themselves struggling just to finish their own jobs; they had little or no time to help each other.

Soon some supervisors, exhausted by the pace, stopped holding after-work group meetings to work out problems. And others, pressured to increase production, began to discourage workers from pulling the cord to stop the assembly line, even when quality was threatened.

Missed by workers

"When the cord went, a lot went with it," said Cathy Lowe, who installs seat belts on the NUMMI cars. "People put a lot of faith in that cord."

The plant stabilized briefly over the summer, when Nova production was scaled back, but it was jolted again in September, when workers began producing two new models—the 1987 Nova and the Corolla FX16, the first Toyota built in America.

Parts failed to arrive on time from Japan, and within two months, the company had fallen 3,000 cars behind its production goals. Many workers—with little time for training on the new, more complicated FX—said they were unable to maintain the quality of their work.

"You can't possibly have quality if you don't have the time to do your job," said Jerry Stearns, a worker on the NUMMI night shift.

Violation of precepts

By early November, hundreds of defective or unfinished cars were stacked up in the back of the plant, employees say, violating a basic precept of the Toyota quest for quality.

"To get the best quality, you want things built in-station, on the assembly line," said John Pesek, assistant manager in the inspection department. "If it's built out back, there are more people climbing in and out of it, more people who can innocently damage it."

Mark Hogan, the top GM executive stationed at the plant, acknowledged that the company violated its own quality procedures, but said he's confident the cars were repaired and in top shape by the time they left the plant.

To make the repairs and catch up on lost production, the management began to require daily overtime in November.

In subtle rebellion, some workers stopped doing calisthenics. Others stopped offering suggestions for making their jobs more efficient. And still others started to criticize their union for not doing enough to improve the working conditions.

By year's end, NUMMI was producing up to 50 percent more cars per person than most U.S. plants. At the same time, many workers who had once embraced the NUMMI concept were wondering whether it was still a system they could trust. "The object is to build the best quality car at the lowest cost so we all have jobs," said Cook, who installs radiators in the NUMMI cars. But "I'm wondering at what cost to the workers."

Morale rising

Since a two-week Christmas shutdown at NUMMI, production is back on schedule and quality has improved, employees say. Morale seems to be slowly rising. Even the disaffected Stevens is considering offering another suggestion to improve his job.

But the culture gap at NUMMI has not been closed.

Workers say they don't want to go back to the old way of building cars, but many, Cook said, "are looking for a median."

The Japanese work pace is the major issue, most workers say, and it's exacerbated by the fact that the average NUMMI worker is over 40—at least 10 years older than the average person on a Japanese assembly line. After months on their jobs, some NUMMI workers say they're still unable to finish their work in the 60 seconds they're allotted.

Clashes with freedom

Another issue, workers say, is that the spirit of the Japanese system sometimes clashes with the personal freedom that most Americans are accustomed to.

NUMMI worker Luis Orozco remembers, for example, that when he returned home from a dentist appointment last year, his mouth swollen and sore from gum surgery, a NUMMI personnel official called to ask why he wasn't at his job.

"I said, 'I work at the plant. NUMMI doesn't own me!'" Orozco said. "You feel you don't have a right to feel sick. They're too strict. There has to be some liberty. This country is based on liberty."

The rigidity of the Japanese system is an issue on the production line, too. Karen Lotoszinski, who builds engines at NUMMI, says it's sometimes difficult for Americans—who are accustomed to flexibility in their jobs—to accept the idea of doing their jobs the same way every time.

'Be like robots'

"They want you to be like robots, basically," she said. "In some ways, it's good. If you get in the habit of picking things up with the right hand, you probably have less chance of messing up. There are some obstacles, though. Some people are left-handed."

But, at least for now, top managers at NUMMI are holding firmly to the Toyota system. They say more training and better communication will resolve most of the problems. NUMMI President Kan Higashi said he runs the company "the way we do it in Japan because I have no knowledge or experience" in the American way. And Gary Convis, who recently was promoted to vice president for manufacturing at NUMMI, said, "We will not waver from the Toyota production concept. It's what will make us successful."

More classes

In that spirit, NUMMI workers and supervisors now are going through another round of classes in standardized work, peaceful problem-solving and other basic Japanese principles, he said.

Hogan, the controller at NUMMI, pointed out that with virtually the same work force, a plant that was losing money five years ago made a $10 million profit in 1986 by adapting to the Japanese way. And he said the company must continue to improve its productivity if it is to remain competitive.

Most employees, Hogan said, understand the situation and are gradually adjusting to the greater demands of the Japanese system. In the meantime, he counsels patience.

"Patience means (waiting) more than six months or a year," Hogan said. "It took 20 years for the Japanese to rebuild their industry. I don't say it will take that long here, but that's the kind of commitment we need to understand."

Japanese auto ideal is hard taskmaster.
Weary workers feel the pressure but hang in there.

Reprinted with permission from the San Jose Mercury News, Monday, February 9, 1987.

By Neil Chethik
Mercury News Staff Writer

They are born-again autoworkers, survivors of the dark ages of U.S. industry, back from the other side of tragedy.

They build cars the Japanese way now, and that means they work harder and faster than ever before. They come in early and stay late. Some work when they're sick. Some work through their breaks

Progress, they are finding, can be brutal.

They are the 2,200 assembly-line workers at New United Motor Manufacturing Inc. Nearly all of them lost their jobs four years ago when General Motors shut its

doors in Fremont; today, in the same vast building, they assemble what's been called one of the best-built cars in the country.

They are proud of the turnaround, but feel its toll. For the workers, steeped for years in the American corporate culture, the Japanese concepts of trust and teamwork have not come easily. Some workers feel exhausted and betrayed, frustrated by a system that always seems to ask for more. Yet most are determined to hang on. They are unskilled workers earning up to $15 an hour in an economy that holds few other opportunities for them. And they are pioneers with something to prove.

Here are the stories of three of them.

Liz Huntington, 34, five years at GM, hired at NUMMI in August 1985.

She comes up the driveway in a new red Nissan Pulsar, stops sharply, bursts out of the car, enthusiastic even in her greeting. Moments later, inside her Castro Valley home, she is full of passion.

"I think NUMMI was the best thing that ever happened to me and to Fremont," she says. "I feel so secure and so content with this company. At GM, every day you go in and hear the rumors they're going to shut us down. Then eventually it happens. It seems like Fremont is born again."

"At NUMMI, we're more involved. When I worked at GM, I didn't know anything except that Friday was payday."—Liz Huntington

She works on the assembly line, building brakes on the Chevrolet Nova, and she likes the NUMMI concept: teamwork, hard work and pride in the product.

"At NUMMI, we're more involved. They tell us what's going on in the company. When I worked at GM, I didn't know anything except that Friday was payday and I probably wouldn't be in on Monday."

She makes these statements in early September, just as NUMMI is gearing up to build its second car, the Toyota Corolla FX16. Two months later, her attitude has changed.

The FX16 is much more complicated than the Nova. Parts are not coming in on time. Many jobs are overloaded. Management has begun requiring overtime every day to catch up on lost production.

"All they want is to take, take, take," Huntington says in November. "You work and do a good job, and what do you get? A (supervisor) who comes up and asks for more.

"This type of work—you just have to have your weekends off. One day of being home just doesn't make it. When I'm (at work), I give my 100 percent. I don't want to give myself on Saturdays. I have nothing left. We're only human. We're not robots.

"Negativity has been setting in like rigor mortis. I had high hopes for NUMMI. It was a pleasure. I stuck up for the Japanese, I stuck up for NUMMI. Now, if my husband got a terrific raise, I'd quit."

Six weeks later, the company is nearly caught up on its production goals. Management has ended the overtime requirement, and Huntington is warming up again. Still, the overtime episode has had its effect on her.

"Things are much better, but I've lost a lot of trust in the company," she says in December.

"A lot of things they said—like having group meetings and being able to stop the line when we got in the hole—a lot of those things haven't come true. I think that's what's making people most upset.

"The quality has gotten lost in the making of the car. Right now, it's quantity, and I think they better realize it. General Motors did quantity and look where they're at." She desperately wants NUMMI to succeed. Both she and her husband, Eldean, lost their jobs in the 1982 GM shutdown. They also lost their car, their boat and their way of life.

At their lowest point, they were forced to sell their gun collection and clean out the $200 a friend had deposited in a bank account for their baby's future. They needed the money for food.

"I think things can work out if they don't push us to the max," she says. "If they do, they won't have absentee problems—they'll have problems with people quitting. People can only be pushed so far before they give up."

Jack McCullagh, 51, 28 years at GM, team leader at NUMMI since October 1984.

A glance at his watch and he's up from the kitchen table, wiping the remnants of a lasagna lunch from his mouth, grabbing his briefcase and sliding out the side door of his south Fremont home.

He wears a gray crew cut, three diamond earrings and the look of a man who loves his job.

"I believe in the Toyota system, and I believe it will work if everybody gives it a

his share of frustrations, but he isn't discouraged. "Maybe I have more patience than other people. I feel that I'm not going to give up on this teamwork and trust and so forth. It's my livelihood. If everybody will go ahead and try it and participate, it would work. I don't understand why other people won't get involved…"

When he was laid off after GM closed the Fremont plant, his wife baby-sat to help pay the bills.

"I used to walk around here with my face hanging to the floor. I'd go out every day and look for a job. After everything ran out, we went on welfare. I don't know how everybody else feels about welfare, but it made me very depressed.

"I don't want to go back out on that street again, believe me. When you work 28 years and then one day find yourself outside the door, you feel like they just threw you on the rubbish pile."

"I saw (the Japanese system) firsthand, and that's why I believe in it. But it's going to take time to get this old way out of our system."—Jack McCullagh

chance… We have a say, which we never had before. We have a say in what we do. There's no locked doors. All doors are open.

"At GM, I used to hate to go to work. I knew I was going to be cleaning up other people's mistakes. I'd be telling people about some problem and nothing would get done. At NUMMI, if you don't ask, it's your fault. If you ask for something, you get it."

As a team leader, he oversees five of his fellow union members on the "final" line, installing seats, hubcaps, steering wheels and carpets. Because of the leadership position, he also got a chance to spend three weeks at a Toyota auto plant in Japan.

"I saw (the system) firsthand, and that's why I believe in it," he says. "I've seen it work. But it's going to take time to get this old way out of our system.

"American people—it's not that they're lazy. They just waste motion. Americans don't understand. If you make every motion count, it's not so hard. It's the flow.

"I tell the people on the line about this. They don't want to listen. They think I want to make them work harder.

"There's more people falling back into the GM ways, and that won't work. They have to have patience… It takes trust. Mutual trust was not at General Motors, but it's at NUMMI if they let it be."

His positive approach has caught the eye of the management at the plant. At various times, he's been assigned to special teams for training and engineering work. He's had

Bill Stevens, 44, 19 years at GM, assembler at NUMMI since January 1985

It is just after work in November, and he is chain-smoking Marlboro Lights in the kitchen of his small Hayward Home, gulping coffee to stay awake. He has friend brown eyes and an easy smile, but anger is just below the surface.

"I don't know if I got the GM attitude," he says. "I'm very bitter inside about the way they're running the plant. I'm very disappointed that they told me one thing and they're doing another.

"They brainwashed me. For one week, every day for eight hours, they talk to you: 'Here's the concept. Let's work together, have these meetings, help each other.' I preached about it. I thought this is the greatest concept. Now, I feel silly…It's blood for blood out there."

Two years ago, NUMMI was the answer to his prayers. Married with two teen-age children, he had been shattered by the GM shutdown.

"During the layoff, I was lost. I was down, really depressed. I didn't know where to turn. I felt I'm not really intelligent because all I know is building cars. When I heard NUMMI was opening, I just prayed I got a job there."

He did, and he was impressed at first. The emphasis on team work and quality made sense to him. For a year, he helped out his fellow workers when they got behind

"I'm very bitter inside. I'm very disappointed that they told me one thing and they're doing another."—Bill Stevens

and made suggestions to improve efficiency in his job.

But early last year, he began to think that the company officials weren't following through on their promises. He also found that he had to come in a half-hour early every day to prepare the stock he used on his job.

"These clips I was using (to protect electrical wires from damage) were too tight and it hurt my thumb to open them. It took them eight months to fix it and that was with me harping on it every day. They kept saying, 'Don't worry about it, we're gonna take care of it.' Yeah, but who's going to take care of my thumb?

"They keep saying it's going to take time, but we're the ones feeling it out there... When I get home, I gotta take a nap. You don't know hard work until you've been at NUMMI."

Two months later, Stevens had mellowed a bit. He's had a two-week break over Christmas, and he likes his new supervisor. Whatever direction his work takes from here, he feels compelled to continue working at NUMMI as long as the plant stays open.

"It's all I know," he says. "I don't have anything else."

Old UAW local ain't what it used to be.

Reprinted with permission from the San Jose Mercury News, Monday, February 9, 1987.

By Neil Chethik
Mercury News Staff Writer

The United Auto Workers in Fremont has a new personality. In five years, it has transformed itself from a militant, anti-management union to one that places the health of the company as a top priority.

UAW leaders say the new look already has saved jobs for workers at the two-year-old New United Motor Manufacturing Inc. At the same time, it is damaging the UAW's credibility among many of its 2,200 Fremont members.

"The union is management. We really haven't got any representation," said Dewish Taitague, who works on the NUMMI assembly line.

"It's a company union," agreed Bill Stevens, another NUMMI worker. "As far as dealing with your problem—if it's not solved by the company, it's not going to be solved at all."

Such opinions have become so common at the GM-Toyota joint venture that local UAW officials, trying to boost support for the union, recently published a list of 50 benefits "you wouldn't have without a union."

"What bothers me most is that more and more people are wondering if it's worth having a union at all," said autoworker Richard Aguilar, who created the list for the monthly UAW newsletter. "To me, that's not a question we should have to ask."

Joel Smith, the national UAW representative who led the transformation at NUMMI, said the union must do a better job educating its members about its new role in the Japanese system. But he said members also must recognize that their leaders no longer can afford a confrontational approach.

"We can go into management, pound the table and demand all kinds of things," Smith said. "But then we risk this plant losing its competitive edge. We have no place to go if this (plant) goes down."

Smith had that cooperative approach in mind two years ago when he helped select a group of NUMMI workers to run for union offices, then helped negotiate a UAW-NUMMI contract based on "mutual trust and respect."

The contract offered wages that were comparable to the rest of the U.S. auto in-

INSIDE NUMMI

TROUBLES IN TRANSLATION

dustry, but it also cut deeply into the 50-year tradition of the UAW. Among other things, the union agreed to assembly-line speedups, drug testing and fewer job classifications.

Traditionally, the latter was a subject of major controversy because it drastically reduced specialization and broadened the tasks that individual workers could be required to do.

At NUMMI, however, union members almost unanimously cheered the new approach at first. Nearly all had been laid off when General Motors closed its Fremont plant in 1982, and many blamed the union's militant attitude for precipitating the GM shutdown.

Some workers still support the new union. They applaud union leaders for no longer defending irresponsible workers, and for taking an active interest in the company's success.

But in recent months, as the production pace at NUMMI has increased, so too have concerns that the UAW has moved too far from its traditional role.

The biggest complaint—from people like Taitague and Stevens—is that union officials no longer act as representatives for workers, but rather as mediators between workers and management. As a result, some workers say they're reluctant to go to the union for help.

"I know I can't depend on the union to get in there and fight for me," said Judy Ward, a NUMMI worker who last year filed a grievance that still is unresolved. "In my case, they've given me lip service, but that's about it."

Bob Silva, a union representative at NUMMI, has formed an opposition group—the People's Caucus—to challenge the current UAW leadership in the 1988 union elections at NUMMI.

Silva said he supports many provisions of the NUMMI contract, but he believes it leaves too much unsaid—and therefore, gives management too much discretion on the job.

"Mutual trust is fine, but I want to see it in writing," he said.

Silva said he believes the current UAW policy is "to keep a lid on this place" so the union will have less resistance when it tries to organize workers at the Japanese auto plants now locating in the United States.

Nationally, the UAW has lost 400,000 members, or more than a quarter of its total, since 1979. Silva said national union leaders believe NUMMI-type agreements will halt or slow down that trend by making U.S. auto plants more competitive.

Local UAW President Tony DeJesus, who led a wildcat strike at GM in 1977, now embraces the cooperative approach. He said he's abandoned his militant attitude because the NUMMI management is trustworthy.

He said NUMMI officials showed their good faith last summer when they decided against laying off NUMMI workers, even after orders for the Chevrolet Nova temporarily dropped off. Instead, he said, the company put the extra workers into training programs until car orders rebounded.

"At GM, we would have had three or four hundred people on the streets," DeJesus said.

"If this company's management ever displayed that (GM) attitude, we'd go back to what we did before," he added. "But I don't think that's going to happen."

While union-management relations have remained cooperative at NUMMI, politics at the union hall have become increasingly virulent since last February, when Financial Secretary Bob Fernandez became the highest-ranking local official to join the People's Caucus.

Most workers, however, have yet to choose sides in the political battle. Many are suspicious of both sides.

The current leaders "want to take their time. They want to grab a cup of coffee and talk about the problems," Aguilar said. "The other side wants to go for the throat—the old GM style. I think we need something in between."

12. Shreveport: No Traditions Here

A visitor to GM's Shreveport, Louisiana assembly plant often hears union members use the word "traditional" disparagingly. At Shreveport, "traditional" represents everything an enlightened management and union would want to get away from. In the summer of 1987, for example, Local 2166 President Dave Hollis complained that the shop committee was having trouble settling the local agreement because some of the committeemen "wanted to go traditional."

Shreveport is GM's flagship team concept plant. Nontraditional ways were an integral part of the plant's functioning from the time it opened in 1981. Long before NUMMI, Shreveport adopted Japanese-style methods in its "participatory" style.

Among those who have a stake in the team concept there is pride that the plant has transcended the traditional. There is disagreement, however, as to how much it has actually done so. On the continuum of team concept plants, Shreveport would rate as intermediate: not as taut as NUMMI, but with more content to the team concept than other plants such as Poletown. Shreveport has a different culture than most of team concept plants.

Shreveport's culture and style were chosen, however, solely by management, which researched other "employee-centered" companies and culled what it deemed best.

Transfers and Locals

The Shreveport plant was originally part of GM's "Southern strategy" to escape the UAW by building new plants in right-to-work states. In 1979, however, the UAW won an agreement that new plants would fall under the national GM-UAW contract. Thus GM lost the opportunity to start from scratch with both a greenfield plant and a brand new, non-union workforce. GM has done well for itself even with the existing workforce, however, initially 60 percent UAW transfers and 40 percent local hires, now about 50/50. For different reasons,

---

- *GM Shreveport Assembly*
- *Location: Shreveport, Louisiana*
- *Employment: 2,500*
- *Product: Blazer sport utility vehicles and pick-up trucks*
- *Production began: 1981*
- *Team concept began: 1981*
- *UAW Local 2166*
  Address: 6881 Industrial Loop, Shreveport, LA 71129
  Phone: 318 / 688-7103

---

both transfers and locals have embraced or learned to tolerate the team concept. Mutual suspicion between the two groups has worked to the company's advantage: management told transfers that the locals were ignorant and would need their help, while telling the locals that the transfers were lazy and had caused their own plants to shut down. Locals resent that the transfers took jobs that could have gone to their friends or relatives. Transfers resent the fact that they are behind the locals on the local seniority list, despite their years of corporate seniority.

The transfers were victims of plant closings or layoffs in their home plants. Some were courted by delegations of management and union members who travelled to recruit workers interested in the new way of working. One group of about 200 "followed their work" from the Baltimore GM plant under the provisions of Paragraph 96 of the National Agreement. They brought their full plant seniority with them. Most others transferred under Paragraph 95 or Document 28, bringing their corporate seniority for purposes of retirement and vacations, but ranking lower than most local hires in plant seniority. At one point former members of more than 60 different UAW locals worked at Shreveport; now the number is around 40.

Almost all the union officials in Local 2166 are transfers from other plants, as far flung as Baltimore, Maryland; Buffalo, New York; Lakewood, Georgia; Anderson, Indiana; and Saginaw, Michigan. Nine of eleven executive board members and five of seven on the shop committee are transfers. The local president is a Louisianan who formerly worked for Ford.

Many union officials say they are not happy with the team concept. "It sucks," was skilled trades committeeman Fred Dean's short-but-sweet comment. Rick McCarthy, a committeeman on the final line, says that general technicians (i.e., foremen, called GT's) overrule team decisions and show favoritism. Greg Hill, McCarthy's alternate, believes most transfers would get rid of the team concept if they could.

But in practice, the union at Shreveport appears quite at home with the team concept. At the union meeting held to decide which local demands to present for the 1987 contract, the demand to keep pay-for-knowledge and the participatory management style passed by a 60-40 margin.

Joe Pietrzyk (he goes by "Joe Paycheck"), who helped found the Together United Group (TUG) within Local 2166 to promote a more "traditional" brand of unionism, says, "The reason the team concept has worked so well in this plant is because the union worked so hard to make it work."

At the union's suggestion, details of team functioning were codified into the Shreveport local agreement for the first time in July 1987 (signed two months before the old contract expired). Shop Chairman J.D. Dalton says the union believed there would be fewer problems with a set way of operating. A memorandum of understanding states:

[B]oth Management and Union agree that team meetings, team duties, and individual responsibilities are a critical part of the Shreveport style of operation. In this regard, teams and individuals have duties and responsibilities to the organization which must be carried out if we are to succeed. The following guidelines are not intended to be all inclusive, therefore when circumstances arise not contemplated in these guidelines the Union and Management expect teams as well as individuals to seek solutions which meet both the need of our business and the need to recognize the worth and dignity of our people. Therefore, both Management and Union jointly encourage all Shreveport employees to participate in accordance with the following guidelines and further agree to address and review any problems or abuses of these guidelines. The parties recognize that these guidelines must be applied so that teams and individuals have sufficient flexibility to respond to the needs of the people or business as they arise and that rules, regulations, or guidelines established by one team on a shift will not apply to other teams without their input and acceptance.

Pay-for-Knowledge

Typical team size is 15, although the range is from four to 28. The jobs in each team of assemblers are broken into three groups of five for purposes of the pay-for-knowledge level progression. All employees hire in at Level III ($14.01). Learning five jobs within the team moves a worker to Level IV ($14.18); those who know ten jobs progress to Level V ($14.29). A worker who knows all the jobs in the team or 15 jobs, whichever is fewer, makes the top Level VI rate of $14.49. According to Lenny Toner, a UAW QWL rep, about 85 percent of the workers are at Level V or VI. The aim of the pay-for-knowledge system is flexibility to move workers from job to job as the need arises. In practice, however, workers are seldom shifted off their regular jobs. Each team has an "absentee replacement operator" (ARO). The existence of this job is a major difference with the Japanese-run plants, and results in less stress than in NUMMI's management-by-stress system.

If two people are absent from the team and a floater must be brought in, it occasionally happens that the floater is put on one of the easier jobs while that worker moves to the absentee's perhaps more difficult job. This is the price paid for being a Level V or VI. Anyone has the possibility of progressing to that level, but a minority choose not to do so in order to decrease the possibility of being shifted.

In the plant's earlier days management pushed workers to rotate through different jobs. Nowadays, some individuals within a team may choose to swap jobs from time to time; the team in Shreveport's tire bay rotates through jobs every few hours. But there is no institutionalized rotation for the sake of rotation. As in other plants, most Shreveport workers prefer a steady job.

Skilled Trades

The Shreveport plant has nine skilled classifications: electrician, millwright-welder, pipefitter-welder, truck repair—gas and electric, toolmaker-jig and fixture welder, carpenter, stationary engineer, painter-glazier, and tinsmith. All are paid the same maximum rate of $16.41. This was done, according to QWL trainer Lenny Toner, to keep one trade from refusing to do the work of another because the other trade was paid more.

When production is running, there are essentially no functioning lines of demarcation; management may cross-utilize trades workers as it sees fit. Only on weekends, when called in for maintenance work, do workers function solely within their own trades. Even then, if there are not enough volunteers from a particular trade, management may call in other tradespersons to "augment" the regular ones. A carpenter, for example, may be called in to augment the electrician force.

Fred Smiley is an alternate committeeman representing skilled trades on the second shift. He says the skilled trades' biggest problem is "job descriptions that are not specific: where a millwright stops and a pipefitter takes over. During the normal 40-hour week skilled trades can flow out quite a ways, but on Saturdays the company is limited. That's when we get the lines of demarcation complaints, when we come in on a Monday."

All training is available to all trades; a painter may take a robotics class, for example.

Team Coordinators

Team coordinators are variously described as "go-fer," "junior foreman," "babysitter," and "facilitator." The duties are similar in many respects to those of a classification which exists in traditional assembly plants, often called "utility man" or "group leader." Coordinators receive a premium of 35 cents an hour over their level rate and are not assigned a regular job on the line. They must know all the jobs in the team. They provide relief for trips to the bathroom or the medical department or when another team member must attend a meeting. They take over a worker's job when he or she is training on a different job for purposes of pay-for-knowledge. They unlock tools and gloves before work. They attend weekly meetings of all the coordinators in their department, run by the department superintendent, and weekly meetings of all the coordinators in the plant, run by the production manager. They chair the team's own weekly meetings.

Many former and current coordinators interviewed at Shreveport expressed frustration with the job. One woman said, "I never knew what I was going to be doing from one hour to the next." No one else in her team was willing to be coordinator, so she eventually transferred out of the department to get away from the job. Another ex-coordinator says, "You're in the middle between the GT and the people. The GT tries to pump information from you, and the people are mad at you because you're running errands for the GT and can't let them go to medical."

Former coordinator Paul Martinski says the worst thing about the job was going to meetings two or three times a week. His replacement, Eugene Williams, likes the meetings. He thinks the worst thing about the job is getting used by your fellow team members. "You relieve one and it's like a chain reaction, they all want to go. Sometimes there's a jealousy."

The main motivation for taking the coordinator job appears to be the freedom afforded by not having a regular job on the line, and, as of the 1987 contract, the extra 35 cents per hour. Formerly the differential was 10 cents. Union officials predicted that the increase would cause more competition for the coordinator job, which had often gone begging.

Becoming coordinator is not a road into management, since due to GM's white-collar cutbacks, GT slots have not been filled from hourly ranks for some time.

Team Offices

Each team must choose its own coordinator, recording secretary, quality coordinator, safety coordinator, timekeeper, salvage coordinator, general stores coordinator, and planner. Their terms of office are up to the team, with a minimum of two months, and they may be removed if the team decides to do so. The selection process is by consensus, or, as several workers described it, "whoever wants it." In some teams a coordinator will remain for a year or more, if the team members are satisfied with his or her functioning and no one else wants the job. Sometimes no one will volunteer for the job, and the lowest-seniority member gets stuck. Sometimes no one volunteers for the other jobs, and the team coordinator must carry out those functions as well. According to QWL staffer Jack Ross, one survey showed 40 percent of the teams to be without a secretary.

Teams also select members, usually in rotation, to participate in the "overnight drive" program: each day management releases a number of vehicles for workers to take home and test drive. The overnight drivers report back to the daily plant-wide audit meeting on how the truck handled.

Each GT is responsible for two or three teams. Many of the foreman's duties have been taken over by various team members. The timekeeper, for instance, checks and corrects each member's hours on the GT's computer and maintains the overtime equalization chart. But it is the team coordinator who is put in the position of being a "junior foreman." Joe Pietrzyk says

that when he was a coordinator, his GT was responsible for two teams; the GT instructed Joe that each of them would run one of the teams.

GT Larry Spinney, who directs three teams with a total of 38 members in the trim department, formerly worked as a GM foreman in Flint, Michigan where he supervised 54 workers. He was asked how his job was different without a general foreman above him (GT's report directly to the department superintendent). Spinney said, "Basically, I am a general foreman."

Team Rules

In the 1987 contract it was decided that teams would commit their rules to writing within 30 days. Rules are to be re-discussed and changed if desired every January and July. Asked how difficult it is to get team rules changed, one coordinator said, "The GT has a lot to say about it." Team rules include:

1. How to fill open jobs within the team. The most common method is by plant seniority, but some teams use team seniority. Sometimes particularly arduous jobs are filled by a method that allows the first person on that job to be the first one off it. In the paint department, for example, some teams use "booth seniority"—first in the paint booth is first out when an opening occurs.

2. How long the team coordinator and other positions serve.

3. Which job the former coordinator takes when a new coordinator takes over. Usually this is a simple swap.

4. How to rotate attending the daily audit and test-driving company vehicles.

5. When the team meeting is held (before or after work).

In theory the practice of "let the teams decide" sounds democratic and empowering. In practice, however, there are serious flaws in the exercise of team power. For one thing, as can be seen from the list above, most of the things teams may decide range from the small to the trivial. Second, lack of uniformity from team to team means that there are no longer any such things as union standards. Third, the supposed existence of team power permits both management and union to slough off the problems of an aggrieved member: "There's nothing I can do, the team decided. Take it to the team." Fourth, through some quirk or unfamiliarity with union principles, a team may democratically make a decision which discriminates against some of its members or takes away some of their rights.

For example, in its new rules adopted in September 1987, Team 25 on the final line set aside 9-11 p.m. every night for "level progression." During that time the coordinator would relieve team members so that they could learn new jobs and move to a higher pay level. But the team also stipulated that during those two hours workers should not call for the committeeman, go to the bathroom, or go to medical.

"Team power" to set rules could be an advantage for workers if they were organized through the union. This is discussed further in Chapter 5.

Team Meetings

The teams meet for a half hour per week, usually after work. Members are paid overtime for attending. Estimates of attendance ranged from 75 to more than 90 percent. One member of an 18-person team, for example, said that two members of his team never came and two came only sporadically. According to all sources, many workers come because "it's the easiest time-and-a-half you ever made." Attendance is higher around model change time or when management changes the model mix, as members have an interest in seeing how the work is to be rearranged.

Attendance at team meetings was made voluntary in the 1984 contract, and it was agreed that no employee would try to convince others not to attend. This clause was followed by a proviso that any "concerted action" of this nature could result in a mutual agreement to make meetings mandatory again. Decisions made in team meetings are binding on those who choose not to attend.

A worker who does not attend meetings is less likely to receive favors, such as excused days off, from the GT. There appears to be little peer pressure to attend, however. Attendance does not seem to break down along militant/non-militant lines. Rather the division seems to be between those who want to get involved and those who don't.

Local 2166 officials point with pride to the voluntary clause. They seem to feel that it solves most of the problems union members may have with the team con-

cept: if an individual doesn't like team meetings, he doesn't have to come. But while making meetings voluntary is an important benefit for individual members, it is not particularly helpful to the union as a whole unless the union makes use of it. If the union were using the team structure to organize, it could, for example, urge members to boycott team meetings when there was a need to pressure management. As it is, team meetings are only a small part of the team concept as a whole. The team structure remains undisturbed by the few dissenters who choose not to come.

The team meeting agenda usually includes reports from the team coordinator, quality coordinator, safety coordinator, and GT. The team coordinator reports the information from the weekly department-wide and plant-wide team coordinators' meetings. This will include how production is doing, the supply of trucks the dealers have on hand, changes in the model, and how well the plant is doing against other plants within GM.

The quality coordinator reports on results of the weekly and daily audits, in particular "discrepancies" found by the management auditors that originated in the team. He or she will tell what is being done to correct those problems. The safety coordinator reports on any accidents or injuries in the department.

If it is near model change time, there will be a report from the planner. This worker is chosen by the team to help implement job redesign required by changes in the trucks or in the mix of pickups and Blazers. Dan Maurin, a former foundry worker from Buffalo, New York, says, "We had a heck of a time getting a planner in our team, because everybody always jumps on the planner. The plant just went to a 50/50 model mix, and they brought the planners in on overtime to discuss the jobs, rearrange them. They give you the illusion that you're participating, but they already know just how they want to do it.

"People do it [volunteer for planner] for the overtime, but along with that comes a lot of people getting upset with you when their jobs get changed. And somehow the planner's own job never gets changed."

The GT's report will confirm information given by the coordinator and tell how certain problems are being straightened out. He or she may announce from time to time that "we need to be more efficient" and that a job must be eliminated from the team. GT Larry Spinney explained the process this way:

> In trim we're becoming more efficient, eliminating operations, and we're not losing quality. The people set up their own jobs. We'll make a presentation to the team: "This is the efficiency of this team"— that's the minutes per hour on your job description. Our goal is to have every job set up so that they're working 48 to 52 minutes out of every hour. For example, if the line was running at one per minute, and it took you 52 seconds to do your job, that's 52 minutes per hour.
>
> So in the presentation we tell them, if every oper-

Very flexible — now kiss your job goodbye!

ation in the team was set at 48-52, it would take x amount of people to do this team's work. That figure could be 12, but there's 15 currently in the team. So they need to eliminate 3.

They have resources they can call in—reliability, the GT [reliability is a management department that deals with parts specifications, proper tools, job sequence]. People will say, "Well, I can take this on my job," and someone else will take another part of it. It's worked out by the team planners.

David Smith, who installs rear bumpers on the second shift, explained what happened when management wanted to cut one job from his team:

> The team experimented with different ways to get rid of the work. We all switched jobs and came up with four or five different plans for cutting a job. At my old plant, management would just have told us to do it their way.[1]

In September 1987 management held departmental meetings to inform workers of annual goals. On the final line, for example, the goal was to eliminate six workers on each shift (two had already been cut that month when the plant changed the model mix). The previous year nine were eliminated on each shift.

During the open discussion period of the team meeting, members may bring up requests for days off, problems on the job such as material not arriving on time, or safety or housekeeping problems such as oily floors. They are not to discuss contractual matters, although virtually anything—safety or oily floors, for example—could be and is a contractual question. Formal grievances are not discussed, however. It is the union's position that absenteeism is "not the team's business," and there is little peer pressure either in the team meeting or on the line over absenteeism. Jim Hodge, the union vice-president, says, "Some of them tried it when the plant first opened up. There was one gal who had a sick daughter, she was retarded, with heart problems. People tried to get on her about missing work, and she told them to stick it."

The 1987 contract says that decisions made at a team meeting are binding and not to be changed by the union or management "unless the change is due to a sound business purpose or the decision is contrary to the National or Local Agreement."

Good Jobs and Transferring

In some team concept plants a common complaint has been that there are fewer good jobs—jobs off the line such as material handling or janitor, or less physical jobs such as inspection, or more varied jobs such as repair. This is partly because many of these jobs have been done away with as separate jobs, and their duties added to assemblers'. Assemblers in team concept plants are expected to keep their areas clean, for example, which cuts back on the number of sweepers. Also, when there is only one classification, it is impossible to move into a more desirable classification by seniority.

In the Shreveport plant there is only one non-skilled classification, "technician," for all production jobs, but there are eight departments—five on the line: cab, chassis, paint, trim, and final, and three off the line: material, salvage, and environmental (janitorial). Workers can transfer to more desirable departments by seniority—e.g., from the paint department to material.

There are no inspection or repair jobs classified as such, except for two special off-line repair sections called Final Reprocess and Paint Reprocess, which management wants to reduce. Some inspection is taken over by regular assemblers: if a worker knows that he or she has made a mistake—leaving a screw loose, for instance—he puts a colored sticker that says "Do It Right" on the car so the error will be caught down the line. Inspection and repair functions on the line are usually combined into one job; one job title, for example, is "quality assurance and repair." Such an operator must inspect the job and either repair it or write it up for reprocess.

It is possible to transfer to a different department or to a different team within the same department. It is not possible to bump a lower-seniority person off a job (except through shift preference) or to transfer to a particular job—only to a particular team.

It works this way: Thelma doesn't like many of the jobs in her own team and scouts around for a better team. She finds one in her own department—the "hot start" team—and another one in the trim department. She puts in two transfer requests at the Personnel Department (she can file a maximum of three requests to a different department and two within the same department). If an opening occurs in either of her desired teams due to a sick leave, a transfer out, a quit, or a discharge, she will be moved to that team if she is the applicant with the highest seniority (but applicants from within the department take precedence over those from outside the department).

The team will first fill its opening from among its own members, according to its particular team rule for doing so (e.g., plant seniority). Subsequent openings caused by this switch are usually filled in the same manner, so that there may be quite a bit of shuffling before the process is over. Thelma gets last pick of the jobs in the team. She can then hope that one of the better jobs in the team will eventually open up. If she gets one she likes, she knows that she can keep it unless she goes on sick leave for more than 30 days (this creates a permanent opening) or is bumped off her shift by someone with more seniority. There appear to be more opportunities for movement at Shreveport than in a traditional plant—although not necessarily to better jobs. The ability to shift around within the team each time there is an opening is one kind of movement. The rule that you lose your job after 30 days on sick leave is harsh, although it creates openings for others. In addition, management is constantly redoing jobs. If 51 percent of the content of your job is moved to another team, you get to go with it and bump someone from that team.

Worker Involvement in Quality

Lenny Toner says with some pride that Shreveport is "a low tech plant," with only 28 robots. "Our creed is to develop the potential of our human resources," he says. "Quality is achieved with people, not with machines." Thus Shreveport management's philosophy is to instill responsibility for quality into every worker. The QWL staff's "Quality Is Not Foreign" training for every employee in the plant, described below, was one part of this. More important, however, is the daily emphasis on quality and the means by which it is achieved.

These means do not include allowing each operator a generous amount of time to do the job. Transfers from GM's Southgate, California and Lakewood, Georgia assembly plants complain of the increased workload. GT Larry Spinney says that the jobs have more work on them than in his former plant in Flint. *Business Week* reported that in the week ending August 2, 1987, Shreveport's labor hours per vehicle were the lowest in GM—and equal to NUMMI.[2]

Shreveport's quality is high, according to GM's internal ratings. Shreveport, along with another GM truck plant in Moraine, Ohio is on a par with NUMMI, higher than any car assembly plant operated solely by GM.[3]

As in other GM team concept plants, management's twice daily audit of randomly chosen vehicles is reported on at an open meeting attended by both salaried and hourly employees. The quality coordinator from each team is supposed to attend (as with many of the team "offices," the chance to get off the line for a break is an incentive for taking the job). The meeting is chaired by one of the "Quality Analysts"; these are hourly workers chosen by management and the committee-person in each department. They are the chief trouble-shooters for quality problems in their departments.

The day shift audit on August 14, 1987, was attended by about 50 people. The plant had failed to reach its goal of an average of 3.55 "discrepancies" per vehicle; its score was 4.50. Discrepancies include loose bolts or screws, fenders that don't fit quite right, and "dings" (tiny dents). The discrepancies in the eight audited vehicles were described one by one, department by department. The quality coordinator from each team where a discrepancy occurred introduced him or herself ("I'm Jill from Team 21") and reported on what had gone wrong.

Usually the cause of the defect was unclear, but there was one formulation that most coordinators used: they blamed the discrepancy on an operator error, but defended the operator in question as a good worker. The representative from Team 57 in trim, for example, said, "Usually the operator is very competent. We will get back with him." The person from Team 31 said, "The operator has been on that job for five or six years and is real good. It could be the torque in the gun." A representative from chassis, which got a round of ap-

THE QUALIGATOR

The Shreveport plant has a mascot, the "qualigator." In the plant cafeteria a stuffed alligator representing the qualigator squats in a glass cage. Until recently the qualigator symbol appeared on the back pockets of the company-issued jeans.

In the 1987 negotiations the union won Local Demand #130: the right for workers to choose either the qualigator or the GM emblem on their pants, to be placed on the waistband rather than the pocket.

plause for scoring .38 against a goal of .50, said, "This is an operator-sensitive area. The operators have been consulted."

The audit ended with the Quality Analyst warning that "Moraine's last audit was 2.8; I don't have to tell you people any more than that." The Moraine plant builds the same pick-up as Shreveport. The meeting lasted 12 minutes.

The meeting, then, was essentially a recitation of operator (occasionally supplier) errors in different parts of the plant, accompanied by promises and exhortations to "watch these jobs a lot closer and try to do better." Although it was not evident that there were any serious consequences for individual workers who were spotlighted, the session had the effect of pinpointing blame on individuals and inculcating the notion that the welfare of the plant was the personal responsibility of each hourly worker.

Shreveport management would like to do away with the "I just come to work, do my job, and mind my own business" attitude. They realize that they cannot do so entirely, and the 1984 agreement to make team meetings voluntary was a recognition of this fact. Most workers firmly believe it is their right to take this attitude, if they so choose. The notion that one should be one's brother's keeper *on management's behalf* and as part of the job description is a new one for American workers.

Why Workers Accept the Team Concept

At the August 14 audit the trim department scored 1.13 against a goal of .70. One of the quality coordinators said, "Trim isn't looking very good this morning, but we're not going to hold our heads down, because tomorrow is another day."

It appears that the majority of the Shreveport workers are truly concerned with quality in a way that workers have never been encouraged or even allowed to be in a traditional plant. Although there are many exceptions, the workforce as a whole has adopted both management's definition of quality and management's drive for efficiency because of a deep-seated anxiety about the future of the plant.

Although the plant is only six years old and consistently ranks first or second in quality, efficiency and attendance, Shreveport workers do not feel secure. Ingrained in the culture of the plant is the notion that it could be chosen for closing at any time if it does not measure up against its competition—other GM plants.

This overriding fear exists despite the fact that there has never been a layoff at Shreveport. Any job cuts made possible by improved efficiency have been handled by attrition. In the 1987 contract

> management reaffirmed its long standing policy that the provisions of the National Agreement notwithstanding: no individual be laid off as the result of improved operational effectiveness gained through employee participation.

In August 1987 union officials said there were 30 surplus people on the payroll, and that 40 more would become surplus in September when the plant shifted from production of two-thirds Blazers and one-third pickups to a 50/50 mix—the Blazer requires more labor because of the many options available. (In the past, however, when the mix changed in the other direction, from 50/50 to two-thirds Blazers, jobs were not added.) Management eliminated jobs from the line in September, but ended up without surplus workers because of sick leaves and transfers to other plants.

THE ROLE OF THE QWL STAFF

As in most other team concept plants, the Shreveport operation includes no separate program for volunteer workers to meet in QWL circles. Such circles are the main aspect of QWL programs in traditional plants. There is a full-time QWL staff, however, consisting of four union and three management employees—much smaller, on the union side, than in a traditional GM plant. Union QWL coordinators were trained in the UAW-GM Internal Organizational Consultant Curriculum through the UAW-GM Human Resources Center.

A major part of the QWL staff's mission is to see that the team concept is implemented properly. The QWL staff has done training for team recording secretaries, for example. Jack Ross, one of the two union QWL coordinators on Shreveport's second shift, believes that the company and the union should have implemented the team concept 30 years ago. He says, "We monitor the team meetings to make sure they're not yelling at each other. The teams or the committeeman can request us as a resource. We're there to help them with their process of problem solving. The biggest thing the teams *don't* do is get their resources involved in time.

"Part of our job is to dilute the grievance procedure. We can mediate between the GT and the employee if it's not something contractual. Or if there's a personal conflict between two union members, we can go in to act as a facilitator."

The QWL staff keeps statistics such as overall plant attendance figures and team coordinators' attendance at department meetings.

Ross and the other QWL staff put the entire plant, in groups of 30, through an eight-hour program called "Quality Is Not Foreign." The course begins with a videotape of economist Barry Bluestone (son of former UAW vice-president Irving Bluestone) exhorting union members to undertake a quality campaign. "We need to set industry share goals for ourselves," Bluestone recommends. "We need to be involved in designing and reviewing [cars]. The key to the '87 contract is to rebuild confidence in what we build."

The program hammered home the Crosby College (a Florida school that conducts management programs) definition of quality: "conformance to requirements." The performance standard, the curriculum argues, must be "zero defects." At the end of the course, participants are asked to write down what they can do to implement the "7 C's of quality: comprehension, competence, communication, correction, commitment, culture change, and continuance."

The QWL staff is also responsible for a myriad of joint company-union activities, from a horseshoes competition to tour guide training (3,700 people visited the plant in 1986) to pre-supervision training.

Like many of the QWL staffers in traditional plants, those at Shreveport have adopted a management outlook on most issues. Jack Ross is a transfer from Saginaw, Michigan. Each summer his wife and children return to Michigan while he stays in Shreveport. Yet Ross believes the fact that half the workforce is made up of transfers who fear for their job security is "a plus for this plant." GM's biggest problem, he says, is that so many of its suppliers are in-house.

Ross approves of IBM's participatory management policy—"a hell of a program." Asked if IBM is a non-union company, Ross says he doesn't know.

The best thing about the team concept, Ross believes, is that it got union and management communicating. The worst thing? "How they communicate."

Surplus workers have been given training, both in technical and "team-building" skills, or, more often, have become "floaters" till an opening is found. There is no JOBS Bank as such.

Anxiety about job security works for both local hires and transfers. For the locals, the job at GM is usually the best-paying job they've ever had, and the best-paying factory job in the area. The average weekly manufacturing wage in the area was $446.01[4] in August 1987, compared to $576.20 for a day shift GM production worker who worked no overtime except the team meeting. A GM job is also a prestige job. Workers say that when transfers first moved down to Shreveport, they found the best way to meet women was to wear their company shirts with the emblem on the pocket.

The transfers are determined not to be the victims of another plant closing. They have moved once to retain their GM seniority, and they don't want to uproot their families again.

Jack Ross, the QWL staffer, explains, "They lost their families and homes once and they don't want to do it again. They got scared, and that's why they're involved more." Joe Pietrzyk explains the effects of the trauma of moving: "Your wife's mad at you and your kids are mad at you because they don't want to be down here. You don't know your neighbors and all the locals are giving you a hard time about your accent, your 'brogue.' So you don't need another aggravation in the plant. You don't want to be fighting everything 24 hours a day. Your committeeman tells you 'be glad you have a job.' So you try to accept team concept. But then management goes back to traditional ways and it turns into a one-way street."

Attitudes Toward Team Concept

Workers at the Shreveport plant display a wide range of attitudes toward the team concept, varying from "this is great—it's like family" to "it sucks," with all shades in between. Most union members interviewed shared one complaint, however: that management was not living up to its promises about the team concept, and sliding back into "traditional" ways.

Shreveport workers, including management, view the team concept as a package which includes all aspects of the plant's philosophy and functioning. That package is supposed to include: 1) an atmosphere where workers are encouraged to have input into decisions and status differences are broken down, and 2) an atmosphere in which "we're all in this together" as the plant strives to beat the competition. In other words, in return for being treated with courtesy, workers are to sincerely adopt management's goals for the plant—even when this means more work for them.

The commitment to equality includes a single plant cafeteria and parking lot. Management personnel do not wear white shirts and ties (but neither, says Lenny Toner with a grin, do they wear blue jeans). Beyond these symbols, the culture of equality wears thin.

Jim Hodge, vice-president of Local 2166, says that the team concept has benefited the workers because it has saved the corporation money. "The teams take care of their own things—there's no stockchasers, the material people bring stock directly to the operator. There's less supervisors, they do their own timekeeping. Plus there's the blanket pay scale."

But Hodge thinks that the team concept in Shreveport is "weaker now than when it first started. I don't see that big a difference with other plants. The foremen now have a bad attitude, and it's tearing down the team concept. Now engineering does a time study and the team has got no say-so."

Rick McCarthy is a committeeman on the final line. His district, he says, is 75 percent transfers like himself. He worked in a foundry in Buffalo, and he finds the transfers from assembly plants more likely to accept the new system. Combined with switching from a foundry to an assembly line, he finds "the new philosophy of working is too hard." In his opinion, the worst thing about the team concept is that the GT overrules team decisions: "As long as the team meeting is going his way, it's okay. But there's still favoritism, who gets the days off, things like that."

Eugene Williams is a local hire who recently became a team coordinator in the repair area. Formerly he was an orthopedic technician in a hospital. He says, "I'm for the team concept. But then I only know one way. I didn't know GM." Williams too complains of new supervisors who don't live up to team precepts. "The new management that's transferred in is not always trained in team concept like the ground floor people—they get back to thinking traditional, they don't know your first name. They'll tell people under them something to tell you; they haven't been trained in the team concept way to be relaxed."

Dan Maurin, who along with Joe Pietrzyk is a founder of TUG, says, "To make this thing work they'd need to teach the management, but they're trying to make it work just with the hourly people. The GT has the attitude 'his way or no way,' 'I'm the boss.' Of course it makes people resentful when they preach participative management and then come in and say 'this is how we do it.' It's the traditional way with a new name, I guess."

Ergonomics in job design was touted as part of the team concept. Maurin says that ergonomics was used as a pretext, however, to eliminate a job in his area. "It was a job where you had to stoop down, but it was hard to do and it was hard on your knees. So they rearranged it and took elements of that job and put them onto other jobs.

"When I first started in 1984, you'd go to your team meeting and say you wanted Friday off. The foreman would say, 'Dan needs Friday off, no problem, but we have to make sure the rest of the team comes in, so when it's your turn we can do the same thing for you.' Now, you're wasting your time if you ask the team. I go right to the GT, because it goes through him anyway."

Some workers, of course, are enthusiastic. Nancy Kirk, who has worked at the plant for three and a half years, says, "This is great, it's like family, everybody pitches in. If you get past your station they help you catch up." Kirk was the Quality Analyst for the Final Line for six months, a job which she thoroughly enjoyed. Complimented on her knowledge of the production process, she replies, "It's my life."

She also spent three months as an instructor in the QWL staff's "Quality Is Not Foreign" program. She is proud of the attitude change the class was able to effect in some of the transfers: "They'd start talking about how they did it at home and I'd tell them, 'We're not home now.' Their outlook after an eight-hour class was a complete reversal."

From a GT's point of view, the worst thing about team concept is that it takes longer to get decisions made and get things done. Larry Spinney says this is outweighed by the best thing about team concept: "When a decision is made, everyone is in agreement." He gives as an example team cooperation in eliminating jobs.

Joe Pietrzyk says, "I came down here with an open mind. In theory team concept seems like a good idea, but in practice it's the same old garbage, more like a management concept. At the New Directions conference in Oklahoma City [New Directions is a caucus within UAW Region 5], it was brought up how can we stop team concept. I said, 'How can you stop team concept when the plants that have got team concept are number one in efficiency?' "

Pietrzyk believes that 95-98 percent of the transfers don't like team concept "because of the competitive edge they always put on you." He believes life under team concept is harder for the committeemen—he was an alternate his first year in the plant—because a worker with a complaint is told, "The team agreed on it, if you disagree, too bad."

Pietrzyk believes that team concept does have one advantage, at least for low seniority people: more opportunities to move from job to job. He contrasts this with the situation his twin brother Jerry found himself in—also a transfer with over 20 years' seniority, but to a traditional plant. Jerry, with little plant seniority, was stuck on a bad job in GM's Leeds, Missouri plant with little hope of improvement.

Two Referendums

One measure of the team concept's popularity was two referendums held in 1982 and 1984. In 1982, the union held a referendum inside the plant on whether the bargaining committee should try to get rid of the pay-for-knowledge system in the next contract. It was seen as a referendum on the team concept. The union maintained a neutral position, and a big majority voted to keep it. The ballot was worded, however, so that some workers thought voting against pay-for-knowledge meant voting for a strike.

By 1984 there was more dissatisfaction. In a similar referendum, pay-for-knowledge passed by only 35 votes. In the team meetings GT's urged members to remember to vote, "so they must have been worried," says Jim Hodge. Union officials attribute the closeness of the vote partially to the "no" votes of 600 transfers who, that same week, returned to their home plant in Lakewood, Georgia. "The 1982 agreement was weak," says Hodge. "It had practically nothing in it. Some people thought that if they threw out team concept and got classifications they'd get better jobs. So the 1984 vote sent a valid message to management to clean it up." It was in the 1984 agreement that management agreed to make team meetings voluntary.

It is difficult to describe an "average" attitude for a "typical" Shreveport worker. It does seem clear, however, that there are fewer workers than in most GM plants with either a militant union attitude or an "I don't care about the job, I'm just here to collect my pay" attitude. Dan Maurin says, "Where I work people don't want to play these team concept games, they don't want to be hassled, but they do the best job that they can. They just want to do their job and go home." In any case, apparently no one feels that it is worthwhile to buck the team concept itself. It appears to be in Shreveport to stay.

Joe Pietrzyk sums up the experience of many transfers: "Either you accept team concept or you don't. And sooner or later, you will."

Team Concept and the Union

Of paramount concern to many local union leaders throughout the UAW is the effect of team concept on the union, both locally and nationally. Team concept may appear to save jobs when the plant is under threat of closing, but are they jobs at union standards? Is the UAW able to survive in more than name only, in a plant supposedly dedicated to worker-management harmony and opposed to the adversarial relationship?

Both opponents and advocates of team concept at Shreveport say that Local 2166 has moved toward a more cooperative relationship with management. Lenny Toner says that before 1984 the relationship was not good: "They were adversaries and reactive as opposed to proactive. Reactive is the way we used to be when I was a committeeman in Baltimore—we *knew* management was going to screw up. A proactive relationship means you talk things over first."

At the same time that the union moves closer to management, workers say that management is moving *away* from the team concept, in the sense of becoming less participatory and more autocratic. It appears that both perceptions are true. At the same time that management is becoming sloppy about preserving some of the positive promises of the team concept—respect for workers' opinions, for example—the union is becoming more and more willing to see management's point of view.

Worker participation in arranging the work illustrates this point: workers say that the team planner's job is now just a fig leaf, that in fact the industrial engineers already know how they want the jobs set up before the planner gets involved. At the same time, the union, as of the signing of the 1987 contract, is committed in writing to "operating efficiency." Which means that a responsible planner should not protest job eliminations anyway.

When the plant opened many workers—at least those with prior UAW experience—were suspicious of team concept. The 1984 referendum on pay-for-knowledge revealed their frustration and was an attempt to do something about the union's direction. But without a conscious plan for organizing, the union fell back on the only plan that did exist—the company's. As the International union moved more and more towards an actively collaborative stance, the Shreveport local was left with no other rudder. Indeed, union leaders seemed to take a rather passive view even of local negotiations. Rather than playing a leadership role by proposing demands that would benefit the membership as a whole, Bargaining Chairman J.D. Dalton told a union meeting that he had initiated no demands in 1987 local bargaining besides those submitted by members.

Watchdog

Among those most disturbed by the direction of the union at Shreveport are members of an informal grouping called the "Together United Group" (TUG). Formed in January 1987, TUG sees itself as a watchdog within the union. It meets monthly before union meetings, and issues leaflets about both local and national UAW events, subscribing to the *Detroit Free Press* to keep informed about national issues. TUG pressured the union to publish its meeting minutes and financial reports in the union newspaper.

TUG members are as concerned as other Shreveport workers about quality. They protested when the shop chairman appointed a plant-wide "Quality Advisor" who had no experience with quality control. (The committeeman chosen had 32 years seniority and was married to a GT.) TUG's leaflet argued:

> At a time when Job Security and Quality go hand in hand it is most important that the most qualified person be selected. Ask yourself, does a person that has 32 years and can retire whenever he wants have the drive to assure this membership that everything possible will be done to improve Quality to the highest degree... ?

TUG members circulated a petition requesting that local leaders let members apply for the Quality Advisor position, as they had for other union appointments such as health and safety rep. They had gathered 700 signatures in two days when TUG member Dan Maurin was stopped by management while talking to day shift workers and told to leave the plant. He was called to the Labor Relations office that evening on his own shift, and told that he could not circulate an "illegal petition," even on his own time. All petitions or flyers would have be to okayed by the shop chairman and the plant manager, but not to bother, because they would not be approved. "We can't allow this," Labor Relations said. "This is not what we're about."

TUG believes that the grievance procedure has become ineffective. Maurin explains what TUG wants the union to be: "If you're going to be committeeman do it right. Here, if you put in a committeeman call, the committeeman will get the GT's side first, and then come and tell you why they can't help you. You'll see them fraternizing with the GT, going down the aisle laughing and slapping each other on the back. That never would have happened in Buffalo. "If you've got a problem your zone man will tell you, 'Just be glad you're working.' Or one of their favorite sayings is: 'You've got to think of the team. The team comes first.' It's gotten so people don't bother to put in a grievance because they'll tell you in advance that it won't do any good."

Lenny Toner says that there are fewer committeeman calls at Shreveport than in traditional plants. One young second-shift worker said, "The union doesn't want to stand up for the people. The committeeman will tell you 'you messed up' right in front of the GT's face." He allowed, however, that the company was less quick to hand out discipline in Shreveport than in his home plant.

Maurin and Pietrzyk are critical of the new union contract, ratified July 20, 1987. For the first time it spells out details of team functioning, such as duties of the various coordinators (see the excerpts at the end of this chapter). Both management and union officials say that this was done to establish more uniformity. The rules created by individual teams were also required to be reviewed and written down. TUG fears that spelled-out rules of team functioning could be used unfairly by the company.

"What I'm afraid of," says Maurin, "is I don't want to be in Labor Relations with them telling me I violated a team rule, when the rules are being violated by the GT's every day. It's just one more rule they can get you on."

Not Convenient

Within a month of the new contract's ratification the shop committee had proposed to modify it. Management had let a new clause slip in which it later decided was not convenient. This clause said that a one-hour difference in starting time would constitute a different shift. The clause was welcomed by some higher-seniority workers because it gave them an opportunity to bump to the paint mixer job, held by 14 people. This was a highly desirable job requiring a great deal of skill and training. It began one hour before regular starting time. Management protested that if bumping took place it would take six months to train new paint mixers, quality could be affected, etc.

The shop committee put out the following memo:

The bargaining committee has carefully considered the impact that would result from repetitive turnover in Team 32-03. Due to the complex nature of the work performed and the long training cycles involved in becoming proficient on operations in this team, repetitive turnover would adversely impact paint quality, which in turn would generate greater repair and lead to production inefficiencies.

Deterioration in our quality and cost in today's competitive environment would only serve to jeopardize the long term security of our members...

Based on the foregoing, the shop committee requests membership support in waiving the one hour starting time constituting a shift preference move for Team 32-03 (paint mix and process attendants—Paint Department).

A special union meeting was called to vote on waiving the clause; the change passed in a 40-minute meeting between shifts, 49-36.

Dan Maurin pointed out that if quality were the concern, it would have been possible to keep the experienced mixers on while training new ones. Maurin said, "They complain about taking so long to train people, but that's what training is all about. They act like there are only 14 smart people in the whole plant.

"Our International Rep said if we left it in it would have to go to arbitration and the union didn't win many of those. The company wanted it changed back, so it was changed back. But what if the union was the one that came back three weeks after the contract was signed

WHAT'S IT CALLED WHEN THE **MINORITY** RULES?

FREE ENTERPRISE.

KONOPACKI
HUCK KONOPACKI
LABOR CARTOONS '85

wanting to change something that was to their detriment? No way the company would have gone along with that."

Using Team Concept for the Union

On paper, at least, the team concept could have some built-in advantages for union organization. Jim Hodge says, "The membership could use team concept to their advantage more than they do. Every day we've got the Creed and the Twenty Points, management'll put that on you every time they get in a corner. Turn it around and use it on them. If the foreman's doing something you don't like, not even necessarily a violation of the agreement, get the team together and nail him in the team meeting. It gets back to group persecution." The Shreveport contract would even seem to facilitate team self-organization with its provision that "teams may request their GT to not be present for a portion or all of a Team Meeting."

In fact there are instances where teams at Shreveport have functioned this way. Hodge says when he worked in Team 63 on the sheet metal line in the plant's early days "we used the team concept for *us*."

"When I was coordinator I was almost a committeeman," says Hodge.

Three new workers who were to work on the second shift when it started up in 1983 were placed in Team 63 for training. "One of them was a black lady," Jim Hodge tells it. "She'd been an English teacher and she'd never worked in a factory before. So the team discussed it and we decided to put her on sealant. That was an easy job and we thought that would let her get her 90 days in.

"A new GT comes in, and he wants to put her on the front bumper job. We tell him she's not going to be able to do it and he says, 'If she can't do it I'll fire her ass.' It was just a sign of power.

"So I go to the superintendent. This is something you'd never hear of in the old plant. And I say, 'Just tell me this, do we have team concept here or not?' And he says we do. So I tell him what his GT is trying to do to this lady, and overriding the team. Well, I don't know what the superintendent said to the GT, but he comes back and tells me, 'Put her anywhere you goddamn want.'

"I think about half the teams would have done something like we did, and the rest would just put the low man on the hardest job. It depends on the leadership within the group; in any group someone will be a leader. Usually it's someone with union background."

Apparently such events are rare at Shreveport now. Nowadays, Hodge says, anyone aspiring to union office would avoid becoming a team coordinator— "they'd label you a red apple boy."

Hodge also tells of an incident on the motor line in 1986. There were four teams of about 11 members each. Management suddenly announced that they would be consolidated into three teams, with no preplanning

or team input. Workers protested by wearing black armbands, as if to mourn the death of the team concept. Union representatives got involved, warning management, "Just let us know if you're planning to quit team concept." They got the change postponed. The consolidation did happen eventually, however, because, Jim Hodge says, it is part of management's overall drive to cut jobs.

Although the union has allowed its role to diminish, it still commands allegiance. Although Louisiana is a right-to-work state, there is only one non-member in the entire plant (a transfer). Attendance at Local 2166's union meetings is 75-100 in a typical month, not different from other locals of its size.

And some members express strong loyalty to the union, or at least to union goals. A woman who had previously been an OCAW member for 18 years said, "I wouldn't want to work in a plant without a union. Without it management do what they want when they want, they make all the rules and break all the rules—we hire you, we fire you. I immediately wanted to be a union member."

Eugene Williams, who had no previous union experience, views the union as essential to keeping the company on track: "If it weren't for the union, the company would have us stretched out. The union is the mediator. I can't see myself working here without a union— not for myself, but for the other people who need the help. Without the union it would be a mess—favoritism, sucking up."

Williams sees the union's power as limited, however. "The company is steady cutting back jobs and the work has got to go someplace—onto the rest of the people. Efficiency is the name of the game and the union can't do anything about it. They really don't have too much to say."

This essentially is the dilemma of the union at Shreveport: having accepted management's competitive imperative as its own guiding principle of day-to-day behavior, and having abrogated many traditional union stands on worker rights in favor of "the team comes first," it is left without a role. Backing up workers who have complaints, as advocated by TUG, would be a step in the right direction. But once the union accepts the view that what's good for the company is good for the workers, its effectiveness is seriously compromised.

An Unsound Trade-Off

The team concept package at Shreveport has worked well for General Motors. Quality is excellent, the head count is low, and the union has been weakened. As a bonus, the Shreveport plant has become a standard that GM pushes other locals to emulate nationwide.

The team concept has certain positive aspects for the individual Shreveport worker: the chance to earn 46 cents more an hour and a few more opportunities to get off the line from time to time through such duties as quality coordinator. Local management has thus far honored its commitment to try to avoid layoffs.

On the other hand, everybody is working quite hard for the money, and has to listen to a good deal of preaching about participation and respect which is not honored in practice. With fewer good jobs, especially off the line, the Shreveport worker has less to look forward to as the years go by than in a traditional plant—especially since jobs are being continually cut back and reloaded.

The immediate trade-off for an individual worker who is not terribly union-minded appears to be a reasonable one: a decent-paying job that is as secure as auto jobs get these days, in exchange for hard work and not much union protection. It is when the bigger picture is taken into account that the trade-off becomes clearly unsound. For one thing, it depends heavily on the good will of management. As we have already seen, the "style" aspects of team concept that were supposed to benefit workers are already fading, as management's manner erodes back towards the traditional.

Secondly, as management asserts its rights, workers are leaving themselves with weakened defenses. One can count on the fact that GM—because of the necessities of competition—will be pushing harder and harder. Without a strong union and with little tradition of opposing the company's desires, Shreveport workers will find it hard to fight back when push comes to shove. For instance, how would Local 2166 respond if management decided, for the sake of efficiency, to eliminate half the Absentee Replacement Operators?

Thirdly, the Shreveport local has made little effort to develop ties with other UAW locals. Jim Hodge says there is an attitude that "we're down here in this utopia, screw the rest of 'em." This attitude leads to getting screwed yourself, as solidarity between locals crumbles. Already, Shreveport, along with NUMMI, sets the standard which other GM locals must try to match. No doubt there will be pressure on Shreveport to stay ahead and to set continually higher standards.

In any case, even if the aspects of team concept that workers liked are fading, *management's* gains are alive and well. The question for Shreveport management will be whether it can retain these gains—top quality, low absenteeism, excellent labor efficiency—if it neglects to keep up the pretense of worker participation. Chances are good that it can, especially since the company has taken the precaution of diluting the power of the one force that could effectively fight for change—the union.

The question for Shreveport workers and Local 2166 is two-fold. One question is whether they will continue to accept the trade-off as the best deal they can get. After all, unions once believed that their job was to seek secure jobs, good pay, *and* a livable work pace and a strong union. For many Shreveport workers, transfers in particular, acceptance of the trade-off was literally a conscious decision. Without a conscious decision, by

workers, to alter the balance of forces, the present trade-off will not change for the better.

It will change, however, for the worse, because management clearly has no reason to honor the current trade-off forever. Thus the second question for the union is: how will it respond when management breaks the unspoken deal?

Notes

1. Aaron Bernstein and Wendy Zellner, "Detroit vs. the UAW: At Odds Over Teamwork," *Business Week*, August 24, 1987, p.55.

2. Bernstein and Zellner

3. General Motors Truck and Bus Group Public Relations Department, October 6, 1987.

4. Louisiana Department of Labor.

Appendix

The contract language reprinted below is excerpted from 1987 Local Agreement between UAW Local 2166 and GM Shreveport.

I. Level Progression Criteria

Technicians in Division I [production] will be eligible for advancement to and retention of higher wage level rates based on their job knowledge and performance of identified operations in a single team. The wage rate percentage paid to new hires at Shreveport shall be in accordance with applicable provisions of the 1987 GM-UAW National Agreement. Technicians in Division I will have the opportunity to progress to higher levels in accordance with the following criteria:

A. Shreveport New Hires
New technicians at Shreveport shall be hired into Level III.
B. Progression to Levels IV, V, and VI
Progression shall be based on the proficient performance of operations arranged in groups as described in Section II.B of this Agreement. Problems concerning the administration of this provision will be promptly addressed by the parties.
    1. Level IV
    Level III Technicians who are proficient at and perform a complete group of five operations to provide flexibility shall progress to Level IV.
    2. Level V
    To provide additional flexibility, Level IV technicians who are proficient at and perform an additional group of five operations in the team shall progress to Level V.
    3. Level VI
    To provide additional flexibility, Level V technicians who are proficient at and perform all of the operations in the team or three (3) groups of five operations each, whichever gives the technician the more favorable treatment, shall progress to Level VI.
    4. Exceptions to the above level progression criteria due to unique situations within certain departments such as Environmental, Material, and Salvage have been mutually agreed to by the parties and are incorporated as an attachment to the Wage Agreement.

II. General Provisions

A. Team Size
It is recognized that team size shall be adjusted to provide an adequate number of operations in each team for meaningful level progression as outlined above. To equalize the time or effort required to achieve Level VI among different teams, Level V technicians can achieve Level VI by being proficient at and performing all the operations in the team or three (3) groups of five operations each, whichever gives the technician the more favorable treatment.
B. Establishment of Groups of Operations Within Teams
Each team shall develop its own groups of five operations to implement Section I.B of this Agreement. Groups shall be designed by the

teams so that the different "job" concept is maintained with like operations placed in separate groups as far as practical in an effort to maximize overall team flexibility.

C. Physical Incapability

Certain technicians due to physical stature or permanent medical impairment may not be able to qualify for level progression by virtue of their inability to perform one or two operations in the team. These instances, when they occur, will be jointly addressed by the GT and Union in a manner consistent with the Shreveport pay-for-knowlege system.

D. Update of Skills

The flexibility achieved as a result of our pay-for-knowlege system is a critical key factor in the successful operation of our Plant. Therefore, maintenance of this flexibility over time is absolutely essential. As a result, and in order to maintain higher levels of pay, all technicians are obliged to keep their job skills current within their team.

E. Temporary Vacation Replacements

Temporary employees hired at Shreveport to facilitate coverage for summer vacation replacements will be hired at a rate in accordance with Paragraph 98 of the National Agreement and will not be eligible for level progression outlined in Section I of the Wage Agreement due to the temporary nature of their employment.

F. Proficiency Credit Outside of Team

In instances where an employee who is assigned to one of the team's regularly existing positions is loaned out of this home team on a regular basis (at least five full days over a continuous four (4) week period), he will be credited for up to two jobs, at which he becomes proficient, for his particular stage of level progression. It is understood that he must be capable of demonstrating this proficiency and the jobs in question must reflect an increase in his job knowledge level consistent with Section II.B of this Agreement. (Example—left and right fender molding install and left and right door window would equate to two jobs credit toward an employee's level progression requirements.) Only two jobs outside the team will be credited toward any particular level. The employee still has the obligation to meet the normal level progression criteria within the team (as outlined in Section I.B of this Agreement) as cross training opportunities arise.

III. Level Treatment Following Transfers, Reassignments, or Recall

Level IV, V, and VI technicians who transfer or are reassigned to a new team or recalled to work from indefinite layoff shall retain the level held in the team from which transferred, reassigned, or indefinitely laid off.

However, the technician must requalify for retention of the level held in the new team based on the criteria in Section I.B of this Agreement. If the technician fails to requalify for the level held within the new team as demonstrated by a refusal to take advantage of an opportunity to requalify, a level reduction shall be made based on the criteria in Section I.B of this Agreement. If the technician fails to requalify, as outlined above, in the new team for any level specified in Section I.B the technician will be reduced to Level III. Technicians requalifying will do so in accordance with the level progression training methods and accommodating schedules established by their team.

IV. Employees hired in Division II [skilled trades] will be paid in accordance with the applicable provisions of the 1987 GM-UAW National Agreement.

V. Team Coordinator Policy Rate

Technicians selected by the team to perform team coordinator's duties shall receive premium compensation for the period they function as team coordinator. In this regard, Division I technicians shall receive $.35 an hour over their current level rate. Division II technicians shall receive $.35 an hour over their skilled trades' rate.

Statement for Settlement Minutes

During the course of these negotiations the parties discussed situations wherein some employees wishing to attain a higher level of pay in accordance with Section I were prohibited, through no fault of their own, from doing so in a timely manner. For example: The parties recognize that in certain instances level progression training requested by some individuals is not accomplished because of the teams' inability to provide training opportunities. In recognition of the foregoing the parties agree that it is necessary for the team to establish level progression training methods and accommodating schedules in order that level progression activities can be properly facilitated. Further, while establishing these methods and schedules, the team should consider their teams' specific needs so as to maintain adequate flexibility and proficiency.

It is further understood that seniority can be used as a tool in determining which team members will be given the first opportunity for training.

In keeping with the spirit and intent of these provisions, when a review of the facts and circumstances clearly indicate an employee was prohibited from attaining a higher level of pay, Management and the Union commit to taking the necessary action to promptly address the situation. During the course of these negotiations, the parties discussed the issue of forced level progression. The union stated that some employees do not wish to increase their pay rate in the level progression process but rather only wish to come to work and build a high quality product in an efficient manner.

In this connection, Management states that such an employee will not be forced to level progress himself but is responsible for training employees on his job and in some instances may be required to temporarily be reassigned to permit another employee to demonstrate his proficiency on the job.

Section VII—Transfer Provisions (Division I)

For the purpose of applying Paragraph 63(b) of the National Agreement both within the department for team to team transfers and beyond department lines, the following procedure will be followed:

A.1. Seniority technicians may make application in the Personnel Department for permanent openings in any other department excluding Final and Paint Reprocess (See VII.B.1). An employee may have only three (3) applications of this type open at any one time, including applications filed under B below. However, an employee may cancel an existing application at the Personnel Department at any time and file a new one if desired.

2. Seniority technicians may make application in the Personnel Department for permanent openings in any other team within their department on their shift excluding Final and Paint Reprocess teams. An employee may have only two (2) applications of this type open at any time. However, an employee may cancel an existing application at the Personnel Department at any time and file a new one if desired.

3. As permanent openings occur, the senior applicant eligible to move under Section VII.A.2 will be permitted to fill the initial opening. Thereafter, the senior applicant under Section VII.A.1 will be permitted to transfer to the department.

B.1. Seniority technicians in the plant may make application in the Personnel Department for permanent openings in Final Reprocess and Paint Reprocess.

2. An employee may have only two (2) applications of this type open at any one time.

3. Applicants will state their qualifications and experience on the application form. Employees with prior repair experience in the Shreveport Plant, will be given preference over employees who cannot demonstrate such skills or prior experience when filling openings in Reprocess.

When two (2) or more employees can demonstrate such skills or experience, a joint decision will be made wherein the most qualified applicant will be transferred. In the event the qualifications of all applicants being considered are determined to be essentially equal, the senior applicant will be transferred.

C. General Provisions

1. Applicants who have made application seven (7) calendar days prior to the opening will be considered for transfer.

2. An employee transferred under these provisions (Section VII) will not be eligible to reapply for a transfer under Section VII A or B for a period of six (6) months from the effective date of the transfer. All other applications for the employee transferred will be voided at the time of the transfer. An employee who refuses a transfer under Section VII A1, VII A2, or VII B will not be eligible to reapply for that respective area for sixty (60) days. In the event an employee is reduced out of the new department, team, or reprocess area, respectively, he/she may reapply at once.

3. All applications for transfer under these provisions will be voided at the end of the calendar year. However, applications filed during the months of November and December will be valid for the following calendar year.

4. It is understood that all transfers will occur as expeditiously as possible. However, it may be necessary to temporarily delay an employee's transfer to accomplish necessary training to maintain the efficiency of operations.

5. Employees must either refuse or accept the transfer in writing within 24 hours of the time the transfer is offered on forms provided by Management.

6. Employees who are granted a transfer under the above provi-

sion of Section VII A1 or B will have a choice of shift, seniority permitting. In the event a different shift is selected, the vacancy created by the transfer under Section VII A2 will be populated consistent with the provisions of the Local Shift Preference Agreement (Section D5 and D4, respectively). The employee transferring under Section VII A1 or B who selects a shift different than his current shift will not be subject to the restrictions on further shift preference moves under Section H of the Local Shift Preference Agreement.

7. It is the responsibility of the receiving team to assign the employee who is transferring under Section VII to one of the team's existing positions, seniority permitting.

8. The transfer application list will be available for review by employees and the Union in the Plant Personnel Office. The Chairman will be provided a copy of the current list.

9. A permanent opening is defined as an opening created when an employee quits, dies, retires, or otherwise leaves the bargaining unit on a permanent basis. In addition, an increase in production necessitating the addition of manpower to the seniority rolls would constitute permanent openings. Furthermore, when an employee is absent for 30 days or more on an approved leave of absence, a permanent opening will be declared.

Any opening created by an employee moving across departmental lines will be considered as secondary under the provisions of Paragraph 63b of the National Agreement.

10. Employees transferred under Section VII A1 and VII B will have their seniority transferred into the occupational group at the time of the transfer.

11. The parties recognize that, due to the application of the definition of openings as contained in Section VII C8 above, situations may occur where, as a result of the volume of employee transfer movement, efficient production cannot be maintained. If this occurs, the parties agree to jointly meet to develop and implement a solution which restores production efficiency. This solution may include the imposition of a limit on the number of departmental transfers that may occur over an agreed upon temporary period.

Section IX—General Provisions

B. Returning to Work from Leaves of Absence

1. Leaves of Absence Other Than Paragraph 106 and 108, National Agreement

Employees who return to work from a leave of absence of less than thirty (30) calendar days (must be at work on the 30th day) will be returned to their former team and operation. Employees who return to work from a leave of absence of thirty (30) calendar days or more will be placed in their respective department, seniority permitting.

2. Leaves of Absence Under Paragraph 106 and 108, National Agreement

Employees who return to work from a leave of absence of less than thirty (30) calendar days will be returned to the operation from which they left providing they remain actively at work for the first ten (10) consecutive working days following the return to work. In the event such an employee is absent for the same or a related illness or injury condition during this ten (10) day period, those absences (including absences which fall outside the ten day period but are continuous from an absence occurring within the ten day period) will be added to the period of absence preceding the return from leave to determine whether the employee's total absence is less than thirty (30) days. If the total absence is less than thirty (30) days, the employee will be returned to their former team and operation. If the total absence is thirty (30) days or more, the employee will be placed in their respective department, seniority permitting.

3. For the purpose of counting days of absence under 1 and 2 above, and Section VII C8 of this agreement, the period of absence will commence with the first full working day absent on an approved leave of absence (or first working day casually absent immediately preceding an approved leave) and will include each calendar day thereafter until the employee returns to work, plus any days absent during or coincident to the ten (10) day period referenced in 2 above.

C. An employee who has been found by his personal physician and the Plant Medical Director to be permanently incapacitated and unable to perform his regular work assignments may be reassigned to other work assignments that he can do.

D. It is agreed that this Agreement governs the layoff and recall of employees while the Plant is engaged in assembling trucks. In the event of complete conversion to products other than trucks, the recall provisions of the Agreement with respect to work on such products will be set aside and negotiations on an appropriate new recall section shall be undertaken without delay. Until such Agreement is concluded, the applicable provisions of the National Agreement will apply.

E. In the event of partial conversion to products other than trucks, negotiations shall be undertaken without delay on an appropriate transition agreement, which shall govern opportunity to transfer, reduction-in-force, and other appropriate items. Until such a transition agreement is concluded, the applicable provisions of the National Agreement and Local Agreement will apply.

F. In those instances when it becomes necessary to reduce a team's size and no employee has volunteered to be reassigned to another team, plant seniority will be utilized as the basis for reduction, provided the team has considered the need to maintain the efficiency of operations.

Memorandum of Understanding Regarding
Team Meetings, Team Duties, and Individual Responsibilities

The local Union and Management recognize that the continued success and growth of the Shreveport Organization into a World Class competitor is dependent upon the participation of everyone. During these negotiations the parties have discussed the subjects of team meetings, team duties and individual responsibilities at great length. As a result of these discussions, both Management and Union agree that team meetings, team duties, and individual responsibilities are a critical part of the Shreveport style of operation. In this regard, teams and individuals have duties and responsibilities to the organization which must be carried out if we are to succeed. The following guidelines are not intended to be all inclusive, therefore when circumstances arise not contemplated in these guidelines the Union and Management expect teams as well as individuals to seek solutions which meet both the need of our business and the need to recognize the worth and dignity of our people. Therefore, both Management and Union jointly encourage all Shreveport employees to participate in accordance with the following guidelines and further agree to address and review any problems or abuses of these guidelines. The parties recognize that these guidelines must be applied so that teams and individuals have sufficient flexibility to respond to the needs of the people or business as they arise and that rules, regulations, or guidelines established by one team on a shift will not apply to other teams without their input and acceptance.

Team Meetings

1. Attendance at team meetings will be voluntary. However, a decision to attend or not attend must be each employee's personal decision. No employee shall seek by any means to cause or influence any other employee to decline attendance at team meetings.

Moreover, consistent with the joint commitment contained herein, such concerted action requires the parties to promptly meet to effectuate a joint resolution of the problems created by the concerted activity. Resolution may include a mutual agreement to suspend this section of this Memorandum of Understanding for a mutually agreed upon time.

If unresolved, the matter will be reviewed by Truck and Bus Central Office personnel and personnel from the UAW-GM Department.

In this regard, the parties commit to utilize the QWL Group [four union and three management employees] to jointly endeavor to increase attendance and participation recognizing that increased involvement is the key to Shreveport's ultimate success.

2. Attendance at team meetings will continue to be paid for by Management in accordance with the National Agreement.

3. Team meetings must not be used to circumvent the grievance procedure or any other provision of the National or Local Agreement. Issues covered by agreement should be resolved by the means provided in the Agreement.

4. Team meetings are normally one-half hour long. However, the exact length of time for a meeting is dictated by the amount of legitimate business the team has to conduct.

5. Each team shall post an agenda prior to the team meeting.

6. Open jobs and team function assignments will be filled by the teams.

7. (a) Team meetings will be chaired and conducted by the team coordinator. In as much as the GT is part of the team, it is part of his/her responsibility to be present at the team meetings to act as a resource to the team. In certain situations, teams may request their GT to not be present for a portion or all of a Team Meeting. If the request is for a legitimate reason, it will be honored.

7. (b) Team meetings will not be cancelled or adjourned except when the cancellation or adjournment is for a sound reason. In addition, emergency team meetings will be approved by the GT if the meet-

ing is required for a legitimate business purpose.

7. (c) Decisions made at a team meeting by the members present will be final and binding and will not be changed by the Union or Management unless the change is due to a sound business purpose or the decision is contrary to the National or Local Agreement. Reasons for the change will be given to the team.

7. (d) Problems with this section if they arise will be jointly addressed.

8. Other members of Management and Union representatives may attend any team meeting provided the team does not object.

9. Team meetings will be held in plant locations suitable for conducting team business in terms of noise, privacy, etc. The starting time for all team meetings is normally dictated by the needs of the business. On a schedule of less than nine hours, meetings are held either before or after work except in the situations discussed between the parties in these negotiations.

Changes in either the team or department meeting schedule will be provided to team members as far in advance as practicable.

10. The team secretary will furnish the committeeman with changes in team rules, regulations, or function assignments. The GT will make certain this duty is carried out in a timely manner. Within thirty (30) days after receipt of notice of ratification, teams will meet to record their rules, regulations, and functions.

Thereafter, during the first team meeting held in each succeeding January and July, teams will again review their rules and regulations and make appropriate changes if desired. Copies of team meeting minutes will be made available to committeemen on request.

Team Duties

1. The team will select employees in the team for the following positions and set a length of term for each position:
   a. Team Coordinator
   b. Quality Coordinator
   c. Safety Coordinator
   d. Salvage Coordinator
   e. Timekeeper
   f. General Store Coordinator
   g. Secretary
   h. Other positions required by the team to perform its duties
   i. Teams will be able to recall or remove team representatives for failure to perform their position, if the team desires.

2. The team will be able to discuss quality, safety, and other issues that may arise on the team.

3. The team will be able to handle early outs when tying up the coordinator provided the GT is informed as far in advance as practicable and team functions have been accomplished prior to the early out. Early outs should be scheduled so that an adequate number of coordinators remain free to handle unforeseen circumstances and maintain efficiency within each GT area.

4. The team will set up guidelines and administer level progression and pay-for-knowledge in accordance with the Local Wage Agreement.

5. The team will be able to request Union and higher Management to help to resolve certain problems when the team does not possess the resources to resolve them on their own.

6. Be aware of and utilize plant information systems required to perform team duties.

7. Be aware of EEO guidelines.

8. Team members are obligated to remain proficient on those jobs for which they have achieved level progression credit. One aim of this practice is to insure that the replacement of an absentee not fall on one employee all the time.

9. Utilizing the information maintained by the team's timekeeper, Management, except in unusual situations, will offer overtime to team members. Management is ultimately responsible to investigate and take appropriate action to correct problems if they occur.

10. Develop work assignments. Operations which occur on more than one shift shall be the same. It is recognized that to accomplish this may require the involvement of employees from more than one shift working together to develop work assignments.

11. Be involved in plant quality standards and daily audit procedures.

12. Appropriate team(s) will be involved in the selection of employees assigned to outside community activities in accordance with legitimate requirements. Examples of these activities are dealer visits, United Way representatives, etc.

13. The Union shall be involved in the final selection of employees for special, or unusual assignments. It is recognized that employees

selected must satisfy all of the criteria for the particular assignment. Both parties agree that these assignments normally are absolutely critical to the successful operation of our Plant and must be treated accordingly.

Individual Responsibilities

In addition to the responsibilities that team members have to be present at work, maintain quality in performing job assignments, maintain a clean and safe work area, and participate in necessary training, the team will select certain individuals to perform the following functions as required:

1. Team coordinator responsibilities
   a. Attend and preside over team meetings
   b. Function as team facilitator. Service the team and provide assistance as required. e.g., supplies, tools, etc.
   c. Transfer information to and from team as required.
   d. Provide relief for situations that might arise in the team.
   e. Acquire knowledge and be proficient on all operations within the team.
   f. Provide training in accordance with the Local Agreement.
   g. Will be used to cover absentees in team when needed.
      1. It is not Management's intent to utilize team coordinators to cover absentees for extended periods of time except in abnormal situations such as excessive absenteeism.
      2. It is not Management's intent to utilize team coordinators to cover for blood drives, dealer visits, and United Way visits except as provided in g.1 above.
   h. Will go over all team rules with new members.
   i. Maintain liaison with other teams and departments.
   j. Train successor as required.
   k. In the event no employee within the team volunteers to be team coordinator, the lowest seniority employee proficient at fourth level or above in the team will be appointed.

2. Quality Coordinator
   a. Function as team representative. Transfer quality related information to and from the team as required.
   b. Assist team members in resolving quality related problems.
   c. Attend team meetings and submit reports as required.
   d. Go to the audit as required.
   e. Provide training for successor as required.

3. Safety Coordinator
   a. Function as team representative. Transfer safety related information to and from the team as required.
   b. Report safety problems to Management or the Union.
   c. Attend safety meetings, team meetings and submit reports.
   d. Provide training for successor as required.

4. Time Keeper
   a. Inspect and correct team time.
   b. Maintain Overtime Equalization Chart
   c. Acquire working knowledge of the CRT and various time codes.
   d. To notify team of their time and corrections if any.
   e. Report all problems to General Technicians.
   f. Provide training for successor as required.
   g. Follow rules outlined in Local and National Agreements.

5. Salvage Coordinator
   a. Tag salvage material in team.
   b. Take salvage material to its designated area.
   c. Provide training for successor as required.

6. General Stores Coordinator
   a. Get dirty aprons, gloves and take to the store room.
   b. Get clean gloves, aprons and tools.
   c. Training successor if needed.

7. Secretary
   a. Keep notes and records of the team meetings.
   b. Safeguard rules and vital information concerning team.
   c. Furnish committeeman with changes in team rules, regulations, or function assignments.
   d. Train successors if needed.

8. All other individual responsibilities deemed necessary due to unique circumstances will be set up by the teams.

9. For individual responsibilities 2 through 7 above, in those instances when no one volunteers to perform a function(s), the team's coordinator will temporarily perform the duties. The parties agreed to jointly work together with the team to resolve the issue of the assignment of these functions.

In support of the foregoing, Management and the Union have agreed that the long term success of the entire Shreveport organization depends, to a large measure, upon the process outlined above. In addition, Management and the Union have affirmed the principle that this process must continue to be jointly developed, implemented and monitored.

Therefore, in this regard, both parties commit themselves to the allocation of sufficient human resources to facilitate the successful growth and development of the individual as well as the organization. Problems shall be jointly discussed and addressed.

81. Transfer of Jobs

In an effort to maintain consistency throughout the plant and to provide continuity of operations, when 51 percent or more of an existing operation is to be relocated from one team or department to another the technician currently assigned to the operation will be afforded the opportunity to transfer with the operation to the new team or department. If such technician elects not to move with the work and it is necessary to transfer a technician with the operation, the team will solicit a volunteer to transfer to the new team. If no technician volunteers, the applicable provisions of the Local Seniority Agreement will apply. In instances where two or more operations are combined and it is possible to identify that 51 percent or more of the work from the original operations remains as part of the new operation, the senior technician will be afforded the opportunity to retain the operation. Thereafter, any job assignments as a result of movement of work will be dealt with by the team in as much as both parties recognize that job assignments within a team are the team's responsibility.

Demand 84—Shreveport Planners

At Truck and Bus-Shreveport, employee involvement is essential to our success. One way employee involvement is assured is through the use of "planners." A planner is a team member(s) selected by the team who satisfies the team's planning needs for a specific plant event, i.e. model change activities, model mix change, etc. This statement is written to facilitate the involvement of employees in the plant planning process. It is the parties' intention that this involvement be significant and meaningful. Selection criteria for planners includes the ability and/or willingness to:

1. Work additional overtime necessary to satisfy requirements of the assignment.
2. Travel to other locations, if necessary.
3. Effectively communicate both verbally and in writing.
4. Analyze technical information and communicate same to the GT and other team members.
5. Remain as a planner for the duration of the assignment. Problems with the functioning of an individual planner will first be discussed and addressed by the team and then by the Superintendent and Committeeman if not satisfactorily resolved by the team. It is recognized that an individual planner may eventually be replaced by the team for good reasons after this problem-solving procedure has been exhausted.
6. Effectively work well with other team members and planners.
7. Good working knowledge of the team and its work.

It is normally expected that the employee(s) selected to function as planner(s) will perform that assignment in accordance with the following guidelines:

1. Keep GT and team members informed of developments which affect them. Decisions will be made consistent with the Shreveport style of consensus decision-making. This in no way infringes on an employee's rights under the National Agreement.
2. Involve other team members to the extent practicable in the decisions related to necessary elements of work which affect them.
3. Be open to alternatives suggested by the team that may serve to meet the plant's objectives.

4. Personal conduct in a manner consistent with the Shreveport Operating Style.
5. Participate in the making of decisions that are consistent with the plant's quality, people, and cost objectives.

It is recognized that there may be instances where planners or coordinators in order to effectively meet the requirement(s) of the job will work additional hours which may occur on the opposite shift. It is recognized that there may be instances where, in addition to planners and coordinators, technicians whose individual operations are changed may be scheduled to work additional hours which may occur on the opposite shift. In those instances such work will be reviewed with the Committeeman for the district in advance. In these instances, other employees have no claim to these particular hours in question. Overtime hours worked by employees performing the planning function will be included on their overtime chart.

Problems that may arise with the Shreveport planning process will be promptly discussed by the appropriate parties.

95. Quality Analyst

Resolved on the basis that each team within a department will be given the opportunity to select their most qualified candidate for the departmental Quality Analyst position. From these candidates the Departmental Superintendent and the District Committeeman will jointly determine the best qualified technician to function in this capacity. Under present operating conditions the term of the quality analyst will be for a period of one (1) calendar year. This period can be altered if the need arises. The former quality analyst will rotate into the team of the new quality analyst. In situations where this would not be practicable they will be jointly addressed by the District Committeeman and the Superintendent.

Demand 131—Memorandum of Understanding Regarding Local Job Security

During the course of these negotiations the parties discussed their mutual concerns regarding plant job security. Local Management reaffirmed its long standing policy that the provisions of the National Agreement notwithstanding; no individual be laid off as the result of improved operational effectiveness gained through employee participation. In this regard both parties recognize that the continued pursuit of attaining world class competitiveness is a key ingredient to job security.

Local Management further assured the Union that it recognized surplus manpower created some inconvenience to employees desiring to transfer to openings under the applicable provisions of the Local Agreement. In this regard the parties have undertaken changes in the current Local Agreement which minimize such inconveniences and yet avoid the layoff of employees.

It is understood that the resolution of any unusual problems with excess manpower related to transfers will not conflict with any agreement. Further, excess manpower related to transfers will not be permanently assigned to a regular job in a team if it results in the permanent movement of a senior employee from a regular job in the team.

Statement for the Settlement Minutes Balancing Manpower

In instances where manpower is being balanced between shifts in a department, the person being displaced from the shift shall have the option of being placed in either the corresponding team or the team in which the least senior employee on the opposite shift in the department is assigned. It is recognized that this placement may then require the reassignment of the least senior employee from the team the displaced employee selects to the team where manpower is needed. It is the responsibility of the receiving team to assign the employee displaced from the shift to one of the team's regularly existing positions, seniority permitting.

13. Chrysler: A De Facto National Agreement

Like many corporations, Chrysler had experimented with versions of the team concept in the past. But in 1986 Chrysler had no significant team production. During the first part of the 1980's, Chrysler focused on financial rescue operations with the government and creditors, slashing its workforce, getting union concessions, and building a new top management. There was little time or resources for dallying with programs such as General Motors' Quality of Work Life (QWL) or Ford's Employee Involvement. The only comparable program, the joint Chrysler-UAW Product Quality Improvement Program (PQIP), had limited funds and scope. Both company and union officials went out of their way to insist that PQIP was not another QWL program and would not stray from its narrow focus on product quality.

However, there were signs that team production was on Chrysler's agenda. In 1979 important changes began appearing in local union contracts. The Belvedere, Illinois local agreed to some reduction in classifications in order to get a replacement for the aging Omni-Horizon line. The new Sterling Heights, Michigan Assembly Plant started up in 1984 with reduced classifications and management flexibility to assign multiple tasks.

By 1986 the company and the leadership of the UAW Chrysler Department appeared to have reached

an understanding and committed themselves to the team concept. Although local contracts did not expire until 1988, Chrysler, using threats of layoffs and plant closings, forced selected locals to reopen and renegotiate their local agreements. So many locals were approached with these new agreements, called "Modern Operating Agreements" (MOA's), that they can be thought of as a second national pattern.

Before 1986, a number of UAW contracts at General Motors and Ford included versions of the team concept. But the union described them very tentatively as "experimental" or required by "exceptional" circumstances. Union leaders insisted that they were not precedents and would be watched very carefully.

At the June 1986 Constitutional Convention UAW President Owen Bieber responded to delegates who were worried about the precedent set by the Saturn contract by saying that the Saturn agreement was "isolated."

"We're not going to Saturnize the auto industry," Bieber assured the delegates. Just three months later, the International was advocating the MOA at Chrysler.

The union held up GM's Shreveport truck plant as the successful model of team concept. The company and the International jointly funded trips of Chrysler local union officers to tour the Shreveport plant.

None of the provisions in the Chrysler Modern

- *UAW Local 7*
  Address: 1551 Hart, Detroit, MI 48214
  Phone: 313 / 822-1744
- *UAW Local 371*
  Address: 201 N. Main, New Castle, IN 47362
  Phone: 317 / 529-6631
- *UAW Local 372*
  Address: 4571 Division, Trenton, MI 48183
  Phone: 313 / 676-9060
- *UAW Local 550*
  Address: 1349 South Tibbs, Indianapolis, IN 46241
  Phone: 317 / 923-5030
- *UAW Local 1183*
  Address: 698 Old Baltimore Pike, Newark, DE 19702
  Phone: 302 / 738-4500
- *UAW Local 1413*
  Address: P.O. Box 1342, Huntsville, AL 35807
  Phone: 205 / 881-8369
- *UAW Local 1700*
  Address: 31201 Chicago Road South, Suite C101, Warren, MI 48093
  Phone: 313 / 264-0333

THE MORE THINGS CHANGE...

The *Wall Street Journal* described some examples of "the overhaul currently under way at Chrysler."

In an effort to involve production employees in the entire production process, workers in one Detroit parts plant were asked to evaluate the entire manufacturing operation. The result: one department was rearranged, eliminating seven jobs; the displaced men were reassigned to jobs where they were needed elsewhere in the plant.

Workers in two small parts departments at a Detroit plant currently work without a foreman. At another Detroit plant, workers and a foreman designed a new engine line and then took it through its "launch" or initial break-in without higher supervision. Both experiments, Chrysler says, have been smashing successes.[1]

This story was published in 1972. Not long afterward the experiments ended, and all but one of the plants mentioned in the story have been shut down.

Operating Agreements was particularly novel. Perhaps the most significant feature was that, for the first time, the International union voiced no tentativeness about the team concept. The UAW Chrysler Department fully backed the contracts, and suggested that teams were the way forward in the auto industry. Union leaders aggressively sought to extend the pattern to other locals.

Jefferson Assembly / Local 7

At Detroit Jefferson Assembly, Chrysler told Local 7 members that there were plans to shut the plant down after the 1987 model. But, the company said, if a new agreement were approved, a $1.2 billion pick-up truck plant would be built next to the old plant, and the old plant would be switched over to full-size truck production. In January 1986, the UAW International proposed that the local allow the International to renegotiate the local contract in hope of saving the plant. In August, Jefferson workers reluctantly voted for the new contract described in detail below. The MOA is supposed to go into effect when the new plant opens, but the company has already begun team training, while at the same time warning that an economic downturn could delay construction.

Trenton Engine / Local 372

In January 1986, Chrysler also approached Local 372 at Trenton Engine in southeastern Michigan and said the company would be willing to invest in the plant for production of a new V-6 engine if the local would agree to let the International negotiate a "modern labor agreement." The company projected declining production for the current four-cylinder engines and claimed the new engine would save 1,200 to 2,000 jobs.

Although local negotiations went on for about six months, the proposed contract varied only slightly from Jefferson's. When put to a vote at the union hall, the proposal failed 527-218. Trenton workers said that the vote might have been close if members had not been angered by what they called the "arrogance" of International representatives in refusing to answer questions and their "take-it-or-quit" attitude.

Following the rejection, Chrysler announced cancellation of plans to build the V-6 engine in the plant. The UAW Chrysler Department made it clear they had no intention of going back to the bargaining table. They blamed "petty local politics" for the defeat, and promoted a "rank and file" petition drive calling for a re-vote. In August balloting was held in company cafeterias to get a bigger turnout, and the members "got it right." The contract was ratified 1,360-610. Chrysler announced the V-6 was back on schedule.

Huntsville Electronics / Local 1413

At the Huntsville, Alabama electronics components plant, Chrysler threatened members of Local 1413 with shifting work to Mexico. But if a new agreement were ratified, Chrysler promised to build a high-tech Electronic City at the plant's location. Huntsville makes ignition controls and radios, and is a part of Acustar, a subsidiary for Chrysler's parts production.

Ann Pollak, recording secretary of Local 1413, said, "Homer Jolly from the [UAW] Chrysler Department came down himself to explain to the people what was the bottom line. Without that, I'm not sure the people would have believed their own bargaining committee."

Dot Byford, a committeeperson, agreed. "It would have been voted down," she said, "but they said we had to accept the MOA or in five years, it would be the end of our plant. The work would go somewhere else." Byford feels that Chrysler's attempt to sell Acustar violated the company's promise.

The local voted 71 percent in favor of the agreement, a five-year contract which takes effect when workers are transferred into Electronic City.

Newark Assembly Plant / Local 1183

In January 1987 Chrysler informed Local 1183 at Newark, Delaware that it had to have a Modern Operating Agreement by March or a new model would not be scheduled to replace the K car (Reliant and Aries)—implying certain plant closing. The company appeared to be playing hardball by demanding the reopening and new contract in such a short period. At one point the company blocked distribution of a leaflet warning of the Jefferson, Trenton and Huntsville contracts. Many members reacted negatively to the company's high-handed tactics. More than 1,000 workers attended the union meeting on February 15, and overwhelmingly voted against reopening.

But the company insisted its threats were serious, and the International pushed for the new contract. According to Committeeperson Pam McGinnis, "When it became clear that the International would not back the local a mood of fear and hopelessness swept the plant and bitter feelings developed between the 'yes' vote and 'no' vote people." On April 5, the local voted 76 percent to reopen. The six-year Modern Operating Agreement was adopted in June, to go into effect when the "A" body car begins production around the fall of 1988.

New Castle Machining and Forge / Local 371

The New Castle, Indiana plant is also a part of Acustar, a wholly owned subsidiary set up by Chrysler in 1987 for its parts manufacturing operations. Parts plants have been under tremendous pressure as the company implements a new "make or buy" policy; each operation and each individual part is examined to determine whether it is more profitable to produce in-house or to buy from a vendor. The corporate reorganization has stimulated fears that Chrysler will try to break off parts production from the national pattern and insist on lower wages and inferior conditions in the name of improving competition.

At New Castle, the MOA was not tied to bringing new work into the plant. Therefore the contract went into effect shortly after the six-year pact was signed in April 1987, and, in August, New Castle became the first Chrysler plant to officially operate with the team concept. The New Castle local thus had the first experience with the MOA's vague and deferred language in areas such as seniority and overtime. These are covered in detail below.

Indianapolis Foundry / Local 550

The Indianapolis Foundry is part of Chrysler's Power Train division, and also under the threat of outsourcing. In 1986 Chysler warned the foundry that it was in jeopardy without a Modern Operating Agreement, and the local union signed up. The agreement took effect in February 1988 when a new impact molding line began operation.

Sterling Heights Assembly / Local 1700

Unlike the other Chrysler locals discussing new agreements in the fall of 1986, the Sterling Heights Assembly Plant (SHAP) was the only one with regularly scheduled local negotiations that year. It was also the only one with experience with some of the features of a Modern Operating Agreement. When SHAP started

operating, the company unilaterally imposed its version of many of the modern features, including greatly reduced classifications (three production, three skilled) and management flexibility to assign multiple tasks.

When formal union recognition was completed in January 1985 the International negotiated the first contract, increasing skilled classifications to seven and production to nine (still a big cut from traditional plants) but leaving in place most of the management flexibility. In the 1986 local elections, partly because of dissatisfaction with the modern contract, virtually all of the original appointed local officers were defeated.

After the election, at the beginning of local negotiations in 1986, the company and the International tried to convince Local 1700 to go with the full Jefferson model team concept agreement. Initially the entire union leadership opposed the team concept agreement, but the International won over the shop committee. The local president and other local leaders continued to oppose the team concept. Compared to the other Chrysler plants, it was easier to resist company pressure at SHAP since there was no way that Chrysler could convincingly threaten to move work. SHAP was a brand new plant, Chrysler's showcase, and the exclusive producer of two good-selling models, the Sundance and the Shadow. Furthermore, management already had a good part of

"A RATHER EFFECTIVE METHOD OF MANAGING LABOR, DON'T YOU THINK?"

the contract it wanted, so there was not as much to gain from a fight for the full MOA.

After considerable debate and division, the local voted overwhelmingly to reject the team concept and to negotiate a more traditional local labor agreement. Unlike the other plants, the International did not push the local to reconsider, and the company made no threats. However, management has stated that it is willing to re-open for team concept discussions at any time, and the team concept continues to be an issue within the union at SHAP.

A Local or National Agreement?

Chrysler's success in re-opening local agreements and bargaining directly with the International threatens all local agreements and the role of local union leaders. Local contracts were supposed to be just that: negotiated by local unions and covering local situations.

But the agreements negotiated in 1986 followed a de facto national pattern, modeled on the Jefferson contract. They were negotiated by the UAW International with Chrysler headquarters and imposed on six Chrysler locals. In every case the new pattern was pressed on an unwilling or at least skeptical local membership.

Where locals rejected the contract, the International did not back the members up. The International could have responded by organizing to stop Chrysler from moving work out, but did just the opposite. The International seconded the company's threats, and made it clear that the local would get no help from the International unless the members voted right. In some cases, the International publicly attacked local leaders.

Pointing out that many provisions in the team agreement required suspending provisions in the national contract, including those covering wages, classifications, seniority, and work standards, International union leaders insisted that negotiations had to be conducted at the International level. Locals were not free to negotiate their version of a team agreement; they could only propose modifications to the Jefferson agreement.

It is certainly correct that if team concept contracts are to be negotiated they should be negotiated on a national or even industry-wide basis rather than allowing the companies to pit plants against each other. But for the union to effectively negotiate on this level means pulling the locals together and hammering out a common program and that locals feel that they can live with, understand and enforce. It means drawing common lines which the union will not allow the company to cross. The fact that representatives of the International union are involved does not itself make for national negotiations. Just the opposite. Because it failed to organize the locals, the International involvement lent legitimacy to and therefore greased the way for the company to whipsaw the locals.

The way the International handled these negotiations was the worst of all worlds. The locals were isolated from one another and, at the same time, lost control over even issues which traditionally unions can deal with effectively at the local level such as specific classifications and work rules.

Ironically, despite the fact that these local agreements follow a national pattern, the result will be weaker national standards in the auto industry because of what the pattern actually contains. The MOA's give new flexibility directly to local plant managements and promise even more with all the language about cooperation or competitiveness. In the next few years we can expect to see a widening disparity in working conditions, job descriptions, union roles, workers' rights and even wages as the company is allowed to freely adapt to specific corporate or market conditions.

Economic Terrorism

Chrysler forced locals whose contracts did not expire for two years to renegotiate and revamp their local agreements. How? In each case, the company threatened to take some economic action which threatened the future of the plant and the livelihood of its workers. SHAP Local 1700 President Bill Parker calls this "economic terrorism." Parker wrote in the September 1987 *Local 1700 News*:

> For over a year this local has participated in the joint UAW/Chrysler Product Quality Improvement Program with the expectation that improved quality would lead to increased job security at this plant.
>
> The decision of Highland Park to place the new production of P-cars for Europe in Mexico is a slap in the face [after] the efforts of our membership.
>
> Even worse are the statements of Chrysler Motors Chairman Gerald Greenwald who stated that the reason for this is to force changes in the tax laws which do not favor exports. But there is a word for using threats to get one's way and that is terrorism.
>
> The use of the threat of moving production out of one plant and into another country is simply a form of economic terrorism which must be resisted. This local will vigorously resist any management effort to reduce production levels at SHAP.

Understandably, when faced with the alternative of concessions or plant closings, people will tend to vote for anything that keeps them working. It's the union's job to build defenses against such threats. This is hard enough at scheduled contract expirations. It is worse when the company can pick the moment to rip up the contract, naturally when it is in the strongest economic position vis-a-vis the union. In the above cases, the company appeared to be deciding whether to schedule new work in the plant or shut down operations.

Further, if a contract can be disposed of so easily, what does this mean for the new contract? If, in practice, the company finds provisions not to its liking, why not insist on re-opening again?

On the Plus Side

The Modern Operating Agreement (MOA) would not have been adopted at any of the Chrysler plants without the company's economic threats and the pressure from the International, but certain features were attractive to certain workers and in many instances were sufficient reasons to vote for the new contracts.

Money was first. The new contract could mean as much as 32 cents an hour more for an assembler and 40 to 50 cents an hour for a skilled trades worker if all the requirements of the pay-for-knowledge arrangement were fulfilled.

Second, the new contract provided what Chrysler workers call a "Sadie Hawkins Day," a one-time opportunity to apply to the department and shift of one's choice and be placed according to seniority. Because of departmental seniority provisions, the layoff-recall cycle often placed workers with relatively high seniority in departments not of their choosing. Further, recalls of high seniority workers from plants that had closed placed many high seniority workers in the least preferred departments. A provision in the Chrysler national contract (66C) does provide for transfers based on seniority, but only when there is an opening in a department after departmental seniority is exhausted. Given the shrinking workforce, various loopholes (such as "temporary assignments"), and the failure of some locals to effectively enforce the complex contract provisions, relatively few workers can transfer under 66C. Thus the Sadie Hawkins Day provision was extremely popular among high seniority workers.

Third, the MOA appealed to many workers' desire to believe that there could be a new, non-adversarial relationship with management, and that problems could be addressed through reason rather than discipline.

Obviously, there is no automatic connection between the team concept and a wage increase or a Sadie Hawkins Day. These features were included to make the agreement palatable despite the team concept. The attractiveness of these features makes the degree of opposition to the MOA all the more remarkable.

Workers who voted against a possible raise of $600 to $1,000 a year, the opportunity to transfer to preferred departments, and a chance to end daily harassment, must have believed that there were real dangers in the Modern Operating Agreement, despite their leaders' reassurances.

Contract and Reality

A contract—particularly a local agreement—does not always describe the reality of life on the shop floor. Much depends on years of precedent and the ability of the local union to enforce its interpretation of the contract, past practice, and what's fair. Sometimes bad contract provisions are simply ignored because management does not want a confrontation with a union which is committed to fighting for certain practices. A classic example is the Chrysler contract provision which requires chief stewards to report to regular jobs, leave only for specific grievances, and report progress on

these grievances to their foremen. In practice, chief stewards have functioned for the union full-time and this clause has been a polite fiction.

Unfortunately, all too often contract provisions which benefit the union also go unenforced. The key is how aware the membership is of their contractual rights and past practices and whether the local leadership sees as its job to continually push for an interpretation of the contract that is to the members' benefit.

Thus, one of the biggest dangers in the MOA's is that they appear to suspend all past practices and at the same time give management more flexibility. For example, the MOA's specifically assign most of the provisions of previous local contracts to "Administrative Procedures." Management would like this to mean that changes no longer require membership involvement, thus down-grading whatever rights and standards the local agreement contained and making it easier to settle issues by quiet deals with the union officers. Traditionally, the local contract is the place where the members finally get to nail management down on the specifics. When members see in writing the number of fans and water fountains specified in the contract, they know what they have won, or what they need to fight for. But the new administrative procedures seem to go back to vague promises or flexibly interpreted generalities.

For example, the Administrative Procedures for both the New Castle and Newark plants state:

> In keeping with our mutual commitment to establish harmonious, non-adversarial relationships...there is no longer a need to cover every isolated incident and situation involving facility, housekeeping and health and safety concerns in a written document.

Both contracts continue with assurances of "management's commitment to work diligently with the union." The New Castle contract goes on:

> The union is further assured that such facilities and equipment as showers, lockers, drinking fountains, lighting, exhaust and ventilation systems, windows, doors, heaters and fans, pans, tubs, conveyors and chutes, machines, transfers, and hammer and press shields... will be maintained in proper condition.

The real effect of the MOA depends more on how the local union interprets the language than on the language itself. But it is obviously harder for members to enforce standards when the standards are not clear. And when the contract talks about "removing any and all impediments to world competitiveness" it becomes even more difficult for members to know what rights they can stand up for. At least in the initial phases of these new contracts, members become more dependent on union leaders to interpret the contract and establish new practices.

Unfortunately, there is likely to be a period of confusion as the new agreements go into effect, during which time the company will no doubt try to press its advantage. Local union leaders are likely to be disoriented by the enormous changes in the contract and the process of its adoption. One sign of the upheaval is that in five of the six Chrysler MOA plants, there have been major shifts in leadership since adoption of the new agreements. Except for Newark, they all have new local presidents.

To add to the problem, the MOA's decrease union representation. The Jefferson Modern Operating Agreement limits the shop committee to four and the ratio of stewards to members will be 1 to 300 when the new plant opens. Previously, Jefferson had six committeepersons, and the old contract set the ratio of stewards to members at 1 to 225 at plants built prior to 1964, and 1 to 250 at newer plants. At the same time, a new structure of "facilitators" is created. Management and the union each appoint a full-time facilitator for each shift. The contract states: "It shall be the responsibility of the facilitators to monitor team activities and to assist teams in carrying out their responsibilities." So while union representation is decreased, this new layer is created to bypass the union in communicating directly with members on the shop floor.[2]

Key Provisions

The following are key provisions from the Chrysler Modern Operating Agreements negotiated in 1986 and 1987. While the agreements are almost identical, quotes here are from the Jefferson Assembly contract unless otherwise identified. The MOA's are vague at several points or refer to agreements to be completed later. Since New Castle is the only Chrysler plant operating under the full MOA at this writing, examples of implementation from that plant will be cited.

1. The agreements are long-term. For example, Jefferson's is a seven-year agreement and Trenton's and New Castle's run for six years. Most of the agreements do not go into effect until some future specified event so expiration dates are spread out from 1993 to 1996, putting the union at a disadvantage in bargaining.

2. The MOA's are openly presented as a tradeoff—the union makes numerous concessions in exchange for new work in the plant. But what work the company will actually bring in and the number of jobs that will be saved is left vague and in management's hands. For example, union members at Jefferson were led to believe that the new agreement meant Chrysler would build a new truck in their plant. The actual contract only specifies that the MOA goes into effect when a "new vehicle" line is put in. Since that time Chrysler's acquisition of American Motors and a decline in auto sales have resulted in excess capacity for Chrysler. While the company will undoubtedly build something at Jefferson (it would betray too many political allies to back out entirely), there is already talk that Chrysler will choose a low volume model or find other ways to scale back operations at Jefferson.

Even when the model is specified, there is no guarantee that the subassembly operations (which can

be highly labor intensive) will be done in the plant. The Newark contract promises the new "A" body car, but the company has decided to shift the cushion room and other work to outside contractors. At Trenton the local union has discovered that Chrysler is planning to outsource a number of important engine component jobs. In sum, the number of jobs "saved" by the deals to accept the MOA will probably be substantially below the current employment in each plant.

3. The contract creates a team structure in the plant. A team is "a group of 8-15 employees performing all of the work in their work area." (5-15 at New Castle.) Each team elects its own coordinator who is paid an additional ten cents per hour. Team meetings may be held on relief time, during breakdowns, and on overtime. (The Jefferson contract specifies that a maximum of 30 minutes relief time may be used for team meetings.)

4. Under the Capability Progression Plan, usually called pay-for-knowledge, workers are paid, not according to the specific job they do, but according to the number of jobs for which they are "qualified." Workers are not required to qualify for more than one job but they may be temporarily reassigned to allow others to learn their jobs. All non-skilled classifications are collapsed into three technician grades (plus a fourth for incentive work at New Castle), although the plants differ slightly in how they assign the old classifications. Typically, Technician III, the lowest paid, includes material handlers, clerks, forklift operators, and cleaners. Technician II includes the bulk of the production workers—assemblers, various machine operators, and inspectors. Technician I includes only jobsetters at some plants and repairers and inspectors at others.

5. The number of skilled trades classifications is reduced, usually to seven:
-Electrical and Electronic
-Tool and Fixture
-Pipe System and Spray Equipment
-Millwright
-Machine Repair
-Gas and Electric Truck (forklift, etc.)
-Facilities (painters, carpenters, etc.)
There are some slight differences between plants. New Castle also has sheet metal and powerhouse workers as separate classifications. Sterling Heights, the first plant with reduced classifications, also has a separate one for sheet metal workers but none for gas and electric truck repair because that work has been contracted out.

The contract contains language intended to break down lines of demarcation even further: "The parties recognize that many tasks are properly performed within the scope of two or more trades." The contract affirms commitment to "efficient work practices," defined as "getting the job at hand completed as quickly as possible." (No mention of quality or safety here.) Lines between trades are further eroded by the elaborate retraining program set up by the contract. To qualify for raises in steps of 20 cents per hour, tradespeople must complete training which includes pipefitting for electricians and electronics for toolmakers and millwrights. Attempts to maintain lines of demarcation are made still more difficult by a provision which refers any disputes in this area to the International and corporate labor relations and forbids filing grievances. Again, what happens with lines of demarcation in practice depends greatly on how the local union presses its interpretation.

Much of the MOA's language on the trades was used in the SHAP agreement when that plant started up. The combination of classifications allowed management to shift work between the trades in order to play one trade off against the other. In its 1986 negotiations the union got a letter committing management to the principle that work should be done by the proper trade.

6. By combining production classifications, the MOA effectively removes seniority as a major factor in assignment for many jobs. The new contract also promises that "a seniority system that permits maximum team flexibility and preserves essential team skills is required." Special negotiations are to be held to create a new seniority agreement based on "occupational groups" to cover layoffs and transfers. If the local union and the plant cannot reach agreement by a specified date, the new seniority language will be written by the International and corporate labor relations.

But with regard to layoff and recall procedures, the specific language at New Castle may turn out to be the same as or even an improvement over previous arrangements. Despite a confusing phrase ("seniority is by team and may be exercised by Technician Group") and possible overriding considerations ("available jobs be filled by employees capable of performing them"), the examples seem to make clear that the lowest seniority person in each of the technician groups will be laid off first. This is similar to the departmental seniority in most plants under previous contracts. Since the number of technician groups is usually less than the number of departments, seniority will prevail more evenly. The language for plant-wide seniority equalization (a person may be laid off while a lower seniority person works in another department for up to 45 days) is similar to the traditional contracts.

The MOA's provide that training may be done without regard to departmental seniority. While it makes sense that different jobs may require different training, training also serves as the vehicle for advancement. Without any union restriction management favoritism will become the basis for assigning training and new jobs to particular teams.

7. The MOA's specifically provide that the overtime provisions in the national contract do not apply. At New Castle, where the MOA is in effect, there are absolutely no contractual restrictions on management's right to schedule overtime.

At Huntsville, the new contract changes the advance notice for working ten hours from one day to four

hours. The plant is 70 percent women, and this has created a special problem for mothers with small children. Committeeperson Dot Byford said, "We have a large percentage of women in our plant, and a lot of them have small children. They have arrangements to take them to a babysitter or a day care center, but they can't pick up their kids two hours later on a moment's notice.

"We complained about this, but management says our plant is unique in Chrysler because of the percentage of women and they can't change the contract because of that. They said it would be discrimination!"

8. For purposes of non-skilled overtime scheduling, each team constitutes an equalization of overtime group. At New Castle, despite the fact that workers have presumably been trained in several jobs, the Administrative Procedures require that all daily overtime be performed by the "individual who performed the required work during the regular shift." Also at New Castle, guidelines for equalizing overtime by teams "must give full protection to efficiency of operations at all times." Under the flexible conditions of team production, overtime work can often be assigned to one of several teams. Since equalization of overtime is only by team there are no provisions to prevent management favoritism in awarding overtime opportunities to specific teams.

9. On the one hand, the MOA contracts contain flowery language about equality, dignity and respect:

A Management-Labor relationship founded upon mutual trust and understanding... and shared responsibilities and decision making.

And later:

The parties acknowledge equity, fair play, and trust as the cornerstones of such a relationship with

I used to spend my evenings at union meetings. Then I discovered teams.

the dignity and respect for the individual paramount to all else.

Some UAW leaders have declared that the MOA's represents an important step toward "economic democracy." But the language which counts is the standard reaffirmation of management's rights:

The provisions and exhibits incorporated herein shall constitute the sole collective bargaining agreement at the plant and, unless expressly limited by this Agreement, the Corporation shall have and reserves the exclusive right to manage the plant and direct its affairs and working force.

The contract is carefully worded to place greater demands on workers without additional power, control or rights. For example, team duties include:
-Process salvage
-Correct minor and report major tooling and maintenance problems
-Monitor and control performance
-Adhere to plant safety rules
-Monitor and report attendance
-Equalize overtime
-Maintain a clean work area
-Administer Capability Progression Plan.

The job demands are definite—team members will be held responsible for doing jobs ranging from production, clean up and maintenance to monitoring and pressuring each other. But when it comes to deciding how to do these jobs, what methods and equipment are to be used, and what production standards should be, the choice of words indicates that real decision-making power resides elsewhere. Workers "assist in development of work assignments" and "assist in methods planning" and "provide input regarding production standards."

When workers can "provide input" in setting production standards, it means that management makes the decision, but teams are responsible for seeing that these standards are met.

10. Given how clear the contract is that management's rights prevail in any area not specifically covered, it is noteworthy that the contracts do not include many of the traditional clauses which limit management's rights. These range from health and safety issues, to equipment, to job definitions. Instead the new contracts mention "Administrative Procedural Matters" or "Administrative Procedures" which include past understandings not to be changed unilaterally. If the local union and plant management do not agree about these, they will be referred to corporate and International representatives. Changes in local agreements have to be approved by the membership, but the company is pushing the interpretation that changes in the issues downgraded to Administrative Procedures no longer require a membership vote. Indeed, even local union officers can be circumvented because management can ask that the issue be resolved upstairs.

This is another case where the significance depends primarily on implementation. Both SHAP and New Castle have printed their Administrative Procedures with the local contract, suggesting that that they are a part of the local contract and subject to a vote.

11. As evidence of "management commitment" the contract includes six points:
-Common cafeterias and parking lots
-Time clocks will be eliminated
-No necktie policy
-Recreation and wellness programs will be offered
-When appropriate employees and management will be trained in the same session
-Enhanced communications will be promoted throughout the plant.

Some of these, like the recreation and wellness programs, are serious. Some are jokes on the surface. Some require a little more information to see the humor. For example, there are no time clocks at SHAP, but employees have to enter the plant through computer controlled gates. When the special identity card is inserted into a slot at the gate, the computer allows the employee to pass and notes the time on a computer database that the supervisor can call up on a video display terminal. Cameras and video tape machines monitor the gates so that management can make sure that workers enter or leave only on their own cards.

12. The contracts reduce the number of stewards and, in some cases, the number of shop committee members. They also reduce the number of first line supervisors in the same ratio. At the same time the contracts create a full-time hourly and a full-time salary "facilitator" on each shift. The contract makes a major point of limiting union representation during overtime periods.

13. The agreement explicitly gives the union stamp of approval to further outsourcing:

It is acknowledged that necessary business decisions will be made relative to utilization of outside sources to perform certain tasks. In addition to outside sourcing historically performed at Jefferson Assembly, such tasks may include:
Direct delivery of material to the line
Building and grounds maintenance
Vendor rework.

14. The contract recognizes that implementation of the team concept will require extensive training programs for employees and authorizes the use of the local and national joint training funds for the purpose. Typically these kinds of joint training programs end up heavily biased toward management.

Notes

1. *Wall Street Journal*, December 7, 1972.

2. For a discussion of the dangers of facilitators, see Mike Parker, *Inside the Circle: A Union Guide to QWL*, Detroit, Labor Notes/South End Press, 1985, Chapter 6.

Appendix

The contract language reprinted below is excerpted from the 1986 Local Agreement between UAW Local 7 and Chrysler Jefferson Assembly.

VII. During these negotiations, the Union expressed concern over a number of subjects which affect their members and which have historically been implemented by plant management during the course of its day-to-day operations. These items, which are best described as Administrative Procedural Matters, provide an orderly and systematic approach to the resolution of everyday business affairs.

Although these matters are not incorporated in the Jefferson Assembly Operating Agreement, these understandings will remain in force as stated, and there will be no unilateral changes to them. Any proposed amendments or modifications shall be mutually agreed upon by both parties. Further, any matters not mutually agreed upon may be referred to Corporate and International representatives for resolution.

XI. The Corporation and the Union have expressed a mutual commitment that employees receive a full measure of job security and mutual recognition. The parties recognize this measure of job security can only be realized within a work environment which promotes operational efficiency and cost effectiveness.

In this regard, it is acknowledged that necessary business decisions will be made relative to the utilization of outside sources to perform certain tasks. In addition to outside sourcing historically preformed at Jefferson Assembly, such tasks may include:

- Direct delivery of material to the line
- Building and grounds maintenance
- Vendor rework.

Exhibit A: Team Concept

During these negotiations, the parties agreed that it would be mutually beneficial to the Corporation, the Union and our employees to develop the full and effective use of human resources. A critical part of that development is the adoption of a participative style of operation. This participative style acknowledges the important contribution that can be made by soliciting input from employees regarding matters which directly affect them in their work environment. This operating style recognizes the need to develop a non-adversarial relationship, based on trust, respect and loyalty, with an aim of enhancing the dignity and self-worth of all employees. In that regard, the parties pledge to resolve or adjust differences that affect their relationship in a manner which exhibits tolerance, patience and objectivity and avoids confrontation. This participative approach to doing business coupled with the large investment being made by the Company and the Union's acknowledgement that the Company must produce quality products at competitive prices make the Union's long term cooperation to continue the principles of flexibility and efficiency absolutely necessary.

Therefore, in order to enhance the long term success of the Jefferson Assembly Plant and to promote the involvement of all its employees in the decision making and problem solving process, the parties agree to begin the establishment of the team concept in the Plant within twelve (12) months from the date of this Understanding. An outside facilitator with expertise in team building may be engaged to assist in the implementation of this concept. It is recognized that implementation of the team concept will require extensive training of all employees. The parties agree that it is appropriate to utilize funds from the national, reservoir and local joint training funds for this purpose.

I. Teams

A group of employees referred to as technicians performing all of the work in an area which might relate to a specific section of the production process, a physical area of the plant or any other logical grouping of jobs that provides meaningful purpose within manufacturing process constraints.

II. Team Development

A. Personal Performance Standards

1. Participate in team concept.
2. Attend work regularly.
3. Produce quality work.
4. Practice defect prevention.
5. Conform to job requirements.
6. Follow safety procedures.
7. Communicate problems.
8. Keep work areas clean.
9. Improve skills and share knowledge.
10. Constantly strive to improve the operation.

B. Team Duties

1. Participate in daily audits.
2. Process salvage.
3. Assist in development of work assignments.
4. Correct minor and report major tooling and maintenance problems.
5. Provide input regarding production standards.
6. Assist in methods planning.
7. Monitor and control performance.
8. Adhere to plant safety rules.
9. Monitor and report attendance.
10. Equalize overtime.
11. Keep overtime equalization records.
12. Support and help train team members.
13. Maintain a clean work area.
14. Problem solving (quality, productivity, etc.).
15. Vacation schedules.
16. Coordinate with other teams.
17. Be aware of and adhere to EEO Guidelines.
18. Assist in employee counselling.
19. Administer Capability Progression Plan.
20. Seek technical assistance where required.

C. Team Size

Appropriate team size will be determined based on a distribution of work which will permit flexibility and efficient utilization of the work force. Generally the Team will be a group of 8 to 15 employees performing all of the tasks in their work area.

D. Team Coordinator

Each team shall select one from among them who will be responsible for all the coordination activities of the Team. The Team Coordinator will be paid an additional ten cents per hour over his established rate. The parties agree that it is desireable to rotate team coordinators. Therefore, elections for team coordinators shall be held periodically.

E. Team Meetings.

1. Team Meetings shall be held by each team for the purpose of resolving various production, quality and maintenance problems.

2. Attendance at Team Meetings will be voluntary; however, it is understood that the decisions of the team shall be binding on all members.

3. A portion of employees' relief time not to exceed thirty (30) minutes per week may be devoted to team meetings. Additional team meetings may be held external to the shift time or during breakdowns.

4. Team Meetings shall not be used to circumvent the grievance procedure or any other provisions of the National P&M Agreement or local agreements.

III. Management Commitment.

To foster participative decision making and the full cooperation the parties are striving to achieve, the Corporation agrees to remove historical differences that have identified and been associated with employees and management. Therefore the following will apply:

1. Common cafeterias and parking lots will be instituted with the completion of the new facility to be built on the Jefferson site.

2. Time clocks will be eliminated.

3. A no neck tie policy.

4. Recreation and wellness programs will be offered.

5. Extensive training of employees and management will be provided in the same session when appropriate.

6. Enhanced communications will be promoted throughout the plant.

IV. Interaction Conduct

As a key element in our new relationship, both parties agree that all interactions will be characterized by:

1. Handling all matters in a common sense way within the bounds of common decency.

2. Using extraordinary effort to maintain and enhance the individual's self-esteem.

3. Listening and responding one to the other with empathy.

4. Asking for help in solving mutual problems.

5. Giving background information and describing why a change is necessary.

6. Remaining calm during emotional situations and discussing such matters in private.

7. Expressing confidence in each individual's ability to carry out his responsibilities.

8. Remaining constantly aware that Management and Union Representatives are the role models for all others.

In support of the foregoing, the parties commit to a joint training effort in conjunction with the work team concept. Such training will work toward enhancing people's ability to deal with one another in a positive way and will include all employees.

V. Participative Style

It is the meaning and intent of this Agreement to recognize certain fundamentals in developing a new participatory style of management based upon the Participation Credo set forth below:

1. Objectives will be shared and there will be a consistent flow of energy toward accomplishing those objectives.

2. People will feel free to acknowledge difficulties because they expect open, non-threatening discussion and problem solving.

3. Decision making will be based upon ability, source and availability of information, timing, and sense of responsibility, and a person's level in the organization will not be considered the sole determinant.

4. The judgment of people at all levels will be respected.

5. People will readily request the help of others and be willing to give help in return.

6. Relationships will be honest with no political games.

7. There will be a high degree of trust among people with a sense of freedom and mutual responsibility.

8. People at one level will not assume that people at another level know why they are requested to do something.

9. Mistakes will be viewed as the opportunity to learn and signal the need for training, counselling, or coaching.

10. Everyone will recognize that threats only cause people to concentrate on the threat and not on the job to be done.

11. Risk will be accepted as a condition of growth and change.

12. Poor performance will be confronted and a joint resolution will be developed.

13. Methods and policies will be questioned and changed if they no longer apply.

The parties have agreed that the long term success of the entire Jefferson organization depends, to a large measure, upon the Participation Credo set forth above. In addition, the parties have affirmed the principle that this process must continue to be jointly developed, implemented, and monitored. Therefore, in this regard, both parties commit themselves to the allocation of sufficient human resources to facilitate the successful growth and development of the individual as well as the organization.

VI. Organization Structure.

Since employees will have a greater decision making role, including selecting Team Coordinators, fewer supervisors and union representatives will be required. The parties recognize that reduction in the first line of supervision and union representation requires effective utilization of the team concept. Accordingly, the parties agree to phase in the reduction of supervisors and union representation.

On the effective date of this agreement the plant shop committee shall be limited to four (4) members and the ratio of Chief Stewards to employees shall not exceed 1 to each 300 employees.

The number of first line supervisors shall be reduced by no less than the same proportion as the reduction in the number of union representatives as set forth above.

VII. Union Representation During Overtime Periods

The Union is in agreement with management that during overtime periods and weekend schedules, Union officials are expected to work. The Union representative shall only handle those matters which arise during such periods.

Management has the Union's assurance that this Agreement will not be abused. Should this become a problem, it will be called to the attention of the International Union for resolution.

VIII. Seniority Application.

A. The parties recognize that if this new and unique organization structure at Jefferson Assembly involving the team concept and a pay-for-knowledge plan is to be successful, a seniority system that permits maximum team flexibility and preserves essential team skills is required.

Therefore, the parties agree to start negotiations sixty (60) days preceding the announced build-out date for the 'K' and 'E' bodies on a new seniority agreement which shall be based on occupational groups and shall govern layoffs and recalls, transfers, and other appropriate seniority matters. The negotiations on such agreement shall be completed by November 30, 1987 and the new seniority agreement shall run concurrently with the term of the Operating Agreement dated July 29, 1986. In the event the Local Union and Plant Management fail to reach an agreement by the agreed to date, the matter shall be submitted to the International Union and Corporate Union Relations for prompt resolution.

B. In view of going to the team concept, Management shares the Union's concern of allowing employees the opportunity to select the department or shift of their choice prior to the new Agreement taking effect. Both parties agreed this must be done in an orderly and efficient manner and on a one time basis only. Therefore, the following understanding has been reached.

Employees will be given the opportunity to apply for the department of their choice, or for the shift of their choice. All applications must be filed out and returned to the Employment Office no later than July 31, 1987. The application will be reviewed by the Employment Office and the appropriate member(s) of the Plant Shop Committee.

Seniority permitting, employees will be transferred to the department or shift of their choice prior to the buildout of the 'K' and 'E' models (presently scheduled for November, 1987). In order to assure a successful launch, employees will not be permitted to exercise shift preference or transfer under section (66)(c) for the first six months following the launch of the new product.

Training may be provided without regard to seniority within the department.

IX. General Provisions

A. All technicians shall be a member of a team.

B. The Memorandum of Understanding on Overtime shall not apply. Each team on a shift will constitute an equalization of overtime group.

C. Transfers at technicians' request may be delayed to accomplish necessary training in order to maintain the efficiency of operations.

D. Union Representatives and technicians who participate on various plant operating committees will accept appropriate responsibilities.

E. Management and the Union shall designate a team facilitator for each production shift. It shall be the responsibility of the facilitators to monitor team activities and to assist teams in carrying out their responsibilities.

Exhibit B. Capability Progression Pay

Capability Progression pay shall apply to all non-skilled trade employees who shall be identified as Technicians. Technicians shall be eligible for advancement to and retention of higher wage level rates based on their job knowledge and performance of identified operations in a single team.

A. Progression Criteria

Rates of pay shall be determined by the number of different operations Technicians demonstrate they can proficiently perform. Team members shall establish qualifying operations under the Capability Progression Plan and determine when Technicians are entitled to wage advancement subject to approval of Management. The table below sets forth the wage rate and progression criteria:

Level	Wage Rate	III Technician	II Technician	I Technician
Level 1	$12.67	Base	N/A	N/A
Level 2	$12.81	Five jobs on one team.	Base	N/A
Level 3	$12.95	All jobs on one team.	Five operations on one team.	Base
Level 4	$13.05	All jobs on two teams.	All operations on one team.	Five operations on one team.
Level 5	$13.13	N/A	All operations on one team plus five operations on another team in the same department.	All operations on one team.
Level 6	$13.37	N/A	N/A	All operations on one team plus five operations on another team in the same department.

B. Rates Upon Reassignment, Transfer or Recall

Technicians who transfer or are reassigned to a new team or recalled to work from indefinite layoff shall retain the level held on the team from which transferred, reassigned, or indefinitely laid off; provided, however, the Technician must requalify for the level held. Based on satisfactory progress toward this goal, the Technician's rate shall not be adjusted; however, Technicians who fail to make progress, refuse to requalify, or are not capable of performing the work shall be reduced to the base level of their team category after a reasonable opportunity in accordance with the Capability Progression Pay Plan Provisions.

C. Conversion

[Not reproduced. Contains language about the mechanism for converting from the classification system to the Capability Progression Plan. For example, which old classification codes qualify for which level of technician.]

D. Qualifying for Higher Wage Level

In the event a Technician does not wish to qualify for higher wage level rates under the Capability Progression Plan, he will not be required to do so. However, such Technician will be responsible for training other Technicians on his operation and, when appropriate, he may be temporarily reassigned to permit another Technician to qualify on such operation.

E. New Hires

Starting wage rates and rate progression for new hires shall be determined in accordance with Section (114) in the Production and Maintenance Agreement except that the applicable percentages shall be applied to the base level for the category of the team to which new hires are assigned. New hires shall not participate in the Capability Progression Pay Plan before they complete the new hire wage progression.

Exhibit C. Memorandum of Understanding on Skilled Trades

I. Skilled Trades Classifications

Pursuant to the provisions of Section (6) and (10) of the Supplemental Agreement Special Provisions pertaining to Skilled Trades Employees, the parties agree to add to the Lists and Schedules in Appendix I the Skilled Trades classifications, related Apprenticeable classifications and complementing Non-Apprenticeable classifications set forth below.

A. Tooling and Maintenance Classifications
Electrical and Electronic Specialist (Apprenticeable)
Related Apprenticeable Classifications
5629 Electrician
5763 Repairer Welder Equipment
Tool and Fixture Specialist (Apprenticeable
Related Apprenticeable Classifications
5365 Layout Metal and Wood
6175 Tool Maker Jig and Fixture Builder
Complementing Non-Apprenticeable Classifications
5520 Grinder Cutter
6270 Welder Tool and Die
Pipe Systems and Spray Equipment Specialist (Apprenticeable)
Related Apprenticeable Classification
5680 Pipefitter Plumber
Complementing Non-Apprenticeable Classification
5751 Repairer Spray and Stripe Glue
Millwright Maintenance Specialist (Apprenticeable)
Related Apprenticeable Classifications
5658 Millwright
5777 Sheet Metal Worker
Complementing Non-Apprenticeable Classifications
5712 Repairer Elevator
6250 Welder Maintenance
Related Apprenticeable Classification
5638 Machine Repair
Gas and Electric Truck Specialist (Apprenticeable)
Related Apprenticeable Classification
5719 Mechanic Gas and Electric Jitney
Facilities Specialist (Non-Apprenticeable)
Related Non-Apprenticeable Classifications
5668 Painter and Glazier Maintenance
5613 Brickmason and Cement Finisher
5617 Carpenter
5671 Painter Sign Hand Letter
B. Powerhouse and Disposal Plant Classifications (All Non-Apprenticeable)
5703 Repairer Boiler
5706 Repairer Compressor
5905 Boiler Operator
5920 Compressor Operator
5942 Sewage Disposal Plant Operator.
II. Skilled Trades Work Practices
The Company and the Union agree to direct their best efforts

toward the full utilization of employees which is inherent in the concept of "a fair day's work for a fair day's pay." The parties recognize that application of this notion requires that each employee exert a normal work effort that is fair to both the employee and employer. Furthermore, such work effort must be in accordance with efficient skilled trades work practices. To this end the parties affirm their commitment to observing efficient skilled trades work practices in keeping with the principles stated in the 1985 P&M Agreement.

In order to clarify what constitutes efficient work practices, the parties recognize that many tasks are properly performed within the scope of two or more trades. In other instances under the following circumstances, skilled trades employees, in order to complete a principal assignment, may properly perform complementary or incidental tasks or series of such tasks that if performed separately may be regularly assigned to a particular trade:

(1) the time required in relation to the principal job is short;
(2) the employee has the capability, e.g., the ability to weld; and
(3) the work can be performed safely.

The following is an example of efficient skilled trades work practices:

A Millwright Specialist is assigned to replace a coupling on a conveyor. The job requires pulling back a motor, removing the brake and uncoupling an air line to gain access to the coupling. It would be expected that the Millwright perform each of these incidental tasks without relying on Electrical, Electronic and Pipe Systems Specialists.

The parties agree that the objective of efficient work practices is getting the job at hand completed as quickly as possible. Everyone should work as a team member for the common welfare of all.

Disputes arising from the above understanding may be referred to the Skilled Trades Representatives of the UAW Chrysler Department and the Corporate Labor Relations Staff pursuant to the work assignment practices provisions of Letter 13 in the 1985 P&M Agreement and shall not be subject to the grievance procedure.

III. Skilled Trades Seniority Application

A. Journeymen on the Related Apprenticeable classifications set forth in Section I., above, as of the day immediately preceding the effective date of said Agreement, be classified on the Specialist classification which is related to their classification. Such employees shall exercise their skilled trades seniority date on the Specialist classification after accumulating three (3) years experience on the Specialist classification.

B. Permanent Employees on the Complementing Non-Apprenticeable classifications set forth in Section I., above, as of the day immediately preceding the effective date of this Agreement, be classified on the Specialist classification which their classification complements. Such employees shall exercise their skilled trades seniority date on the Specialist classification after accumulating four (4) years' experience on the Specialist classification.

C. Permanent Employees on the Related Non-Apprenticeable classifications set forth in Section I., above, as of the day immediately preceding the effective date of this Operating Agreement shall, as of the effective date of said Agreement, be classified on the Non-Apprenticeable Specialist classification which is related to their classification. Such employees shall exercise their skilled trades seniority date on the Specialist classification after accumulating two (2) years' experience on the Specialist classification.

D. Skilled Trades Temporary Employees shall not be classified on Specialist classifications unless and until they acquire the right to exercise skilled trades seniority on one of the Related Apprenticeable or Non-Apprenticeable classifications or Complementing Non-Apprenticeable classifications set forth in Section I. above.

IV. Skilled Trades Compensation and Training

A. Journeymen and permanent employees classified in accordance with the provisions of Section III., above, shall be paid the applicable hourly wage rate specified on the Classification and Rate Table as set forth in Attachment I.

B. In order to provide employees with opportunities to acquire the broader skills required to maintain high-tech equipment and earn hourly wages commensurate with increased responsibilities, the Corporation shall establish a Skilled Trade Rate Improvement Program (STRIP). The program shall consist of three (3) levels of training for each new classification. Employees shall receive an increase to their hourly wage rate when they successfully complete the specified training for the applicable level. The training content and the amount of the applicable increase for successful completion of the training are set forth by classification on Attachment II.

14. Oklahoma City: International Changes its Tune

The UAW International was not always as favorable to the team concept as it is now. When the union was trying to organize General Motors' new Oklahoma City plant in 1979, getting rid of the team concept was one of its main talking points.

The Oklahoma City plant was part of General Motor's "Southern strategy" to escape the UAW by building plants in right-to-work states. The UAW was determined to organize the Oklahoma City plant to prove that GM could not run away from the union. The corporation's heavy-handed imposition of the team concept was used as an argument for why the workers should go union. And the Oklahoma City workers were convinced that a union would be better for them than team concept.

GM began hiring workers to build Chevrolet Citations in October 1978; production began in April 1979. From the beginning, the plant operated under the team concept. In lieu of a union contract, workers were given a booklet outlining the team concept and their responsibilities.

Workers were organized into teams of 15 to 30 members, and each team chose a leader. The leader, who made an extra ten cents per hour, made job assignments and kept overtime records, leaving the "area advisor" (foreman) with little to do, as each supervised only one team.

Many GM workers from other plants had transferred to Oklahoma City. At first they thought the team concept sounded good: they wanted the chance, for the first time, to make decisions about their jobs. They soon discovered, however, that management was willing to let them make decisions about only the most trivial things.

Darold Dye, a pipefitter who started at Oklahoma City in January 1979 and was instrumental in the UAW organizing drive, related one incident that happened early on, before production began:

I was on second shift in the skilled trades. They had us coming into the plant ten hours a day, seven

---

- *General Motors CPC Oklahoma City*
- *UAW Local 1999*
- *Location: Oklahoma City, Oklahoma*
- *Employment: 5,500 workers*
- *Product: Chevy Citation, Buick Century, Pontiac 6000*
- *Production began: April 1979*
- *Team concept began: November 1987*
- *UAW Local 1999*
  Address: 7125 S. Air Depot Blvd., Oklahoma City, OK 73135 Phone: 405 / 732-7330

days a week, but there were no tools assigned. They were starting to bring in the equipment we would be servicing, but we got no instruction.

So our team asked that we come in early and overlap with the first shift to become familiar with the equipment. They told us that we could decide what color the restroom would be painted or the texture of the toilet paper, but when it came to what time we were going to come to work, they'd tell us.

So there was a motion to disband the team, it passed unanimously, and from then on the foreman had to give us orders as to what to do.

In other cases management tried to give teams decision-making powers that were completely inappropriate. Dye gives an example:

One woman transferred to a new team where she was the only woman; all the rest of the people were young males. When she'd been there about two weeks, she was told by her doctor that she needed an operation, a hysterectomy. She told the foreman and he said she would have to get permission from the team to be off, because they'd have to do her work while she was gone.

The first members hired onto a team would tend to divide up the work so that all the hard work was loaded onto one job which became virtually impossible to do. Someone who came in later would get stuck with that job.

UAW organizers sent from Detroit, along with the union's in-plant supporters, argued that a grievance procedure would provide better protection than the team concept. They explained that under the UAW contract you could file a Paragraph 78 grievance if your job was overloaded, while under the team concept you were not supposed to complain about workloads because "the team had decided."

As in most other union organizing drives, the slogan that "management is our best organizer" was true in Oklahoma City. "If it hadn't been for team concept there wouldn't have been a union in Oklahoma City," Dye said.

Along with the team concept went a drastic attendance control procedure: after four absences or tardinesses, for any reason, a worker was discharged. There was no step procedure as in a traditional plant.

When the union won the recognition vote by 79 percent in July 1979, team concept was abolished as soon as the International-appointed committeepersons bargained a new local agreement. Classifications, including both skilled and production, were increased from 10 to 130. A traditional local agreement was signed by the

TEAM CONCEPT: THE PHOENIX

by H.C. Shearer

The big man entered the room wearing a worried look. There, sitting around tables, laughing and joking, were 15 of his fellow workers. One of the supervisors in the room quickly called the group to order when he saw Dale come in the room.

"The team," said the supervisor, "has a decision to make. Dale has been absent for three days, and the team has to decide whether or not he is excused. It's your decision," he told the group.

Then he nodded to Dale, as if to say, stand and explain your absence as you were trained to do.

Dale's big frame unwound from the chair he had taken. He stood before the group and in a soft, apologetic voice, explained that his family needed him. His young daughter was in the hospital and he had spent most of the past three days with her.

No one thought too hard about the absence because Dale's reason was good and because the new OKC-GM plant had not started up.

Using the power given to them, the group unanimously excused Dale. Everyone seemed to feel good about the decision as they went back to talking and joking. The supervisors and the team leader had taken a table close to the others, but it was a little off to the side. One of them spoke out: "Dale, can I see you over here for a minute?"

Dale went over to the table and, at their suggestions, took a seat with them. In a smooth low tone of voice, the supervisor began the interrogation.

"Dale, you were gone three days. Couldn't you have come in at least part of the day Tuesday?"

Dale replied that for most of the day, he had stayed at the hospital. In the afternoon he went home to rest.

"What about Wednesday?" the supervisor continued.

Dale's face began to turn red as he told about his activities on Wednesday morning and afternoon.

The supervisor pressed him further. "Well, what about Thursday?"

At that point, Dale got up from the table. He didn't say a word to anybody. He just walked out.

I never saw Dale Grey again. I wonder what happened to him, especially now that the team concept has risen from its grave.

This is a true story about one experience that occurred in March 1979. I thought team concept was dead when the union was approved the following

July. Alas, like a Phoenix*, it continues to rise from its own ashes.

Workers are given no significant powers under team concept and those given are easily corrupted, circumvented, or taken back at management's whim.

Take Dale Grey's case: the team excused him, but management went around the team decision and used humiliation to drive Dale out, thus taking from the workers the power to excuse.

Dale didn't have anyone to help him at that time. He was a probationary employee; his peers were as weak as he, and the union was a distant hope.

Some may say that we all give up dignity in order to work. Wrong. There is no box on your paycheck that lists loss of dignity and a dollar amount to pay for it.

One sells his labor, not his dignity.

Team concept, I'm convinced, offers better treatment only to a few, while the majority receive worse treatment and less quality in their worklife.

We didn't need team concept in 1979 and we don't need it now.

* *Editor's note: According to an Egyptian myth, the Phoenix was a bird that lived for 500 years, consumed itself in fire and then rose again from the ashes.*

This article is reprinted from Newsline 1999 *(Volume 7, Number 7, August-September, 1987), the newspaper of UAW Local 1999. H.C. Shearer is on the Newsline staff.*

newly-chartered Local 1999 on December 3, 1979.

When the UAW beat GM and the team concept in Oklahoma City in 1979, it was the beginning of the end for the Southern strategy. In the National Agreement signed that fall, the company agreed that any new GM plant that opened would automatically recognize the UAW and fall under the National Agreement.

This agreement was not without its ironies. Afterwards, the union did not seem to mind the team concept so much. The very next GM plant to open—the Shreveport, Louisiana truck plant—was both team concept and UAW from the very beginning. It seemed the union was against the team concept only where it didn't have a contract.

Team Concept Once Again

Team concept eventually came to Oklahoma City after all—but under a different name.

In 1987 GM once again began to insist that the plant adopt teams. Because of the previous fiasco, however, the company insisted that the new plan would be nothing like the earlier team concept; instead management wanted a plant just like NUMMI. (For those familiar with NUMMI, this hardly seems like a convincing argument.) The shop committee of Local 1999 printed T-shirts that proclaimed "NO NUMMI."

Insisting all the while that it was not team concept, management and the local union began a pilot project called "Employee-to-Employee" in the paint department. Two supervisor's groups on each shift held voluntary half-hour meetings on overtime once a week. A pamphlet issued by the company and the local union said the program was to achieve "rights of employees to participate in decisions that affect their working lives."

At the same time, the UAW International was pushing Local 1999 to adopt team concept throughout the plant. An International Rep from the union's GM Department told members that if the local did not switch to team concept the plant would close.

Discussion in the plant during local negotiations in the fall of 1987 centered on the team concept. "All the people who were here when team concept was in are against it," said Darold Dye. "But the entire second shift wasn't here then, and many on the first shift." Members of the New Directions caucus passed out blue tags that read "Count Me With Those Who Oppose Team Concept." Local 1999 Vice-president Steve Featherston wrote in the local newspaper that most team concept agreements at other GM plants were "take it or else" propositions. Featherston noted that most workers at team plants received a pay increase and expanded recreational and training facilities. He contended that labor-management relations had improved at team concept plants, and that the plan needed more time before its success could be judged.

In November the shop committee brought back a local agreement that included a plan called "Voluntary Input Process"—VIP. It contained all the usual features of a team concept contract except the name. It called for "units" (rather than teams) of six to ten workers, plus a "support person" (rather than team leader). The foreman was renamed "group coordinator."

In the assembly line departments, classifications were reduced to "participant" and "non-participant." Participating VIP operators were to rotate through all the jobs in their unit, attend unit meetings, do housekeeping, inspect and repair their own work, and "seek constant improvement." Non-participants were those who chose not to learn all the jobs or to attend unit meetings. Like participants, they were responsible for self-inspection and repair. VIP would not apply in skilled trades.

Although the Local 1999 by-laws call for the full text of local agreements to be available 48 hours before a ratification vote, only "highlights" of the agreement were distributed this time. Informational meetings were held department by department, with staffers from the UAW-GM Department in Detroit explaining the new contract. It was ratified by 66 percent in skilled trades and 72 percent in production.

"It was sold as *not* being team concept," said Darold Dye. The shop committee's brochure stated:

> This process in no way resembles the team concept that management unilaterally forced on us in 1979. Rather than a plan designed to keep the union out of the plant, this new agreement assumes that the union will be the architect of the boldest experiment in the corporation's history.

A principal reason for the ratification was the pay raises. All unit members who chose to participate in VIP would receive a pay raise to $14.49, which was 20 cents more than the higher classifications such as inspection were making before (base rate, 1987 National Agreement). Support persons would earn $14.99 and "non-participants" $14.29.

Another reason for the yes vote is that many members believed team concept was inevitable anyway, given the commitments made by the International in the new National Agreement. "The International said if we didn't have an agreement they'd negotiate us an agreement," said Dye.

Although at the time of this writing it was too early to draw conclusions, VIP seems designed to create divisions between participants and non-participants. In other team concept plants, all workers are considered team members whether they participate in pay-for-knowledge or not, and all are encouraged to attend team meetings. In Oklahoma City the contract states:

> If a non-participant wishes to attend the meeting, he/she may do so provided he/she gives prior notice to the Group Coordinator and does not disrupt the meeting.

15. Fairfax II: New Plant, New Contract

By Bob Kutchko

In January 1986, UAW Local 31 in Kansas City, Kansas ratified a new team-style contract by a two-to-one margin. The contract was part of a deal whereby General Motors promised to build a billion-dollar plant to replace the aging Fairfax facility in exchange for a hefty package of tax breaks and union concessions.

An announcement of the contract approval, signed by the company and the union, congratulated Fairfax workers on the vote:

Congratulations to all Fairfax employees on making the decision for your future. Without this decision, all of the work of others would have been fruitless. We have always had faith in your intelligence and fairness. When given an opportunity, Fairfax employees will do the right thing.

But was "the right thing" for GM also "the right thing" for the workers and the community? GM admitted that there would be at least 1,000 fewer jobs in the new plant; critics charged that the figure would be closer to 1,500. The city of Kansas City, Kansas granted more than $200 million in tax breaks and outright gifts to General Motors.

The union and the city were promised jobs in return for their sacrifices. But there would be fewer jobs, and the tax breaks meant belt-tightening for a fairly small city. The net result seemed to be a smaller payroll and dwindling tax revenues.

GM was so confident that its demand for the team concept would be met that, by the time of the contract vote, construction was already under way next door to the old plant.

The new contract was full of nice language about "mutual trust," "respect" and "cooperation," but the evidence indicates that GM pulled no punches to get the contract ratified.

Bob Kutchko is a former committeeperson at Fairfax I and was a member of UAW Local 31.

- *Fairfax II Assembly*
- *Location: Kansas City, Kansas*
- *Employment: 3,800 hourly*
- *Product: Pontiac Grand Prix*
- *Production began: May 1987*
- *Team concept began: May 1987*
- *UAW Local 31*
  Address: 500 Kindelberger Road, Kansas City, KS 66115
  Phone: 913 / 342-7330

For a number of years, Fairfax management hinted that the plant was on its last legs, although when convenient, GM lauded the versatility and tradition of the decades-old plant. During World War II Fairfax produced bombers. After the war, the government sold GM the plant for the grand sum of one dollar, and automobile production began. During one period, cars and jet fighters were built simultaneously.

But increasingly, management implied that the plant's better days were long gone. Although GM never claimed to be losing money at Fairfax, management officials said that slacking sales of larger cars threatened the plant's future. In the daily plant newsletter, management wrote that it would cost more to convert the old plant to front wheel drive production than to build a new plant.

As the 1970's came to a close, the community speculated that GM would build a brand new plant across town in western Wyandotte County. GM finally announced such plans, and movement in real estate and infrastructure increased. However, as suddenly as the announcement was made, some months later GM cancelled its plans.

The announcements back and forth sent Fairfax workers and their families on an emotional roller coaster of concern, relief, and then anxiety again. More than 5,300 hourly jobs seemed to slip through the community's fingers. General Motors cavalierly described the perceived threat to jobs as a "significant emotional event."

A Glimmer of Hope

Did Fairfax have any chance at all?

General Motors was planning a new nationwide project to build smaller, front-wheel drive cars called GM10. Initial plans for the GM10 cars included coupes available by the 1988 model year, sedans available by 1989, and wagons and diesels by 1990. The Pontiac, Olds, Buick, and Chevrolet divisions would all be involved. In the first year of full production, GM anticipated North American volume at 1,901,000 vehicles, representing almost a third of its sales.

Did Fairfax have a shot at GM10? At management's coaxing, UAW Local 31 officials were convinced to participate in a joint committee to explore future possibilities. And so the Fairfax GM10 Project Committee was born.

A recently defeated shop chairman was appointed to coordinate the local's side of the project, and another eight members representing various departments were also assigned. Beginning in early 1985, these members worked full-time on the committee. The GM10 Project began to develop a life of its own, separate and apart from the daily drudgery of life on the line. Project members downed their tools and and picked up notebooks, escaping the line to attend meetings and travel across the country to visit other GM plants such as NUMMI, Poletown, Orion, Twinsville, and Willow Run. Some of these trips were made to see the team concept in action; others were to observe state-of-the-art automation. For example, Project members went to Willow Run to see the robots in the sealer paint department.

GM10 Project committee members were introduced to "new ways" of building cars. The GM10 cars were to be built without defects. "No level of non-conformance to specifications is acceptable," Project members were told over and over. Other plants in the U.S. and around the world could achieve these standards with different production methods. Other union locals in the U.S. and around the world had a new type of contract that seemed to ensure success. Project members were told that these changes were necessary in "today's modern world" if an auto plant were to survive.

Management saw to it that the GM10 Project members were led to certain conclusions. "Impartial" experts and consultants all told of a new, cooperative way to stay alive in the automobile industry. But this would mean a big departure from the way things had been done at Fairfax. In essence the company said that if auto workers tried hard enough, if they were more efficient and flexible, if they understood that their goals were the same as management's, then maybe there was a chance for a new plant.

GM made it clear that the GM10 cars had to be built in this new atmosphere. With a "many are called but few are chosen" attitude, GM suggested sites around the country that might accommodate GM10 cars. A renovated plant here...a new plant there...high tech for tighter fits and better quality...combined with better labor relations and worker attitudes... Management told union representatives that if they couldn't make the changes, then maybe the workforce at the Arlington, Texas plant would. Or Oshawa, Ontario...or Shreveport, Louisiana... Local unions were "whipsawed" against one another to see which would give the most for a secure future. Without a firm stand by the International union to coordinate the locals in a united fight against GM's demands for concessions, locals could be picked off, one by one. Temptation to make changes was strong.

Tax Giveaways

GM also placed great demands on the city, claiming that keeping Fairfax's huge payroll in the community required a tax break. So politicians put together a big package of taxpayer money to appease the corporation, including $136 million in tax breaks through a $1 billion

industrial revenue bond; $20 million in infrastructure site improvements such as road expansion and repair; and Fairfax Municipal Airport as the building site.

Giving away the airport had to be one of the most blatant, symbolic acts of prostration any city government has ever made. Fairfax Municipal Airport was the city's only public aviation facility, and it dated back decades. Leases were broken with a string of companies along the airport corridor, all of which had to relocate. A modern fire station was demolished and rebuilt a few blocks away. One day the huge runways were torn up; the next day they were pulverized and transformed into concrete for the new plant. And for the icing on the cake, GM wrung a no-strike agreement from construction unions.

Two years later, Kansas City was still debating the wisdom of its deal with GM. Although he voted for the tax breaks, Councilman Ron Mears told the *Kansas City Times*: "This cost the city, and I hope we can recover what we put into it." Mears did not speak out at the time, but he later said that a high-ranking GM official told him the city gave away far more than was necessary to keep the plant.[1]

Contract Battles

When negotiations began, GM made bold demands, confident that union leaders at Fairfax would support the drastic changes that were being studied by the GM10 Project. GM put issues on the table such as automation; outsourcing of jobs like the cushion room to lower-wage, non-union companies; replacement of tag relief by mass relief; fewer seniority rights for job assignments and shift preference; elimination of many classifications; and an intensified job pace.

But not all members of the GM10 Project were pleased with what they considered to be huge concessions. Opposition to a team-style contract developed both on the committee and in the plant. Hundreds of Fairfax workers were "migrant" auto workers from the closed down GM plant at Fremont, California. Fremont had since re-opened as NUMMI with Japanese-style production. Many Fairfax workers heard from their friends and family members who worked at NUMMI that the work pace was vicious, management intimidating, and the union ineffective.

Dissenters on the GM10 Project were not appreciated. One outspoken critic, John Herrera, who had been recording-secretary at the Fremont plant, authored a letter signed by 13 union members of the GM10 Project stating that the company was not seriously interested in the input of the union. The incident that sparked the letter was a management decision to eliminate a parking lot in the rear of the plant, which would mean that those working in that area would have to walk three-quarters of a mile. The writers complained that a decision made jointly was revoked unilaterally, and requested "that any decision that has not been 'jointly' considered be nullified and renegotiated 'jointly.'" The letter was mailed to officials of the company and the union, including GM Vice-President Alfred Warren and UAW Vice-President Donald Ephlin. Many of the signers of the letter threatened to go back on the line, and it wasn't long afterwards that Herrera was eliminated from the committee. The explanation he was offered was that the committee was too large and he was the low seniority person.

Later, Herrera looked back on the union's work in the GM10 Project committee and said:

> We were more of a token than anything. We really didn't get to do anything. Everytime we wanted to give input we had to go through a whole bunch of red tape. We were just there to show that there was joint participation. If we weren't traveling, we were basically sitting at our desks doing nothing. The company worked with IE [Industrial Engineering], and we kept going back to them to get information about what was going on. We argued for things like a parking lot in the rear of the plant because the plant was so big, or bathrooms downstairs. But our arguments didn't mean anything. They did what they wanted to do.

Fairfax II worker, illustrated in a Future 31 leaflet.

They put the parking lot in on the blueprints like we wanted it, but the next day it was gone.

Future 31

An opposition caucus formed at Fairfax called Future 31. The caucus began to put out informational leaflets explaining what the team concept would mean. With the Saturn and NUMMI contracts in hand, and inside information from the GM10 Project, Future 31 publicized details of the negotiations and the contract well before management or Local 31 officials did.

In its first leaflet, Future 31 warned that the new agreement would eliminate jobs through automation, outsourcing, and replacement of tag relief with mass relief. The leaflet went on to explain some of the drawbacks of eliminating classifications:

> Lumping everyone in the same classification and rate of pay means: a) Transfers throughout the plant will be non-existent (what you see is what you get!). b) By overlapping classifications Management will have you doing all types of work but at one single pay rate. c) Management will have the sole right to move you around on any job they want, totally disregarding seniority rights (their "pay-for-knowledge" scheme throws a few more cents an hour your way; the UAW went on strike at Wentzville last year when 80 percent of the workforce had become this super-pool people without a job to call their own). Management's equation: one rate, one classification equals no advancement, no movement; which equals big bucks for GM. And it is Management's intention for you to do your own assembly, inspection, and repair with a reversible gun, at 75 jobs an hour. Goodbye to inspectors and repairmen. More work for less people. This is the "Quality of Work Life" we hear so much about.

Another leaflet criticized the proposed disciplinary procedure, pointing out that the plant had never before had a written procedure. A caucus leaflet warned:

> Our local contract has never had any such punishment section! Shop rules are Management's to enforce, NOT the Union's! We don't pay union dues to have a district committeeman "jointly counsel" us in cooperation with Management! And don't believe the story about us now having an "eleven step" procedure instead of eight; this contract language agrees to a five-step for absenteeism, and a six-step for all other shop rules. Lighter steps such as "balance of shift and a day" and the "balance and two days" are gone! We have for years held Management's punishments back; now we are in writing agreeing to punishments and making them more severe! And Management has the LOOPHOLE word "severity" with which to skip steps anyway! OH NO!

Potentially the union was in a strong position as the company was investing millions every day in construction. Each passing day made it harder for the company to threaten not to finish the plant if management did not get everything it wanted in the contract.

But the local union leadership took the line that it might be dangerous to call the company's bluff; GM might sell the new plant or perhaps make it a joint venture. From time to time, construction was stalled—officially due to material shortages, but these explanations did not quell the rumor mill.

GM appeared fair and impartial, but evidence mounted that the company was pulling strings behind the scenes. For example, contract booklets were issued to every worker two weeks in advance of the vote, supposedly with the word-for-word text. Later it came out that a series of negotiations "minutes" also applied, yet these were not available.

The "migrant" workers from California were played against the locals. Rumors circulated that if the team agreement were voted down, the California workers would be called back first because, although their plant seniority was low, their corporate seniority tended to be higher than the locals'.

Joint union-management pro-contract presentations were made at a local hotel to several hundred key workers, such as elected officials, QWL reps, and GM10 Project members. These workers were given time off with eight hours pay to attend the presentations, which lasted about half a day. No dissenters were invited to the meetings. Back in the plant, Future 31 members asked their co-workers, "Doesn't it strike you as funny that they're paying people to go hear how good the contract is?"

When all was said and done, the contract was ratified. Members, through whatever combination of fear of losing their jobs and faith in the union leadership, voted two-to-one in favor.

School Days

The old Fairfax plant shut down on May 8, 1987, and Fairfax II opened its doors a week or two later with the new contract in effect. Before they were allowed to put a wrench to a car, Fairfax workers, in groups of a hundred or so, were sent to school for training in the team concept.

Team leaders, who were self-selected on the basis of seniority and got paid an extra 50 cents an hour, took five weeks of classroom training. Team members took a four-week course. (Six months later, training was reduced to two weeks.) There were no other pay differentials among production workers, including no pay-for-knowledge, although job rotation "to retain proficiency" on all jobs in the team was required by the contract. The contract provided for two percent relief workers, again without more pay, but also said that team leaders were responsible for "providing unscheduled relief."

Hourly workers were appointed as facilitators to conduct the classes. Facilitators led exercises designed by managerial consulting firms like Zenger-Miller and Kepner-Tregoe. Emphasis was on joint management-worker problem solving techniques, but the criteria and guidelines of the problems always met the company's goals of saving money, increasing efficiency, or meeting production quotas.

There was little traditional union influence in the classes even though it was supposed to be a joint program. One 25-year man who consistently raised provocative points in class said, "I'd be surprised if 10 percent of the facilitators have ever come to a union meeting. I never see them there. And I'm probably being generous by saying 10 percent!"

The facilitators used exercises printed in a slick booklet titled *Managing Involvement* published by Kepner-Tregoe. The first exercise described recurring fires in an area where chemicals were being used. The reader is the plant manager. Several department heads have come to the plant manager with different ideas about how to solve the problem. The manager has been allocated $25,000 to solve the problem, and wants to arrive at a solution that others will be committed to and that stays within the budget. How to do it? The "right" solutions are always those that use group consensus. "I suppose," said one committeeperson later, "if there was another fire, or an explosion, and someone was killed, we'd all feel guilty since we agreed to those conditions in the first place."

During a training session for committeepersons, someone complained that all of the exercises were written from management's perspective. The reader becomes the plant manager, the production manager, nursing supervisor in a hospital, head of the advertising department—but never someone working on the line. The next day the facilitators brought in a mimeographed version of the book which changed some of the protagonists to hourly workers: "Ralph is a module leader." "Pete is lead operator of a production molding machine." "Sally is the senior quality control inspector." This mimeographed version disappeared when team member training began.

Some time in classes was spent overviewing safety procedures, but the emphasis was in other directions. An entire book titled *Fairfax Industrial Engineering Training Program* was issued, full of charts and graphs and tables. The book instructed team members on how to eliminate unnecessary motions and steps. Demonstrations with wooden blocks on a tabletop were used to figure out the quickest way to do a job. One block represented the worker, one the line, another the workbench. The blocks were repositioned so the job could be performed in the fewest steps possible.

During one session the facilitators announced that the local contract would be discussed on the coming Friday. A team member asked whether contracts would be distributed. When the facilitator said no, the union brother insisted that contract pamphlets be passed out to improve the discussion. Finally, the facilitators okayed that request. For some reason, the company was very reluctant to allow the contract to be seen, despite the fact that the tentative agreement had been given to everybody in notebook form prior to ratification! In the old plant, management tried to fire a committeeperson for passing out the new contract, saying it was stolen property. During class that Friday, the booklets were handed out, but the four-hour session was spent with the head of labor relations reading the entire contract aloud word-for-word! Union representatives stood in the back of the room, on rare occasion making comment. It was definitely not a forum for airing one's views on the agreement.

Back to the Future

The Fairfax contract promised employee involvement and input into the decision making process. Many workers thought they would be setting up their own jobs, but they were surprised to find out that industrial engineering had already broken down initial job elements and laid out the jobs on paper and even on overhead projector transparencies.

The only real "input" workers were allowed to exercise was to make one's job "more efficient." Then management would shift more work to that job—otherwise known as speedup. Workers were not invited to have input into investment decisions or line speed. In order to gain workers' complicity in speedup, management openly stated that, in order for the plant to be competitive, each job must work a person 56 seconds out of the minute; the previous average at the old plant was 42 to 45 seconds per minute. In some team training classes students were told that to really ensure the new plant's future, the workforce must be pared down to 2,800 to ensure the plant's future—2,500 fewer jobs than the old plant.

The local leadership has solidly maintained its commitment to the Fairfax II team concept contract, despite management provocations such as switching to mass relief three months after the contract was bagged (and ten months earlier than they had verbally promised), which eliminated more than 400 jobs.

Will the team concept in practice be accepted by the workforce? Only time will tell. As of March 1988 Fairfax II was only approaching about three-quarters of the proposed line speed of 75 cars per hour.

Notes

1. "Verdict still out on breaks for GM plant," *Kansas City Times*, March 30, 1987.

Appendix

The contract language reprinted below is excerpted from the 1986 Local Agreement between UAW Local 31 and GM Fairfax II.

Team Concept

During the course of these negotiations the parties have discussed innovative work approaches which provide for a world class quality product at a competitive cost at the Fairfax II facility. These approaches were jointly developed and necessitate a high degree of mutual trust, respect and understanding. The cornerstone of this Agreement is the Team Concept, in that the parties recognize that the catalyst for our success is our employees. The very core of the Team Concept is the Team Members and Team Leader whose duties, responsibilities and training have been defined as follows:

Team Member

-Understand and support Team Concept.
-Attendance and participation in all team meetings and training sessions.
-Be proficient at all operations in the Team and rotate to retain proficiency.
-Individual and Team safety.
-Maintain the cleanliness of the area through good housekeeping.
-Maintain regular attendance.
-Provide training for others as required.
-Cost reduction in areas of material, labor, scrap, and processing supplies, etc.
-Quality, which includes knowing the job, specifications, use of SPC [Statistical Process Control], use of audit information and CAMIP [Continuous Automotive Marketing Information Program], self inspection, and repair on parts and product before it leaves the work station.
-Participate in job design utilizing available information through time study, methods, layouts, and ergonomics.
-Contribute to efficiency gains through job improvement.
-Operate equipment to its design intent.
-Additional duties as may be jointly developed by the parties.

Team Leader

Inasmuch as the Team Leader is the foundation on which the Team is built, his duties and responsibilities include those previously listed for Team Member and additionally will include:
-Direct responsibility for the morale and performance of the Team.
-Providing unscheduled relief.
-Evaluating other training needs and making necessary arrangements with proper resource.
-Procuring necessary tools, supplies, etc., for the Team.
-Maintaining Team records.
-Communicating with Group Leader, other Team Leaders and Team Members to improve the overall effectiveness of the Team, the Departments, and the Plant.
-Ensuring constant improvements in the effectiveness of the Team in the areas of quality, cost, and productivity.
-Resource to other Teams and Group Leader.
-Promoting new methods, processes, and employee suggestions.
-Coordinate Team activities and ensuring job rotation within the Team.
-Planning, scheduling and conducting Team meetings.
-Performing all duties associated with time and attendance for the Team.
-Additional duties as may be jointly developed by the parties.

The following list of general training subjects are necessary to prepare the Team Member and Team Leader for their respective roles within the Team Concept. The parties will mutually develop such curriculum.

Training for Team Member

Curriculum consisting of:
-Definition of Fairfax II Team Concept.
-Problem solving.
-Group dynamics.
-Communication skills.
-Team building and human relations.
-Safety/ergonomics.
-Job training techniques.
-Understanding costs.
-Role of the Team member in cost reduction.
-Specifications/engineering documents.
-Statistical process control.
-Understanding audit and CAMIP.
-Time study and job evaluation.
-Methods analysis.
-Operation design and improvement.
-Self-inspection.

Team Leader Training

A curriculum consisting of:
-Intensive Team Member training (expanded coverage).
-Expense material inventory control.
-Facilitator training (work with groups).
-Stand-up speaking skills.
-Proper record keeping techniques.
-Plant systems, process and controls.

-GM Suggestion Program.
-Job design training.
-Methods improvement training.
-Personal development skills training.

Team Size

It is the intent of the parties to establish the size of teams between four (4) and ten (10) members and to have a Team Leader for each Team. Any deviations of this intent necessitated by unusual circumstances will be a subject of discussion between the parties.

Team Meetings

In order for the Team Concept to function to its design intent the parties recognize the need to provide time for the teams to meet. Accordingly, teams will be allowed to meet for thirty (30) minutes each week at a time and day mutually established by the parties.

Rotation

During these negotiations, the parties have discussed at length team concept and job rotation as being an integral part of that concept. The parties recognize that in the establishment of jobs within the team a concerted effort will be made by team members to balance the work loads in a fair and equitable manner. To address concerns raised during these negotiations regarding seniority assignments it is understood that once all employees within a team have become proficient on all the jobs within a team, seniority employees within the team will be given consideration for working on a specific assignment until it again becomes necessary for team members to rotate to retain their total proficiency within the team.

In the event that remote work assignments exist which would make it impractical to include into a team concept, it is understood that seniority employees desirous of such assignments will be given preference to fill such jobs.

Skilled Trades Memorandum

The purpose of this Memorandum is to provide a basis of understanding for the operating of skilled trades activities in the Fairfax II facility. This document is intended to be flexible as the parties recognize they are embarked on a critical and historic course. In beginning this journey, the parties again re-commit themselves to the business goals of a world class quality product at a competitive cost, and the philosophy that those goals can only be attained through the cooperative efforts and dedication of the workforce.

As conditions may change or issues not addressed in this document arise, the parties are resolved to meet in a spirit of mutual understanding for one another's concerns and respect for the principles of Fairfax II.

A. The parties recognize that within the skilled trades classifications there are certain skills and knowledge that are unique to individual trades and not commonly shared. However, the parties also recognize that many skills are common among a variety of classifications and individuals possess both the knowledge and skills to perform work in a variety of trades.

Accordingly, the parties agree that under normal conditions, skilled work will be assigned to employees within the classification that such work is commonly recognized to fall as outlined in the General Job Description to be jointly developed between the parties, and which becomes a part of this document by reference. However, it is understood that such assignments will include the right to access and perform incidental work that falls within the knowledge and abilities of the tradesman while working in a safe manner.

B. The parties recognize that Fairfax II will be a highly automated facility utilizing "state-of-the-art" technology. In order for this equipment to operate with maximum up time and to its design intent, the role of the skilled tradesman becomes more vital than ever before. It is the intent of the parties to approach this automated facility through dedication to a system, as in the laydown side frame system and robagate system.

Accordingly, the parties agree to assign skilled tradesmen by teams to the various systems. These teams will be made up of the trades necessary to maintain the system and each tradesman will receive extensive training to enhance their ability to fully maintain the system. When it becomes necessary to replace a team member it will be by the trade in which the opening exists.

16. Van Nuys, Part I: Teams Divide the Union

By Eric Mann

How to stop a plant from closing? At General Motors' assembly plant in Van Nuys, California, two very different strategies have been proposed. One strategy was to adopt the team concept, increase cooperation, improve productivity, and prove to GM that Van Nuys is a great plant with a hard-working workforce.

The other strategy was conceived before the company made any overt threats to close, and before the team concept became the latest fashion in the auto industry. In 1982, workers at Van Nuys started the Campaign to Keep GM Van Nuys Open. They knew there was a possibility the plant would close; five out of six of California's auto plants had been shut down over the previous two years, and GM had been rumbling about the inefficiency of having an assembly plant on the west coast.

The Campaign got an appropriate kick-off when GM laid off the second shift in November 1982. Second shift workers became a core of activists for the Campaign. They formed a coalition with supporters from the Black and Chicano communities, which had already had to deal with previous plant closings and high unemployment. The Campaign organized a series of militant rallies and marches. Its strategy was to head off the closing by threatening a boycottt of GM products in the Los Angeles area—the largest new car market in the United States. Along with business students and small business people, the campaign developed a plan for GM to build a stamping plant in Los Angeles and buy parts from local contractors. Workers from closed plants would be rehired and GM would not have to ship parts from the Midwest and then "back-ship" completed cars east of the Rockies.

At a meeting with Campaign members in January 1984, then-GM President F. James McDonald confirmed that the plant was in danger of being closed and boldly asserted management's rights. The coalition, in an equally bold style, went into detail about its commitment to carry out the boycott. As the meeting broke up, Assemblyperson Maxine Waters confronted McDonald and asked if she could tell the press that the plant would be there for at least two more years.

McDonald paused, and then said, "Yes."

Waters turned to coalition members and said, "Now here I am in the legislature trying to get 90 days advance notice on plant closings, and they say my bill is 'too radical.' But our coalition just got two years' advance notice from GM."

After the meeting, GM changed its strategy towards Van Nuys. A new plant manager, Ernest Schaefer, was brought in to quarterback the local situation. Schaefer had formerly been the plant manager in GM's Fiero plant in Pontiac, Michigan. He had a reputation for actively intervening in the politics of the local union to advance the company's interests. Gregarious and outgoing, Schaefer was schooled in the jargon of nonadversarial labor relations. He walked the assembly lines, shook hands with the workers, and invited himself to lunch in the plant cafeteria: "Hi, I'm Ernie Schaefer; mind if I join you? I want to know your opinions about how we can improve things around here."

Schaefer's first effort was to develop the *Positive Press*, a glossy handout that ostensibly was a publication of both GM and the UAW under the "joint activities" provisions of the 1982 contract, but in actuality was a propaganda organ for management. While not attacking the Campaign by name, Schaefer consistently editorialized against those who spread "negativity." In his early articles, he said he didn't want to talk about plant closings. If the workers had a positive attitude, they could raise quality, show the Detroit headquarters that Van Nuys was a "world class plant," and avert the unspoken plant closing.

Part I of this chapter is adapted from the book, Taking on General Motors: A Case Study of the UAW Campaign to Keep GM Van Nuys Open *by Eric Mann. Mann is a member of United Auto Workers Local 645 in Van Nuys, California and a leader of the campaign to keep the plant from closing.*

- *GM Van Nuys Assembly*
- *Location: Van Nuys, California*
- *Employment: 3,800 hourly on two shifts*
- *Product: Chevy Camaro, Pontiac Firebird*
- *Production began: 1947*
- *Team Concept began: May 1987*
- *UAW Local 645*
  Address: 7915 Van Nuys Blvd., Van Nuys, CA 91402
  Phone: 818 / 782-5362; Shop Committee: 818 / 782-2811

Cooperate or Else

But soon Schaefer began to spread a little negativity of his own. With support from his allies in the local union, he began to put out leaflets warning the workers that the plant was indeed in danger of being closed and that their only chance to save their jobs was to adopt a Japanese-style management system called the team concept. While the system claimed to be based on labor-management cooperation, Schaefer emphasized that if the workers did not choose to cooperate, the plant would be closed.

Schaefer began telling the Van Nuys workers that the car they were producing, the Chevrolet Camaro, was going to be manufactured through a new process with an all-plastic body and would be phased out of Van Nuys, probably around 1989. If they wanted a new car—that is, a job—they would have to agree to many work rule changes, a.k.a. the team concept.

Whereas in the past the Campaign distributed magazine and newspaper articles warning of future plant closings, while the company denied the stories, this time the company was reprinting those articles. An *Automotive News* article distributed by management with the headline, "10 factories may go dark in 4 years," explained:

> William R. Pochiluk Jr., president of *Autofacts* and author of a report on plant capacity, said that based on his analysis the following General Motors plants are the top candidates for closure: Van Nuys, Calif.; St. Therese, BC [sic]; Detroit (Clark Street); Arlington, Texas; one J/N car plant such as Leeds (Mo); and one A-car plant such as Tarrytown (NY).

The threat by itself would not suffice. Schaefer needed a philosophically sympathetic union leader to help carry out his plan. He found one in the plant's newly elected shop chairman, Ray Ruiz. Ruiz, who had in the past taken a sympathetic stance toward the Campaign, underwent a transformation shortly after his election in May 1985. He explained that although he previously had been a militant, now he had come to believe that people (such as Local 645 President Pete Beltran) who retained an adversarial stance towards the company

were "dinosaurs." He pointed to NUMMI as the cooperative model of the future. Ruiz told the workers that the Campaign had been a useful tactic to draw attention to the problem, but the team concept was the only way to solve it.

On December 9, 1985, Schaefer and Ruiz organized unprecedented mass meetings on each shift. The goal of the meetings was to ask the membership's permission to "explore" a new local contract based on the team concept. Many workers who attended the meetings reacted angrily. "Why are these meetings being held in the plant instead of the union hall?" "Why is the company paying us and stopping production to have these meetings?" "We already have a ratified local agreement that doesn't expire until September 1987. Who gave Ruiz the authority to reopen it?" The meetings broke up in angry debate, with many workers booing Ruiz and accusing him of cutting a deal with the company.

President Beltran explained his opposition in greater detail:

> This reminds me of how GM got the concessions at the national level in 1982. They came to us and said, "We don't want concessions, we just want to 'explore' new ways of being efficient." The next thing we knew, GM had $3 billion of our money. The shop committee does not need a membership meeting to "explore" anything. They can explore all they want. But if they want to reopen the contract they have to come to the membership, explain why they want it and get a vote. But why would the company want to reopen the contract—to give us more? The whole thing is a disgrace.

Ernie Schaefer put out an issue of the *Positive Press* explaining his position:

> We have developed a proposal to build A-cars (Buick and Oldsmobile Cutlass) along with our current Firebirds and Camaros. This plan would cost about $200 million to implement at Van Nuys and would provide products for us to build well beyond 1990.
>
> In discussing our proposal with Detroit we were told that for General Motors to invest $200 million in our plant we would need changes in our local contract that would allow us to implement a team organization. The team organization is needed to allow the flexibility necessary to build two car lines in our plant. We were told that if we did not have such an agreement, there was no need for us to come to Detroit. Consequently, the meeting for Wednesday, December 11 to review our plans in Detroit was canceled.
>
> The bottom line is if the Van Nuys Plant is to be considered for a new product line, we must introduce new and innovative work concepts at our facility.

Beltran attacked the "captive audience meetings" as a "deal, negotiated secretly and privately, without the knowledge of the local union president or other members of the shop committee." After raising initial criticisms of the team concept, he indicated a willingness to try it. He focused his criticisms on GM's unwillingness to make a long-term commitment to the plant in return

SHHH, IF HE'S WARNED, IT COULD CAUSE US GREAT PAIN!

HUCK/KONOPACKI LABOR CARTOONS

KONOPACKI

1987 THE IUE NEWS

for workers' acceptance of the team concept:

> Accepting the team concept is not the major stumbling block, instead it is GM's open-ended guarantee...GM's so-called guarantee is meaningless if it rests on consumer demands and if there is no other commitment to re-tool again, if necessary, to keep GM Van Nuys open into the 1990s.
>
> For these reasons, a more appropriate exchange for the Team Concept would be a GM guarantee that the GM Van Nuys plant would remain open for at least ten years so that everyone now employed, if the plant should close, would qualify for a guaranteed SUB benefit for a full 52 weeks, followed by Guaranteed Income Stream Benefits for an additional nine years at 50 percent of their present wages without having to transfer out of state to another GM plant.[1]

Beltran did not attack the team concept frontally, but instead demanded a long-term commitment from the company in return. GM, however, was not negotiating. Essentially, it was demanding teams without conditions. For those familiar with GM's decision-making structure, the entire plan was based on a deception. Central staff on GM's Executive Committee in Detroit make decisions about long-term capital investment and disinvestment. Plant managers such as Ernie Schaefer are low-level line officers whose responsibility is to implement decisions made in Detroit. Local plant managers have no authority to decide whether plants will be kept open or closed.

Under the new politics of the GM-UAW "joint activities," however, local plant managers and shop chairmen are encouraged to come to Detroit on pilgrimages to present competitive bids for their plants. And, as Schaefer had argued, if the workers would not agree to the plan ahead of time, the pilgrimage would be cancelled.

But even if the workers agreed to his demand, the very terms of the competition made it impossible for any one plant to ever achieve job security. Since GM had at least four new plants due to come on line, which would add far more productive capacity than market demand warranted, at least four plant closings were assured. As long as local concessions would determine who would be kept open and who would be closed, as soon as one local gave concessions and returned home thinking they had saved their plant, another local would appear in Detroit offering more, and the cycle would continue.

Shop Floor Debate Rages

For several months, the workers debated the issue. In the first stages, everyone in the plant was asking, "Are you for or against the team concept?" and in the next breath wondering, "What the hell is the team concept anyway?"

Many committeemen and foremen who supported the teams focused on the ability to "weed out the bad workers." They argued that while most of the workers were hard working and dependable, there were "five per-

cent" who were not doing their share. These slackers, through poor workmanship and high absenteeism, were threatening the livelihoods of the "95 percent" by making the plant "uncompetitive." This was a clever formulation. In reality, the company (and the company-oriented committeemen) knew that far more than five percent of the workers would be cut. But it allowed them to appeal to the votes of the mythical "95 percent," with each person, of course, believing it was "the others" who would be eliminated.

It also set the stage for attacks on the seniority system with the argument that "only poor workers have to hide behind seniority." When some of the workers began to say, "I'm going to vote for the team concept so I can get rid of Willie (or Mary or Jose)," the danger of "the team" turning worker against worker and breaking down even the most minimal union solidarity became apparent.

But the underlying point in every discussion was the company's ultimatum. As Kelley Jenco, a leader of the Campaign who later became the first woman elected as committeeperson, explained: "With most of the people on my line, a few are gung ho for it, a few are really dead-set against it, and the majority are just resigned to it. They say, 'If GM says give us the team concept or we'll close the plant, why are we pretending we have a choice in the matter?'"

Beltran's Strategy

Beltran was portrayed by the opposition as a hardliner who dogmatically opposed any cooperation with the company. In fact, he had a complex and well thought-out strategy. He was willing to make certain concessions to GM, out of necessity. Without a strong movement led by the International union or by a coalition of UAW locals to fight plant closings, he believed that some compromises with the largest industrial corporation in the world were inevitable. What he feared most, however, was the complete disintegration of collective bargaining as he knew it:

> No one even knows what the team concept is, and neither Ruiz nor Schaefer wants to be very specific. If we can stop all the generalized discussion and get down to specifics, we can bargain over classifications, line speeds, job descriptions, and even manpower levels. But with workers running around the plant asking, "What the hell is going on?" and Ruiz and Schaefer saying, "Trust us," the whole process of collective bargaining is going down the drain. Since when do we reopen contracts every time the company asks? Since when do we package a whole series of company proposals under the name "team concept" and ask the workers if they want it on an all-or-nothing basis?

Beltran's plan had two elements: 1) to make the Campaign to Keep GM Van Nuys Open more visible so that the workers would feel that they had an alternative to the company's threats, and 2) to engage both the committeepeople and the membership in a discussion of the team concept's *provisions*, so that the mystique of the team concept could be broken down and the individual elements of the team concept could be bargained one at a time.

But, despite Beltran's flexibility and moderation, the faction of the union allied with the company began a systematic campaign to discredit him. The verbal attacks on Beltran followed a consistent theme: "Beltran is a hard-headed egotist who doesn't care about the membership. He wants to stick it to GM and doesn't really care whether they close down the plant." The company advocates were trying to set up Beltran and the Campaign activists as the scapegoats for a future plant closing.

Campaign Regroups…and Miscalculates

Opinion in the plant, according to most estimates, was split into three roughly equal camps. One third of the workers were genuinely in favor of the team concept and felt it was in their interest. Another third opposed the team concept but favored voting for it to avoid a possible plant closing. The remaining third was adamantly against the plan, arguing that, while it was risky, the union should call the company's bluff. Thus, in early 1986, most of the seasoned union veterans held a common assessment that the team concept was disliked by the majority of the workers but would pass by a two-to-one margin.

The Campaign activists made two proposals for action. First, acting as individual union members and not in the name of the Campaign, they proposed that the union elect a rank and file delegation to visit several plants that already had the team concept, and then report back to the membership. They proposed that the delegation visit the GM plant in Wentzville, Missouri. This plant had been the scene of an eleven-day strike that led to the company modifying some details of the team concept. The goal was to support Beltran's idea that the workers had to take a hard look at the plan in practice before they decided whether they wanted it.

Second, they proposed another large Campaign rally in opposition to GM's latest round of threats. For over two years, the Campaign had not called any major demonstrations because the company was denying that there was any danger to the plant, and the workers themselves did not see a need for dramatic action. It was hoped that by bringing back the community support and the threat of the boycott the workers who wanted to resist the team concept at all costs, along with those who would agree to it in return for a long-term commitment from GM, would be strengthened.

Many of the Campaign activists, as individual union members, put out a signed leaflet urging that the local send a delegation of ten workers, five from each shift, to investigate the team concept and visit the Wentzville plant. They demanded that Shop Chairman Ruiz stop his efforts to force a vote before such an investigation. The idea of the "rank and file investigating group" was proposed to counter the shop committee's plan to investigate "for" the members and report back.

After the leaflet, however, the pro-team concept committeemen changed their position from opposing the "rank and file" delegation as an intrusion into their bargaining power, to opposing the proposal for ten delegates as "limiting the delegation to a small clique."

In a shrewd tactical maneuver, they proposed voting down the motion to send ten workers and substituted a motion for two workers per department on each shift—a total of 34. When Beltran's supporters argued that sending 34 workers would cost the local more than $60,000 and was a transparent effort to decimate the funds of the local, the "cooperation faction" was able to turn the debate around: "What are you afraid of? Don't you want the membership to see for themselves as you claim?" The motion for the $60,000 plan passed with little opposition.

But the vote was won by more than clever argument. The team concept was attracting new supporters from the shop floor and was developing the character of a mass movement. Unfortunately, in the view of many Campaign activists, it was a right-wing movement. At union meetings, the team concept advocates openly argued: "Look around the country. Yesterday's militants are today's flexible thinkers. The days of confrontation are over." "Seniority is important, but it's time that we allowed the best people to rise to the top. My foreman says that I have a lot of potential, but people who don't give a damn are standing in my way just because they have more seniority." Members who had not attended union meetings came into the union hall and demanded to know why the union was spending money on trying to organize immigrants at the nearby Superior Industries. They called for an audit of the Campaign's books. They attacked every line of the monthly financial statement that involved the payment of "lost time" to CAP activists who had been paid by President Beltran, as was standard procedure, to work for the local. Union meetings were taking on the character of an inquisition, and the Campaign activists were very much on the defensive.

Delegate Elections

The Campaign organizers, who had in the past been very attentive to changing conditions in the local, were unable to unravel the rapidly unfolding events and resorted to mechanical thinking. In 1983, the Campaign had held a big rally a few days before the UAW convention. In 1986, with the convention planned for nearby Anaheim, California, the organizers resorted to a similar tactic. In early February, the organizers fixed April 26 as the date for a large rally. The organizers focused almost all their attention on the upcoming convention, again hoping somehow to spark a broader movement within the UAW.

But they paid scant attention to the fact that the local's elections for convention delegates would be held on April 22. To the degree that they thought about the delegate elections at all, they assumed the usual results: both President Beltran and Shop Chairman Ruiz would win, along with a relatively even split between committeemen opposing the team concept and those supporting it.

Two weeks before the delegate elections it became clear that the "cooperation team" had put together a very strong slate, called "Responsible Representation." With strong backing from the company and the International, they put out attractive literature and argued that if the workers wanted to save the plant, they should send a signal to Detroit that they had elected a team that was willing to cooperate with management.

During the delegate election campaign, a series of mysterious leaflets appeared attacking President Beltran. The leaflets raised a series of unsubstantiated and personal attacks against Beltran, red-baited both Beltran and Eric Mann, and charged that "Pete wants the plant to close. He has everything to gain (at your expense) and nothing to lose."

The leaflets were signed by "Tom D. Torquemada, the Grand Inquisitor." Recording secretary Mike Gomez researched Torquemada and found the following biography:

Torquemada, Tomas D. First Grand Inquisitor of Spain....During his 18 years in office he burned

10,220 persons and condemned 6,860 to be burned in effigy... His later activities were directed against the Jews and about 1,000,000 of them fled the country to escape his persecution. He was one of the most bloodthirsty fanatics in history.[2]

Under this type of attack, Beltran retreated into a shell. He argued:

I have served these people for two terms as president. I have handled people's unemployment claims, fought to get them reinstated when they were fired, stayed up until midnight with the families of injured workers, and worked many seven-day weeks when that was needed. Right now, I'm fighting to save the union from being destroyed. If, after all these years, people can be swayed by this type of garbage, they can have the damn election.

Beltran was a savvy political operator. He knew that, while virtue may be its own reward, many a virtuous candidate has gone down to defeat because of poor campaigning. Still, despite increasingly desperate urgings from his closest friends and allies, Beltran did not put together a slate, did not put out one piece of campaign literature—and lost! The Responsible Representation slate, led by Ray Ruiz, won a clean sweep of all

seven delegates. It was an impressive organizing victory and gave the cooperation faction a valid mandate for its strategy.

The Campaign organizers had tried to separate the debate over the team concept from the upcoming rally. They argued that whether one was for or against team concept, community pressure was in everyone's interest. In retrospect, there were two reasons why the Campaign activists were slow to oppose the team concept directly.

One, through years of organizing they had become adept at the art of coalition building—uniting people with sharp disagreements among themselves. Because the team concept was new, they didn't want to make the Campaign a partisan issue, and they knew that many of those who were open to the team concept were also very sympathetic to the Campaign. The subtlety of their outlook and their patience were clearly virtues.

On the other hand, part of the "subtlety" was not very different from old-fashioned fear. The team concept supporters were aggressive, angry, and often willing to physically attack those who did not agree with them. It appeared that there was a landslide of support for team concept, and those who didn't like it were intimidated into silence. Thus for a time Campaign activists misread the extent of anti-team concept sentiment.

Campaign's Strengths and Weaknesses

The election results became known on Wednesday, April 23. The Campaign's rally took place the following Saturday at noon. The crowd was well over a thousand people and reflected many organizing accomplishments. The most important step forward was that, for the first time in the Campaign's history, there was significant participation from the higher seniority workers on the first shift. Traditionally, they had seen the Campaign as primarily a second shift movement, because of its roots in the 1982 layoff of the second shift and because they had felt more secure about their future. But in the growing debate over the team concept many of these workers, with greater ties to earlier and more class-conscious times and a greater knowledge of trade union principles, began to see the Campaign as a necessary tactic in the battle against concessions.

The rally had a last minute addition—the Reverend Jesse Jackson. Jackson's moving words reflected another step forward for the Coalition. At the rally he pledged himself and the resources of the Rainbow Coalition to a boycott of GM products if that became necessary. Looking out at the coalition represented by the rally, there was no question in anyone's mind that it had the capability to carry out a successful boycott of GM products in Los Angeles.

Later several foremen, whose jobs would also be lost in a plant closing, told Campaign organizers, "Detroit was very impressed with the rally." Only half-jokingly they added, "Maybe you troublemakers will save our jobs after all."

However, in the eyes of some allies, the Campaign organizers had compromised their political influence because they had virtually ignored the delegate election race, and had severely underestimated the growing strength of the cooperation faction. As one experienced labor leader in the city assessed: "The company and the Ruiz faction are spreading the election results all over the city. While Beltran is still president, they are talking like he's a lame duck. You people had better give top priority to his reelection campaign for president or your movement is as good as dead."

The next day's *Los Angeles Times* placed more emphasis on Beltran's electoral defeat and Ray Ruiz's new-found expertise on preventing plant closings than on the views of the rally organizers:

> Ruiz's stance is gaining favor in the plant according to him and a number of others in the union. They said the growing sentiment for accommodation was manifested last week when a slate of delegates headed by Ruiz defeated Beltran's slate to be the local's representative at the UAW convention in Anaheim this June.
>
> Ruiz opposes the boycott, explaining, "We would be boycotting products built by our brothers and sisters in other GM plants." Ruiz also said he fears that the threat of a boycott would have the opposite effect to what its advocates intend because General Motors, not wanting to appear to be bowing to pressure, would be more likely to close the plant.

Ruiz's public statements sharply contradicted his statements to the Van Nuys workers. Contrary to his protestations about his "brothers and sisters" in other plants, Ruiz urged the Van Nuys workers to "look out for number one." As Pete Beltran explained, "In public he claims he is for solidarity, but at every union meeting, when he tries to sell the team concept, he says it's us versus Norwood [GM's other Camaro plant in Ohio]." Ruiz's supporters echoed those sentiments by putting out leaflets arguing, "We are in a Superbowl competition where there can only be one winner—us or Norwood. The choice is up to you."

Ruiz and his slate had won the delegate election and Beltran and his allies had not. Until that balance of forces could be reversed, the Campaign to Keep GM Van Nuys Open was in a state of decline.

And if the Campaign wanted to rebound, it could no longer count on the help of the press. Armed with the option of the far more palatable team concept and a union faction advocating it, the press became a combatant in the struggle, placing even more pressure on the workers to accept the company's plan. A *Los Angeles Daily News* editorial titled "Change or Die" reflected the public pressure that was placed on the workers:

> Auto workers concerned about bread on the table got an earful of baloney from the Rev. Jesse Jackson on Saturday... The troubles of the Van Nuys plant are more fundamental than anything that might be solved by community action... The Van Nuys plant in its present form lacks a strong economic reason for being.

Either it cuts its costs or it closes. Realistic union members realize this... For the union, the choice is between changing its work rules and meeting management halfway, or dying. It's not a choice that can be scared away with a rally.

A Hinged Acceptance

In every political battle, as long as the issues are not resolved there is the possibility of reversal. As the UAW convention approached, the "cooperation team" leaders felt it would boost their standing with the International if they could get the membership to ratify a team concept agreement and deliver that package to the convention. But there were two problems with that plan. First, the 34 workers who had recently returned from their investigation of the team concept had not finished their reports to the membership. Second, there was no logical reason, except for the "deadline" of the UAW convention, to push through a vote.

The 34 workers who had been elected to investigate the team concept were rerouted away from the Wentzville plant where, GM management told them, "labor difficulties" made a visit impossible. Instead, they were sent to the Pontiac, Michigan Fiero plant, which coincidentally was Ernie Schaefer's former plant.

The majority of the workers elected were sympathetic to the team concept to begin with, but most of them tried to approach the task with an analytical and open mind. They took the job of representing their departments very seriously, taking copious notes on the trip and preparing their reports when they returned. In that the union had spent $60,000 for their trip (including a week's compensation for lost wages), some very strict ground rules had been set up: every observer would write a report expressing the pros and cons of the plan. The union would print the reports in a special edition of its newspaper, *The Fender Bender*. The reports would form the basis for an informed vote by the membership on whether to adopt, modify, or reject the team concept.

Before this process could be completed, however, Shop Chairman Ruiz distributed a leaflet announcing that a ratification meeting would be held on Wednesday, May 28. Members would receive the shop committee's report, followed by an immediate vote. Many of the elected observers, who were still in the process of finishing their reports, explained to Ruiz that his planned meeting was before the agreed-upon deadline for *The Fender Bender*. They asked him to postpone the vote until one week after the union newspaper was distributed to the workers. Ruiz overruled their objections.

In a surprise development, more than 20 of the elected observers, many of whom had supported both Ruiz and the team concept, signed a leaflet criticizing him for preventing a democratic ratification process. Others on the shop floor went further, angrily criticizing Ruiz for squandering $60,000 of the local's money for

reports which he had no intention of listening to.

The uproar grew louder. Workers demanded that the vote be postponed at least until the day after they had heard the shop committee's proposal for a new contract, so that they could have time to digest the information and talk among themselves. Ruiz backed down and agreed to the one-day hiatus between the report and the vote.

At the mass meetings at which the proposed contract changes were presented, there was an effort made to prevent President Beltran from speaking, which ended when Beltran fought his way to the microphone. He spoke against the team concept and urged a "no" vote, pointing out that behind all the talk of democratic cooperation in the workplace was a heavy-handed effort to impose a contract on the workers. He taunted Ray Ruiz, asking, "What is the hurry for this vote?" The workers already had a local contract in place and there was no "deadline" in Detroit except one that Ruiz and Schaefer were artificially creating.

In a prophetic observation, Beltran pointed out that if Ruiz and Schaefer could dictate the reopening of the contract any time they wanted, there was no guarantee that they wouldn't try it again. Finally, while expressing his strong opposition to the plan, he took up the Campaign's demand for a ten-year commitment to the plant, and challenged Ray Ruiz and Ernie Schaefer to come back with such a commitment.

Beltran's challenge went a long way toward shaping the debate that followed. Beltran repeated that even those who wanted the team concept should demand a long-term commitment in return for their vote. Schaefer and Ruiz, sensing that the pendulum was swinging away from them, promised the workers that they could vote what was called a "hinged acceptance"—that is, the new team concept agreement, if ratified, would not go into effect unless and until GM made a clear commitment to bring in a new model. The exact wording of the proposed contract was, "If ratified, this agreement will become effective only when a new product is announced for the Van Nuys Plant."[3]

While this helped get more votes for the team concept, it was a far cry from GM's original demand, "Vote for the team concept or we will close the plant." It reflected a significant modification of their position because of Beltran's, and the Campaign's, pressure.

Several months before the vote, most observers had predicted the team concept would pass by a margin of two to one, and those estimates were even higher after the Responsible Representation slate's delegate election victory. But in just one short month, the undemocratic measures against the membership had taken a toll. The team concept contract passed by a narrow margin of 53 percent "yes" to 47 percent "no."

One night-shift worker who had planned originally to vote "yes" explained why she changed her mind:

I have always been active in the Campaign and you always tell us how GM may close the plant, and I agree. So when they told us to vote for the team concept or they would close the plant, I figured that I would give it a try. If it was very good, which I don't expect, then that would be a plus. If it is a little bad, well, life is sometimes a little bad and I can live with that. And if it turns out terrible, then we can vote it out and tell them, "OK, close down the plant; I'm tired of being threatened."

But when I got to the meeting I could tell they weren't being honest. Every question we asked they said, "That hasn't been decided yet" or "The team will decide that." All they told us is that we will eat in the cafeteria with our foremen. But I don't want to eat with my foreman; I like it better when they eat in their cafeteria and we eat in ours.

And you know they aren't making such a big fuss to get us to vote for this thing just so we can all eat together or use the same parking lot. I want my job, but when I left there I didn't think that Ray Ruiz was telling me the truth. I think the company knows exactly what the team concept will be like but they don't want to tell us everything. So I voted "no."

The worker next to her on the line explained why he voted "yes":

To me, "team concept" means "speedup." But I still voted for it. When GM says they may close this place they aren't kidding. I was at Southgate for twenty years and I saw what it was like when they closed that place. It may be when they finally get the system organized, the jobs will be so hard that I won't be able to do them. But that won't be for a few years, and by that time I'll be close to retirement.

As far as Beltran is concerned, that was the first time I had heard him speak. They say he's hard-headed, but he was the only one up there who seemed to believe in what he was saying. I voted "yes" on the team concept, but I'll vote for Beltran when he runs again for president.

During the summer of 1986, both sides maneuvered for position. On July 3, 1986, five weeks after the vote, GM laid off the second shift because of poor sales. The team concept advocates argued that because of their better working relationship with the company the second shift would be brought back as soon as possible. The team concept opponents argued that the second-shift workers had been used. The company had pushed through the vote, taking advantage of the lower seniority workers' insecurity to pass the team concept by a narrow margin, and then laid them off.

The Ascent and Decline of Ray Ruiz

A few months later, the balance of power in the local changed once again. In late September 1986, Chairman Ruiz argued that conditions had changed dramatically, and urged the workers to allow him to implement the team concept immediately, without the guarantee of a new model. In a leaflet to the membership, Ruiz raised the following arguments:

We are in a drastically different position today than that of four or five months ago during negotiations. First of all, we were running with two shifts of production...There is also a major concern that when the 2.9 percent interest rate is discontinued...the sales projections seem even worse than originally anticipated.

Further, while in May when our contract was ratified we were on the leading edge of innovative contracts and were viewed in a very positive light, since then...the St. Therese plant in Canada recently ratified a new agreement, as have Janesville and Fairfax. On October 8 the Arlington plant will take a ratification vote on the issue of the team concept....

I have been exploring ways of bringing a significant number of our members back to work through a training program designed for the team leaders and group leaders....Thus, I will propose team concept implementation at today's meeting.

Ruiz's plan produced an uproar in the plant. Many of the workers who had voted for the team concept had done so only because of the promise of a new model. Now Ruiz essentially had negotiated another new agreement with the company that superseded the "hinged acceptance" agreement—which had superseded the regular local contract.

Beltran's warning that the practice of acceding to company demands for reopeners would lead to the disintegration of even minimal contract protections had proven accurate. Even before the team concept took effect, it became apparent that the perpetual breaking of the contract and its eventual replacement with "informal understandings" between union and management had become tantamount to policy.

Many of the workers on the first shift took the contract and its provisions very seriously. They carried their contracts in their overall pockets and could quote chapter and verse to any foreman. On Thursday, October 3, almost 400 workers stormed across the street to the UAW hall and voted unanimously to remove Ray Ruiz from office for improperly using his office of shop chairman to deny them their right under the UAW constitution to ratify their contracts. Ruiz and his supporters boycotted the meeting.

The following day, the International union ruled that Ruiz had been removed through a "procedural error" and that a trial had to be held to remove him from office. Some angry workers felt this was an effort by the International to protect Ruiz on a technicality, but without orderly rules, groups of 300 or 400 workers could come across the street any time they wanted to and take turns removing Beltran and Ruiz.

A recall movement was organized to carry out Ruiz's removal according to the local's bylaws. "Let's do it right this time," his opponents said. The odds-makers in the plant gave the recall an excellent chance to succeed. Ruiz's credibility had reached an all-time low.

One worker who voted for Ruiz's recall explained:

Hell, in recent years we've had some sell-out contracts, but they've still been contracts. This team concept movement tears up contracts as quick as we can vote them in. Under the new system, any time the shop chairman and the plant manager cut a deal, they tell us the conditions have changed and the deal becomes legal.

On October 30, after qualifying petitions had been circulated in the plant, a mass meeting was held in the local's parking lot to vote on a recall of Ray Ruiz. This time it was an official meeting of the GM Unit attended by more than 1,000 workers. President Beltran charged Ruiz with violating his duties as shop chairman and abrogating the membership's right to ratify all local contracts. Ruiz sarcastically thanked the members for showing up for his "party" and dismissed the meeting as illegal.

The chair called for a "division of the house." Approximately 800 workers walked to one side of the parking lot to indicate their vote to remove Ruiz, while approximately 200 walked to the other side to vote to retain him. The political message was clear: Ray Ruiz had lost the confidence of the membership less than six months after he had been elected delegate with the highest vote total. While those voting for recall had more than the necessary two-thirds margin, there were legitimate questions about whether the total votes cast were sufficient for a legal quorum. But this time the International union chose not to overturn the election on a procedural issue. Ruiz's influence having waned, he was given a job with the International union in Detroit.

Notes

1. Pete Beltran, "GM Van Nuys Report," leaflet distributed to the membership, December 17, 1985.

2. *Encyclopedia Americana*, Volume 26, 1966, p.78.

3. "Summary of Proposed Agreement," May 1986.

Van Nuys, Part II: Union Alive and Well

General Motors implemented the team concept at its Van Nuys, California plant in May 1987. But the company has not gone unchallenged. Part II of this chapter describes how shop floor union officials have worked to curtail the team concept and maintain decent working conditions.

The company broke its agreement with UAW Local 645 that introduction of team concept was "hinged" on announcement of a new model to be built at the plant. Instead, GM extended for an indefinite period the Camaro and Firebird, products which were supposed to be dropped in 1988.

The sentiment at Van Nuys against team concept did not go away, despite the "hinged" approval of the plan and its "unhinged" implementation. To express their feelings, many workers urged President Pete Beltran to run for chair of the shop committee, challenging incumbent Richard Ruppert, who strongly favored teams.

Of course, Beltran would have to give up his position as president, but in GM-UAW locals the shop chairman runs all in-plant business such as the grievance procedure and negotiations, while the president administers other affairs of the local from the union hall. Thus electing Beltran as shop chairman would make possible a strong union presence on the shop floor and would help build resistance to the team concept.

Fighting Back

Beltran ran for shop chairman on an explicitly anti-team concept platform. Four caucuses merged to form the "Fighting Back" group with Beltran at its head. Beltran's campaign literature said that he would not implement the team concept, or would at least modify it. However, team training began during the election campaign.

It is likely no coincidence that management brought the second shift back from layoff only three weeks before the election. It had been the second shift which provided the team concept its margin of victory in the vote only a year earlier. While the shift was laid off, from July to May, shop chair Ruppert and plant manager Ernest Schaefer sent workers no fewer than five co-signed letters, vowing that they were both doing their best to bring them back to work. Union activists estimated that, when first recalled, the sentiment of second shift workers was running nine to one to re-elect Ruppert as chairman.

The second shift workers received team training away from the shop floor. They heard promises of a new company attitude, a new spirit of teamwork. However, some were turned off by the training; one called the exercises "hokey." When told the team concept was based on trust, they asked, "Then why do we have to punch in and sign two attendance sheets, and why are there guards at every gate?"

Beltran's supporters made the most of the three weeks before the election, both in the team classes and on the shop floor. They were able to convince a sizable number of second shift workers that with the team concept in place they would need a strong union presence in the plant more than ever. Beltran won the chairmanship by 117 votes out of more than 3,000. The second shift voted 60/40 for Ruppert, while the first shift, with a higher turnout, went 60/40 for Beltran.

Why were the Van Nuys workers willing to elect a shop chairman strongly opposed to the team concept, when the company had warned them that without a "successful" team concept their plant was in jeopardy?

Pete Beltran's long history of service to the membership had a great deal to do with it. The insulting nature of the company's team training program also played a part. The major factor was the Campaign to Keep GM Van Nuys Open. The four-year-old Campaign had convinced workers that they had an *alternative* means of saving their plant besides team concept. Workers were presented not only with a critique of the team concept, but with an alternative strategy—the community coalition and boycott threat. The Campaign had also developed a core of experienced activists who campaigned hard and well for Beltran.

Although fear of a plant shutdown had led the Van Nuys workers to vote for team concept the year before, they were not willing to give up all their union protections. It was as if the average Van Nuys worker reasoned, "All right. If the company wants team con-

Ted Rall

cept so bad, let them have it. But in the meantime we'll try to keep them from messing with us any more than we can help."

Living with a 'Living Agreement'

A small majority of the committeepersons and shop committee elected along with Beltran were from the Fighting Back slate. (New President Jerry Shrieves, however, was from Ruppert's pro-team concept Responsible Representation slate.) With this backing, Beltran's initial desire was to dismantle the team concept entirely. He planned to negotiate a new local contract to begin in September 1987, at the regular expiration date, that would supersede the team concept agreement.

After the election, however, the company announced that the team concept agreement was good till September 1990. Unknown to the members, documents to that effect had been signed by the old shop committee. In November 1987 management even began to insist that the contract was good through 1993!

When the team concept contract was first accepted, because of the "hinged acceptance" it had no set starting date. Now it appeared that the expiration date was equally flexible—the "living agreement" taken to its logical conclusion.

When Beltran asked the UAW regional office for strike authorization (over production standards and safety and for a new local agreement), he was turned down. Both management and higher UAW officials had invested a lot in getting team concept accepted. Beltran and the Fighting Back caucus were stuck with a system they despised.

But unlike some local leaderships who have thrown up their hands when team concept came in, the Fighting Back committeepeople have maintained that team concept is not written in stone; the union can shape how team concept is implemented in practice. Mark Masaoka, a member of the Fighting Back caucus and an apprentice electrician on the second shift, said, "The membership elected a shop leadership which opposes team concept. That created the conditions for a host of other strategies to be played out in some way. Then you have some control. Then you can seriously talk about raising some demands."

How Teams Function

Van Nuys' team concept was modelled after NUMMI's and adopts several of its important features: small teams, a single pay rate, and appointed team leaders. As at NUMMI, workers were told in their team training that they could stop the line if they had trouble with a job. The Van Nuys plant does not go as far as NUMMI in "management-by-stress," however; there are still some workers designated as absentee replacements.

Both salaried and hourly employees from NUMMI came down to Van Nuys to assist in team leader training. Although the union members were basically positive about the team concept, they were not cheerleaders. They did not try to sugarcoat the fact that they were working much harder than before. Their message to Van Nuys workers was: it beats being laid off.

There are two production and six skilled classifications (electrician, carpenter, millwright, toolmaker, pipefitter, air conditioning) in the Van Nuys plant. In production, the team member classification makes $14.49 and the team leader $14.99. Assembly line workers are told to inspect and repair their jobs and clean up their areas.

Teams are made up of three to 17 workers, but most are in the range of five to eight. Teams are told what operations they need to accomplish, with the jobs specified, but they may redivide the work. "The thing is, the teams get more work," said one worker. "It's just up to them to decide how to do it." During start-up team members were expected to learn all the jobs in their teams, but now that the plant is at full production this often does not happen. Production stops for a half hour per week for the mandatory team meetings, where the status of production and defects are discussed.

Team leaders are appointed by management from among applicants; initially they received 160 hours of training. They were called back from layoff out of line of seniority to get that training. A number of full-time positions were created under team concept, such as trainers and facilitators, newsletter editors, a cafeteria committee and a ventilation committee. These positions were filled as patronage jobs by the outgoing chairman. The number of such positions has now been reduced.

Problems with Team Concept

Pete Beltran was on sick leave for a time during the early implementation of the team concept. He says, "The way the media presents the team concept is way off-base. It gets people thinking that they're going to have input. Team concept as it was sold to the people simply never took place. People are not rotating jobs or anything like that. When I came back from sick leave, I told management, 'I'm still looking for a team and I can't find one.' In practice, the only time the teams exist is when they meet. Team concept was used as a ruse to cut manpower."

One of the union's big complaints about team concept is the company's policy on replacing absentees. For one thing, the number of Absentee Replacement Operators (now called Team Member Replacements—TMRs) has been cut back. "Say we had 20 in chassis," says Mike Velasquez, a Fighting Back committeeperson on the first shift. "Now we have 13." TMRs operate department-wide. Now that they receive no more pay than a regular team member, fewer workers want the job, and so low seniority workers or those returning from sick leave are forced to be TMRs.

Second, team leaders must cover for unscheduled absences. Mike Velasquez says:

The policy here—which we don't agree with—is

that even if I'm hospitalized and they know my leg is broken, if I haven't taken out papers officially, I'm not replaced. One has to trigger the other. But once you give your papers to the receptionist at Kaiser [HMO], it may be a week later before the company gets the paperwork. In the meantime, the team leader's doing your job and the people aren't getting their emergency phone call relief, etc. That's where we get involved as a union. The team leader can't service the team if he's tied to a job.

The company wants the team leader to do some of the foreman's duties: keep track of overtime, pass out payroll checks and medical passes. We do not agree with that. We don't want to put our people in the position where if somebody's check is lost, or if someone doesn't get to go to medical, he's responsible.

Clarence Benton, a team leader on the chassis line and chairman of the local's veterans committee, says:

I keep a very clear line between what my job is and what management's job is. I'm not going to ask the guy why he wasn't here yesterday, because it's not my job.

We have a lot of grievances that haven't been resolved, and most of it's based on manpower. We have a lot of people out on disability or sick leave, and that means I have to go on the line. When I'm on the line that means I'm not going to do all the repair work that I would normally be doing. I refuse to do that. I think we have to keep management in line, otherwise we're going to be doing two-for-one jobs.

Mike Velasquez agrees: "The big problem is manpower. The last team meeting I went to, the team had drawn up a whole list of demands—manpower, and things they were told in class that were not happening. They were told the responsibility would be with the team, that the team would make decisions, but instead it's going to the group leader [foreman], he's saying, 'We'll set up the job *this* way.' Management is not listening to them. We as union representatives had to get involved, and some we did turn around."

Pete Beltran describes, "In some areas where the work standard was pretty good they got teams to decide where to eliminate jobs. But then the foreman made the decision anyway."

Management has also cut back on "team-building" activities. Velasquez says, "Also, every team was supposed to be given $15 per member, and the team would make a decision on what to do with it. Some went for pizza, some went to the executive lounge for lunch. But as quick as the $15 came, the company did away with it. Just a handful of teams got to use it. The company said they were losing money, that because of the line stops and the backlog of production they had to put it on hold."

Job Overloading and Job Cuts

Jobs are more heavily loaded than before, although the changes vary from department to department. Areas such as the motor line which have been re-organized have seen a good deal of job consolidation, while in the body shop the heavy welding guns make it difficult for management to shuffle the jobs much. There has been a good deal of turnover among team leaders in areas with the worst job overloading.

Pete Beltran says: "This term they use, 'standardized work,' it seems to mean you don't have a standard. They're always adding work on. Take the tire-changing job. It's a heavy job. There were two guys on it, and they'd work a half hour on and a half hour off. Now they want the guy who's off to load rims while he's supposed to be resting."

Beltran points to safety problems caused by combining some of the skilled trades: "When they combined the classifications they didn't provide cross-training. So some are not trained in lock-out and tag-out [of power sources], there are skilled trades people that don't even have locks to lock out with, who don't know where the power source is. And team leaders and foremen have keys to the line now, so a real lock-out becomes impossible. The result is we've had a number of close calls. People who were working on conveyor line motors, because it was not locked out, they had close calls when other people started up the line."

Mike Velasquez says, "The jobs in production are heavier. Both by the fact that you can measure it, as far as the job elements, and the stress factor. Now you have not only the capability of building it, but also inspecting it and repairing it if necessary. We used to operate with 4,300-4,400 on two shifts. Now we're at about 3,850." (Cuts were also made possible by a reduction in the number of options available on the product.) Line speed has remained at 62.5 jobs per hour.

Velasquez points in particular to cuts in TMRs, repair and material. "It used to be you had one that drove a hi-lo, one that unloaded from the boxcar, one that did checking of serial numbers, another they called a right hand man that took care of all the paperwork and used the computer. Now a person has to do all those functions. Not only the physical work but the computer and paperwork puts more stress on."

It is also harder to get a good job. Whereas before team concept there were over 100 classifications to which workers could transfer, now they can transfer only to departments, such as trim, paint or maintenance. Velasquez explains:

Under the old system if you put in a transfer say to the trimmer classification, you knew where you were going. Now, you can put in an application for the trim department, but as just a team member you could wind up anywhere in the department. You can also file an application to go from team to team, but not to any particular job. So people are more reluctant and more selective.

It used to be that if two people were both transferring, the one with more seniority got the opening. Now the person from within the department has preference. But in some departments we've been able to hold that back. You may have three things happening

Ragtop / TDU Convoy-Dispatch

at the same time: an application from another department to go to Department 15, Team 4; an application within the department from Team 5 to Team 4; and an employee that just requested from the group leader, "I'd like that particular job in line with my seniority." Out of those three, the person with high seniority *should* get that job.

The Fighting Back members feel that their ability to represent members is restricted by the new contract. Pete Lopez, a shop committeeperson on the first shift, said:

Before, your seniority was protected. Seniority ruled number one—although there was still discrimination. Now, there's a lot of favoritism under the team concept. Before, when there was an opportunity for a particular job, there were certain measures the company would have to deal with to try to get away with putting on one of their favorites. We could catch them. Now there's a limit on the moves we can make.

Take a reduction in force. The procedure in the book is extremely advantageous to the company. Say there's 20 people. If the company didn't like one person, they could eliminate her job and give the elements to the other 19 people, even if she had more seniority than ten others. The contract says a person whose job is eliminated must bump the low seniority person in the department. Now you take the worst job in the department, and you'll usually find that the lowest seniority person in that department is on it. Under the system she would be stuck there. The company can really do a number on a particular person.

Mark Masaoka notes:

People can still write 78's [production standards grievances], but in effect the new arrangement has rendered that nearly useless. Because it's your own workers who in some way impacted the decision on how that job was structured. Recently a woman got injured and had to have 16 stitches. The foreman said, "Don't blame me, the team set up the job."

Besides, the whole process has created an atmosphere where filing 78's is not viable. There's an attitude of "We've got to keep this plant open, it's all right to be pro-company and pro-union at the same time, we've got to save the company money."

Confronting the Team Concept

Although the internal battle in Local 645 over team concept was intense—and is still ongoing—management's own actions turned many workers away from team concept. Five months after its implementation Mike Velasquez said, "If we had an election today I feel no doubt they would get rid of it." Mark Masaoka believes, "Because of team concept people do feel more pressure and in some ways there is more support for the union now than when they came back, because people realize team concept is an effort by the company to save money. They see quality as a hollow promise."

The Van Nuys committeepeople have stepped in to deal with team concept in an aggressive way. Despite the strong upper hand that the contract gives management, they have been able to bargain for certain arrangements that benefit workers more than the contract would indicate.

The bottom line, explains Masaoka, is that committeepeople continue to write grievances and deal with management "in a way that's still recognized as an adversarial relationship." The committeepeople spot check the team meetings, for example, to see whether any of the teams needs a union rep. They defend members whom the company tries to discipline for not attending team meetings. They have gotten the company to pick team leaders by seniority, from among applicants plantwide. This should help to alleviate the problem of company-selected team leaders acting like junior foremen.

Team concept is famous for its use of peer pressure among team members; at least in one department at Van Nuys the team leaders use peer pressure among themselves. Clarence Benton explains: "One of the things we try to do as team leaders in chassis is when we see guys that are stepping over the line trying to be junior foremen, the team leaders get together, we meet once a week, just the team leaders—no management involved—and tell this guy, 'Hey, that's not our job, let's not step over that line.' "

In addition, an informal agreement was reached

on reductions in force. Pete Lopez explained, "The way we're doing it, if your job is eliminated and you have more seniority than someone in your team, you stay in the team and bump the lowest person in the team. If you don't, you bump into your section (a group leader's jurisdiction) and bump the lowest person there. Then it goes to the department, then to the plant." Management, of course, continually tries to renege on this understanding.

In some cases, at the committee's insistence the company has agreed to certain arrangements that benefit the membership simply because management, too, needs a stable mechanism that keeps the shop floor functioning.

For example, under the old system, management's objections to classifications and transferring were: 1) restriction of its ability to add more work onto jobs by the classification title, and 2) the time required to train people who transferred to new jobs. Under team concept, the "team member" classification is so broad that almost any kind of work can theoretically be added to it. Likewise, with only one production classification, the number of transfers has been reduced greatly. Thus, having won most of what it wants, management does not particularly mind having jobs filled by seniority.

The shop committee wants to hold further discussions with management about aspects of the team concept that they "can't live with."

Mike Velasquez said, "If the past administration had stayed as the leadership here, probably there would not have been too many changes. But with Pete as chairman, and with the current attitudes within the committee, our regional director has got to live with us. We went to one meeting with him and he said once we compiled a list he would sit down with us with the company and back us up." This has not happened. Instead the shop committee has been told to fall in line with team concept or the region would appoint a new chairman (while Beltran was on sick leave).

Two of the important things on the committeepeople's "list"—which they've submitted to Labor Relations—are better transfer procedures and more classifications, including TMR, inspector and repair. Lopez says, "We want to meet with the company and the International and have them recognize the fact that having inspectors would be beneficial to them in terms of money.

"Inspectors historically have been very valuable for the company. They insure a high quality product. Repairmen too. They don't want to recognize the fact that we have repairs, but we do. And they are higher skilled than the regular operator. If you don't have repairmen recognized as having a lot more knowledge than the regular guy on the line, if you don't have inspectors who are trained to check and recheck, quality goes down."

Workers' Right To Stop the Line

Meanwhile, GM is unhappy because workers have taken one of its team concept promises seriously.

Workers were repeatedly assured during training that they could and should stop the line if they ran into a problem. They were told they would have a say in what kind of car was built. Now, a large part of team meetings is spent going over when it is okay to stop the line and when it isn't.

The plant manager put out a letter to employees explaining that too many line stops were putting the plant behind its production schedule; the stop button should be pushed only when the problem was critical. Some team leaders stop the line when management ignores their requests for more manpower. A small scandal was created when word got out to the local media, which had strongly supported the team concept, that management wanted to restrict this supposed right.

"It's ironic," says Mike Velasquez, "that three weeks ago one of the committee members was taken in the office because he saw a defect going down the line, out of the area where the team could correct it, and took it upon himself to stop the line. He was brought down for a discussion in Labor Relations and verbally penalized."

The Van Nuys committeepeople will continue to pressure the company to make informal arrangements that make the plant more livable. Their ability to do so will depend on the backing they get from the membership, their ability to organize the membership, and their own tenacity.

In September 1987 six members of the Fighting Back Caucus put out a leaflet which suggested improvements in the team concept:

1. Reinstate a fair and effective seniority structure of at least fifteen production classifications. This will provide equal basis for promotion, and with the incentives of higher pay, it can enable and encourage our more experienced and qualified workers to take the more difficult positions of repairmen, TMR's and inspectors/monitors. Some supervisors have privately acknowledged that the lack of these experienced mechanics are part of the problem with the high down time.

2. Maintain lines of demarcation in the maintenance skilled trades.

3. Automatic allocation of PAA [Paid Absence Allowance] pay for the first five absences per year, if requested. Workers with excellent records are being denied PAA pay and Perfect Attendance Awards because they lack or have insufficiently filled out doctors' excuses.

4. Give the teams the authority they were verbally promised earlier—to be able to reject additional work assigned to their team, in production and maintenance. Hire more manpower if needed, and at the very least, teams should be able to turn down work for 30 days, to allow time to find a better solution. Any increases in line speeds should be reported and done after consultation with the teams in the department.

These and other creative ideas will be necessary if the shop floor representatives are to carry out the membership's mandate to keep team concept under control.

Appendix

The contract language reprinted below is excerpted from the 1986 Local Agreement between UAW Local 645 and GM Van Nuys.

The framework for change is a team organization. In a team organization, the work performed in the various departments will be assigned to business teams. Each team will consist of a Team Leader and Team Members. Their activities will be coordinated by a Group Leader. Each team will be responsible for such things as safety, product quality including specifications, cost reduction, meeting budgets and schedules, overtime equalization, training, job rotation, absentee coverage, job layout and methods, inspection, repair and housekeeping. Team leaders will guide and coordinate the activities of the team. The Team Leader will provide unscheduled relief, training, and where necessary, cover for absentees. Based on the guidelines discussed between the parties, team decisions in the areas outlined in this paragraph shall be implemented by the Group Leader. Effective implementation of the above concepts will require changes to be made in our Local Agreements. It is recognized that the team concept will dramatically change the existing system and structure, expanding the responsibilities of all employees. Accordingly, higher rates of pay will be justified.

The CPC Van Nuys Plant recognizes that job security is essential to an employee's well being and acknowledges that it has a responsibility, with the cooperation of the Union, to provide stable employment to its workers. The Union's commitments in this agreement are a significant step towards the realization of stable employment. Hence, CPC Van Nuys agrees that it will not indefinitely lay off employees unless compelled to do so by severe economic conditions that threaten the financial viability of this facility .

Management agrees that before it is necessary to indefinitely lay off bargaining unit employees, the parties will implement any jointly agreed upon affirmative measures as are appropriate for the local parties to discuss such as, returning outsourced work to the bargaining unit which they are capable of performing competitively, alternative layoff programs and other cost saving measures. In this regard, the parties recognize that all employees should share in adjustments necessary to avoid indefinite layoffs of large groups of employees.

Team Concept Operational Structure

The parties discussed at length the Management structure which might logically result from the implementation of a Team Concept. It was recognized that to produce the lowest cost product, it is advantageous to create a structure which results in the minimal number of salaried employees required to service the needs of the manufacturing operation. Inherent in this philosophy is the need to delegate the authority to implement decisions consistent with the responsibilities which have been assigned to the teams.

At the same time, the Union requested it be involved in redefining of the resulting structure. Management responded that it would welcome the Union's input and agreed to review its plans as they are being developed and to give substantial weight to the Union's comments.

Team Organization Guidelines

1. The plant will set aside one half hour per week in order to hold team meetings. The time set aside will be either part of the eight-hour shift or prior to or after the shift depending on the needs of the team and the organization.

2. Meeting areas will be established throughout the plant to accommodate the meetings. These meeting areas should be kept clean and orderly.

3. It is mandatory that employees attend the team meetings—employee participation is important.

4. It is part of the Group Leader's responsibility to monitor team's progress and act as a resource (not as a Team Leader). The team may request that anyone not a member of the team leave the team meeting.

5. The Team Leader will be selected based on criteria jointly developed by the Union and Management.

6. Teams will preferably consist of 4 to 8 people each.

7. Minutes will be taken at each meeting. The Group Leader for the area and the District Committeeman will be given a copy. A master log of meeting minutes will be maintained in the Joint Activities office.

8. Contractual issues such as D.L.O.'s, Paragraph 78 grievances, Local or National Bargaining issues will not be discussed in team meetings. District committeemen may be invited to the team meetings to explain contractual issues or answer general contractual questions.

9. Names and telephone numbers of in-plant resources, as well as outside vendor resources, will be made available to all teams in order to help resolve problems.

10. A resource meeting (Group Leader and the Team Leaders and the District Committeeman) will be established and will meet at least once per week to discuss and resolve problems as well as share and exchange information.

11. A meeting will be established between the Team Leaders and the District Committeeman to discuss and resolve problems and share information.

12. Existing business team meetings consisting of the Department Superintendent, Group Leaders, and the various support department personnel will be expanded to include the District Committeeman and Team Leaders.

13. The Joint Steering Committee consisting of the Shop Chairman and the Shop Committee and the Plant Manager and his Staff will meet on a weekly basis to monitor the process of team organization. Any changes in team organization guidelines will be by mutual agreement and in response to the needs of teams.

Memorandum of Understanding

In developing the Team Organization Guidelines, the parties agreed that the selection of Team Leaders would be based on criteria jointly developed by the parties. The parties recognize that they must be guided by the provisions of Paragraph 63(a) of the GM-UAW National Agreement. In this regard, the parties agreed to jointly develop the criteria for determining merit, ability and capacity and to participate jointly in the selection of Team Leaders. The parties recognize that some skills can be learned while some skills must be present prior to training. It is those skills that training cannot provide or that are necessary for training to be effective that the parties must jointly determine in developing the criteria for Team Leaders. Accordingly, the parties are committed to develop both the criteria and the selection process for Team Leaders in accordance with the above guidelines.

Memorandum of Understanding

During the discussions regarding the Team Organization Guidelines, the parties agreed that small teams were critical to the effectiveness of a team organization. Team Leaders can better service the needs of small teams due to the fact that the larger the team, the more the Team Leader would be required to perform a regular operation. The parties recognized that while teams might preferably be no larger than 8 or smaller than 4, there would be occasions that teams might consist of less than four people or more than eight, depending on the proximity and/or nature of the team responsibilities. Therefore, the parties agreed to work jointly in the formation of small effective teams utilizing where possible existing resources.

17. Mazda:
Choosing Workers Who Fit

Officially, the new Mazda plant in Flat Rock, Michigan is not a joint venture. But for many Ford workers, it feels that way. Ford owns 25 percent of the Japanese parent company of Mazda Motor Manufacturing (USA) Corporation (MMUC). The new assembly plant, located 30 miles south of Detroit, is on the site of the former Ford Michigan Casting Center.

MMUC president Osamu Nobuto says that MMUC and Ford "are freely providing the opportunity to observe each other's plants."[1] Ford will purchase about two-thirds of the production of MMUC and will market the car as a Ford Probe. This will allow Ford to maintain less of its own assembly capacity and will probably lead to the closing of the Rouge Dearborn Assembly plant. In effect Ford has arranged for the replacement of one of its current assembly operations with a new one that is under a very different kind of union contract. Furthermore, Ford workers had no right to move with "their work."

Because of its ties to Ford and its location in the center of U.S. auto production, MMUC's operation will provide strong precedents for the rest of the auto industry.

Mazda Goes Union

The deal to bring Mazda to Michigan was constructed in 1984. The state of Michigan put together a package of inducements totalling more than $120 million. This included $16 to $18 million for job training, $30 million in funds for improvements to roads, railway spurs and other infrastructure, and about $80 million in tax abatements from Flat Rock and Wayne County.

But Mazda was not about to open its first U.S. plant in the Detroit area, home of the United Auto Workers, and face an all-out struggle with the union. Before the Michigan deal could be consummated, the company required that the union issue be settled. According to the *Detroit Free Press*, "State officials worked directly with the UAW on the job training program and

---

• *Mazda Motor Manufacturing (USA) Corporation*
• *Location: Flat Rock, Michigan*
• *Employment: 3,500 hourly and salaried projected*
• *Product: Mazda Mx-6, Ford Probe*
• *Production began: 1987*
• *Team Concept began: 1986*
• *UAW Local 3000*
  Address: c/o UAW Region 1A, 9650 S. Telegraph Rd., Tayor, MI 48180
  Phone: 313 / 291-2750

---

on concessions sought by Mazda on work rules and job classifications."[2]

A "letter of intent" between Mazda and the UAW was drafted in September 1984. They agreed on recognition of the UAW, hiring preference for laid-off Ford workers, and some points to be contained in a future collective bargaining agreement:

The Collective Bargaining Agreement will provide for the Union's long term cooperation in the recognition and commitment to the principle of flexibility that the company must have to maintain and improve quality and efficiency and to the implementation of work practices and production systems similar to those used by Mazda in Japan. This flexibility includes, among other things, a minimal number of job classifications, flexibility in job assignments and job transfers, employee training, the performance by employees of different jobs, an effective cooperative work relationship among the employees, the use of the team concept, and an active and meaningful employee involvement program.

The union made major concessions on seniority language. For example, management would have the right to designate the departments from which new job openings will be filled rather than allowing plant-wide bidding. Layoffs and recalls would give "consideration to such factors as employees' abilities, qualifications, experience, physical capacity, and length of service." The understanding also included a wage structure with starting pay at 72 percent of Big Three wages, increasing to 85 percent after 18 months. The letter contained a commitment to raise the pay scale to the level of the Big Three during the course of the first three-year contract.

No formal signing of the letter of intent was ever announced. Suits by the anti-union National Right-to-Work Committee over terms in the UAW-GM Saturn contract forced the UAW to be more cautious about pre-production agreements. No UAW or Mazda spokesperson would comment on the letter. But in public statements made in 1986, UAW officials clearly regarded the plant as organized.[3]

Some provisions of the letter were not carried out. A special letter was sent to all laid-off Ford employees inviting them to apply. But as a group it does not seem that they were given preference over other applicants. A Mazda spokesperson declared that the number of previous Ford employees was "proprietary information,"[4] but workers estimated the figure at about ten percent in early 1988.

On the other hand, Mazda adhered to the wage structure in the letter, and the UAW never challenged management's flexibility or work arrangements. Mazda publicly announced a policy of strict neutrality on whether its workers joined the union. The UAW, although not formally recognized, participated in new-hire orientation sessions.

Throughout the start-up period, the UAW got workers to sign authorization cards. To help avoid challenges, the company and the union agreed to a secret ballot election conducted by the American Arbitration Association. The UAW magazine *Solidarity* described the election campaign as a "low key, word-of-mouth effort describing the benefits of unionization."[5] Announcements of the election were posted in the plant, but there was no campaign literature either pro or con. On September 11, 1987 the vote for union representation was 717 to 92.

Following the election the local began to hold union meetings. Several hundred attended the first meeting which included dinner, and large numbers attended the next two. The meetings provided many members with their first opportunity to get answers to their questions. How were the appointed local officers selected? What could they do about how team leaders were selected? What was the relationship of the local to Ford workers? UAW Regional Director Ernie Lofton reassured anxious workers that if there were a Ford strike, Mazda workers would not go out with Ford workers despite the fact that the Mazda plant's main product would be sold by Ford.

The union officials include a benefits representative, a health and safety representative, five committeepersons and a president, all appointed by the UAW regional director. Workers complain that they do not get to talk privately to their committeepersons unless they insist. As at NUMMI, the committeepersons share offices with their management counterparts, and in some departments they respond together to problems or grievances.

No Burned Out Bulbs

The atmosphere and organization of the plant are much like NUMMI's. Like NUMMI, the plant is strikingly clean. Those who have worked in other auto plants comment that oil leaks or burned out light bulbs are taken care of right away. The plant is modern, with about 350 robots and some automatic guided vehicles (AGV's) in the stamping operation.[6] MMUC President Nobuto says, "Yes, we'll have some robots and state of the art machinery but it won't be space age equipment that requires a lot of experimentation."[7]

There are 15 minute mass relief breaks in the morning and afternoon and a 40 minute lunch time (ten minutes paid). There is a single production worker classification and no pay-for-knowledge.

Teams consist of four to eight members with some teams expanded in prepartion for adding the afternoon shift. Management selects the team leaders, who are paid an additional 42 cents an hour. Team leaders

keep track of attendance, provide relief, replace absentees, train new team members, and help establish programmed work standards.

The lowest level supervisor is called the unit leader, who is in charge of two to four teams. The original unit leaders and team leaders were sent to Mazda's plant in Hofu, Japan for training.

Team meetings are scheduled regularly. Production workers gather every morning before the start of the shift for ten minutes (unpaid) of exercise and meeting. Once a week the team meets for a half hour. In addition there are periodic department or "town meetings."

Weekly "diagonal slice" meetings with the plant manager involve about 20 people, including managers of different levels and selected team members (different people each time). The meetings are mainly for workers to raise problems directly to the highest levels of management. Most of these problems are usually referred to departmental management but workers speak positively about the meetings.

The diagonal slice approach apparently was an important part of Plant Manager Dennis Pawley's popularity in the plant. Workers comment that Pawley, with his earthy language and knowledge of the shop floor, was one of the few managers comfortable "not wearing a tie" and was very approachable. (In February 1988, Pawley, who previously had been plant manager of GM's Fiero plant, quit Mazda to become a vice-president of United Technologies' Otis Elevator.)

Skilled trades for the entire plant, including plastics, stamping, and assembly, are in a single classification referred to as maintenance. This includes tool and die makers (who have a separate classification at NUMMI). The total skilled trades workforce at full staffing will be 180-200, less than half the number most assembly plants of this size. It is especially low given the amount of technology and normal start-up problems.

This low number is achieved in several ways. Everyone in the maintenance classification is cross-trained. Work traditionally done by trades such as glaziers and carpenters is contracted out. Production workers perform some traditional skilled trades jobs, such as replacing weld tips, changing hoses and reprograming robots. Construction and maintenance jobs that require more than a few hours are assigned to outside contractors. Furthermore, management attempts to apply the principles of "programmed work" (detailed specifica-

> Jane Doe
> **mazda**
>
> Team Member
> Maintenance
> Manufacturing
>
> Mazda Motor
> Manufacturing (USA) Corporation
>
> 1 Mazda Drive
> Flat Rock, Michigan 48134

Production workers are issued "business" cards at Mazda.

tions which break down every step in a job, also called job charting) to maintenance procedures, especially preventive maintenance.

Maintenance teams meet every morning for 10 to 45 minutes. Often the meetings are brief, taking up only team leader reports and the day's assignments. But frequently maintenance teams will have discussions about problems with specific machines, safety problems, or company policies like lack of adequate tools.

Cultures Mix

When the Flat Rock plant started, Mazda brought from Japan 500 "dispatchees"—engineers and advisors. The plan is to slowly phase out all but a few of them. Most of the U.S. workers seem to enjoy the contact with a different culture. Many of the workers recently moved to the area, and there is a fair amount of social contact outside the plant between the U.S. workers and the dispatchees. There have been some reports of racial incidents—anti-Japanese slogans scrawled on the walls, for example—but they seem to have come from workers employed by outside contractors doing construction in the plant. U.S. Mazda workers were genuinely angry and apologetic about these incidents.

In management, there is a division of labor along racial lines. The Japanese handle most of the manufacturing and technical questions, and the American managers take charge of the internal human relations, hiring, orientation, and public relations.

The dispatchees also serve as role models. Many U.S. workers comment on the dispatchees' loyalty and commitment to the company. The dispatchees often put in extra hours without pay and think nothing of suggesting that workers study materials at home. Many workers tell stories of dispatchees doing dangerous feats to get the line moving again, such as riding on a moving platform through an automation area or reaching into a powered-up machine to unjam it.

Gold Braid

As at NUMMI, many of the status symbols that differentiate management from hourly workers have been removed. But subtle distinctions still exist. All levels wear the same uniform of brown shirt, blue pants or skirt, and blue cap (unlike NUMMI, the uniform is required). But department managers and higher all have a gold braid around their name badges.

The uniforms are a source of considerable controversy. In the summer the nylon jumpsuits required in the painting areas are oppressively hot. In other departments the company insists that workers wear their caps at all times. Bracelets, chains, watches, and rings are prohibited because they are possible safety hazards or because they might scratch the cars.[8]

Everyone eats in the same cafeteria. But many management people have sufficient flexibility on their jobs that it is possible to get to the cafeteria a few minutes early, avoid the rush and get the best seats. Hourly workers must keep working until the last minute before lunch. No matter how fast they run to the cafeteria, they still have to stand in line. Similarly, salaried workers have sufficient flexibility that they can manage to have lunch at outside restaurants.

Life in the Start-Up Mode

As of February 1988, the plant was still in a start-up mode. While it has a full complement of workers for the one shift it is running, the line speed is only around 40 cars per hour, as compared to the projected 65. As in all start-ups there are quality problems and bugs to be worked out.

There are many features of life in the start-up mode which will not exist once the plant gets to full production. The line speed is slower so workers have the time to help one another out. There are frequent problems, and the company truly needs and wants workers' input to solve them. The continued expansion of the workforce plus the turnover of a new workforce create openings for new team leaders and group leaders and plenty of opportunity for the company to reward those it wishes. There is an air of excitement about being involved in something new.

But as the NUMMI experience illustrates, most of these attractive features will disappear once the plant gets up to full production. Workers will find that they have no time to help one another and that the interesting parts of the job—like problem solving—are pushed to the background. As the workforce stabilizes, promotional opportunities will diminish to a trickle. The main task will be keeping up with a fast line every day, something that gets old very quickly.

Even now problems show up. Occasionally a team makes a proposal which is ignored by management, and members feel resentful. Such resentment is frequently expressed by reduced participation in voluntary activities like pre-work exercises.

Consider the Errors

Mazda's disciplinary procedure begins with the standard list of offenses that bring immediate suspension or firing: illegal activities, theft, fighting, "falsifying or omitting any information on a company record," and encouraging any "illegal strike, slowdown or other interruption of work."

-Next there is a list of "employee expectations" which contain rules like:

-No food, beverages, or smoking in non-designated areas.

-No reading materials in non-designated areas.

-Working hours may be varied by the company to meet its needs.

-Strict attendance required with no tardiness.

-Uniforms must be worn at all times.

The three-page list of employee expectations is summed up with:

Mazda employees are also expected to be flexible

in job assignments, to have near perfect attendance, and be responsible for the quality of all Mazda products. In short, all employees are expected to be active contributing members of the Mazda team.

Failure to live up to these employee expectations or to neglect or disrupt the performance of your job responsibilities or the responsibilities of others will be addressed through the Code of Conduct.[9]

The Code of Conduct explains how violations will be dealt with. Mazda's procedure has been used by other U.S. companies and is described in the *Harvard Business Review* as a "nonpunitive approach to discipline."[10] It is a five step procedure.

1. Oral reminder.
2. Written reminder.
3. Second written reminder.

These first three steps are designed to gain the "worker's agreement to solve the problem" and develop "a new action plan to eliminate the gap between actual and desired performance."

Step four is a *discussion with labor relations*. This is the point from which the procedure gets its "nonpunitive" name. After the discussion, the "disruptive" worker is given a day off *with pay* to consider the error of his ways. After the paid day off, the worker reports to the unit leader with the decision to either change his ways (with an acceptable plan for correction) or quit.

If another incident of disruptive behavior occurs, the company takes it as a decision to quit and, after review of the incident, the fifth step, the *worker is "self-terminated."*[11]

One of the 96,500

NUMMI was forced by union pressure to hire mainly from the workers laid off from GM's Fremont plant, but Mazda had virtually unlimited freedom to hire whomever it wished. Considerable effort and expense went into designing and running the selection and orientation programs.[12] In full-page ads Mazda proclaimed:

At Flat Rock, Mazda launched what may well be the most painstaking recruitment and training program in automotive history. An intensive five-stage screening process was used to select 3,500 workers from a mass of 96,500 applicants. Those hired then participated in a rigorous 10 week training course followed by off-line training with a team leader. Throughout, the new workforce was introduced to The Mazda Way of Open Management and Worker Participation.[13]

Because the selection process reveals so much about the kind of workforce Mazda desires and the kind of management Mazda uses, we describe it at some length. Both successful and unsuccessful applicants were interviewed for this chapter. However, most of the detail offered below is available because one of the authors of this book, Mike Parker, went through the first four steps of the selection process. The following account is based primarily on his notes.

Stage 1: A Message from Debbie

Mazda starts hiring in 1986. I send in a letter requesting an application. I never get a response, but most people receive a standard job application form which asks for previous work history, schooling, and three references.

During the last week of March in 1987, Mazda runs an ad specifically looking for journeymen electricians or welder repairers. I send in a copy of my resume and a photocopy of my journeyman's card.

I assume I have a fair chance of getting a job offer. Things are going pretty well for electricians in the area and I know there would not be many electricians with experience in heavy industry or construction applying for jobs that started at two-thirds the pay of the Big Three. (I did not know Mazda was advertising and sending recruitment teams to other areas of the country.)

I have not made up my mind whether I will take the job if it is offered. Plus side: interesting technological problems of a new plant, being part of building a new union, and I would not be on the bottom of the seniority list. Minus side: less money, long distance from home, concerns about how the plant would be managed, and whether I would actually get to work on the technology.

Sunday, five days after I mailed in the application, I receive a message on my tape machine to call Debbie from Mazda. In all my experience at Ford and Chrysler, I have never had an official company call on the weekend or in the evening. On the one hand, it might make more sense to call when people are more likely to be home. On the other hand, the blurring of company time and personal time gives me some pause.

I call Debbie on Monday. She tells me to come to Cadillac School at 5:00 p.m. that day with two #2 pencils and a picture ID.

Stage 2: Two #2 Pencils

Mazda uses Cadillac elementary school, no longer in regular use, for its extensive selection and testing program. The other applicants and I take every other chair at long tables in a large gymnasium and have a few minutes to talk before the test starts. It seems that everyone has applied for a skilled job so perhaps this battery of tests will be only for skilled trades. (Production workers later told me they took the same tests.) Most had their applications in months ago. The only other person who had applied recently is also an electrician. I figure they must be hurting for electricians so my chances are pretty good.

Three Mazda people, wearing the company uniform, administer the test. I later find out that all three are unit leaders, the lowest level of supervision. They check our picture ID's, record our Social Security numbers, and then the tests begin.

Test 1: A 15 minute Mazda Math Test checks for basic addition, subtraction, multiplication and division skills, and ability to read simple graphs.

Test 2: A Flanagan Industrial Test[14] tests for observation of "quality." There are diagrams of the correct part or object and then a number of similar ones next to it. I am supposed to circle all those which have a defect (i.e., some difference with the model). I find this test very difficult, and I probably spend too much time on the first few problems.

Test 3: Another Flanagan Industrial Test. This ones shows bunches of parts with letters indicating how they are to be put together. The object is to choose which of five diagrams looks most like the assembled item.

Test 4: A 10 minute listening test. A tape recorder in the middle of the room is turned on and we listen to various instructions and then write the correct answers on our answer sheet.

Test 5: A 30 minute mechanical aptitude test. The questions measure basic knowledge of gears, electricity, levers, and temperature.

The tests are run in a no-nonsense, machine gun fashion. While one test is going on, the unit leaders are placing the next set of test materials, exactly counted out, at the outside ends of the tables. When each test is over, we immediately pass our materials to the center where the piles are collected. At the same time, the new test materials are moving into place right behind. There is never a mistake, the unit leader begins instructions for the next test within a minute.

The next day there is a message on my tape asking me to call Don at Mazda. There is a later message—Don giving me his home phone. I have mixed reactions again. On the one hand, I am pleased that I do not have to wait until the next day to find out what is happening. On the other hand, I feel a bit uncomfortable intruding on someone's private life with something from work which is clearly no emergency. It turns out Don is playing basketball, and his wife thinks he will be home late. Don and I cross calls a few times the next day. When we finally connect, Don apologizes. He is an electrical engineer and was out on the floor because of breakdowns.

Don tells me I passed the test and wants me to come in for a personal interview. Since I have not actually filled out an application form, I should come early to take care of that. We schedule an interview.

Stage 3: Ever Been Written Up?

While driving back to Cadillac School, I decide to be very careful at the interview. I don't want to lie, but at the same time I do not want to volunteer any more of my views on unions or industrial relations than necessary.

After filling out an application form, I go to an empty classroom with one table and three chairs in the middle. Two Mazda engineers interview me. They explain that they will be asking me questions from a typed script so that, in the interests of fairness, everyone will

be given the questions the same way. They also explain that they are writing down my answers so that they and others can evaluate them.

Why did I apply at Mazda? They ask about my present job, my absence record, my tardiness record, and whether I have ever been written up. They ask about my hobbies and community activities. I mention working in a group on a job, and they ask me if I am familiar with the "team concept." I say that I know something about working in groups but don't know anything about how it works at Mazda.

Then they read some descriptions of hypothetical situations: *I am working at my job, and I notice the parts coming from the station before me have occasional defects. It does not affect my job. What do I do about it?*

They record my answer and probe a bit, then present me with a second scenario. *My job is putting heat shields on one side of the car. A woman I don't like is putting them on the other side. She misses bolts, and I have been adding them. I have tried talking to her but it doesn't work. What do I do?*

I don't like the question, and I think it shows. I figure that they must surely know that only the most disgusting apple polisher would volunteer to fink. I finally mumble something about talking to her again about taking responsibility for herself, and, unless she took her problem to the team to solve, I was not going to continue covering for her. I don't think they consider it a good answer.

We move on to a section of the interview where they read a series of statements and ask for my response. The wording here is approximate.

Mazda is aiming to achieve the same efficiency and productivity as they have in Japan.

The Mazda way is no idleness.

We discuss this a bit. At one point I am asked if I ever made a suggestion to increase productivity or efficiency. I describe some suggestions I have put in. The interviewer interrupts to explain that he did not mean a technical suggestion, but have I ever suggested a way that we could do a job with one fewer person? I think for a moment and reply that I can't recall having done so. They make a note.

Being on time and present for work is important.

What would I do if my neighbor were having problems with a Mazda car?

I honestly do not understand the question. They explain that Mazda expects its employees to stand behind the company and help out wherever there is a problem. I am beginning to realize just how strongly I feel about the separation of work and private life and how much the "Mazda way" seems to blur that distinction.

When they finish, they offer me an opportunity to ask questions. Some answers:

There is no guaranteed job security. They will try to do it "like in Japan" (presumably meaning no layoffs), but no promises. They do not expect any layoffs because 60 percent of the product will be bought directly by Ford. (I do not understand the logic—surely Ford is not guaranteeing the cars will sell—but I do not pursue it.)

There is no seniority at the plant as yet. There is no union. The UAW participates in the orientation, but it will be up to the people to decide whether they want a union or not. Mazda has good relations with its union in Japan and has no problem with having a union here if that's what the workers want.

Teams meet for ten minutes every morning and one-half hour (on company time) on Wednesdays. Neither could give me much description of teams since they are not regular members. "We can sit in on teams and are often requested to meet with the teams."

They answer my questions for about a half hour. There is no hype. They want to make sure that I understand that skilled trades work is done differently at Mazda from my experiences at traditional plants.

They leave the room while I wait. Five minutes later they return and schedule my appointment for an "assessment."

Stage 4: Dinner with the Plant Manager

Twenty-one of us hopefuls gather in a waiting room on the appointed Saturday afternoon. This is the first time that any of us are on the Mazda grounds. Conversations are quiet and nervous. No one knows what the assessment will be like.

All the people I talk to are applying for production jobs. They say that they had put their applications in some time last year but were called only recently for interviews. Most have friends who never even got interviews. One man, in his forties, has driven 250 miles from Norwood, Ohio. This is his third trip in the application process, and he is pleased to get this far. A uniformed Mazda person, Carl, comes in, joking about how we may not make it through the day. I ask him how far people travel to go through this application process. Carl responds that people have flown in from California and Florida for a crack at these jobs.

Finally they take us to a large room where they explain how the assessment works. We will be evaluated in groups of five or six by two assessors. Group members and assessors will be shuffled for each of four exercises. All sessions will have the same structure. At the beginning, the assessors will explain what we are to do and we can ask questions. After that, we can ask no more questions.

We follow the shuffling instructions on the sheet and go to our first assignments. Mine is called "Rewards" which, like all the others, is held in a windowless conference room just big enough for one long table.

Shuffle 1: Rewards. We are told to assume that we are a functioning team. The plant manager wants to set up a rewards program, and our team has been asked to suggest a system. We are given a list of activities and told to prioritize them, suggest appropriate rewards, and decide whether these should be individual or team

TEAM CONCEPT INCENTIVES

Choose one of the following rewards:

DREAM VACATION

OUR MOTTO: "SHUT UP, GET BACK TO WORK, HERE, THANKS"

YESTERDAY'S PAPER

SACK OF LEAVES

MATCHES

DINNER AT THE BOSS'

DOLLAR A DAY

LIVE LOBSTER

10¢ PER HOUR

BAR O' SOAP

CAN O' COKE

USELESS PLAQUE

COMPANY "STOCK"

BEST SPOT ON THE BUS TO WORK

SHOW TICKETS

TED RALL

rewards. We should take about ten minutes to read the materials and use our work sheets and then 35 minutes to come up with our group answer on a sheet of paper.

The list of items to be rewarded includes:
- Most cooperative
- Highest productivity
- Highest team spirit
- Most work related suggestions
- Most improved individual or team
- Best attendance
- Highest quality
- Highest score in company team sports

The list of possible rewards includes:
- Ten cent per hour raise
- $100 U.S. savings bond
- Plaque
- $500 shopping spree
- Best parking space for a month
- Dinner at the plant manager's house

The assessors sit back and take notes during the session. From the scratch of their pencils at certain intervals, I assume they are making notes about the role that each member of the group plays—surely they don't care whether we think "highest productivity" rates above or below "best attendance."

The group starts its discussion. One person volunteers to lead off, someone else offers to be recorder and write the final report. One person will keep track of time. Everybody is aware that they are being measured

by their participation and is trying to play the role the examiners are looking for. It's a challenge because no one is quite sure what it is. I am trying to play the role of someone who is helpful in resolving disputes and familiar with team procedures like brainstorming.

After our team has several false starts I suggest that we all make known our individual priority lists to see where we are in general agreement. Two people make "highest productivity" their number one choice. I assume this was to impress the assessors. I suggest adding safety to the list as number one. Some group members are nervous about agreeing that the most important item was not on the original list, but nobody has a good argument against it. After some discussion we get consensus to make safety number one. I also suggest that "most improved individual or team" should rank high, but find no support. I try a second time, then drop it.

Shuffle 2: Group Assembly. The group is to act as a team to assemble an "airboat" using toy blocks (like Leggos). We must use all group members and assemble the airboats as quickly as possible. The assessors show us a completed model and demonstrate how to check it for "quality." They explain that since the parts are so worn, the quality check almost always fails. Our instructions are to pass it after one check and one repair. (Now this sounds like the auto industry I know.)

For 25 minutes we devise and rehearse our assembly technique. Then they give us the rest of the parts for our time trial. It takes us four minutes and 30 seconds to assemble our units. The assessors examine them and show us a couple of "quality" problems where the constructed units are not exactly like the models. They ask us whether we want to try another model or work more on this one. We choose to improve, and we reorganize our assembly process slightly. In addition to improving our quality check, we also make sure that everyone makes sub-assemblies as well as participating in final assembly. Our time for the second trial is 45 seconds more than the first, but our quality is 100 percent.

One of the assessors senses that our team is discouraged and says that we have done it in good time. Later in the hall I hear of teams that made 100 percent quality in three and a half minutes.

Pat is a Good Worker, But...

Shuffle 3: Problems. We are a team of Mazda production employees. Four problems have come up. We are to prepare a brief outline for the team supervisor on how we think the problems should be handled.

1. The plant manager wants us to participate in a volleyball tournament because volleyball builds team spirit. Some people on our team do not like volleyball and would prefer baseball or bowling. Some even object to the use of outside time for company activities.

2. Pat (male or female carefully avoided) is "a bright, alert, and reliable worker." Pat has saved the plant thousands of dollars through suggestions and has helped our team "turn out more work than similar teams at Mazda." But Pat has a problem of "complaining" and being "rude and nasty" to others. The supervisor sent a letter to the team leader asking the team to deal with Pat's attitude problem and that "Pat must show more cooperative and flexible attitudes." The team is meeting without Pat, who is on vacation.

3. It is too hot in our part of the plant and there are three alternatives: request permission to wear shorts or go shirtless, investigate the causes of the heat, or air condition the plant.

4. Lee is a good member of our team—the written story is lavish in its praise. But Lee's daughter has severe asthma which sometimes means that Lee has to take her to the hospital. "The lateness is far in excess of what can be tolerated and the plant's production schedule does not permit Lee to make up lost time on other shifts."

We prioritize the problems to deal with the most important ones first. Most think that the heat question is trivial, and when we get to it, it takes only a couple of minutes to agree that the obvious reasonable answer is to investigate the causes before making any proposal. It is an indication of just how far from reality the assessment procedure is. Trying to work at full speed in overheated plants is excruciating. Short term solutions—more break time, reduced line speed, fans to move the air, rotation to cooler places—are essential. I bite my tongue on this one. (The issue of deviation from the uniform would be a big issue in the plant that summer.)

The volleyball question also takes little time. Of course, we tell the plant manager, we would like to participate in his tournament, but add that some of our group would like to suggest that the next tournament be baseball or bowling.

The other questions, the group feels, are tough. Most of our time is spent on the Lee and Pat problems. The few suggestions that even remotely challenge the company are extremely tentative. My suggestion—maybe whoever decided that Lee's schedule could not be "tolerated" might be wrong and that we should inquire how this was determined—is completely ignored. The group focusses on how we might be able to give Lee some assistance. One guy volunteers his wife: "I could have my wife drive Lee's kid to the hospital." Someone else says, "Maybe Lee could hire a live-in nurse and we could raise money."

Shuffle 4: Mazda Philosophy. "Mazda wishes to be sure that new employees have no problem adjusting to work at a plant that uses new philosophies and methods." Our team is given a list of possible problem areas in the Mazda philosophy and asked to rank these in order of difficulty and suggest ways that might ease the difficulty.

The list includes:
-Expect workers to make lots of suggestions
-Expect workers to do many jobs
-Trust between workers and management
-Flexible jobs and a variety of tasks
-High degree of work commitment
-No waste of material or motion
Needless to say, no one challenged any of these. All the suggestions were the same: more training and better communication.

At the end we reassembled in the original big meeting room. This was it, we were told. Those rejected would receive a letter in the next two months. Most of those accepted would be called within the next week to make appointments for the medical exam. (The medical tests include screening for drugs.) After the physical, people would be called for a one-day "stamina, coordination, dexterity" exam where they would work with tools and materials used at Mazda. Someone asked at what point one was hired. The assessor answered that she did not know of anyone called for the stamina exam who was not hired, but it was possible.

Stage 5: Still Waiting

I do not receive a call, but neither do I get a rejection letter. Maybe there is still hope.

From talking to other applicants, I learn that in this final phase of the screening a mock car is set up. The applicant is given a job assignment with several specific steps: assemble the dome light, get into the car, install it, get out of the car, get back in, remove it, and disassemble it. The work varied. Sometimes it was carpet installation. Some workers recall they did this for an hour, others for four.

A Giant Game

The Mazda screening process is a giant game. An applicant has to invest up to five trips and sixteen hours of time to be considered for a job. The applicant is going to say and do what he or she thinks the company wants. The company knows this. The applicant knows the company knows this. Are the interviewers and assessors, themselves newly hired unit leaders, well enough trained in assessment and interviewing to judge who would be a good worker from this game? In mid-1987 Mazda switched to professional interviewers, but most of these had no experience on the shop floor.

From the tests and from comments made by company officials, it seems that the qualities the company was looking for were communication skills and the likelihood of developing company loyalty. The tests seemed to have a cultural bias in favor of middle-class verbal skills. Factory experience—surviving in a plant for five to twenty years—counted for little and may even have been considered a negative factor, implying habits that would have to be unlearned.

In any event, the results of the screening are interesting. The number of Black workers is 10 to 12 percent, low considering the number of unemployed Black auto workers in the Detroit area. Some Blacks—both unsuccessful applicants and current Mazda workers—believe that the interviewers, almost all white, reflected racial bias in their judgments. Some point out that a lot of workers who "proved themselves" through years of ex-

perience at Ford were denied jobs at Mazda. Less than 25 percent of Mazda workers have previous experience working for Big Three companies.[15] Many have no factory experience. Almost half the employees are women.

Orientation: The Will to Participate

Like everything else at Mazda, the three-week "common" orientation which all new employees attend is executed with precision scheduling. The printed program is adhered to closely during the eight and one-half hour day. Actually the day is slightly longer; a ten minute "exercise/team meeting" period is scheduled before the program officially begins.

The orientation includes welcoming remarks and procedural and administrative details. Paperwork is filled out, benefit programs explained, uniforms fitted, and safety shoes ordered. One session deals with compensation, and a UAW representative explains the relationship of the company to the union. Several sessions teach proper lifting techniques and health and safety. To ease communication and relations with the large population of Japanese "dispatchees," one session is devoted to Japanese culture.

Some sessions elaborate on the Mazda philosophy. Over and over they hammer away at the idea: Where you worked before it may have been all right just to come to work and do what you are told. That is not enough at Mazda. Here part of your job is to contribute ideas to improve productivity and quality.

For example, the conclusion of the presentation

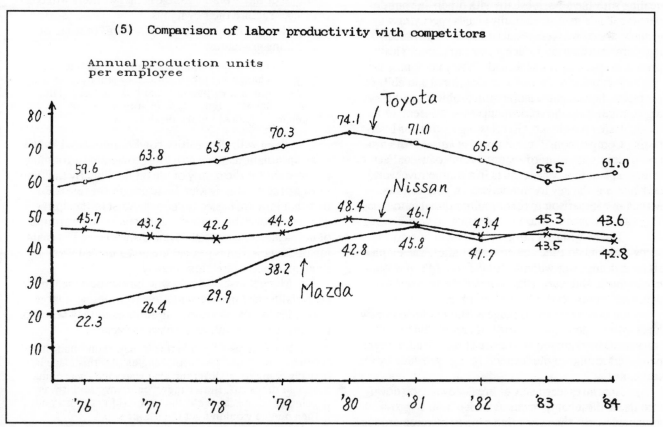

Productivity competition is stressed in Mazda Kaizen Simulation Training Manual.

on how the MMUC Manufacturing System works contains a warning: Mazda "cannot accept people who have the following characteristics." The manual lists five. The first four are the standard offenses for which one can be fired in most plants— absenteeism, fighting or property destruction, use of alcohol or drugs, disregard of company regulations and safety rules. The fifth is the clincher: "Those who don't have the will to participate in work accomplishments or *kaizen* activities."[16]

Whatever your specific job assignment, everyone is an inspector for every operation. If "a defective component is discovered coming from the previous process, the team member should press the button..."

One important message of the training program is that at Mazda the teams make important decisions. Teams design the production process and specific jobs. Partly this message is explicit and partly it is implicit in the kinds of examples and situations used in training.

Three days are spent on "interpersonal" training. Most of the examples in the manual involve the type of situation and degree of decision-making power typically reserved for management. For example:

Your department just went over the top in the United Way campaign... Jean volunteered to help you out without being assigned and did a lot of work after hours. [How do you provide recognition?]
This morning you see next month's budget and your boss has not given you your own maintenance budget. [How do you approach your boss?][17]

While some of the problems specifically mention dealing with the boss, most are with others in your department. The manual carefully avoids specifying whether these are co-workers or subordinates. The Mazda new hires work on skills such as how to communicate problems specifically and directly, how to give positive reinforcement, how to deal with emotional and ability problems, how to solve motivation problems, and how to "communicate the consequences for failure."

Using the slogan, "Everlasting Efforts for Everlasting Competition,"[18] the concept of *kaizen*—the process of continuous improvement—is introduced. Facilitators explain that Mazda exists in a competitive world and *kaizen* is the key to productivity. A graph shows Mazda in comparison to other multinational auto firms. Toyota is the leader. Mazda must catch up with Toyota.

The new Mazda workers are taught how to use a stopwatch and do time and motion studies. The emphasis is on doing away with the "Evil Three M's of waste— *muda, mura,* and *muri*" (translated as waste, overburden, and unevenness). (See Chapter 9.)

In order to learn to judge a "standard pace," new hires watch video tapes of work situations and rate the workers as working too fast or too slow. Then they compare their ratings to the "expert" ratings provided by the company.

New hires learn how to break down a job down into its smallest components, describe it on a "programmed work" sheet, and find ways to increase produc-

tivity. Then the jobs of the team are "balanced," and the search to remove idle time begins again. Programmed work is described in Chapter 9.

For several days the team members practice their new understanding of programmed work by assembling flashlights. They are given the parts and a detailed explanation of the specifications for the final product. For example, the flashlight is packaged in a pouch with the rear end in first and wrapped twice with a rubber band. They practice breaking down the assembly operation to its smallest steps and *kaizen* the operation over and over. Using cardboard and tape they devise and build fixtures to increase productivity. Video cameras record their assembly operations so the new hires can study the tapes to find wasted motions.

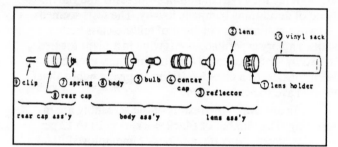

Flashlight diagram from the Mazda training manual.

Reality Hits

The training and manuals make the point that the unit leader is "charged with making the final decision."[19] Yet the overall message is that workers will control and structure their own jobs.

One worker describes the illusions of some of the training graduates:

They think they will be meeting all the time and they can change the job or shift to another job or just stop the line if they find out that it is too hard. They don't understand that this is an auto plant and the company is going to make production.

Even with the positive conditions created by the start-up situation, many new hires come out of training unprepared for the reality of life on the line. By the time most workers actually join the teams on the lines, they find that jobs are basically defined. Most of the "programmed work" has been carefully specified by groups of unit leaders, team leaders and dispatchees. The main job of the new hire is to read the programmed work sheet and follow directions exactly.

Many Mazda workers who have experience in auto plants take these orientation activities with large quantities of salt. Yet during training even they begin to look forward to a different work experience:

It would have been better if they hadn't had that orientation. They kept promising us that this place is really going to be different, that everybody was equal and all that stuff. Better they would have said it was going to be the same old shit as at GM and Ford and then people wouldn't get their hopes up.

In March 1988, the UAW and Mazda reached agreement on their first contract, which was ratified 1,492-172. The contract provided for wage parity with Ford by 1991 and a $750 signing bonus. It also included a system of "union coordinators," a "problem resolution" procedure, and job security language similar to NUMMI's. While skilled trades will remain a single classification for purposes of seniority, it will be divided into three Section Occupational Groups—electrical, tool and die, and mechnical.

Notes

1. Louise Kertesz, "Mazda Plant Nears Job One," *Automotive News*, June 29, 1987.

2. Paul Lienert, "Governor's Role Held Key to Mazda," *Detroit Free Press*, December 9, 1984.

3. For example, see the remarks of UAW Vice-President Odessa Komer, "The Transplants—Threat or Opportunity for U.S. Workers and Suppliers?" in *The UMTRI Research Review*, University of Michigan Transportation Research Institute, September-December, 1986.

4. *Detroit Free Press*, December 17, 1987.

5. "A New Car with a UAW Label," *Solidarity*, October 1986.

6. *Manufacturing Week*, October 25, 1987.

7. *Detroit Free Press*, June 1, 1987.

8. *MMUC Newsletter*, May 22, 1987.

9. "Employee Expectations," MMUC, February 25, 1987.

10. David N. Campbell, R. L. Fleming, and Richard C. Grote, "Discipline Without Punishment—At Last," *Harvard Business Review*, July-August, 1985.

11. The procedure allows for union representation at all levels. As described here, it is the procedure followed before the formal recognition of the UAW in September 1987 and before the adoption of a local contract in March 1988.

12. Kertesz, June 29, 1987.

13. *Detroit News*, October 16, 1987.

14. Published by Science Research Associates, a division of IBM.

15. *Detroit Free Press*, December 17, 1987.

16. *MMUC Production System: Concept and Outline*, Mazda Motor Manufacturing (USA) Corporation, 1986.

17. *Interact Interpersonal Problem Solving*, Interact Performance Systems Inc., 1987.

18. *Kaizen Simulation Manual*, Production Engineering Department, Mazda Motor Manufacturing (USA) Corp., p.10.

19. *MMUC Production System: Concept and Outline*, Mazda Motor Manufacturing (USA) Corp., 1986, p.34.

18. Wentzville: Strangest Job Training Ever

By Peter Downs

The night I heard the news that GM was starting up a second shift at its Wentzville, Missouri assembly plant, I had just been laid off from my job as a machine set-up person at a cabinet factory. The next morning, February 1, 1985, I applied for a job. The state employment office was packed. People huddled in cars parked two deep in the street or crouched on the sidewalk, pressing against the side of the building to escape the biting wind as they filled out applications. About 100,000 people applied for 2,400 jobs.

When the Wentzville plant was opened a year earlier, General Motors hailed the facility as the most advanced in the corporation. The factory had more robots than any other GM assembly plant, and it was organized into Japanese-style work teams. The company hoped that the teams would lead to a new era of labor-management cooperation in which shop floor conflict would be a thing of the past. Slightly more than three years later, however, the local union had a backlog of 11,000 unsettled grievances, more than two for every worker. Corporate consultants warned that GM would close the plant if the workers' attitudes didn't "improve."

For 25 days after submitting my application, I blindly stumbled through the five-step hiring process. The first step was applying to the state of Missouri, where state personnel weeded out those without a high school diploma and two years of factory experience or college. The second step was a four-and-a-half hour battery of manual dexterity and intelligence tests. Passing this step entitled you to apply directly to GM, which was followed by an interview. Step four was an essay test. I watched a 25 minute videotape of people performing their tasks at GM and answered six questions. "You have just seen a film about GM, how do you feel? Do you prefer to do one job continuously or move around

---

Peter Downs is the recording secretary of UAW Local 2250 in Wentzville, Missouri.

- *GM Wentzville Assembly*
- *Location: Wentzville, Missouri*
- *Employment: 2,540 production, 280 skilled*
- *Product: Buick Park Avenue, Oldsmobile 88, Olds 98*
- *Production began: December 1983*
- *Team Concept began: December 1983*
- *UAW Local 2250*
  Address: 1395 E. Pearce, Wentzville, MO 63385
  Phone: 314 / 327-5796

to different operations? Do you prefer to work in a team or as an individual? Describe yourself, strong points and weak points. What makes you suitable for GM? What are your goals?" Step five was the physical.

When I finally heard the words "report to personnel next Monday" I still wasn't sure I was hired. I later realized that management at GM cultivates that uncertainty.

A management spokesman told those of us who made it through the testing and interview process that we were "the best and the brightest." I just felt lucky. At the cabinet factory, I was making $6.75 an hour, which was a better than average wage for factory work in Missouri, but, still, it was hard to support my family of five. The starting wage at GM was $11.18 an hour. Unimaginable wealth!

Dozens of people from the cabinet factory applied, but many gave up before completing the interview process. One guy told me: "I can't afford to miss five days of work and possibly lose this job only to be told I didn't get that one."

People who were hired screamed for joy and jumped in the air, like winners on a TV game show. Gerald Horton had lost his job after 19 years when the Carter Carburetor plant closed. Horton said he was so happy to get hired at GM "I would have done anything they asked, and for less money."

How to Build a Car

General Motors rented an elementary school for our training, and it was the strangest job training any of us had ever experienced. For six days, ten hours each, our time was divided between lectures and small group discussion. Four more days were spent listening to lectures at the plant. The union made a half-day presentation at a local restaurant.

On the first day, our facilitator, Dave Brandt, instructed us to pair off and prepare to introduce our partner. After the introductions, we counted off by fours to form discussion groups. Then, while we were still trying to figure out what such things had to do with building cars, Brandt began to tell us how bad it used to be to work in an auto factory.

The auto industry grew up on the Ford system, he explained, which "produced more cars, but was based on supervisors being dictatorial. They used intimidation, harassment, and favoritism. They treated workers as interchangeable parts of a machine, as if workers were lazy and stupid.

"But that system had two consequences, poor

quality and the rise of the union. That led to strikes and grievances. Unions chose their leaders on the same model as the supervisors, and both ignored the workers. The union disrupted production so the industry couldn't compete with the Japanese, the Swedes, and the Germans," Brandt said.

"The old methods didn't work, so management changed. It now believes that all people are deserving of respect and have ideas that can help people. It now believes that everyone should participate in decision-making. The union has to change too, and cooperate, if we're to defeat foreign competition.

"There are still some dinosaurs," Brandt added. "Some supervisors use the old ways, but they'll retire soon. And some workers try to sow distrust of the company. But if we can't get this new process to work, we'll lose to the Japanese and you'll be out of jobs."

Dinosaur Practices

Confrontational or "dinosaur" practices included grievances, strikes, and calling the committeeman. "Anybody defending traditional practices," Brandt said, "will not have a job." As if to give his argument more weight, Brandt explained that he used to be a committeeman at GM's Leeds plant in Kansas City, but he went over to management because he thought he could do more good for the workers there. He added that GM has nothing against the union, and that the training we were receiving was paid for jointly by union and management out of the Joint Skill Development and Training Fund established by the 1984 National Agreement.

After the lecture, we broke into "work groups." The stated function of these groups was to discuss the lecture with a facilitator present "as an observer." Dave Brandt was the observer for my group. On the first day he strongly implied that individuals who did not actively participate in the "team" would not have a job. Two of the group members took the cue and began discussing how teams, along with the new company philosophy of treating workers with dignity and respect, made the union unnecessary.

Before we got too carried away, we got a few examples of the company's idea of how to express their high regard for workers. Brandt told us that one guy in the class got fired because a facilitator overheard him say that the team concept was "bullshit." "We were instructed to watch out for negative comments and negative attitudes," Brandt explained.

The next morning the facilitators surprised us

with a lecture on the necessity of strict obedience "because you don't have jobs yet." It seems that the day before someone had fallen asleep during a lecture. He got fired. Another person missed the company bus that morning and drove his car to the school. He too lost his job for not obeying the rules. We quickly developed a buddy system to keep each other awake during the deadly boring lectures.

In contrast to the lectures, the discussion groups became a place where we could relax and joke while playing the games assigned by the facilitators. The facili-

tator began the group by having each member introduce him or herself. We were to include such information as birthplace, number of brothers and sisters, whether our siblings were older or younger. Then, starting with a different person, each of us was asked to talk about our first paying job and how we felt about it.

Sue Brand, a member of my group, recalls that she was apprehensive at first because she was the only woman in the group. The exercises relaxed her and helped her to feel a part of the group. Then, she remembers, "we just laughed and joked and had a good time."

The Games Workers Play

The games we played in the groups were designed in part to strengthen group identity and in part to illustrate the importance of worker-management cooperation. One game we played was "A Plane Crashes in the Desert." We were given a list of objects that we had with us after the crash. Individually, we rated the objects in order of importance. Then we got together in our group and rated them. The game was designed to show that by cooperating we could come up with answers that would give us a better chance of survival.

In another game, each group had to draw up arguments to defend a controversial political position, such as gun control. We were told that we would be debating other groups also defending gun control. When we got together, individuals in different groups began shouting and screaming at each other that "we" were right and "you" were wrong. The facilitators drew the moral that, like management and labor, the two groups wanted the same thing, but were fighting simply because they were different groups.

Another game was called "The Prisoner's Dilemma." The facilitator explained: "You are one of two people arrested following a bank robbery and immediately held in separate cells. The prosecutor goes to each of you and says exactly the same thing: 'We can't pin the robbery on you unless one of you cooperates and gives us a full confession. But if neither of you confesses we can get you both on the less serious charge of driving a stolen car. If you confess and the other does not, you will get off free for giving evidence and he will get 25 years. If both of you confess you will each get 20 year sentences. If neither of you confesses you will both get two years for the stolen car charge."

You have to assume that the prosecutor has described the situation honestly and accurately and that each prisoner will have to decide alone—they cannot communicate with each other.

THE CASE OF THE UGLY ORANGE

One of the games played in the Wentzville team training was "The Case of the Ugly Orange." It involved two discussion groups.

One group was told that there was a deadly new flu epidemic in the United States and 100,000 children would die unless a vaccine were found. The group was to play the role of university medical researchers who had just developed such a vaccine using the juice of the ugly orange. The only available crop of ugly oranges, however, was controlled by a Brazilian, a Mr. Lopez. The group had $100,000 with which to buy the whole crop of 10,000 oranges, which would produce just enough vaccine. Unfortunately, a group from a chemical warfare laboratory in Denver also wanted to buy the oranges. Mr. Lopez insisted on meeting representatives from both groups at the same time. He would only meet with them once.

The other discussion group was told that a toxic nerve gas had leaked from a weapons depot and that 10,000 people would die unless they received the antidote. This group's role was to be a group of researchers from a chemical warfare laboratory who had developed an antidote to the nerve gas from the peels of the ugly orange. The rest of the information given was the same as for the first group.

At the meeting, Mr. Lopez told the representatives of the two groups that he was not willing to sell his crop for as little as $100,000.

The problem was to figure out how to get a purchase agreement for the ugly oranges.

To complete the exercise successfully, each group had to listen to the other and figure out that each wanted different parts of the orange. That would lead them to pool their money to buy the crop of ugly oranges. Each group could then take what it wanted and they would be able to save the United States from nerve gas and influenza.

In practice, our groups fell into the expected traps. The meeting with "Lopez," played by a facilitator, was carried out by a representative from each group, with everyone else watching. One of the representatives refused to shut up. He kept increasing his bid in a futile effort to get Lopez to sell. First he offered $100,000, then $150,000, then $200,000. When he offered $250,000 and a night in New York's finest hotel with two prostitutes, the facilitators called a halt to the game.

The facilitators explained that management and workers were like the two groups in the exercise. They fought each other because they didn't communicate enough to realize that they were not competing with each other for the same thing. They actually wanted different things, different parts of the income from selling cars. Workers, they said, want good wages, and management wants decent profits, which are different parts of the company's revenues. If workers and management could learn to cooperate, both of them would win. If they continued to fight, both would lose.

If you are only interested in doing what's best for yourself, your best alternative is to confess because, regardless of what the other prisoner does, you will get a lighter sentence (zero years instead of two if the other prisoner doesn't confess, 20 years instead of 25 if he does). Our facilitators stressed that the prisoner comes out ahead by being cooperative and honest, by "trusting the process." If the other prisoner thinks the same way, however, you both will get 20 years instead of two. So, if the prisoners had been able to communicate and make a deal with each other, they both would have gotten off much easier.

Cures All Ills

Ken Wigger, who was a team coordinator (TC) for 14 months, recalled that what he liked about the training was "the idea that there would be a mutual effort of people and management towards the success of the operation. They told us up front that they would be using our brains and not just our brawn because the people on the jobs can see problems as they arise. They told us that what we said would mean something." Ken worked in industry for 32 years before starting at GM. He was in the Oil, Chemical and Atomic Workers and the United Steelworkers, and spent 14 years in management. "I was so very impressed by what they told us in school," he says, "that I actually shed tears. I was convinced that the team concept was the answer to our national economic and industrial ills, because the ideas and efforts of each individual worker would be sought out and appreciated, and this would strengthen our economy and preserve our jobs."

Brandt told us that there would be problems, but he exhorted us to "trust the process" instead of calling the union. In other words, we were supposed to put our trust in the good feeling generated by the group. That good feeling does fill a need. There are more than enough things at work, and in everyday life, to make us feel bad. We liked the team concept because it promised to make us feel better about ourselves and our work. Many teams at Wentzville even celebrate their members' birthdays and spend some holidays together.

For many of us, however, the promise of the teams is unfilled. Tommy Poole, for example, says the teams have become "nothing but a way for management to show favoritism." Tommy, an easy-going guy originally from Arkansas, was a team coordinator for six months. He thinks "the teams would work all right if the foremen didn't interfere...but all our foreman wanted to do was use it to get his favorite people off the line."

A Rock and a Hard Place

In January 1985 Wentzville workers went on strike to get their first local agreement. Since opening, the plant had been operating under management-imposed rules, as the national contract provides that management be given a year to get things started. When the strike took place the team system was a big issue, but it was settled with an agreement that didn't mention teams or team coordinators. The union agreed to let management implement the team system on its own. As one committeeman told me, "We just decided to ignore them and pretend they weren't there." This led to many problems. New employees heard from management that they had to learn many jobs, do whatever the foreman said, could not take time off for any reason without advance permission from the foreman, and should not file grievances. The shop committee made no effort to teach new hires their rights, though some were helpful if called about a specific problem.

Team Coordinators in the Middle

The team coordinators felt caught in the middle. Coordinators did not have a job description. Supervisors could tell them to do anything, and frequently had them doing work traditionally performed by foremen. Workers, on the other hand, thought the team coordinator's main duties should be to provide bathroom and emergency breaks, and to keep the work stations stocked with the tools, gloves and other supplies necessary for people to do their jobs. At first the workers in a team elected one of their own to be team coordinator for six months, and they could recall the coordinator at any time.

The first team I was in went through three team coordinators in six months because we felt they were doing too much for the supervisor and not enough for us. That kind of turnover was common so management changed the rules: there could be no recalls without the approval of the department supervisor. That still didn't stop the conflict over the TC's duties, so in January 1987, management extended the TC's terms to one year.

Even that didn't isolate TCs from pressure from their workmates, so in April, management went a step further. It instructed TCs to keep track of the incidental costs (e.g. gloves and nondurable tools) and the product defects associated with each individual job in their team (management already kept track of defects through a computer system, but now TCs were to keep a cumulative record over time for the team). Then management issued a warning: the TCs would do as they were told or the supervisor could remove them and appoint someone else. Several TCs chose this time to resign, and management has yet to get TCs to record the data it wants.

Many TCs made an effort to represent the interests of their teams when dealing with the supervisor, but they complained that they got no support from the union when conflicts developed with management. Many committeemen just ignored the TCs' problems. One result was that TCs played an important role in the wholesale defeat of incumbent union officers in local elections in May 1987. In my area, many TCs supported a candidate who was widely regarded as pro-company. Before the elections, he inspected for mutilations; that is, he walked around and tried to find out how cars were getting scratched. He worked directly with the TCs on this, and reported to the foremen. Not all the TCs supported candidates who preached more cooperation with management. For example, I was elected recording secretary with a lot of support from TCs, on a platform of getting more information to the members and not giving in to management. The common thread running through the campaigns of the ultimate victors was the charge that the incumbents had failed to inform or involve the members in union business.

Team Spirit

Team coordinators were not the only ones with problems. Gerald Horton discovered that foremen can use the team system to punish someone they don't like. Part of the team concept is "pay-for-knowledge" or variable classification. Workers who choose to go into the variable classification at Wentzville must learn eight different jobs, after which they get a 19 cent raise. Traditionally, workers choose a job by seniority and stick to that job until they bid on another one or get bumped by a layoff.

Horton chose the variable classification. At first he was a TC, but he resigned because he got into arguments with his foreman over favoritism and what he saw as the foreman's failure to live up to the team concept. Horton became a hood fitter, but he was still on the foreman's bad side. The foreman pulled him off hood fitting, and put him on a fender job, where he had to bend over and reach up under the fender and shoot some screws. Horton stands about 6'2" and weighs 268 pounds, and the new job was bad on his back. When he filed a grievance against the move, he discovered that since he was in the variable classification, his foreman could ignore seniority and place him on any job for any length of time. Horton says he still thinks the team concept is a good idea "if only management would abide by it."

Variable classification was a key issue when the union struck in 1985. In the first year of the plant's operation, when there was no local agreement, management set up a pay-for-knowledge program in which 16 jobs had to be learned to obtain the variable classification and the top rate of an extra 44 cents. In the summer of 1984, the local held a referendum on pay-for-knowledge, which the membership rejected by more than 80 percent. When the shop committee came back with a tentative agreement after a two-week strike, they claimed the new agreement went a long way towards eliminating the program and the members voted it up.

Under its new guise, workers only had to learn eight jobs to get the variable classification, and a top rate of 19 cents. More workers decided to enter the program since most of those classified as variable still got to stay on the same job anyway. Management refused to let people move the other way, however, unless their supervisor found they couldn't perform the jobs they claimed to know. And in that case, management claimed the worker could be required to pay back all the pay-for-knowledge money received. Management told those of

us who hired in new in 1985 that we had to go variable. We didn't know there had ever been a choice.

Looking Into It

The most common complaint about the team system at Wentzville is that management is not really interested in quality. Management lectures us several times a week about the importance of doing a quality job, but when problems are brought to their attention, usually nothing gets done.

I had a job installing the left shoulder harness. Two molded plastic pieces were supposed to fit together, but frequently did not. I brought it to the attention of the foreman, the department shift supervisor, and the engineers, and they always said they'd "look into it." They didn't look into it until the problem became so bad that I had to ship the jobs without securing the harness. First, the foreman tried putting other people on the job, but they couldn't do it either, so an engineer "looked into it" and agreed there was a problem, and I was put back on the job. The only thing that changed is that nothing more was done to me.

Millie Donnelly, who was a TC for eight months, reported that when she brought up quality problems with the foreman, he would tell her to build it anyway. Donnelly said: "They don't want to accept our ideas. They always say they wanted our input, but I was TC through two line changes and what we said went in one ear and out the other. They did whatever they wanted. This last line change, in January, they didn't even ask for our suggestions." Even when they asked her to do something, Donnelly said, such as developing a process document (a check-off list on which workers can mark defects in the car as it goes down the line), they ignored what she did without offering her an explanation.

Ken Wigger agreed that management is "frustrating on the team concept. They didn't ask for our input on the line change. They arranged jobs however they wanted. We made several good suggestions that they rejected without even sending them to the engineers." Before the line speed change in January, Wigger went into the plant three times on his own time to get advisors to listen to the team's suggestions, but to no avail. That, he said, "was the culmination of my frustration." Now, he believes that management does not have a good plan for the teams. "They're just going to use them against the union."

Other events also have been common enough to undermine employees' belief that management wanted to cooperate. For example, supervisors have refused to allow employees to use contractual days off, so they will have enough people "just in case" absenteeism is high. Supervisors award overtime to a few favorite people, instead of equalizing it throughout the team as required by Paragraph 71 of the national contract. Plant management has also refused to honor transfer requests, refused to fill open jobs, and supervisors exhibit favoritism in enforcing company rules. These problems account for a large portion of the unsettled grievances.

Such problems do not mean that the teams have failed completely from management's point of view. The team is but one part of the company strategy to reintroduce competitition among the workers. That strategy is working. When we hired in, we were told we were competing against the Japanese. By the second year, we were competing against Ford. Now our competition is other GM plants. Local unions bid against each other for work. The company also encourages teams and individuals to compete for doing the most and best work. Workers are blaming each other for not being able to take days off or for management's threats to close the plant. I've seen workers ask supervisors to discharge fellow employees who became sick or injured because "if they can't do the work they shouldn't work here. They're going to cost us our jobs."

X, Y and Z

The competitive strategy works because management is able to place workers in a "prisoner's dilemma" and control the information they receive. Management isolates workers from each other so that they think they have to cooperate on management's terms to keep their jobs. The fear of informers, for example, which was nurtured during our training, isolates individuals from each other. When I changed teams in January 1986, I moved into a team in which the foreman awarded overtime to just four people instead of equalizing it. As I talked to people in the team about putting a stop to that practice, I'd hear from X, "I'm in favor of what you say, but no one else will back you up. Don't tell Y, she'll tell the foreman." Y would say, "I agree with you, but don't tell Z, he'll tell the foreman." Z would also agree with me, but add, "You can't get these people to do anything, and X will tell the boss first anyway."

Some of the team members had filed a grievance on the problem a year earlier, but nothing had changed. I suggested we call the department shift supervisor into our team meeting to discuss the problem. After getting an agreement from most of the rest of the team, I did so. Then I looked up our committeeman and told him what we were doing.

When the time for team meetings arrived, our committeeman showed up. At least nine of the 18 team members stood up and loudly complained about the unfair distribution of overtime. At the end of the meeting, the shift supervisor came. Within 20 minutes, we had an agreement that the four people who had worked the most overtime would not get any more until overtime was equalized in the team. Almost everyone in the team was surprised that we had stood together. They were encouraged by that and, as individuals, they began to challenge the foreman on other things they thought were wrong and to insist on their individual rights.

19. Buick 81: Granddaddy Team Plant

Factory 81, part of the giant Buick complex in Flint, Michigan, was one of General Motors' first tries at the team concept. It was an experiment with a workforce which had a long and militant union tradition.

The Buick complex includes Hydra-Matic and Delco parts plants and the Buick City assembly plant, which builds LeSabres. It employs 11,000. Besides Factory 81, teams now exist in parts of three other manufacturing plants in the complex and in Buick City.

In 1975 the Buick complex was in trouble. Employment had fallen from a peak of 27,000 workers to 9,000 in the 1975 recession. The plant had a reputation for bad labor relations and there were threats of losing more work.

Following an annual General Motors Executive Quality of Work Life Conference, the general manager approached Local 599 and proposed a QWL program to save the plant. The union agreed.

Factory 81's "work unit" (team) system was a direct outgrowth of the UAW-GM Quality of Work Life (QWL) efforts in the 1970's. Although QWL had been negotiated in the 1973 contract, there were few serious efforts to use it in unionized plants until the 1980's.

Relations between the union leadership and the company changed dramatically. When the foundry in Plant 81 was scheduled to be phased out, management assured the union that they would make every attempt to find new business to replace the jobs.

When GM decided to modify the foundry to build torque convertors, the QWL structure was used to help design the work unit system. When the plant opened in 1981 it was considered way ahead of its time. While most GM plants were just beginning QWL activities, Factory 81's work units, pay-for-knowledge, and absence of time clocks were all long term goals of QWL. The plant was hailed in management and academic circles as a success story embodying a new way to work. This new way was supposed to satisfy the needs of both the company and the workers.

Representatives of UAW Local 599 and local

- *GM Factory 81*
- *Location: Flint, Michigan*
- *Employment: 2,200 hourly (November 1987)*
- *Product: Torque converters for Hydra-Matic Division*
- *Production began: 1981*
- *Team Concept began: 1981*
- *Part of UAW Local 599*
  Address: 812 Leith Street, Flint, MI 48505
  Phone: 313 / 238-1616

management were invited to many conferences to spread the word of the new vision of cooperation. At the Second U.S.-Japan Automotive Industry Conference, for example, held in March 1982 at the University of Michigan, Local 599 President Al Christner said, "My perspective is to make the workplace the kind of place where people *want* to come to work....It's a pleasure to deal with a management which is people-oriented."

At the 1981 GM Executive QWL Conference, Bob Roth, QWL Coordinator for the local, said:

> I must give credit to Buick management. Their support of the programs has made this a most cooperative movement, and together we cannot help but succeed. The overall response from both hourly and salaried people at Buick is, "It's about time. Why didn't we do this five or ten years ago?"
>
> None of these enthusiastic people are saying, "What's in it for us?" We don't think of what's in it for the union or for each individual, or for Buick or GM—we think of it as all one united group of management and workers accepting the challenge.

For 13 years Bob Roth was a committeeman in the plant which was later dubbed Factory 81. In 1980 he was appointed Local 599's full-time Quality of Work Life coordinator for the whole complex. As such he played a big role in the design and initiation of Factory 81. He became one of the UAW's and GM's well-known public advocates for QWL. In 1984 he returned to being committeeman in Factory 81, and in May 1987 was elected to the full-time job of local education director.

Lessons from Granddaddy

As one of the granddaddy team concept plants, Factory 81 contains lessons for others now dealing with the team concept. We asked Roth about the evolution of this early team experiment.

Question: How did the "work unit" system start?

Bob Roth: Factory 81 had been a foundry, but it closed. They got some new business, a torque converter, and management and the union wanted to do something different and unique. They jointly selected a design team and took us offsite for a week for training.

Q: What kind of training?

BR: Group development training, problem solving. They used "STS" [sociotechnical systems] and the bullseye concept—ways to work out your goals.

What we said was: take the roof off the building. Pretend it's in the middle of a cornfield. There'd be no constraints. The design team went to different plants in the South. I went with them and I saw plants that looked like a McDonald's—they were beautiful.

When the plant opened we made a two-day presentation to workers and management. We told them it would be different. The people who got the first chance were the ones who were laid off from the foundry. They'd been out six or eight months, and they all went through the two-day seminars. Then they signed whether they wanted to work there or not. Ninety-six percent wanted to, but they didn't have to—only if they liked what they were hearing.

Q: What were they hearing?

BR: Bullshit. The company raised expectations so high. They told them there would be no shop rules and no time clocks. We were the first factory to do that. It was supposed to be the honor system—"we trust you."

Management said they would be very highly motivated toward education. There would be full-time training for hourly and salaried to teach problem solving—how to brainstorm. It was definitely valuable for the people, including on the outside. They got a chance to learn listening skills—how to listen to their wives, their kids. If they wanted to, they could translate it to their everyday life.

Management said there wouldn't be any production standards set, it was left to the group. "We'll tell you at the beginning of the week what the schedule is and you decide how to meet it." The concept philosophically was great. Sometimes the people could meet the schedule in four and a half days and then clean up.

A Feeling of Freedom

Q: How was production organized in Factory 81?

BR: We had about eight "product areas"—like assembly, pumps, covers. This was equivalent to what would be under a general foreman in a traditional factory. Each area was responsible for a specific part of the process and it could be a couple hundred people. We started out with 100 people and slowly built up. Currently we've got 2,200 on three shifts.

Q: Did the people get a say in designing their jobs at all?

BR: The design team did. But when the people started to work the jobs were already set up. They were not changeable.

Q: Did the people like the new system?

BR: Yes. They had some autonomy to make decisions, a feeling of freedom. They could take their break when they wanted to, the group would decide when. They could work through lunch if they wanted to and leave early, take their break at the end. Now, the new superintendent says, "The people will be on the machines." They want you to take your 23-minute break before lunch, your 20-minute lunch, and your 23 minutes after lunch. And stay to the end.

Q: Could the work units initially make decisions about things other than their breaks?

BR: They were led to believe they could. If it wouldn't affect other shifts, they were supposed to be able to change their work hours. But it didn't work be-cause of the schedule—one work unit would be affected by the others.

Q: What were the work units responsible for?

BR: Each one had a coordinator, elected. The coordinator and the advisor [foreman] both went to a meeting every day. Then the work unit would have one or two meetings a week. They'd tell us, "The customers need 5,000 this week," and the work unit had to meet that schedule. The meetings would go over "quality, cost and schedule." Because the work units were responsible for quality too. It worked great for about three years.

Q: How big was each work unit?

BR: Ten to fourteen.

"A" Is Above Average

Q: Did the plant have a pay-for-knowledge system?

BR: There was just one classification—everyone was called a "quality operator." This was an advantage because whenever there was a reduction you'd have plant-wide seniority and there wasn't much bumping around.

There were seven pay levels depending on the number of jobs you knew, with about a dime difference between each level. The sixth pay level right now is at $13.30 [base rate, July 1987]; that's if you know all the jobs in two work units. Then the coordinator is the seventh level, he gets $13.40. Supposedly, you hire in at the lowest rate, you learn a couple more jobs, you go up to the next level. But actually anybody who transfers from another plant in the complex comes in at a three or a four.

Throughout the complex they have what they call A, B and C level. "A" is above average. Metal finishers would be an example. In a traditional plant you've got about 20 to 25 percent of the people at A level. $13.30 is like an A level in a traditional plant, but in Factory 81 about 70 percent of the people are at that rate. So people liked the pay-for-knowledge. It was an opportunity for advancement in the pocketbook.

Q: Did having so many pay levels create any problems among the people?

BR: Not really, because the group had to say whether you were qualified to move up. If you're new it's up to the coordinator and the advisor to move you from job to job to get trained. You work with another operator to learn a new job. But lots of times you don't get the chance to train on more jobs because of high absenteeism or because the foreman or advisor doesn't like you. So the committeeman will get you a raise every few months anyway.

Q: What about rotation?

BR: There was a rotation system set up in the beginning. The group decided how often to rotate, usually weekly or biweekly. People wanted to learn other jobs at first, but once you made top rate, you wanted to stay put: "This is my job."

Q: How long is the coordinator elected for?

BR: Whenever the group wants to change. Some have been in since it started, some only last a month.

Q: What kind of person runs for coordinator?

BR: Some suck-asses. Mostly it's popularity. Someone who knows the jobs.

Q: Does the coordinator work on a regular job?

BR: Each shift is different. On my shift he worked and got replacements when he went to meetings. On first shift some work and some don't. It's left up to the work unit.

Q: How are jobs assigned?

BR: When it started in 1981, the work unit got together and decided who would do what job, who would get trained on what job, promotions. Since then, we are almost back to a traditional way of operating. On 99.99 percent of the jobs, it's "I got the seniority, that's my job." The team doesn't have anything to say about it.

When it first started, it wasn't a problem to transfer. You'd just let your advisor know you wanted it. But because management people are so traditional, they put us in the position that we have to get everything in writing. And we do enforce it. They fill jobs in line with seniority by application. You can transfer within the work unit, from one work unit to another within a product area, or to another product area.

Q: What about the "creature comforts"?

BR: They have a weight room because the people themselves got pissed off and built it. Before they could

have radios and TVs, but they took them out.

The plant is nice on the outside. Inside, compared to the foundry, it's better. It's relatively clean, it has a nice air-conditioned cafeteria, the work unit rooms are air-conditioned. We used to have a library but it was cancelled because the books got stolen. We wanted a full-time hourly person in charge of the library and the weight room and all the non-work activities, but management said no.

There still aren't any time clocks, but they want you to wave to the advisor to prove you're there.

Q: Is there any peer pressure about absenteeism?

BR: It was designed that way. They wouldn't replace the absent people and then still try to get out the parts. People who ran other machines had to make it up.

At first it didn't bother them because they were never messed with. They could work straight through and get done early, go to the weight room or the library. But since then management has been saying they have to work whistle to whistle. So now their attitude is, "If John Doe is absent you'd better have someone to cover him, because I'm not doing it."

Q: How has the plant changed?

BR: When 81 first opened, six or seven out of ten managers really tried to work well with the people. But then foremen began to be forced into 81, and they were more traditional.

Plus, when people from other plants in the local

bumped into 81 by seniority, they hadn't been through the training.

Management at the top kept changing plant superintendents—they moved the good ones. We got a so-so one, then the next one was terrible. The autonomy has almost completely gone. The whole concept is gone, other than everyone being one classification and the chance to get top pay.

The work units still exist. They still have their weekly meetings, but the training has gone downhill. It was supposed to be ongoing, but they only have one full-time trainer for the whole factory, and he can't service the whole plant. The groups don't make decisions like they used to. The advisor has the last say.

They raised expectations so high about the autonomy, the decision-making process which the people were supposed to have. And then management took it back. The groups used to talk about who was going to work on what specific jobs, scheduling for the day, when they would take their breaks, what time they would go to lunch. Management just said, "Hey, this isn't working, we're not getting the schedule." So the union said, "The hell with you if you're going to be that way…" That's when we started with the written applications for transferring and all that.

Q: Why did management cause the relationship to deteriorate?

BR: As the plant got bigger, there was more pressure on the plant managers to produce. People were supposed to count; now it's just "schedule, cost, quality." It used to be that when you were free you could go to the weight room or the oasis or whatever. Pretty soon management said, "We can't afford to have you off the job for this length of time." Now it's just numbers, numbers, numbers. Quality is important, but it doesn't stand in the way of the numbers. They keep upping the schedule. It was 15,800, then 16,000, 16,200. Now it's 16,400 a day.

Q: How do the people who work there feel about it?

BR: The ones who were there from the beginning had high expectations. They were very distraught about seeing management's traditional foremen come in— "I'm going to tell you how it's done—it's my ass that's hanging out there." This person, his enthusiasm is gone.

Q: Were there any open signs of discontent with the system?

BR: Committeeman calls went up. And the attitude change. In the work unit meetings at first, the people worked well together. Now they're bitch sessions. There's a lack of training. New people are supposed to get a week of training, but they don't because of the needs of production.

Q: What was management's motivation in starting Factory 81?

BR: Profit. They were hoping to improve productivity, up time on the machines—and "quality, cost and schedule." So they seized on QWL.

Q: Have they succeeded from their point of view?

BR: Yes. Not 100 percent, but they haven't lost any money.

Q: How about the people?

BR: Overall, it's been beneficial to the people because of the pay structure. But the freedom, the autonomy—that's gone by the wayside.

Bottom Line: It's Their Plant

Q: How did you come to be appointed QWL coordinator?

BR: When the president appointed me full-time QWL I didn't even know what it was. I learned fast. One of my prime responsibilities was to act as a consultant from the union side, an OD person [organizational development].

Q: I understand you've been fired five times. You had a history of being adversarial with management. What did you think of QWL when you were first put in charge of the program?

BR: I understand why [UAW Vice-president Irving] Bluestone put it in the contract. Philosophically I believe in the concept. Seventy to eighty percent of the rank and file would try to work with management to make things better for everybody if they could see benefits to themselves. But in management, it's reversed. Twenty percent of management believes there should be a change, and 80 percent are assholes.

But management does forward planning. That's where the union falls short. We just look ahead three years, contract to contract.

The bottom line of QWL is this: anything joint should be 50-50. But in reality it's 51-49. When it's a question of "quality, cost, schedule," *they'll* make the bottom line decision. It's their plant. That's not jointness.

I'll give you an example. When I was on QWL, GM had the Organizational Development Department in the GM Building. They had approximately 20 staff people. The union had one guy. Management worked well with me for the four years I was on QWL (although it was still 51-49). I was important, I was somebody. But after I was out, they wouldn't even talk to me. I felt like I was used.

Q: Did you have a transformation, like you sometimes hear about, when you started in QWL?

BR: Do you mean was I brainwashed? As a committeeman you're in your own little factory. You're just like the rank and file, you come in and you go home. The four years I was on QWL gave me an opportunity to see firsthand the broad picture of the auto industry and the problems we have. I'm not so negative against change. I got a broader perspective of the concerns the UAW's faced with. I didn't know it was as bad as it is.

As far as Factory 81, though, it isn't any different from a traditional plant. The money is about the only thing good about it.

CHOOSING SIDES: UNIONS AND THE TEAM CONCEPT
Labor Notes, 7435 Michigan Avenue, Detroit, MI 48210 313/842-6262

20. Poletown: High Tech Headache

General Motors' Detroit/Hamtramck plant was born in controversy. An entire neighborhood—Poletown—was razed to build the new plant, including 1,200 houses, 144 businesses, 16 churches, two schools and one hospital.[1] Before construction could begin, elderly Polish protestors had to be dragged from their neighborhood Catholic church, arrested and carted to jail. To this day the plant is called "Poletown" by everyone except management.

The justification for such a drastic move was to create employment for a job-poor city. Poletown replaced two existing 60-year-old assembly plants employing 9,000 workers on Detroit's west side with a state-of-the-art facility employing 5,500 on the east side. The six hundred million-dollar plant was to be so technologically advanced that workers there would have more job security than in the older plants.

As it turned out, Poletown's high technology has been a medium-grade nightmare for GM. In management circles Poletown has become a symbol of the wrong way to use technology—too much and too fast. The *Wall Street Journal* called the plant a "headache" and said that the experience at Poletown helped convince GM to slow down introduction of new technology:

> So far, the Hamtramck plant, instead of a showcase, looks more like a basket case. Though the plant has been open seven months, the automated guided vehicles [AGV's] are sitting idle while technicians try to debug the software that controls their movements. In the ultra-modern paint shop, robots at times have spray-painted each other instead of the cars. Some cars have been painted so badly that GM had to ship them to a 57-year-old plant to be repainted.[2]

In September 1987 the bugs were still there: a trade magazine headlined what it called "GM's AGV Debacle."[3]

But technology was not management's only failure. Because GM tried to save money by having many nameplates across different divisions share the same basic styling, its luxury cars were no longer distinctive. "It doesn't look like a Cadillac anymore, so why would anyone spend money on it?" said one union official. Because of poor sales, the second shift was laid off in February 1987, reducing Poletown's workforce to 3,400 workers and 260 robots.

Poletown's team concept has not fared any better than its new technology or its sales. The forms exist—team coordinators, team meetings—but the content is lacking. Workers say the biggest differences between Poletown and the traditional plants they transferred from are 1) there are fewer classifications, more job overloading, and consequently fewer good jobs, and 2) the union accepts management's actions as "the way we do things over here."

If we wanted to compare different team concept plants to each other to measure how fully they have implemented the team concept, several different scales could be used. For now, let's look only at a scale that would indicate how firmly the team system is ingrained in the culture of the plant. Let's consider such questions as: Does management consistently use the rhetoric of participation? Do the workers themselves feel they are involved in something different and use the team concept rhetoric? Do the teams have a life of their own? How much do workers and management share a common outlook on efficiency (workloads) and quality?

Measured on this scale, NUMMI would be at the high end of a continuum and Poletown at the other.

Ray Church, who was the first unit shop chairman at Poletown and is now a vice-president of UAW Local 22, emphasizes that management unilaterally introduced team concept in the new plant. When Church was appointed shop chairman and transferred there from the Fleetwood body plant in February 1984, team training was already in place. "They didn't ask us about team concept, or pay-for-knowledge, or combined classifications. We never as a local union signed team concept or pay-for-knowledge, we weren't given the option. In two years as chairman I never negotiated team concept."

Virtually all Poletown workers transferred from traditional Detroit-area plants, chiefly the Cadillac and Fleetwood sister plants which closed in December 1987. Church says that Poletown workers don't trust the team concept. "People have seen so many damn programs at GM. They believe it's all a plan to get more work out of you. It started even before QWL, but QWL was the main thing. They saw how QWL caused favoritism and split the membership at Fleetwood."

- *GM Poletown*
- *Location: Hamtramck, Michigan*
- *Employment: 3,400 on one shift*
- *Product: Cadillac Seville, Eldorado, Allante, Buick Riviera, Olds Toronado*
- *Production began: 1985*
- *Team Concept began: 1985*
- *A unit of UAW Local 22*
  Address: 4300 Michigan Ave., Detroit, MI 48210
  313 / 897-8850; Poletown Work Center 313 / 972-6459

Bill McGuire, a former Fleetwood worker, agrees: "If QWL was phase one, this is phase four or five over here." (Bill McGuire is a pseudonym. Some Poletown workers requested that their names not be used.) Craig Nothnagel, a former team coordinator, says: "They feel like they've been lied to." Ray Church: "They don't buy team concept overall. They don't trust it."

Team Functioning

Initially teams had 20-30 members, except in the separate Allante section of the plant, where cars costing $54,000 are produced. In the October 1987 local agreement it was agreed to reduce team size throughout the plant to the four to eight members that Allante had been using. Shop Chairman Ronnie Martin said that although the proposal for smaller teams came from management, the shop committee accepted it because they calculated it meant more team coordinators and would therefore increase plant population.

Team coordinators are paid 50 cents an hour more than the rate for team members, which is $14.49 for production workers and $16.41 for all skilled trades. All production workers are classified "technician." Unlike a true pay-for-knowledge system, where workers must demonstrate that they know a number of jobs in order to make the top rate, at Poletown the shop committee insisted on a flat wage for everyone. In team orientation, workers were told they had to know at least three jobs to earn the top rate. In practice, however, by 1987 workers had regular individual jobs from which they were seldom moved.

Ray Church says: "They do move people, but not on a wide-scale basis. Management doesn't need that much flexibility, they can't live with it. I believe pay-for-knowledge can be implemented so you get the money and you stay on your job 90 percent of the time. *We* need that flexibility. The company has always moved people off their jobs. If they needed you somewhere else and it was a question of production, they'd move you and take the grievance. The difference was we always ended up fighting a grievance on it."

Church adds, "The majority would choose classifications over pay-for-knowledge. The Fleetwood people think that the alternative to pay-for-knowledge is individual job rights. But we'll never get back to that."

Hopeful at First

A minimum of two weeks training was provided for transfers to the new plant, conducted jointly by the union and management. "The training was mainly about the team concept," says Ron Banks, a former Cadillac worker, "along with rotation and ergonomics."

Many workers were hopeful that management meant what it said during training. Banks explained: "They said it would be different, that besides appearances—things like no ties—there would be more cooperation, you could take your problems to the team. The supervisor's decision would still be final, but that would be rare. They gave the example that if two people wanted to take their vacations at the same time, this would be something the team could solve. They said the team could assign jobs if it wanted to, or let the foreman do it."

Banks began on the afternoon shift when production was only three to ten cars per day. Management was very lenient at that point. By the time he switched to days in May 1986, the line on afternoons was running at its regular speed—60/hour—but with many stops. The shift was producing only 100-125 cars per day, but workers were already complaining about their jobs being overloaded.

On the afternoon shift, Ron's team assigned jobs by seniority. "That was the only thing our team did," he remembers. "But when I came on days and went into a new group, over half the people were new. I had the highest seniority but the second worst job, installing the rear axle. The foreman mentioned in the team meeting that there were two good jobs that he wanted to assign by seniority. I talked to him later and told him that I had the highest seniority in the team. But the people already on those jobs had the second and third highest, and he wanted to keep them on.

"I called the committeeman. He didn't want to handle it, he wanted to wait till after model changeover. He said he would canvass the department on whether to choose jobs by seniority, but he didn't. Finally it was agreed that as jobs came open they'd be filled by seniority."

Most workers attend the weekly team meetings, which are held on Tuesdays during the half hour before the morning break. "We're usually out within ten minutes," says one worker. "Our foreman is good, but some make you stay the whole half hour.

"We don't discuss much. The bathrooms are dirty, there's trash in the parking lot. This is our input. Can we get more tissue paper in the bathroom? Nothing meaningful. Nobody pays any attention to whether it's a contractual issue or not.

"Questions about the job never come up. I can't recall a time when it has. Sometimes we'll watch a taped message on our TV from the plant manager, a pep talk on absenteeism or quality."

Craig Nothnagel says that meetings are mainly a way for coordinators to pass on the information they've received at the coordinators' meeting the day before. "The meetings are kind of short. We go over things like no reading newspapers on the job, no leaving early, we're going on a 12-hour schedule, we'll get our paychecks on Thursday. If someone in the team is having a problem with someone in management, they'll bring it up. But the coordinator tries to steer away from union issues, he'll tell him he'll put in a call for the committeeman."

Banks has several examples of how he tested management's supposed commitment to treat workers with dignity—before giving up in disgust. Banks recalls:

When I was on afternoons, our last break was at one a.m., an hour or so before we went home. This suited everybody I knew fine. Then they changed it to midnight. I went to the superintendent and asked wasn't this something we could vote on? He said management had talked to the shop committee and the shop committee said they'd canvassed the membership and the majority wanted it earlier. Management wanted it earlier because they wanted production to take the same break as repair.

So then I asked the committeeman about it. *He* said management had just told them they were going to change it.

Another time I was working QIS [quality inspection system], punching a VDT, and I had to stand on concrete all day. My knee hurt; it would throb at night. In the training they had emphasized ergonomics—'don't work harder, work smarter,' 'fit the job to the person.' So I thought sure I would get a stool. First I brought it up in the team. The foreman said it couldn't be done. Then I asked the health and safety committeeman, and he practically laughed. He said, 'They'll never give you a stool.' So then I went to the management health and safety guy, while the union health and safety man just sat there and grinned, he didn't say a word for me. The management guy sent me to another management guy, and that one got real belligerent. He acted like I had to be crazy to be asking for a stool.

After we voted down the local agreement, our committeeman came to our team meeting and asked us to turn in suggestions for local demands. I put in my stool, which they never got.

Banks knows of one example where a team was able to win something, though not through the team structure. Management provided very few benches near the line, telling workers they should use the team rooms if they wanted to sit down during breaks. One team in the body marriage area was located a long walk away from its team room. So team members did use the team room for breaks—and walked back to the line only when break was over. They got their benches.

Slipping By the Wayside

At Poletown many of the features which are supposedly basic to the team concept have been allowed to slip by the wayside. These include rotation, team responsibilities, and worker involvement in job design.

Rotation, as at many other plants, is just about nonexistent. When production began and the line was slow, workers learned all the jobs in their team and switched jobs regularly. Mary Kowalski (a pseudonym) says that when she started on the second shift in February 1986 she had to learn all 21 jobs in her team. When the line got up to speed, however, management ordered rotation to stop because of quality problems.

"When it started again we never could get a good rotation plan going. The jobs in our team were so diverse—either real easy or real hard, either for a real short person or a real tall one. The men didn't want to get stuck just on the heavy jobs and the women couldn't

do the real heavy jobs. So we never could work out a plan that would satisfy everybody.

"They split our team into three sections and we were supposed to rotate within those sections. I said I didn't want to, and some people were mad at me for not being part of the team. Then a few other people said they didn't want to rotate either, and pretty soon the whole rotation caved in and people stayed on their same jobs.

"Nobody wanted to rotate through all 21 jobs. They didn't even want to rotate through half the jobs. They might have liked to do three jobs, to break the monotony. But that was never tried.

"One of the main things at our team meetings was the company trying to get rotation going again. They said if you didn't rotate within a year your pay would be cut. But they didn't enforce it. The cars were coming out so bad they couldn't put people on different jobs. You can't go from job to job and do a quality job quickly."

Kowalski believes that management would prefer to have workers rotate: "They want the flexibility. They don't care whether you take pride in your job or not. You don't have the pride of saying, 'This is *my* job.' A certain job belongs to you, but when other people come on it who don't have to do it all the time, they see ways work can be added onto it."

Bill McGuire believes that GM's initial emphasis on rotation had an additional motive: "Say they've got ten people in the team. They've got five good jobs and five bad jobs, including one or two *real* bad. They want to see who will do the real bad jobs. Everybody will say, 'I can do this for one day, or one week.' You want to keep it up, because you want to be equal with the rest of the team.

"Before long more of the jobs are bad."

Craig Nothnagel says, "I know a girl that works at Mazda. When somebody in their team takes a day off, the other team members have to fill in. That is just not going to happen at our plant. People like to have something they can call their own—their own job and no more."

When workers try to assert team rights, they are rebuffed. McGuire says he argued in team meetings that special assignment people should be brought under the jurisdiction of the teams. Jobs such as "mutilation committee" and other quality assurance jobs should be open to team members by seniority and not handpicked by management. After several fruitless attempts, McGuire's zone comitteeman told him, "The company's throwing you out if you keep bringing that up." The zone man referred him to Paragraph 7 of the National Agreement: "Neither the Union nor its members will intimidate or coerce any employee in respect to his right to work."

There is no pretense at Poletown that workers help to design their own jobs, although team coordinators do work on eliminating manpower during changeover. Management would like to have the teams implicated in speedup decisions, however. Bill McGuire tells a story of a woman whose foreman (no one says "team manager") told her that four items were to be added to her job. When she protested that there was no way she could do more work, he told her, "Then take it to the team and divide it up among whoever you think can do it."

Favoritism

Both Banks and McGuire say that favoritism—and the number of jobs available for "kiss-asses"—is much greater than in their former plants. "It seems like the only way you can get a good job any more is to become a Human Resources Advisor," says Banks. "You see all these people walking around with clipboards, like the World Class Quality Council.

"To get a job like that you have to be part of their propaganda machine, write little articles for their newspapers: 'If everybody just did a little extra... find that scratch and report it to the hot line.' There was a big stink about the World Class Quality Council. So they had a screening process, everyone could apply, and they would pick a new World Class Quality Council on the basis of seniority and qualifications. Well, they just picked a new team, and their first assignment is to go to Mexico and Texas.

"And yet they're eliminating jobs like crazy. How can you have so many hourly people do nothing but kiss ass while everybody else is working their ass off?"

Craig Nothnagel became enthusiastic about the team concept when he worked at GM's Livonia, Michigan engine plant. When he transferred to Poletown he was elected a team coordinator. He volunteered for the World Class Quality Council because "I really thought we could make a difference, being the liaison between management and hourly." Nothnagel was on the World Class Quality Council until September 1987, before the union insisted it be chosen by seniority. He explains the Council's functioning:

Management asked the team leaders to come to a meeting on a voluntary basis to talk about the quality problems of the plant. We started out with close to 50, but after a while it dwindled to 20 or 25. Out of that came a charter and our philosophy of the plant and things of that nature. We were offered full-time jobs. I took one of those jobs...

We started having what we called the 9:00 Business Meeting on Fridays. We would get a review of the audit for that week, and out of that report we'd take 10 of the top items and go back to the teams, invite them to a meeting, discuss the problem with them. The meeting would include the plant manager, production manager, superintendents and team leaders.

We used different kinds of charts like a fishbone

chart, and asked the team to go over this in their team meeting. Then somebody would represent their team as to why they were having a problem in that area, usually the coordinator.

It was an effective method if all parties involved did what they agreed to do at this meeting. But a lot of times the information never made it all the way back. The management communication line was not effective as to the team members. If someone came in and really raised a lot of hell, you could get a response from management. But it was a slow, slow process.

There was a lot of politics involved. A lot of people in higher management positions didn't like hourly employees telling them they were doing something wrong.

People get real upset about things like the World Class Quality Council. They feel these people are working for management even if they're union-appointed.

From five full-time members when Nothnagel was participating, the World Class Quality Council has grown to twelve.

They're Coming After Your Money

The foundering of the team concept at Poletown is due to two factors: 1) an old-fashioned management is not interested in getting workers involved on a day-to-day level (much less in sharing power), and 2) the company pretty much has what it wants even with a bare bones version of team concept. (Quality is an important exception.) Even with the minimal variant of team concept, Poletown management has achieved some important goals: it has gotten rid of troublesome classifications. It has the right (though seldom exercised) to move workers around at will. And it has a more cooperative union. With these successes, it is not crucial to management whether workers feel betrayed or not.

Poletown committeemen visited the NUMMI plant in 1986, and seemed to feel that problems at Poletown paled in comparison to NUMMI. They returned with this message for their constituents: "You think you've got it bad... "

According to some Poletown members, union officials are disinclined to challenge management even when members insist. Workers who want to file grievances on overloaded jobs are told by their committeemen that "we don't do that over here." When Mary Kowalski tried to get her committeeman to write such a grievance (Paragraph 78), he took her into the foreman's office where both tried to talk her out of it. "Day shift does that job with no problem," they said. When Kowalski came to work early to talk to her counterpart on the day shift, workers told her that people had a very hard time with that job. The union, however, had told them they couldn't file a grievance because they did not yet have a contract (in fact, the grievance procedure was operating even though no contract had been signed).

The kicker for Poletown workers is not only that they are suffering under speedup. Without a strong union presence on the shop floor and worker loyalty to the union, they also face much worse erosion of their conditions in the future. As Bill McGuire summed it up, "Once they get your power away they're coming after your money."

Poletown workers overwhelmingly voted down the shop committee's first attempt at a local agreement in October 1986 (a contract was finally ratified in October 1987). According to Banks and McGuire, there was not a great deal in the proposal besides the team concept. Team coordinators' pay differential would have been raised from 10 cents to 50 cents, which was widely resented. "There was nothing weird in it," Banks says, "They just needed something to latch onto as a reason to vote it down. It was just a vote against Poletown."

Notes

1. Jeanie Wylie, *Community Betrayed*, Champaign, University of Illinois, forthcoming.

2. *Wall Street Journal*, May 13, 1986.

3. *Manufacturing Week*, September 28, 1987.

21. Orion: Early Disenchantment

General Motors' assembly plant in Orion Township, Michigan was one of the earlier team concept plants. A clone of the Oklahoma City plant, it opened with team concept on October 17, 1983. Orion has much in common with Poletown, its sister plant an hour south in Detroit. As at Poletown, workers transferred to Orion from traditional GM plants, and they were initially enthusiastic about the new relationship promised by management. Also as at Poletown, they are disillusioned.

Skilled trades workers at Orion waged a successful three-year battle against the "general maintenance" concept—management wanted to collapse their lines of demarcation. Their fight is described at the end of this chapter.

Work Groups

In early 1986 leaders and members of Local 5960 were particularly disturbed about job overloading, relations with top management, and management's attitude towards work group coordinators (what other plants call "teams," Orion calls "work groups"). When a work group manager (foreman) assaulted a worker in April, the anger crystallized in a 97 percent strike vote. The strike was not called, but the plant manager was removed and later the production manager as well. Orion management and UAW Local 5960 negotiated guidelines they hoped would improve the functioning of the team concept.

One modification was to change the work group coordinator's term of office to one year, to run from January 1 to January 1. Before, management had said that each group could choose the length of its coordinator's term of office and could recall the coordinator if necessary. The union felt that there was too much turnover and thus negotiated the one-year rule. One possible problem with this approach, of course, is that it would be much harder for group members to get rid of a coordinator they didn't like.

"I knew one group that changed their coordina-

- *Orion Assembly Plant*
- *Location: Orion Township, Michigan*
- *Employment: 5,800 workers on two shifts*
- *Product: Cadillac and Oldsmobile C-cars (Coupe de Ville and Olds 98)*
- *Production began: October 1983*
- *Team concept began: October 1983*
- *UAW Local 5960*
  Address: 180 East Silverbell, Lake Orion, MI 48033
  Phone: 313 / 377-2520

---

tor every two weeks so they could all get the opportunity to train for pay-for-knowledge," explained Chris Altemann, formerly a committeeperson in the chassis department and now on the Local 5960 executive board. "So we negotiated this guideline for more stability, so the coordinators could serve without fear or intimidation." (The "intimidation" in this case was coming from fellow members, not from management.) Coordinators may be removed by the superintendent and committeeperson if they are not doing their jobs properly, but this rarely if ever happens. In the January 1987 elections 70-80 percent of the coordinators were re-elected.

The guidelines also included a definition of the coordinator's job. "The coordinator has maybe 15 things he's supposed to do," says Altemann, "but the first-line supervisor thinks he's only responsible for one thing—'whatever I say.' "

Unlike other team concept plants, where the pay differential ranges from 10 to 50 cents, Orion coordinators receive no extra money. They are elected by secret ballot in a group meeting. Previously, the work group manager voted as well, but this was disallowed under the new guidelines. Local 5960 President Ernie Emery explained, "He would have his certain segment that he could more or less direct his favoritism to. He could more or less control who got in."

Group meetings were also made voluntary. Groups of 15 to 24 members meet for a half-hour per week before or after work, during lunch or on break. Workers are paid time-and-a-half for attending. Each work group manager supervises one or two groups.

Old Man with a New Face

Once a year coordinators go through a three-day training class. Chris Altemann helped to design that class and taught it jointly with a salaried person. They started by asking the coordinators to draw a picture of their job. The coordinators learn "team building" and how to control their groups, although, Altemann says, the large size of the Orion groups makes them hard to control.

Jerry Overfield has been a coordinator in three different work groups. He has coordinated his current group on the chassis line since early 1987. He described his job this way:

> Basically what it is is a go-fer. I do bathroom relief, get stock, gloves, tools, anything to run that department. It's the same as a utility man, which it was called a long time ago. Everything in the plant is an old man with a new face.

Once a week all the coordinators from chassis meet with the superintendent for half an hour, before the group meeting. They tell us what's going on, how the plant is doing on quality, when the vacation checks will come out, if there'll be a shortage of gloves.

The difference between a good coordinator and a bad one is a good one will get out your stock, fix your trays, get it the way you like—it only takes a few seconds more. A bad one will just throw it on the table and leave.

I work on the line maybe an hour and a half a day. The rest of the time I'm getting stock, dealing with problems on the line. Like if someone puts on the wrong bumper, I have to run to the other department to change it if it gets out of our department. There are days you run your butt off all day long, other days you don't.

The work group managers treat you different if you're a coordinator. They value your opinions. That's good for the coordinators, but it shouldn't be for one individual, it should be for the whole group, for all the good workers.

At Overfield's June 24, 1987 group meeting he relayed the worrisome information he had been given at the coordinators' meeting: GM was considering eliminating one of four BOC Division plants. Orion, he told group members, was at the top of the endangered list because of absenteeism and medical leaves. Members were perturbed and wanted more information, including the names of the other plants. Management, however, had not seen fit to provide details.

Pay-for-Knowledge and Rotation

The "Innovative Wage Plan" (pay-for-knowledge) at Orion provides for three wage levels for production workers: an assembler at the lowest rate must know two jobs and earns $14.29. Knowing five jobs earns $14.40, and eight earns $14.49. Some classifications, such as stockman or sweeper, earn less at the two-job level, but all jobs collect $14.49 at the eight-job level. (See the contract language reprinted at the end of this chapter. Rates shown there are for the 1984 National Agreement, which was superseded in September 1987.)

The percentage of workers who choose to be "variables" differs among departments, but is probably 80 percent plant-wide. The contract provides that a worker can switch from base rate to variable rate or back again every six months. Although the contract refers to the variable assignment as "rotating" and says such employees "will be regularly assigned to perform such assignments within their group," in practice employees stay on one regular job. Workers may rotate among themselves, but seldom do.

Asked why management does not take advantage of its ability to move workers around, Chris Altemann says, "It's the resistance of the people, they don't want to move. And management has the belief—I don't know if they're right or not—that the best person for the job is the person who does it every day."

Ernie Emery says, "It kind of bothered me that GM liked that system. We always preach quality, but when you have someone doing different jobs, he may be *adequate* at all the jobs, but maybe not proficient. Management has gotten to realize that, so they do have the flexibilty, but they don't make use of it."

Asked how the workers like pay-for-knowledge, Overfield says, "They don't. Not for 20 cents an hour. It's not worth the aggravation."

Classifications and Transferring

The Local 5960 contract is different from other team concept contracts in that it contains 25 classifications in production, such as assembler-trimmer, metal finisher, paint booth and oven cleaner, and utility operator-soft trim. Most team concept contracts contain only one to three classifications for all production workers.

However, the classifications at Orion do not serve much purpose. They make a difference in pay only at the two and five-job levels; all eight-job "variable" operators are paid the same. Nor are classifications used for transferring. As in other team concept plants, workers may transfer to a different department or another work group, but not to a different classification.

An opening in a work group does not necessarily go to the most senior person who has an application in. When an opening occurs, the highest seniority person *in the group* may take that job if he or she wishes. *That* person's job is then open to the next senior person, and so on. A person transferring into the group from outside gets last pick of the jobs. This shuffling process is known as a "circle jerk."

Jerry Overfield and former Vice-President Jerome ("Butch") Craft said that at Orion many of the good jobs have been eliminated. The job of line sweeper is gone, for example, as work groups are now responsible for housekeeping in their own areas. Although a Quality Control classification exists and a "finesse" repair classification was added in the 1987 agreement, workers are still expected to "perform miscellaneous repair, in-process repair and/or inspection duties in conjunction with such employee's primary job duties."

Craft said, "At my old plant [Fisher Body in Pontiac] it took you seven to ten years to get a decent job. Here, it's 15 or 20." Overfield says, "They eliminated a lot of sweepers by getting people in the group to sign up to sweep. The coordinator relieves them and they sweep for up to an hour. It works, it keeps the department clean."

Chris Altemann explained the Quality Control job as opposed to the former "inspection": "It's not your old traditional guy at the end of the group checking things out. Instead he reads off a repair ticket and inputs [into a computer] the things already generated on the tickets." The repair tickets have been marked by the operator who made the error or by other workers who noticed a defect as the car went by. At the end of the line, there is one final repair ticket for all the accumulated defects. Clearly, the quality control job is designed to be replaced by a bar code reader or optical scanner.

How Well Does Team Concept Work?

Despite management's early promises of a friendly working relationship, workers and union officials interviewed at Orion say that the plant is not different in this regard from a traditional plant.

Besides his involvement in coordinator training, Chris Altemann is involved in the Quality Network and other joint programs. He has visited several other plants to study chassis quality, including ones with team concept. The plants he found to work best were NUMMI, GM's Grand Am plant in Lansing, and the Delco plant in Moraine, Ohio. Asked how team concept is working at Orion, Altemann said, "It has a lot of room to grow. The concepts have not been adhered to.

"The difference between plants that work and those that don't is a resolve to get things settled quickly at the lowest level, by management and union. In Lansing, both the superintendent and the committeeman say that when someone approaches them with a problem, they ask them first if they've approached the foreman on the problem and tried to rectify it right there. They won't talk to him till he does that. Here, I've been trying to get a drinking fountain for four years, and just a month ago I was finally told I would get it."

Asked whether Orion workers are able to use the group meetings for their benefit, Altemann said, "No, because there's no response [from management]. They can bring up problems in meetings and that's all the further it gets."

Ernie Emery was asked how different Orion is from a traditional plant. He said, "Before the work group meetings were made voluntary, there was a lot of difference. There were a lot of people unhappy because they didn't want to be involved. A lot of people just want to do their job for eight hours and go home.

"But some are legitimately concerned about the product. And some want to be the foreman's go-fer. It's an opportunity for those who choose to become involved. I couldn't be the judge whether that's good or bad."

Jerry Overfield says that when workers first transferred into Orion, "the excitement was, finally, somebody's going to listen. But when they saw they didn't have any say-so in how things were going to be done, they got disappointed and angry. People feel like no one listens, nobody cares about me, I'm out there by myself."

Overfield, who is not active in the union, does not believe that Local 5960 is an effective counterweight to management. "The union doesn't give a damn. When you hear people around here talking about how the union used to be in their old plant, they say the committeeman would come in kicking down the door, grab the foreman by the throat, and make him do what's right. Now they tell you why the company's right."

Butch Craft says workers liked the teamwork idea at first. "At one time they almost had us. They brainwashed a lot of our people. People were enthused, it was a new idea, till management promised too much and didn't deliver. It backfired on them. At first, people thought they could work with management and they wanted to. Now they just want to do their job. They're getting paid for it or they wouldn't participate."

It appears, then, that Orion workers do not perceive their new team concept plant as much different from their old ones. What about management? Has the team concept at Orion met management's goals?

'86 FOR LABOR NEWSPAPER/HUCK-KONOPACKI LABOR CARTOONS
KONOPACKI

MANAGEMENT KEEPS AN OPEN MIND ABOUT EMPLOYEE IDEAS.

If one of those goals is maximum efficiency, the answer is no. According to one study which adjusted for vehicle size and complexity, it took the Orion plant more labor-hours to build a car than most other GM plants in North America. Orion took 34.5 hours, compared to NUMMI, the low plant at 19.[1]

Skilled Trades and 'General Maintenance'

From the time skilled trades workers first transferred to Orion when the plant was under construction in 1981, management wanted to blur lines of demarcation and operate with a concept called "general maintenance." This meant that electricians, pipefitters, millwrights and toolmakers would receive cross-training and all do each other's work. All would receive the same wages.

It took the skilled trades a three-year "war" and two contract rejections to convince management to let each trade do its own job. Their rebuff of "general maintenance" meant that some trades were willing to accept a lower pay rate than they could have gotten under management's plan.

"It was a battle to defend your trade, to not be given a job assignment you weren't trained for," said Marvin Whiteman. Whiteman is a millwright and a trustee of Local 5960. In his former plant he was a committeeman; today he is coordinator of a ten-person skilled trades group which includes toolmakers, pipefitters, electricians and millwrights. He believes the work groups "offer a vehicle for workers to work together and enhance the workplace for themselves. It's good to understand the system, know the company's problems. There is a risk, though, as a coordinator, in becoming company-oriented. Ideally the coordinator should serve only as a messenger."

Whiteman described how Orion management tried to implement "general maintenance":

Management would tell you to look at something that was out of your trade, "Here, go help that electrician." But it wasn't blatant. They didn't use discipline. Their definition of 'general maintenance'—and this is a quote—was "to do whatever you feel comfortable with."

We were smart enough to realize that "whatever you feel comfortable with" would not produce quality skilled work. Besides, if you weren't comfortable with the given job assignment and did refuse it, from a management perspective you were judged lazy or uncooperative. In reality, it's just the opposite, skilled workers enjoy the work of their particular trade and like nothing more than to display the craftsmanship involved.

Being a new plant there was no contract to enforce, so the committeeman was between a rock and a hard place. Then when there was a local agreement, it wasn't traditional. Lots of things were pre-arranged and were part of the GM-UAW agreement on transferring in Paragraph 96. Right from the start we gave up welders, machine repair and the 'WEMR' [welder/electrical maintenance repair] skilled classifications, to name a few.

Speculation on the floor was that the International union saw that the company needed a competitive, technologically advanced auto plant and believed that the trades had become a burden. So when the conditions were set forth for transferring into the new plant, it was agreed to use general maintenance. The rank and file suspected union cooperation above the local level.

Regardless of what may have been discussed beforehand, the plant was built here, and that was what was most important to all of us. It had now become our job to dig in and fight for our needs. Most of the time we know what's best for us, as well as the company, in the everyday running of the plant. I just wish they [GM] were more willing to honestly accept this hourly input. We do have a lot to offer.

Ernie Emery, also a millwright and formerly the skilled trades committeeman, said, "Plant management had orders from the corporation. They had four new plants that were supposed to get this in, including us, Buick City and Wentzville.

"I sent a letter on December 4, 1981 to our regional rep, when there were only 42 tradesmen here. I said management was manipulating the hourly employees, trying to 'flex lines of demarcation of those assigned to work groups.'

"People would always respond to each other, we're not rigid. If an electrician needed help lifting a big piece of conduit, he'd get it. But before long management came to realize that each individual possesses different skills. There's more downtime if people are not capable of performing. After the first contract was voted down they realized at the corporate and plant level that general maintenance was not such a great idea. We were able to convince them about skill levels and safety, and that happy employees work better."

Whiteman described how the skilled trades united to resist general maintenance:

When we arrived we got six weeks of training, not specific to trade. They gave us training in robotics, computers, they wanted to familiarize you with other trades. There wasn't resistance to that; people were cautiously optimistic.

The social training, the group dynamics didn't go over, though. There was distrust there. The teachers didn't have any credibility—this was all new to them too. At that point the work groups were seen as synonymous with general maintenance, so people were against them both.

The first 40 or 50 guys got along well, and that set the ground for the people who came in later. A handful of people saw fit to enforce lines of demarcation and to take charge of communication.

We called trades meetings in the plant. Each trade elected two representatives to meet with management; we called it the "steering committee." We did this twice, in late '81 and March '82. I was on the latter for the length of its existence.

We met with management and told them what we thought it would take to run the plant in terms of manpower and training. We took a stand from the beginning against general maintenance. If management tried to tell you on the floor to do something that was out of your trade, you'd refuse. Ernie Emery, our committeeman at the time, filed numerous Paragraph 182 grievances on the lines of demarcation and did his best to stay on top of it.

At first quite a few people wanted to cooperate with management on general maintenance. Maybe they were tired of the adversarial relationship, the ulcers, the heart attacks, the things that go with the "I'm the boss, you're the worker" relationship. But they weren't accepted by the others. And after seeing the company's methods, most of the people who wanted to cooperate were won over.

In the spring of 1982 six of us went to [GM's] Shreveport, [Louisiana plant] to report on the work groups and general maintenance there. But we're not like those people; we came from traditional plants. We told 'em to bag it.

In the fall of 1984 the skilled trades overwhelmingly voted down their part of Local 5960's first contract. It would have made general maintenance part of the agreement. The second try was also voted down overwhelmingly a few months later.

Finally, management gave in. "It was as hard on them on the floor as it was on us," says Whiteman. "There was almost a complete turnover of management in three or four years—the superintendent and his assistant, as well as the general and floor supervisors, seemed to do their best to leave the Orion plant. They bailed out.

"We had no choice, we had to stay. It took three and a half years to win, but the trades persevered and the union listened. I always knew they would if we stuck together."

A contract which included eight trades—millwright, pipefitter, truck repair, electrician, toolmaker, carpenter, painter, and powerhouse operator—was ratified by a two-thirds margin in April 1985. Millwrights, pipefitters and truck repair were all to do welding. Wages ranged from $14.84 for painters to $15.15 for electricians and toolmakers (1984 National Agreement).

Whiteman believes that "in terms of cost effectiveness, time to complete a job, the traditional lines of demarcation prevail. There are things I couldn't teach someone, shortcuts—those save time, which is money. The company could pay three or four hundred people to do general maintenance and waste time and money. And we would be deskilled."

Notes

1. Daniel Luria, "Work Organization and Manufacturing Performance in the U.S. Automotive Sector, 1982-1992," paper prepared for WZB Conference on The Future of Work in the Automobile Industry, Berlin, November 1987.

Appendix

The contract language reprinted below is excerpted from the 1984 Local Agreement between UAW Local 5960 and GM BOC-Orion.

Memorandum of Understanding
Regarding the Orion Innovative Wage Plan

The Orion wage plan was conceived to balance the needs of employees who desire traditional work assignments and the needs of employees who want to participate in more varied work. As such, this entirely new agreement is without precedent in the American automobile industry. In order to ensure that it is implemented in a manner consistent with the parties intent, the parties have agreed to semi-annual review meetings. These meetings will be scheduled at locations mutually agreeable to the parties. Representatives of the UAW Region 1B Office, Solidarity House, and the Industrial Relations Staff of the Buick-Oldsmobile-Cadillac Group general offices may be invited as appropriate.

A joint agenda will be developed for each meeting defining administrative problems surrounding the agreement. It will be the purpose of these meetings to resolve these problems and to make this new agreement an effective part of the Orion Union/Management relationship.

It is further understood that this memorandum is in no way meant to circumvent the grievance procedure.

Wage Rules

A. The intent of this agreement is to allow employees the opportunity to select either fixed or rotating assignments. Accordingly, both base and variable assignment classifications have been established. The attached classification and rate schedule establishes rates for base classifications and rates and progression criteria for variable assignment classifications.

B. Employees who desire to be assigned to the base classifications set forth in the attached classification and rate schedule shall be paid the corresponding job classification rate.

C. Employees who desire to be assigned to the base classifications will be placed on an assignment by supervision. It will be the responsibility of employees assigned to a particular job to be proficient on one other operation and to train other employees as required on the operation to ensure flexibility. Such employees may be reassigned to allow other employees the opportunity to demonstrate proficiency on the job or to ensure the efficiency of operations.

During the negotiation of this Agreement much discussion was had concerning claims that employees who did not desire to be reassigned were reassigned for no good business reason. Management assured the Union that employees who do not desire to rotate, but instead desire to be assigned to a base operation, will be assigned under the circumstances described in Paragraph C above, or some other sound business reason. Any alleged abuses of this will be brought to the attention of Labor Relations and corrected, where warranted.

D. Employees who desire to be assigned to variable assignment classifications shall be paid the job rate set forth in the attached classification and rate schedule based on the following conditions.

1. Employees will be assigned to perform the number of jobs consistent with their job rate preference.

2. Employees who are assigned to variable assignment classifications in accordance with (1) above who thereafter elect to perform a base assignment shall be paid the job rate for the base classification in accordance with the attached classification and rates.

3. Department supervision will discuss the clustering of job assignments with the District Committeeperson in an effort to establish a rotational matrix that provides for employees a broad base of job experience.

E. Employees who desire to perform work within a variable assignment classification will be regularly assigned to perform such assignments within their group. However this does not preclude employees from receiving credit for performing up to 25 percent of their assignment outside of their group within their department in order to attain their job rate preference.

F. The parties recognize that one of the primary concerns of employees who desire to perform work within the variable assignment classifications is the opportunity for advancement to a higher job rate for performing such assignments. In that regard seniority will be given primary consideration in those groups where there is more than one employee who is desirous of receiving the necessary training in order to progress to a higher job rate.

G. Employees in variable assignment classifications who are assigned to a new cluster of operations must learn the number of jobs consistent with their job rate preference. As long as such employee remains willing to learn jobs in the new cluster as opportunities are presented, they will retain the wage level earned within their previous cluster.

H. Variable assignment job rate increases shall become effective the Monday of the week in which the employee qualifies for progression.

I. An employee who is assigned to a higher rated classification more than one hour, and who satisfactorily performs the operation assigned, will be paid the job rate of that classification or their own rate, whichever is higher, for the hours worked on that shift.

J. Employees who request to change their classification within a group from a base assignment to a variable assignment or vice versa may do so once each six (6) months. Such request will be made to the employee's supervisor on forms supplied by Management and a copy will be provided to the employee.

Classifications and Job Rates

Classifications	Job Rates
Assembler-Chassis	$13.09
Assembler-Trimmer	$13.09
Assembler-Trimmer-Seats	$13.09
Body Framer-Schedule Parts, Seal, Caulk, Grind and Assemble	$13.09
Fire Equipment	$13.09 Minimum
Janitor, Sweeper, Laborer, or Cleaner	$12.56
Janitor, Sweeper, Laborer, or Cleaner-Utility-Variable Assignment	$12.56 Minimum
Metal Finisher	$13.09
Paint Booth and Oven Cleaner-Utility-Variable Assignment	$12.82 Minimum
Paint Mix, Bonderite, Elpo Attendant-Utility-Variable Assignment	$13.09 Minimum
Sand, Seal, and Prepare Body for Paint	$13.09
Spray Gun Repair-Booth Monitor-Utility-Variable Assignment	$13.09 Minimum
Sprayer-Prime or Finish Coat	$13.09
Stockman	$12.98
Stockman-Utility-Variable Assignment	$12.98 Minimum
Utility Operator-Body-Variable Assignment	$13.09 Minimum
Utility Operator-Chassis-Variable Assignment	$13.09 Minimum
Utility Operator-Cushion Room-Variable Assignment	$13.09 Minimum
Utility Operator-Final Process-Variable Assignment	$13.09 Minimum
Utility Operator-Hard Trim-Variable Assignment	$13.09 Minimum
Utility Operator-Soft Trim-Variable Assignment	$13.09 Minimum
Utility Operator-Paint-Variable Assignment	$13.09 Minimum
Utility-Quality Control-Variable Assignment	$13.09 Minimum
Welder-Spot, Arc, Gas, etc.	$13.09

Rate Progression for Utility Variable Assignment classifications will be based on the minimum rates established for the classifications and jobs learned as follows:

Jobs Learned

	2 Jobs	5 Jobs	8 Jobs
Minimum rate	$13.09	$13.19	$13.28
Minimum rate	$12.98	$13.13	$13.28
Minimum rate	$12.82	$13.09	$13.28
Minimum rate	$12.56	$12.82	$13.28

Division II
Departments 30 and 40 Skilled Trades

Classification	Job Rate
Toolmaker	$14.95 - $15.15
Electrician	$14.95 - $15.15
Millwright-including Welding	$14.81 - $15.01
Pipefitter-including Welding	$14.81 - $15.01
Truck Repair-Gas & Electric- including Welding	$14.81 - $15.01
Carpenter	$14.70 - $14.90
Painter	$14.64 - $14.84

Department 42 Powerhouse

Powerhouse Operator-Stationary Engineer-including Welding	$14.81 - $15.01

22. Pontiac Truck and Bus: Strike Against Team Concept

At GM's Pontiac Truck and Bus Plant, the story of the team concept is the story of how the local union got rid of it.

General Motors tried to use whipsawing to convince UAW Local 594 to agree to the team concept. The local, however, refused to re-open its agreement. GM unilaterally started teams in one part of the complex anyway, forcing the local to strike. GM gave in after four days and agreed to stop all contract violations and to compensate workers to the tune of $1.5 million.

It was the strike which ultimately caused GM to back down, but it was Local 594's consistent policy of membership education which made the strike possible—and solid.

The story begins in mid-1986 when management at the Truck and Bus complex in Pontiac, Michigan approached Local 594. If the union would open its local agreement and combine job classifications, the company said, the plant would be "in the running" for placement of a new medium-duty truck. Local 594 was already building a medium-duty truck, but rumors had been circulating for almost a year that GM wanted to move production to Janesville, Wisconsin. The Janesville union, Local 95, had already agreed to teams.

Local officials asked what guarantees they would get if they did change the local agreement. The company response? "Absolutely none. You'd be in the running."

"We felt that the company had already made the decision on the fate of the medium-duty and just wanted to milk our agreement," said Jim Simmons, a zone committeeperson. "You look across the nation at the plants that have opened and you look at the plants that have closed. Anderson, Indiana had a great amount of people working; they opened their agreements, now they're half. They don't gain anything, they just lose, it's a no-win situation. So why the hell would we do something like that when you see what's happening?"

The local leadership said absolutely no on opening the agreement. "GM has embarked upon a program

that pits local against local," said President Don Douglas. "And we thoroughly believe that this must be stopped."

Perhaps to drive its point home even though the whipsawing had not worked, the company announced that the medium-duty truck would be built in Janesville.

Unilateral Implementation

Meanwhile, GM unilaterally began to implement the team concept in one of the plants in the Pontiac complex, Plant 6. Plant 6 was slated to begin building a new full-size pick-up, the CK-400. GM apparently decided that it wanted the new product to start off on a different foot. Workers who transferred to Plant 6 from Local 598 in Flint, Michigan were required to undergo three weeks of training in the team concept.

Carl Forester and Jim Simmons were the zone committeemen for Plant 6. They were against the team concept and the training from the start. "We had heard from other plants at [UAW] subcouncil meetings that they had real bad experiences with it," Simmons said. "It was a nightmare for some of the members. We sent people to Shreveport to see their product, and they reported back to us that no, their people were not happy."

Simmons and Forester called the training ("Modules 1, 2, and 3") "brainwashing." Simmons said:

> They talked about working together, building a better product, what they could do to improve it? They did exercises like: what part of a boat would this person be—would he be the chain, or the anchor?
>
> In some classes they would pick people out of the crowd and ask them how they felt about their family life. If people didn't want to participate, the teacher would say, 'Look—this guy doesn't want to participate and the rest of us do. We can't work that way, we have to work as a team.'
>
> There were people who couldn't read and write, and the teacher would be saying, 'What do you think of this?' on the page. If the guy would say he didn't want to participate, they'd stick him in the corner and go on. The teacher didn't even realize that's what was going on.

When production began in Plant 6, it began with teams. Innumerable articles of Local 594's contract were violated. Simmons and Forester, backed up by the rest of the 594 leadership, took the position that the contract was sacred and that any violation of it would be protested. The battle was on.

The company organized the Plant 6 workforce into teams of 15 to 20. Each one elected a team coordinator. Coordinators, or TC's, had to get to work early

- *GM Pontiac Truck and Bus*
- *Location: Pontiac, Michigan*
- *Employment: 8,700*
- *Product: full-size and compact pick-ups, utility vehicles, medium-duty and full-size trucks*
- *Production began: pre-World War II*
- *Team Concept began: 1986; stopped in 1987*
- *UAW Local 594*
  Address: 525 East Blvd. South, Pontiac, MI 48053
  Phone: 313 / 334-2557

and hand out gloves, tools and coveralls. They worked with the foremen (called "area specialists" in the team language) to keep the line running, such as filling in for people who had to go to sick bay.

In many ways the duties of the TC's were similar to those of a classification already existing in Local 594's contract—"group leader." Group leaders made 16 cents per hour more than assemblers, and the jobs were filled by seniority. But there were no group leaders in Plant 6, only the team coordinators, who were chosen by the team and could be recalled. The union would not permit the company to pay the TC's extra because, under the contract, a person on a higher-paying job had the right to keep that job as long as he or she wanted it.

But some workers still ran for TC. According to Forester and Simmons, mostly it was the "fair-haired boys," people who were looking for a promotion to supervision. Sometimes the teams would refuse to elect anyone, as a protest against the system. Sometimes they would elect the most union-conscious person. The committeemen say that if someone was elected that management didn't like, often he or she just wouldn't get used. "We're not going to have a TC this month," management would say.

The TC had a regular job on the line but had to attend daily one-hour meetings with management. Management also chose "quality coordinators" ("big fair-haired boys") who met with the general manager every day. The union didn't object to these "QC's" because they carried the proper job classification—inspection.

The weekly half-hour team meetings were mandatory. Pay was docked for missing a meeting.

Yellow to Blue to Yellow

Besides the teams, management set up committees. Jim Simmons recalled: "They had one committee I called the color committee. They decided to paint all the yellow warning stripes on the floor blue. I tell them they have to change them back, and the following day they're yellow again. Then a few months after that, this color committee decides to paint blue stripes *inside* the yellow stripes. I didn't know how to combat that so I left it, as long as my yellow ones were still there.

"The clothing committee decided that everybody should get three pairs of pants and shirts a year, with 'Pontiac East' on the rear end and on the pocket. But they had to sign to give up their coveralls that are in the local agreement. We told them, 'Take the pants, but you're entitled to the coveralls too.' We lettered the plant notifying the people that the company wasn't relieved of the obligation to provide coveralls and aprons."

One of the main changes in Plant 6 was the company's policy of eliminating many classifications. There were no group leaders, sweepers, or line inspectors. And all stockkeepers were made "chief stockkeepers" and paid an extra 16 cents, so that the company could have each one do all stock-type jobs. "These chiefs had to do everything," Simmons says, "the chief's job, forklift driv-

ing, going out on the docks and bringing in material. Half the guys making $12.98 as chiefs wanted to go back where they were from.

"After the strike we made them break up the classification and bring in stockkeepers. We took the luxury away from the company of assigning all the stock-keepers' work to a chief. They had to bring in 12 people, including six drivers."

Carl Forester explains: "Besides getting people to do more work, their main reason was to prevent other people from bumping in from other plants. If you're paid top rate, someone from another part of the plant needs more seniority to bump you than if you're a plain old stockkeeper. They didn't want other people coming in and breaking up their happy home.

"There was no way we could stand for that. Can you imagine a 20-year man walking by a 1978 man that's working in Plant 6 and he has no way to bump him? Our contract says complete plant-wide seniority with immediate bumping rights. And that's what we got."

Meanwhile, GM was giving the lie to its rhetoric about "cooperation" and "respect for the employee." Management took away a five-minute morning break that had been a past practice at Pontiac for 20 years. It forbade reading of newspapers or sitting down while the assembly line was not moving (and since the product was new, there were many breakdowns). "A member would be socializing with a friend 20 or 30 feet down the line while the line was broken down and they'd stop his time," Simmons said. "They had to pay for that later. Some 15 individuals got compensated one-tenth of an hour for management stopping their time."

Forester added: "The mask came off. People said, 'Hey, you didn't preach that in the school.' "

"The company said they wanted to make it nicer for people so they'd come to work," Simmons said. "And it is a clean plant, it's a beautiful plant. But they had all kinds of safety problems. There were 17 or 18 major safety problems they refused to look at until we struck them."

At the same time, the company's own system was breaking down. After production began in earnest, workers no longer rotated jobs. And team training gave way to the needs of production. New people transferring into the plant were put directly on jobs without benefit of Modules 1, 2 and 3.

How They Stopped the Teams

Local 594 was able to beat back this unilateral brand of team concept through a concerted effort that involved not only the directly affected members in Plant 6, but the whole local. The local educated the entire membership on all the related issues: why GM's whip-sawing had to be combatted, how company decisions on placement of work are made, the futility of making deals which encouraged locals to bid against each other. The local did not allow the company to put it on the defensive, but aggressively defended members' rights to maintain their negotiated conditions, and put the blame for any job loss on the corporation.

Local 594's resistance to contract concessions did not start in 1987. In 1982 Local 594 President Don Douglas co-chaired Locals Opposed to Concessions (LOC), the group which agitated against the UAW's first national concessions to GM, and in 1984 Douglas co-chaired Restore and More. The local's history in leading resistance to GM's demands played a big part in memers' readiness to take the company on once again.

In 1985 the local started a "union awareness" program. This program was designed to reach every member of the local who wanted to participate, and it was expensive. Education Director Bob Schroeder and union trainers Mike Caverly and Ralph Isenbarg designed an eight-hour class to teach union history and current union issues. In groups of 30 or so, union members were called out of the plant on union business and paid lost time while they attended the class. In addition to films and videos, union officers made presentations on their duties and were available to answer questions about anything the members wanted to ask.

The classes were extremely popular. Members had a degree of access to their elected officials which can be rare in such a large local. Their questions about company rumors and threats could be answered from a strong union point of view.

Seniority System Is Worth Fighting For

When the local was criticized for its strong stand on not opening the agreement, the officers came back aggressively. In a statement widely publicized in the media, Michigan Department of Commerce Director Doug Ross attacked Local 594 for not giving up job classifications to "save jobs." Ross called the local's refusal to open its contract an "outrage" and claimed that union leaders said they "prefer to lose the 2,500 jobs."

President Douglas responded both in the press and to his members. "Apparently, Doug Ross does not think our work rules and seniority system are worth fighting for, but we do," he told the *Detroit News*. "We

told him we've got more than Michigan jobs at stake; we've got union democracy and union integrity at stake."

The local made use of the occasion to draw the issues out. In a special bulletin to the membership, union officers and rank and file members took on the arguments one at a time. Foremost on members' minds: Was GM's decision on placement of its medium-duty truck really dependent on Local 594 opening its contract? The bulletin argued:

> Decisions of this magnitude are not made just prior to announcement. GM has known for a very long time their intentions relative to the future of medium-duty products. In fact, testimony before Federal Court Referees by GM executives clearly indicated that the decision on placement of medium duty products was formulated as early as 1982. Obviously, all the commotion since has resulted from GM's clever campaign to milk from this situation all the benefits possible.

Next, Education Director Bob Schroeder placed the blame for lost jobs squarely where it belonged—on the company.

> Where was [Ross's] "outrage" displayed when GM made announcements of moving U.S. manufacturing operations to Mexico, Japan, Korea, Brazil and other foreign countries?
> Where was his outrage displayed when GM announced the elimination of thousands of jobs and the shutdown of many plants where employees had previously given extra concessions across the nation, including plants in Michigan like Pontiac Motors, Orion, Fiero, Buick City, Flint Truck, Grand Rapids, Detroit and others? Concessions have not saved one job!!

Douglas continued:

> When Ross publicly puts the blame on the local union because we will not give our agreement away, then he relieves any social pressure that could be applied to GM for running out on an excellent work force and a very responsible community...
> The local union contract is one of the last considerations in making a decision to move a product. However, if it became a flip of the coin between us and another location then Ross has given them [GM] the out.

"TEAM CONCEPT" TO SUPERSEDE PAR. 78?

As production in Plant 6 escalates towards final production goals, paragraph 78 (speedup) violations are "popping up," not only in Plant 6, but in the other plants as well, as enterprising supervisors and management personnel start looking at the "new" Plant 6 concept.

We refer to the recent incident this past week in Plant 6, when an entire "team" of hourly production workers was called into a meeting to resolve a paragraph 78 (speedup) situation. Isn't that beautiful? Now, management is intent upon superseding the vital provisions of paragraph 78 and 79 of the National Agreement by invoking a "team vote" on whether or not a paragraph 78 violation exists.

Realize that this concept pits worker against worker, with each vying for the position of team leader, and makes rats out of union members who set themselves up to judge their brothers and sisters on such things as attendance, job performance, rights to take a vacation or get a pay increase, and now, if management has its way, to determine whether or not a speedup exists.

Not only is this illegal and a violation of law and contract, it is downright sickening.

UAW Local 594 called for strike authorization in February 1987. The above is from a four-page leaflet on the issues.

A letter from rank and filer Robert Willett revealed Ross's true sentiments. At a Democratic Party meeting in August 1986, Willett wrote, Ross had told him that "the age of well-paid industrial labor is over" and that today's industrial workers "would soon be paid like some of the people at Wendy's or Pizza Hut."

The local leadership's strategy was effective. The Doug Ross incident—rather than panicking the membership into wanting to open the contract—strengthened their understanding that they were in an ongoing battle with the corporation.

Meanwhile, Committeemen Simmons and Forester, backed up by the rest of the local, were filing grievances on the contract violations in Plant 6. They distributed leaflets informing members of their contractual rights and urging them not to give those rights up.

It became clear that GM was not going to cease the contract violations inherent in their version of the team concept. The local leaders knew that only force—a strike—would make GM change. They began to plan to take the members out.

Strike

Timing was important. As President Douglas explained afterwards, "We had everything lined up. They were just introducing the full-size pick-up which they knew was going to be a heavy seller. The dealers weren't fully supplied yet. The S-truck Blazer that we build is a heavy seller too.

"We knew when the profit-sharing would be announced," Douglas continued. "And we knew it would be little or nothing. That would give our members another incentive. And then we had another card to play if we were still out—the executive bonuses would be announced soon."

In addition, Douglas said, "We were right on every issue." The committeemen documented every violation carefully, even down to estimating the amount of back pay for which GM was liable. Thus the local was not worried that the International might be reluctant to grant strike authorization. The clarity of the contract violations was underscored later when GM gave in on every issue with little argument.

The idea of a strike was discussed at the January and February 1987 membership meetings, both standing-room-only. Local officials urged those present to talk up the strike vote back in the plant.

The local-wide vote to strike was 97.6 percent. "The rest of our people were smart enough to see that the rights were being deleted in Plant 6 as an avenue to get to them," Simmons explained. "People knew it would filter to the other plants."

As a result, Local 594 wasn't subject to the divisiveness that the team concept often causes. "We got it before it took," Forester said.

The strike began Thursday, March 26 and ended Sunday, March 29. Local 594 won on every demand. The company had to promote 60 people to group leader and pay them retroactive to October 21, 1986. It had to make whole transferred employees whose seniority, promotion and recall rights had been violated. It had to bring 16 more classifications into Plant 6, including sweeper, repair, inspector, clerk, and stockkeeper. There are now 60 more inspectors in Plant 6 than before the strike.

GM had to compensate employees who were misclassified. It had to repay $550,000 to skilled trades workers as compensation for subcontracting and return the work to the bargaining unit. The five-minute break was restored, and Plant 6 workers got $90-95 apiece to make up for the period it was suspended. Certain assemblers who had been ordered to seal floors received a total of $143,000. Attendance at team meetings and at training was made voluntary. Management's total liability for all the contract violations was $1.5 million.

Since the strike, President Douglas says, the foremen's attitude is, "We just want to get along. We had our marching orders from above." The team coordinators still exist, but Committeemen Simmons and Forester believe they will fade away. Teams continue to meet on a voluntary basis, after work, on overtime.

Simmons and Forester were asked if the team concept in Plant 6 had been cleansed of its objectionable content. "We'll have to police it forever," they replied.

Postscript

In January 1988 Local 594 was ready to hit the bricks again over the team concept—but management backed down five minutes before the strike deadline.

According to Don Douglas, management began to "hit around the edges" in Plant 6, trying to plant the seeds of team concept once again. Workers were called off the job to meetings and classifications were infringed upon. The local made the contract violations in Plant 6 part of its contract package in 1987-88 bargaining. Ten months to the day after the first strike began, Douglas said, management "decided to give up the fight on it."

The frosting on the cake came in April 1988, when Douglas's point on how GM decides to place work was proven. GM announced that it would start a second shift in Plant 6, to built more full-size pick-ups. GM chose Pointiac in spite of the fact that two other GM plants were also already building the pick-up—Ft. Wayne, Indiana and Oshawa, Ontario—and both of those plants used the team concept.

23. Warren Hydra-Matic: Just Say No (Four Times)

At General Motors' Hydra-Matic plant in Warren, Michigan the team concept went down to an overwhelming defeat, not once but four times within five months. The proposal created an atmosphere of strife in the plant—but it also mobilized rank and filers to organize on a level not seen before.

The contract was first jointly proposed by management and the UAW Local 909 shop committee in Otober 1987. Its most important features were a four-day, ten-hour work week and the "Bullseye Concept," an advanced version of the team concept. (Why would management tempt workers with a name that begs to have the final three letters changed?)

The Local 909 shop committee and Hydra-Matic management had begun joint exploration of "innovative" ideas in the summer of 1987. They visited three of GM's team concept plants: Janesville, Wisconsin; Bay City, Michigan; and Tarrytown, New York. The Janesville plant has a four-day, ten-hour work week. The company newsletter reported on the trip:

> The Warren team was particularly impressed with Janesville's union and management relations. They report that distinguishing between the two groups was a challenge. Janesville's union and management both supported the same things and treated each other with respect. Both union and management also dressed in casual clothes...
>
> Human Resource Manager Floor Operations, John Oakley said, "We also went there to look at what that plant did to get new business. They recently acquired new truck business out of Pontiac."[1]

Bullseye Concept

The "Bullseye Concept" goes further than most team concept contracts in eliminating an independent role for the union. If adopted, it would have completed a process already begun by Hydra-Matic management of breaking the plant down into "business teams." The business team structure means that managers in each area of the plant—such as subassembly, final assembly, stamping, wheels—run their areas to a certain extent as

---

• *GM Warren Hydra-Matic*
• *Location: Warren, Michigan*
• *Employment: 3,500-3,700 hourly*
• *Product: transmissions, wheels, and other parts*
• *Production began: 1961*
• *Team Concept: voted down 1988*
• *UAW Local 909*
  Address: 24249 Mound Road, Warren, MI 48091
  Phone: 313 / 759-4320

---

separate businesses. The profit or loss of each business team is reported separately. The Bullseye language claimed that "team members of the Warren plant will be the owner-operators of their function."

For a union, buying into business teams means the erosion of solidarity. If Warren workers as "owner-operators" began to identify with the profit goals of their business teams, they would have a material interest in competing with each other. The final assembly team, for example, could make a higher profit if subassemblies were "cheaper." It would be in the final assembly team's interest to cut jobs in the subassembly team.

It has been traditional for unionists to oppose "enterprise unionism"—identifying with the company and its goals rather than with fellow workers in other companies. Business teams go one step further—to "department unionism."

The role of the district committeeperson under the Bullseye Concept was to be "a joint business partner with the business team manager in the areas he/she is elected to represent. They should, while still maintaining the role elected to, assume more direct involvement in the matters of business that affect the team they represent."

Team captains (equivalent to what is usually called team leader or coordinator) were to "function as a joint partner with area advisors [foremen]." In addition, the proposal called for hourly "group leaders" who would serve as joint partners with the "area coordinators" (general foremen). The Bullseye language describing the roles of teams, "team captains," group leaders, advisors, and business team managers is reprinted at the end of this chapter.

The aspect of the Bullseye proposal which most disturbed Local 909 members was that all of the hourly "partners," except the committeepersons, would be appointed by the shop committee. (In most other team concept plants these positions are elected by fellow team members, and in some they are chosen by seniority.) Shop Chairman Carl Eden at various times defended this proposal on the grounds that 1) management did not want elections, 2) elections would play into the hands of management, and 3) these employees worked for the shop committee, so the shop committee had to feel comfortable with them. Because of obvious membership dissatisfaction, before the first vote the proposal was changed so that the lowest level "partners," the team captains, would be chosen by team members.

Team captains, group leaders and district committeepersons were all to find "ways for constant improvement in uptime, cost, SPC [statistical process control], safety, housekeeping, running of meetings, communications with necessary parties to insure the success of team members they serve."

Originally, the job description for all three "partners," plus committeepersons, the local union president, and the shop chair, included the sentence, *"They must support the joint process."* In the final version this sentence was changed so that committeepersons were only "encouraged" to support the joint process.

Four-Day Week

Hydra-Matic first floated the idea of a four-day, ten-hour week in July 1987. Management saw it as a way of combatting absenteeism. When it was proposed in the contract in October of that year, it was even more controversial than the Bullseye Concept. Working ten hours per day at straight time, production workers would have received only the 58 minutes of paid relief time mandated in the National Agreement, with no unpaid lunch break. The example given in the shop committee's summary said that this "grand total" of 58 minutes would be divided into a half-hour lunch break and two 14-minute breaks.

The contract also contained provisions for recre-

ational areas including a basketball court, putting green, shuffleboard and horseshoes. The joke in the plant became: "When are we supposed to use them—during our 14-minute break? Or are we supposed to come in on our day off?"

The new schedule was to run for a six-month trial period, followed by a vote on whether to continue it.

In the skilled trades, only workers assigned to construction and cribs would be on the four-day schedule. Preventive maintenance workers would remain on five days. According to the shop committee, this would practically eliminate skilled trades overtime.

During weeks with holidays, the plant would work four eight-hour days—that is, workers would not get an extra day off. Or, by mutual agreement, the plant could work two 11-hour days and one 10-hour day (a total of 32 hours), all at straight time.

Bereavement leave would remain at 24 hours. Thus a worker would either have to come into the plant and work six hours on the third day of his or her bereavement, or take that time as Paid Absence Allowance.

The contract also stated that management would be liable for no back pay resulting from grievances over the four-day week.

Hydra-Matic workers were horrified at the idea of working 10 hours with less break time than they'd had before during an eight-hour day (a half-hour unpaid lunch and two 23-minute breaks). Women workers in particular did not like the idea of a ten-hour day because they would get home too late to spend time with their children. President Frank Hammer, who opposed the contract, wrote, "The people that agreed to this have *forgotten* what it's like to put those kind of hours in on assembly lines such as ours!"

A Progressive Plant

At some plants, the team concept has been sold as a somewhat bitter pill the union must swallow in order to save the plant from closing. Union officials recognize that team concept is not what they or the members would prefer but they support it because it seems like the only viable alternative. Not so at Warren. The Local 909 shop committee maintained throughout that the Bullseye Concept and the four-day, ten-hour week were *workers'* demands.

"This is without question the best Local Agreement ever negotiated at Hydra-Matic Warren," said one shop committee leaflet. "We want to emphasize how proud we are of what we have achieved...the real value of this contract lies in the fact that employes will now have a

...AND BEST OF ALL, IT PUTS THE UNION RIGHT IN THE CENTER OF THINGS!!

BULLSEYE CONCEPT

© '89 UE NEWS HUCK
HUCK-KONOPACKI

say in the way things get done around here, and in the committees to get new business and keep the business we have."

Management stopped production lines for a half hour for the shop comittee to hold informational meetings. These meetings were attended by management personnel. The Local 909 executive board estimated that the shutdown cost a quarter million dollars worth of production.

After over two weeks of heated discussion in the plant, the membership voted the proposal down 1,868-177—91 percent "no." It was the largest ratification turnout in the history of 909, twice as large as for the previous contract. Two days later, the size of the membership meeting—450—set another record. Angry members passed motions for the shop committee to set up shift meetings to get input from members and to bargain a new contract.

However, claiming "confusion" over the defeated proposal, the shop committee scheduled a second vote. They received the backing of the UAW's regional office. The shop committee and management published a six-page glossy brochure they called "a joint local negotiations summary." Again management stopped production lines for half-hour meetings—losing another quarter million dollars worth of production. The only change made from the first proposal was that the four-day week would get a 90-day trial period instead of six months.

This time around scare tactics were added to the hard sell. For several years plants in the Hydra-Matic Diision had been quite vulnerable to loss of contracts. A competitive mentality existed among the different plants. Local union leaders had been taken to Mexico to observe how much cheaper GM could do their work there. Thus workers were already attuned to threats of job loss.

The shop committee argued that the new agreement was needed to "change the image of this plant from a non-profitable, dying plant to a progressive, innovative plant." A committeeman from Eden's Blue & Gold caucus put out a leaflet which said, "When this contract was voted down the first time, I feel it gave this plant and our jobs a sentence to death row, by highlighting this plant across the country. Vote it down again and we will probably put the death switch to this plant and our jobs."

Many 909 members were angered at being asked to vote again after the overwhelming rejection. On the second vote, held in the plant this time rather than at the union hall, production workers voted down the four-day week 1,342-707 and the rest of the agreement 1,169-876. Skilled trades were not asked to vote on the four-day week again, but rejected the rest of the agreement 627-67.

What Made the Difference

While the vote was closer the second time, it is in striking contrast to other locals which have voted twice

on team concept, such as Chrysler's Trenton and Newark plants (see Chapter 13). In those plants a heavy dose of threats that the plant would lose work or close altogether achieved ratification the second time around.

The difference at 909 was the open, organized, active and well-researched opposition, both from a section of the local union leadership and from the rank and file. Before the tentative agreement was even reached, the Bullseye Concept language was leaked to the membership and widely circulated in the plant. President Hammer and the local executive board put out a total of nine leaflets explaining the proposed contract, informing members of the status of events, and urging workers to attend meetings.

One of these was a detailed, five-page analysis of the contract by Hammer which came out before the first vote. The analysis went through the proposal item-by-item, and contrasted the verbal and written claims made about the agreement with the actual language of the contract.

In addition to the executive board, rank and file workers were active on their own. T-shirts were printed up in blue and gold which read "1987 Shop Committee Bullseye World Tour" and listed the plants the shop committee had visited. Stamped across the front were the words, "SOLD OUT."

Many cartoons were drawn, copied, and passed around the plant. "Vote No" was painted on transmission cases as they moved down the line. Someone took out a "Sweetest Day" ad in a Detroit daily newspaper (Sweetest Day is similar to Valentine's Day). It read:

> Carl E. & Shop Committee
> Roses are red
> Violets are blue
> We on management
> Really love you

One hand-lettered leaflet addressed to the chair of the shop committee asked, "Carl—What exactly was it you didn't understand? Was it the 'N' or the 'O'?"

After the second vote, more than 100 workers picketed the UAW regional office to protest interference in the local's affairs.

Third Time Around

When negotiations resumed after the second defeat, management continued to insist on the Bullseye, unchanged. They also wanted to institute the four-day, ten-hour week as a "pilot program" in one area of the plant. The shop committee organized supporters to come to a union meeting, which mandated yet a third vote on the Bullseye Concept. The proposal also would have allowed an area of the plant to petition for the four-day week.

Big signs appeared in the plant calling for the recall of the shop committee. One worker remarked that he had voted for the contract the first time, but would vote no this time because of the unfairness of bringing it back again. On January 21 the Bullseye went down by 66 percent—the same margin as the second vote.

Four's the Charm?

It is hard to believe, but the shop committee still did not take no for an answer. On March 20 a relatively small membership meeting made up mainly of shop committee supporters voted to schedule a *fourth* ratification vote. The 10-hour day was no longer part of the proposal, but the Bullseye Concept—including "group leaders" appointed by the shop committee—was unchanged.

However, three things happened between the third and fourth votes which helped members to understand the true nature of what the shop committee wanted from the Bullseye Concept.

One was that it became widely known that the rejected contract included some language which the shop committee had not told anyone about. President Hammer, in a report to the membership, publicized the fact that the contract would have let management split Department 88 (transmission final assembly) into four overtime equalization groups, one for each line. And, as Hammer wrote:

> Even though the contract was rejected three times, management—with the Shop Committee's blessing—split Dept. 88 into four equalization groups anyway! This is the same Management and Shop Committee that talks about a new era of "JOINTNESS" based on "TRUST" and "WALK LIKE YOU TALK."

The second thing was a petition by members of Department 88 to keep their overtime equalization department-wide. President Hammer's report tells the story:

> 274 workers from Dept. 88 signed a petition requesting that the Shop Committee take out the language in the new agreement setting up the four separate lists.
>
> The hundreds of Final Assembly workers who signed the petition were concerned that management would play favorites by forcing the four lines to *compete* for the overtime, thus eliminating any hope of solidarity and equity between the lines....
>
> In the course of this petition getting signed, the workers in Dept. 88 got a good taste of what Team Concept and the Bullseye Concept are all about.
>
> One of the workers who helped initiate and circulate the petition is an individual by the name of Ray Eaton....He happens to be the "Line Chairman" for Final Assembly Line #3. [This department had elected "line chairmen" approximately a year previously, as part of a management quality campaign.]... Concerned about the fate of his Department and responsive to the workers who elected him, he took it upon himself to get signatures on the petition—which, when completed, were submitted to the Shop Committee.
>
> According to Ray, Shop Committeeman Art Dennis and his own District Committeeman, Frank Warren [both from Eden's Blue & Gold caucus], got all over him for daring to circulate the petition. Among many other things, he was told that *as a line coordina-tor, he could not get involved in union activities, and was threatened with being removed from the job* he was elected to do.
>
> He was told that his petition was most unwelcome because it was contrary to what his District Committeeman and management wanted to implement. Dennis and Warren let Brother Eaton know that circulating a petition was not "appropriate" to a Line Chairman, and was counter to the "program."
>
> If that wasn't enough, Brother Ray Eaton was called into the office where his General Foreman, Mitchell Budzynowski ("Area Coordinator?") and his foreman ("Team Adviser?") got all over him, too.... Budzynowski told Brother Eaton that he should *stop his union activity or else be subject to being removed....*
>
> According to the Agreement on the "New Bullseye Concept," the concept is intended to "insure employes some authority in the quality of the product, the cost of the product, *and the working and personal environment of his work place."* It's clear that Management/ Shop Committee mean just the opposite. Judging from Brother Eaton's experience, the Bullseye Concept will work to strip employes of any and all authority if the employes' actions/activities... don't coincide with Management's (and the Shop Committee's) directives.

The third thing that happened was that President Hammer discovered a document which had been signed by the Shop Committee on September 28, 1987, before the first vote on the agreement. No member of the Local 909 executive board had seen it before. It essentially made the contract a "living agreement." Hammer warned that such clauses had been used at other plants to reopen and waive the contract without the approval of the membership.

Management, perhaps embarrassed by the shop committee's continued pushing of a lost cause, refused to let the fourth vote be held in the plant. Nearly 1,600 members came to the union hall to vote—and turned down the agreement by 81 percent.

Within a few weeks a strong movement was under way to recall the shop committee.

Remarkable Persistence

Those who oppose team concept and other concessions have a tough row to hoe these days. The companies do not want to take no for an answer, and it sometimes seems that UAW locals are falling like dominoes. Up against these odds, the stand taken by the members of Local 909 is even more remarkable.

Important aspects of the Bullseye proposal and its companion, the 10-hour day, are reprinted below. Although the language was rejected, it is an instructive example of what management might have in store for local union members less persistent than those at Local 909.

Notes

1. Oakley's comment refers to GM's whipsawing of the Janesville plant against Pontiac Truck and Bus. See Chapter 22 for details.

Appendix

The contract proposal printed below is excerpted from "A New First: A Joint Local Negotiations Summary," published jointly by GM Warren Hydra-Matic and UAW Local 909 in October 1987. This proposal was rejected by Local 909.

Memorandum of Understanding on Alternative Work Schedule

1. This agreement is temporary, to apply for two 90-day trial periods commencing on the date of implementation of the Alternative Work Schedule. Prior to the expiration of the trial period, the parties will hold a conference to review their experiences with the Alternative Work Schedule and to discuss extending the Alternative Work Schedule beyond the two 90-day expiration dates by mutual agreement in writing. In the event of failure to extend the Alternative Work Schedule, the provisions of the GM-UAW National Agreement shall be reinstated on the first Monday following either of 90-day expiration dates.

2. In accordance with the 1984 GM-UAW Contract Settlement Agreement, item 12, "National Agreement Changes and/or Waivers," the purpose of the Memorandum is to provide for an Alternative Work Schedule for all employees regularly assigned to designated plant operations on the first, second, and third shifts as designated by Management. However, the provisions of this Memorandum shall not serve to modify, alter, or supersede any provision of the GM-UAW National Agreement unless specifically stated herein.

3. The Alternative Work Schedule shall consist of a regular forty (40) hour weekly work schedule, starting on Monday of each week, based on four (4) ten (10) hour working days as follows:

Regularly Scheduled Shift Hours

MO	TU	WE	TH	FR	SA	SU
10	10	10	10	X	X	X

WEEKLY WORKING HOURS: 40

Furthermore, the normal allocated relief time will be redistributed not to exceed the relief time provided under the National Agreement. Management will continue to administer scheduled production so as to guarantee no loss of production.

For example, this could mean a schedule wherein 30 minutes of the allocated 58 minutes tag relief, as provided for a 10-hour shift, could be utilized for a mid-day break/lunch period, and the balance of the 58 minutes, or 28 minutes, could then be divided into two breaks of 14 minutes each.

It is understood that the provisions of this Memorandum do not prejudice management's exclusive right to schedule and determine the working hours pursuant to Paragraph (8) of the GM-UAW National Agreement and the "Working Hours" provisions of the GM-UAW National Agreement and management's exclusive right to determine and assign manpower to the above four (4) day, ten (10) hour schedule and/or the regular five (5) day, eight (8) hour work schedule.

4. For the Employees working the (40) hour work week based on the five (5) and eight (8) hour working days, the Paragraphs of the "Working Hours" section of the GM-UAW National Agreement shall apply.

5. For the employee working the forty (40) hour work week based on the four (4) ten (10) hour working days, the Paragraphs of the "Working Hours" section of the GM-UAW National Agreement shall apply *except* as modified below:

a. For the Purpose of Computing Overtime Premium Pay:

(81) For the purpose of computing overtime premium pay, the regular working day is ten hours and the regular working week is forty hours.

b. Straight Time:

(84) (a) For the first ten hours in any continuous twenty-four hour period, beginning with the starting time of the employee's shift.

c. Time and One Half:

(85) (a) For time worked in excess of ten hours in any continuous twenty-four hours, beginning with the starting time of the employee's shift, except if such time is worked on a Sunday or holiday, when double time will be paid as provided below.

d. Night Shift Premiums:

(89) A night shift premium on night shift earnings, including overtime premium pay, will be paid to an employee for time worked on shift scheduled to start in accordance with the following chart:

Scheduled Shift Starting Time Amount of Premium

1. On or after 11:00 a.m. before 7:00 p.m. —five percent
2. On or after 7:00 p.m. and before 4:45 a.m.—ten percent
3. After 4:45 a.m. and before 6:00 a.m. —ten percent until 7:00 a.m.

When an employee covered by (1) above is scheduled to work more than eleven hours and until or beyond 4:00 a.m. he/she shall be paid ten percent for the hours worked beyond 2:00 a.m.

In applying the above night shift premium provisions, an employee shall be paid the premium rate, if any, which attaches to the shift he works on a particular day.

e. Holidays:

During any week in which any of the holidays specified in Paragraph (203) of the GM-UAW National Agreement fall, management may schedule the forty (40) hour work week based on the regular five (5) eight (8) hour work days schedule. In such event, the paragraphs of the "Working Hours" section of the GM-UAW National Agreement shall apply.

The parties may, by mutual agreement, elect in advance to waive Paragraph 5.E above and schedule an Alternative Work Schedule, as provided in this Memorandum, for a week in which any of the holidays specified in Paragraph (203) fall provided, however, that eligible employees receive eight (8) hours holiday pay for each of the specified holidays, computed at their regular straight-time hourly rate exclusive of overtime premium.

During our discussions, the parties agreed that in weeks where Holidays occur, if the union requests and the parties agree, the following schedule will apply: two (2) eleven (11)-hour shifts and one (1) ten (10-) hour shift, with no added shift premium or overtime premium applicable during this period.

6.a. Notwithstanding the provisions of this Memorandum, employees eligible for bereavement pay pursuant to Paragraph (218b) of the GM-UAW National Agreement, will continue to be compensated on the basis of the amount of wages the employees otherwise would have earned during their straight-time hours on the three (3) excused bereavement days, subject to maximum of twenty-four (24) hours per eligible death. The employees who receive pay pursuant to the provisions of the GM-UAW National Agreement for such absences will have the following two options to supplement the hours worked or paid in a given week in order to equal forty (40) hours:

1. Employees may apply for unused Paid Absence Allowance providing they have met eligibility requirements as outlined in the GM-UAW National Agreement, or

2. Employees may take two (2) ten (10) hour days and one (1) day of four (4) hours as excused bereavement absences and work the remaining six (6) hours.

b. Jury duty pay and short term military pay will be compensated on the basis of the amount of wages the employee otherwise would have earned during straight-time hours subject to a maximum of ten (10) hours per day for any day eligible under the provisions of the GM-UAW National Agreement.

7. For the purpose of administering the Vacation Pay Allowance and the Paid Absence Allowance provisions of the GM-UAW National Agreement for employees on the Alternative Work Schedule, an employee may use his paid absence allowance credit and his vacation pay allowance in accordance with the provisions of the National Agreement, with the understanding that employees will be credited as having used such allowances at the same rate as the amount of scheduled working hours that they do not work.

8. It is understood that implementation of the Alternative Work Schedule may impact the administration of GM-UAW Benefit Plan Agreements. Therefore, the parties agree that, if necessary applicable provisions associated with such benefit plans will be administered in a manner which does not increase the cost to the Corporation or loss of pay to the employee in comparison with the application of such benefit plan provisions to employees who work a regular five (5) day, eight (8) hour work schedule. In addition, the same treatment shall apply in the administration of Workers' Compensation and Unemployment Compensation Laws.

9. Issues that arise as a result of implementation of this Memorandum will be discussed at the Management/Shop Committee Step of the Grievance Procedure. If such issues are not resolved, they shall be reduced to writing and presented at this step of the Grievance Procedure. There shall be no liability as a result of implementation of this Memorandum.

10. The local parties, by mutual agreement, subject to the approval of the Corporation and the International Union, are specifically author-

ized on an ongoing basis to review, evaluate, and effect other changes or modifications to National Agreement provisions necessary to facilitate successful implementation and maintenance of the Alternative Work Schedule provided for herein.

11. Either party may elect to cancel this Memorandum by presentation of written notice to the other party. Thereafter, this Memorandum will be void effective the first Monday following the fourteenth day subsequent to the receipt of such written notice.

The New Bullseye Concept

For the first time, all workers will have a real opportunity, if they so desire, to have a voice in their work area and be a part of the decisions that affect them on a day to day basis.

This new concept provides for a team of eight to twelve people, who will select their own Team Captain from among themselves. The team will discuss their job, work environment, and make suggestions for improvement or changes they think are necessary.

The team and Team Captains will be assisted by a group leader who will be selected by the Shop Committee. The team will have access to "all" information relating to the area they work in, in addition to plant information, the team concept is strictly voluntary.

The exact langauge reads as follows:

A. The purpose of the Bullseye concept is a commitment by Union and Management to provide employee involvement in the operation of each Business Team area. This new concept is intended to insure employees some authority in the quality of the product, the cost of the product and the working and personal environment of his workplace.

B. Team members of the Warren Plant will be the owner-operators of their function and will be supported in a new way by the organization. Teams will be composed of 8-12 members whose focus will be quality and cost effectiveness of the parts they manufacture, and their working and personal environment, looking for ways of achieving constant improvement.

They will help to find ways for constant improvement in quality, cost, uptime, training, SPC, safety, and housekeeping, to become key parts of each team member's day, working in a team atmosphere.

They will have all necessary business information; they will be asked to be a part of business decisions that need to be made on a short- and long-term basis. The organization focus will be to insure the success of the team members and the team's business to insure the overall success of the Warren Plant's future. They will be encouraged to support the joint process.

C. Team Captains are leaders chosen by their peers. These people will function in a role to help coordinate the overall needs of team members. They will function on a part-time basis as a joint partner with area Advisors when needed or continue on regular assignments.

They will provide leadership by having the skills to train fellow team members to be knowledgeable and involved in the areas of quality, information sharing, helping to find ways for constant improvement in uptime, cost, SPC, safety, housekeeping, running of meetings, and communications with necessary parties to insure the success of team members they serve. They will be encouraged to support the joint process.

D. Group Leaders are chosen by the Shop Committee and reviewed by the Joint Steering Committee.

This person will function on a full-time basis in a role to help coordinate the overall needs of all Team Captains in their Business Team when needed or to continue on regular assignments. They will serve as a joint partner with the area Coordinators. They will provide leadership by having the skills to train team Captains and other team members to be knowledgeable and involved in areas of quality, information sharing, helping to find ways for constant improvement in uptime, cost,

SPC, safety, housekeeping, running of meetings, communication with necessary parties to insure the success of team members they serve. As group leaders they will be direct line to the District Committeeman. They will be encouraged to support the joint process.

E. The District Committeeman's role will be one of a joint business partner with the Business Team Manager in the areas he/she is elected to represent. They should, while still maintaining the role elected to, assume more direct involvement in the matters of business that affect the team they represent.

They should lead in areas of team concerns and problem solving, insuring trust is the cornerstone of each Business Team, looking for ways to have constant improvement in quality, cost, uptime, being involved in short-and long-term planning, safety, housekeeping, training, SPC, helping decisions to be made at the lowest possible level. They will be encouraged to support the joint process.

F. Advisor will replace the traditional concept of a supervisor. Their new role will encompass a much larger span of control (e.g., 1-50 as compared to 1-20) as we improve. They will function as joint partners with the Team Leaders.

They will assigned to areas by Management's staff and will be reviewed by the Joint Steering Committee.

They will provide leadership by having the skills to train fellow team members to be knowledgeable and involved in the areas of quality, information sharing, helping to make job assignments, helping to find ways for constant improvement in uptime, cost, SPC, safety, housekeeping, running of meetings, communications with necessary parties to insure the success of team members they serve. They must support the joint process.

G. Coordinator represents the direct line support to the Business Team Manager, District Committeeman, and the Shop Committee.

They will be assigned to Business Teams by Management's staff and will be reviewed by the Joint Steering Committee. They will function as a joint partner with the Group Leaders. They will coordinate in a role to support Advisors in their short-term and long-term needs and goals of the organization. They should be able to train, provide leadership to Advisors, and to insure the success of the team members. They must support the joint process. In addition, Group Leaders will be appointed for Skilled Trades, Material, and Sanitation.

H. Business Team Managers will have a greatly expanded role in this matrix organization. They will be expected to work jointly with a District Committeeman, and the Shop Committee where needed, to interface and manage a business function with total responsibility to joint leadership for those operations. They will be expected to foster a team relationship based on trust, quality, maintain a budget, meet productivity goals, develop short and long-term plans, look for ways for constant improvement, safety, housekeeping, uptime, inventory levels, training, SPC, and to force decisions to be made at the lowest possible level. They will also insure compliance with the Local and National contract provisions. They must support the joint process.

I. Functional Staff Heads will continue to coordinate staff support areas. They will interface with the staff support individuals assigned to the Business Teams. They will also be responsible for long range planning and coordination with divisional resources in each functional group. The functional staff will also be responsible for a regular interface with the Shop Committee in his/her area of responsibility (e.g., manufacturing engineering). They must support the joint process.

J. The role of the Plant Manager's Staff, Shop Committee, Local Shop Chairman, President, Region 1 Representative, under the Warren Plant concept, requires a commitment to create the environment for change and to reward those behaviors which lead to employee involvement and world leadership as described in the Joint Memorandum of Understanding. They must support the joint process.

24. Hermosillo, Mexico: Concepto de Grupo

Auto workers in the United States and Canada live under the specter of runaway plants. One of the multi-nationals' strongest weapons in their battle to convince U.S. employees to work for less is the threat of Third World workers who work for pennies an hour. It's not surprising that the companies look with favor on countries where they can pay workers $166 a month.

What is surprising is that even labor this cheap is not cheap enough for the multinationals. In Mexico, Ford and Volkswagen have both forced their employees to strike because the companies refused to pay legally required cost-of-living increases. And as if chiseling on wages weren't enough, the "team concept" (*concepto de grupo* in Spanish) has been introduced.

Production of the subcompact Tracer for export to the United States began at Ford's new plant in Hermosillo, Mexico in November 1986. The company announced proudly that because of new labor relations methods, the plant would be immune from strikes. A year later, the plant was producing 300 Tracers a day, all for export to the U.S., but it has not been strike-free.

With 1,300 employees, Ford is the largest employer in Hermosillo, a city of half a million. The surrounding state of Sonora, which borders the U.S., is largely agricultural. The first Ford workers were hired in 1984. They were told they would have unlimited opportunities to advance and a chance to participate in decision-making. Relations between management and workers were to be those of colleagues, not adversaries. Many of those hired were middle class young men who thought working for a multinational, even in a factory, would be the way to get ahead. The average age was 22.

High Caliber, Low Pay

Bert Serre, a Ford public affairs manager, explained the set-up of the Hermosillo plant: "Our employees there received the highest level of training of any assembly plant employees anywhere. We have a very high caliber of individual, either with a high school degree or high school equivalent. Our training program is very stringent. We took them through two special training centers.

- *Ford Hermosillo*
- *Location: Hermosillo, Mexico*
- *Employment: 1,300*
- *Product: Tracer*
- *Production began: November 1986*
- *Team Concept began: November 1986*
- *Sindicato Nacional de Trabajadores de Ford Motor Co.*

"With a new workforce there are not the rules and classifications that you encounter here [in the United States]. They have more flexibility in how they approach their jobs, they can do things that classifications do not allow people here to do. It's more along Japanese lines. There is only one classification—technician—and no special category for skilled trades. And our training is ongoing."

The first workers hired were trained for six months. Many were taken to the Mazda plant in Hiroshima, Japan, or to Ford plants in Belgium and Spain. Later, training was cut to three months, with a week spent on group problem-solving techniques.

The trainees were divided into groups and given a variety of games to play and tasks to accomplish. They ranged from constructing a cube out of paper to deciding what to do with a lazy worker. The groups were told that they would solve technical problems that might arise on the assembly line, figure out how to cover for absenteeism, decide who should get days off, and decide on the correct punishment for a worker who made too many mistakes.

Demian V., a young Ford worker who was present when the plant opened, explained the plant philosophy this way: "We were supposed to believe that as an individual it was the responsibility of each of us to contribute to resolving the problems on the line." The team concept was enthusiastically received by the workers, most of whom had not worked in a factory before.

Teams in the Hermosillo plant were large—20-30 members in the assembly department. Each team elected a leader, called an "especialista de producto" (product specialist), who was paid slightly more and then became part of management. According to Demian, management usually had its own candidate in mind for this position. If management and the workers chose the same candidate, fine. If not, management prevailed.

Management initially wanted the teams to meet during their ten-minute break or their half-hour lunch period. (Lunch breaks are usually for one hour in Mexican factories.) The paid work day was nine hours, 7:30 a.m. to 5 p.m. When workers were reluctant to use their breaks for team meetings, it was decided that the specialist would call meetings as needed, to solve problems as they arose. In fact, of course, it was the superintendent or supervisor who decided when meetings should be called. And before long, only the specialist and facilitators were asked to stay after work to solve problems.

Job rotation was supposed to be one of the important features of the team system. There was no pay-for-knowledge system as such (although workers were to receive yearly raises if they kept up with their training and had good records), but the workers wanted job rotation as a way to combat the boredom of the assembly line. At first the workers rotated but as production increased, the right to rotate became the say of the specialist.

As in many U.S. plants, during training the Hermosillo workers were told that "Quality Is Job One" for Ford, and that therefore they could stop the assembly line if they ran into a problem. The problem would then be corrected right away. Once production began, however, if a worker stopped the line the specialist and the supervisor immediately turned it back on again. A utility worker was brought in to try to fix the immediate defect while the line was moving. The original idea of taking time to *solve* the problem was out the window.

The supposedly harmonious relationship between management and workers began to break down fairly quickly. For one thing, the workers knew that the Hermosillo plant was way behind Ford's other two Mexican plants in pay: 108,000 pesos per month vs. 180,000 in October 1986 (108,000 pesos at that time was equal to $138.36). And Ford was stingy about raises and about providing benefits. For another thing, the jobs were overloaded. For a third, all the promises of getting ahead and a consultative relationship between management and workers proved, in practice, to be false. Even such simple requests as the right to rotate fell on deaf ears.

Using Teams to Organize

When the harmonious relationship began to break down, there was, as Demian points out, a pitfall—from management's point of view—in the team structure. "Once the worker realizes what the philosophy means, and rejects it, then the structure of the group can help the workers to achieve union goals.

"We took advantage of the group structure. We democratically elected a union representative in each group, and they even rotated. When we had group meetings they took on a union character. Our idea was that every member should participate.

"The company threatened us. We went to our union officials and asked them to call a general assembly. We told them that they themselves were in danger of being displaced by the very philosophy of the group concept."

Like most Mexican unions, the National Union of Ford Workers (Sindicato Nacional de Trabajadores de Ford Motor Co.), is tightly controlled by an entrenched bureaucracy which is intertwined with the ruling political party and the government. The Mexican workers call their union officials *charros*, which can be translated as "corrupt, pro-company bureaucrats."

The *charros* in the Hermosillo plant were not anxious to get into a confrontation with Ford. They asked the membership to place their trust in their officials for negotiation of a first contract. The young workers, however, insisted that the general assembly (membership meeting) should be the highest authority, so that everyone could have a voice in what the union would do in bargaining.

In October 1986 a spontaneous work stoppage protesting the low salaries spread throughout the plant. At the plant's official dedication on November 14, attended by the President of Mexico and Chairman Donald Peterson from Ford World Headquarters, workers in the assembly division wore red armbands as a protest against their low pay. In early 1987, as the speed of the line was increased, spontaneous work stoppages over job overloading broke out.

When the union contract came due for a wage reopener on March 1, 1987, Ford offered only an 18 percent increase. This was despite the fact that the company had not paid the government-decreed 20 percent increase due in January (because of runaway inflation, the Mexican government orders cost-of-living adjustments for all workers every three months). Workers had to strike for 39 days to finally receive a raise of 54 percent, which included the 20 percent cost-of-living increase due in April. Their increase brought them up to 166,320 pesos per month—by that time worth only $143.

Immediately after the strike Ford fired 13 members of the strike committee, and then two more workers who participated in a protest against the firings.

According to Demian, the teams at Hermosillo still function, but the workers no longer believe in them. "They had already begun to see the real nature of the Ford Motor Co.," he says, "but the strike confirmed it."

The Hermosillo plant is still not on a par with Ford's older plant at Chihuahua. As of October 1, 1987, they were earning 255,717 pesos a month, equivalent to $166.55.

Never Too Cheap

The Hermosillo story, which is far from over, contains two lessons for North American workers:

One, Ford's attempts to get more work for less pay out of its Mexican workers illustrates the futility of U.S. workers trying to "compete" with Third World labor. Labor will *never* be cheap enough to satisfy Ford (or GM, or Volkswagen), no matter how many concessions U.S. workers make.

Two, Mexican workers (and Korean workers as well, as the militant strikes there show) cannot be bamboozled any more easily than workers anywhere else. Indeed, if the events at Hermosillo are any indication, they are ahead of workers in the U.S. in understanding the team concept and reacting to it.

25. Nissan: Teams Without Unions

By John Junkerman

Jackie Dixon is a 47-year-old mechanic. He owned an engine-repair shop in Union City, Tennessee until 1983, when he moved 150 miles across the state to take a job at Nissan Motor Company's assembly plant in Smyrna.

Because of his experience, Dixon was assigned to train other employees before production began. Once the plant started operating, Dixon assumed he would check and repair engines. Instead, he was placed on the assembly line. Younger, less qualified workers landed the job he thought he deserved.

Dixon requested a transfer, availing himself of Nissan's widely praised open-door policy of worker-management relations. "I kept asking, and I kept getting deeper and deeper in the hole," he recalls. "I was following the open-door policy, but from then on, the judgment fell on me."

When Dixon pinched a nerve in his shoulder and was taken off the assembly line on doctor's orders, his supervisor ridiculed him in front of his co-workers. "He would say things like, 'Jackie's bones are getting old,' or, 'Jackie's got a little ache, so he's going to the doctor again.'" Dixon was reassigned to a job supplying the assembly line with parts. But word that he was a troublemaker followed him.

A month later, Dixon was called into the supervisor's office and told that he was not doing his job. Dixon protested that there had been no complaints about his performance, and then, in anger, told the supervisor he would file suit for harassment.

His supervisor didn't flinch. "He said, 'Go for it,'

John Junkerman, a free-lance writer, reported on labor-management relations at Nissan for PBS's "Frontline" in 1984. The research was supported, in part, by grants from The Dick Goldensohn Fund and Essential Information, Inc. This chapter originally appeared in The Progressive *in June 1987 titled "Nissan, Tennessee: It ain't what it's cracked up to be."*

- *Nissan Motor Company*
- *Location: Smyrna, Tennessee*
- *Employment: 3,300 on two shifts*
- *Product: Sentra and hard-body pickup trucks*
- *Production began: 1983*
- *Team Concept began: 1983*
- *UAW Organizing Office*
  Address : Route 12, New Highway, Smyrna, TN 37167
  Phone: 615 / 459-2292

Dixon recalls. "It was like he was saying, 'I'm Nissan. I'm God. Nobody can whup us.'" Later that day, Dixon was fired for threatening his supervisor and insubordination.

"It's a total nightmare," says Dixon. "I wish I had never seen the place. I wish I had never heard of Nissan." Dixon is suing Nissan for libel and slander.

Fall from Grace

Nissan's Smyrna factory is the flagship of some 500 Japanese assembly and manufacturing plants in the United States today. As many as 250,000 Americans now work in these plants, and that number is likely to surpass one million in the next decade.

When the Smyrna plant opened as the largest single Japanese investment in the United States, it was hailed as a model of worker-management cooperation. Nissan stressed a system based on teamwork, cooperation, and trust. "People are our most valued resource," the Nissan creed read.

The superiority of this Japanese approach to management was accepted as gospel by most Americans. The media, from *60 Minutes* on down, came to Smyrna to witness the introduction of the new industrial revolution, complete with uniforms and morning calisthenics, common cafeterias and parking lots, team organization and open communications. Smyrna mayor Sam Ridley told reporters that looking down from the overpass at the shining white factory made him understand how Moses must have felt when he gazed down from the mountains on the Promised Land.

The first 2,000 employees also seemed to equate their initiation into the Nissan "family" with entering a state of grace. Selected from a pool of 130,000 applicants after an endless battery of interviews and tests, many had vaulted from minimum wage or unemployment to one of the best-paying jobs in Tennessee.

Four years later, the mystique that once surrounded Nissan has dissolved. "In this area, it was a prestigious thing to have a job at Nissan," says one former supervisor. Now "it's got such a bad reputation, it's pathetic."

At grocery stores and on bank lines, clerks once responded with envy when a Nissan employee entered. Today, they are more likely to whisper sympathetically, "I hear they're killing you out there." And the barber near the railroad crossing at the center of town tells people he can spot Nissan workers even when they're not wearing their telltale blue uniforms: They're the ones who fall asleep in the chair when they're getting their hair cut.

By all external measures, Nissan's Smyrna plant is a success. Quality and productivity have reportedly matched or surpassed Japanese levels. And Nissan management has added a car line, the Sentra, and a second shift, boosting its investment to $850 million and employment to 3,300. The operation even turned a small profit in 1986.

Success the Old-Fashioned Way

Innovative Japanese management had little to do with this success, however. It was achieved the old-fashioned way—through speedup. "Eight-hour aerobics" is how one employee described work on the production line. In parts of the plant, employees have to run from one task to the next to keep up with the line.

"You don't have time to unwrap a piece of chewing gum and stick it in your mouth until the lines stops," says one assembly worker. Adds another, "You feel like you've done three days' work at the end of the shift."

Tellingly, the morning calisthenics were dispensed with about 14 months after production began. But there is still evidence of the Japanese influence. Employees are called "technicians" and are organized in small, closely supervised work groups. Their bosses are called "area managers" and "operations managers," and they pick up the tab for regular beer and pizza parties.

Most of all, there is an expectation—common in Japan—of loyalty, gratitude and enthusiasm from the employees, despite the intense production pressures. Those who fail to show the proper *esprit de corps* are routinely told, "If you don't like it, here's the door. There are 80,000 people out there who want your job."

Many employees have chosen to leave. In a recent one-year period, 235 quit or were fired, including a significant number of top managers. Some of those who have not left have been subjected to harassment and transferred to the most demanding jobs in the plant.

Heart, Soul and Body

Peter Harding (not his real name) came to Nissan five years ago with decades of experience in the auto industry. Last fall he quit.

"I put my whole heart, soul, and body into that plant," Harding says. "What they preached at the beginning, it would have been a beautiful company, but it is

---

SEXUAL HARASSMENT AT NISSAN: THE OPEN DOOR CLOSES

Four women have sued Nissan and 16 current and former company employees for sexual harassment and for management's lack of action to prevent the alleged abuse. Each suit asks $1.25 million in real and compensatory damages. Nissan has denied the charges.

Patricia Stafford worked as a forklift driver at Nissan's Smyrna plant from August 1982 until May 1985. She first complained of sexual harassment after a supervisor repeatedly threatened to make her job difficult if she did not go out with him. She notified his manager and then told the human resources officer. Finally, she went through the "open door" to see President Marvin Runyon. He had her transferred from the shop floor to the receiving deck.

"Because I had gone to see Runyon, I knew I was on the blacklist," she says. A friend in lower management warned her to watch her step after she was identified as a troublemaker in a management meeting.

On the receiving dock, one of Stafford's co-workers soon began making "sexual remarks and four-letter requests," she says. "I couldn't bend over a box without him coming up behind me and hunching me, right there, in front of everyone, he would touch me, grab me."

Again she complained to management, but without result. "It went from bad to worse," she says. "they made him a supervisor. Everyone was in shock that they would do that." The very day he was promoted, says Stafford, he "came by and said, 'Now you're going to have to let me fuck you.'"

It got so bad that Stafford would drive away on her forklift at full speed when she saw him coming. "Finally," she recalls, "he came one day and grabbed me between the legs, and that was the last straw."

A meeting was held in a glass-walled office with Stafford, the co-worker, and two higher-level managers. One became extremely agitated and accused Stafford of trying to frame the man. "He told me, 'I've had trouble with you since day one,' even though they had always told me I was the best worker, even better than the men," she says. The manager "got so mad, he had spit coming from the corner of his mouth. He backed me up against a filing cabinet, flailing his arms, and then he hit me and bloodied my nose." After reporting the incident to the human resources office, Stafford was again transferred. "When they moved me to quality control, I had high hopes," she recalls. "But they put me way off in a dark corner, in a repair-parts crib, like I was a time bomb. I felt like an animal. I asked the supervisor why I was put out there in a cage, and he told me, 'Everyone knows you've had trouble. You're on the blacklist. You're never going to go anywhere.'"

During the height of her troubles, Stafford received several anonymous phone calls late at night, threatening her and her daughter. The emotional stress began to take its toll.

"I had knots in my stomach when I walked through the front gate," she says. "I dropped from 120 to 98 pounds. I looked like a walking skeleton. Fi-

absolutely the worst company I have ever worked for. I was ashamed to tell people I was a manager at Nissan."

Hired as a supervisor, Harding spent his first seven months at Nissan interviewing prospective employees for his department. "We hired exceptionally good people, people we thought we could keep for the rest of their working lives," he recalls. "I ran into one of them at the pharmacy the other day. He looked like he was dead. He's lost 30 pounds, he's had a shoulder operation, and now he's taking medication for his hand. He said to me, 'I think they've got us on a four- or five-year cycle. They'll wear us out and then hire new blood.' I think he may be right."

Employees would call Harding on the phone and begin weeping. "They're pushed to the limit," he says. "They say they have to quit or they'll be dead in a year. What are people going to do 20 years from now?"

When the Smyrna plant opened, Nissan had a policy prohibiting workers from doing heavy physical labor for more than two hours before rotating to lighter tasks, Harding says. This policy has been abandoned, and work loads have steadily increased, especially over the last two years.

Even Nissan advisers from Japan, where the intensity of work is legendary, are startled at the Smyrna work loads. After observing the underbody line where engines are installed in the Sentra sedan, a Japanese quality supervisor took Harding aside and told him, "You're crazy. Only 17 doing the job. In Japan, we have 22." That job alone has accounted for 15 injuries in the past year, Harding says. The employees work with their hands over their head 80 percent of the time, and the constant repetitive motion wears out their joints. Two of the workers have had shoulder operations.

"As soon as people are injured, they have no use for them," says Harding. "You take the best employee, a hard worker with a good attitude, and say an elbow goes out from overwork. They'll say, 'Get him the hell outta here.' It's hard for me to believe it, and I have seen it. It seems so far out, but it's the damn truth."

Harding is not hopeful for Smyrna: "Nissan will ruin more people and lives than the good it will do in Tennessee, and that's a hell of thing to say."

'You'll Be Out'

Jerry Bowman grew up on a farm in Wartrace,

SEXUAL HARASSMENT continued

nally, my nerves got the best of me, and I quit."

Stafford has had difficulty landing a new job. At one plant, she was told she wouldn't be hired because of her problems at Nissan. Eventually she eliminated all mention of Nissan when she applied for jobs.

"They told me I'd die without Nissan, but it's not true," she says. "One thing they can't strip me of is my dignity and self-respect. I just pray to God it will come out in public. If I can save the heartbreak of just one other woman going into that plant, it will be worth it."

Fueled the Fire

Teresa Caudill had a similar experience at the Nissan plant. A quality inspector since April 1984 who still works at the plant, she says she was repeatedly touched and approached sexually by a co-worker. After Caudill complained several times to management, a meeting was held. Caudill's managers accused her of lying and said "two or three other girls who had been mistreated were also lying," she recalls. "They made him apologize, for the record. That just fueled his fire, because he knew he could get away with it."

Like Stafford, Caudill took her complaint to Runyon. "I talked to him for an hour and a half," she says. "He seemed appalled, and he said he would take care of it." Some time later, however, the trouble resumed.

"He started in again, putting his hands on you, in front of others," she recalls. "They would just laugh and humiliate me." Caudill went to see Mary Parker, the lawyer who is handling the suits of all four women.

After Caudill sued, an announcement was made at her work-group meeting. The supervisor told her co-workers not to talk with her.

In a closed-circuit television address to the plant, Runyon told the employees that all of the allegations had been investigated and were untrue. Runyon accused the women of trying to ruin Nissan's public image, she says.

"They make you feel so awful you could die, like you've betrayed the Nissan family," she says. "People will make awful faces and say things like, 'I can't believe you would do this to our company.' My manager went around and wished everyone a Merry Christmas, but he just looked at me with death in his eyes." In its court filings in response to Caudill's suit, Nissan charged that she brought on the sexual advances by "wanton" behavior. This outrages Caudill.

"I had dated my fiance for three years before we got married," she says. "Not once did I date a person at the plant; I don't believe in dating people I work with. I even had a policy of not going to lunch with men."

Since she sued Nissan, Caudill has been transferred to the paint department and has not encountered problems. But three women in the paint area have complained to her of sexual harassment. "They're frightened and they tell me, 'I don't know what I'm going to do.' It's happening throughout the plant."

about 35 miles south of Smyrna. "Me and my grand-daddy don't get on too well," Bowman says, so he left the farm and headed for Smyrna. Through some fishing buddies in management at Nissan, he was hired on at the plant in early 1985.

A year or so after joining Nissan, Bowman start-ed attending union meetings and talking with other em-ployees about the United Auto Workers. "You'll be out of here before you know it," Bowman was warned by a foreman he used to fish with.

Bowman's job was to install heavy steering gears on the Nissan pickup. One day, he wrenched his back while lifting a gear and doubled over in pain. He was rushed by ambulance to a hospital in nearby Murfrees-boro.

Nissan wanted him back on the job the very next day; he was put to work opening boxes, but he could only stand five minutes before the pain forced him to sit down. Finally, Bowman was allowed to see a doctor, who ordered him off work for five weeks and restricted him to light labor when he returned.

Several weeks after he got back to work, he was transferred to the Sentra trim line, where he installed radios and performed three or four other tasks on a 96 second cycle. "It was the hardest line," Bowman recalls. "You had to be real fast. I had to jump in the car and lie flat on my back. It was hurting worse and worse, but I kept trying. I didn't want to be laid off again."

Bowman pressed himself, dreading the thought of another layoff. He had collected only $29 a week in workers' compensation payments, and his wife had just had a baby. Managers would come by and ask him how long it was going to take for him to learn his job. They told him other workers had mastered it in just a week.

"I was busting butt, but I just couldn't do it," he says. Eventually, Bowman was called up to the front of-fice and fired for inadequate job performance. Nissan took away the car he had leased from the company at a discount and escorted him out to the highway.

Now Jerry Bowman spends his days trapping fox in the woods around Wartrace and runs a video store at night. He filed charges before the National Labor Rela-tions Board that he was fired for union activities, but his case was dismissed.

"They're all big wheels up there," he says of Nis-san management. "They run all over people, and there's nothing to stop them."

Out of the Family

Nissan's "open-door" policy, which ostensibly al-lows any employee to bring a complaint to management without fear of retaliation, is a fraud, employees say.

"The open-door policy just lets them know if you're going to be a 'troublemaker,'" charges Juanita Brown, the pseudonym of a quality-assurance inspector at Nissan since 1984.

"When you first start, they tell you, 'If you ever have any problems, just come to us and we'll do every-thing in our power to clear them up, since all of you are now members of the Nissan family.' But when you do have a problem, it's like you're betraying them. People with problems are immediately cut out of their so-called family."

Former supervisor Peter Harding recalls at least 15 times when employees with complaints were trans-ferred to the most difficult jobs in the plant, without ro-tation, for months at a time. Employees who speak up "are identified as having an attitude problem," Harding says. "If you don't think exactly like they do, you're out of the ballpark. What we've got there is management by intimidation."

Human resource managers act as the enforcers of the system. Intended as employee advocates, "now they are nothing more than a Gestapo for manage-ment," says Harding.

"The human resource people would try to get on the employees' good side, get them to open up to them," says Larry MacArthur (not his real name), a manager in the engineering department. "And the next thing you know, your boss is calling you into the office." MacArthur recalls one human resource manager who "went on a witch hunt to find out if two of my people were sympathetic to the union, strictly because they were in the habit of voicing their opinions. He would drag their names through the mud during meetings with other managers, until I got him to stop. There were no grounds for it."

Distrust and fear pervade the plant. Even co-workers are suspicious of each other. "You can't trust the person working next to you," says Steve Cobbs, the pseudonym of an assembly worker. "You want to put your confidence in them, but then they'll turn you in."

Repairman Dennis Boyd (not his real name) cites a recent management effort to have workers "re-strict their intake of liquids" before the shift so they won't have to take breaks. "They don't try to tell you that you can't go to the bathroom," says Boyd. "They try to put you on a super guilt trip. I actually saw a man wet his pants on the line. There was a relief man right there, but they had said at the morning meeting that people were abusing their breaks."

A recent company-wide attitude survey reflected a drop in satisfaction levels, compared to the previous survey, in virtually every area tested. In a talk with the engineering department after the attitude survey was re-leased, Jerry Benefield, Nissan's vice-president of manu-facturing, upbraided the employees. "He told us basical-ly that he liked to see people with smiling faces, and if you can't come in here and smile, get out," recalls Mac-Arthur.

Revert to Type

Why has Nissan strayed so far from its benign im-age of cooperative management? One explanation is that many of the senior company officials, including President Marvin T. Runyon, are former Ford Motor autocrats who brought with them the worst tendencies of traditional American management.

"The so-called 'new concept' doesn't exist," says MacArthur. "It broke down six months after we started production. The people in charge of the plants just reverted back to type, back to the only system they ever knew. The only difference is that here the people on the line don't have a union."

But it's too easy to blame former Ford managers. The Nissan plant here is remarkably similar to its counterparts in Japan. The abuses at Smyrna are not an aberration, nor are they a betrayal of the promise of the Japanese model; they are a natural consequence of the Nissan system.

Consider this remark, from a Nissan worker I interviewed in Japan in 1982. "There's a pretense of 'family' at Nissan, and workers are forced to put on a good face. The definition of the 'Nissan man' is one who is never late, never takes a day off, and never complains."

If Japanese management is more productive, it is not because workers are more loyal or committed. It is because they are tightly controlled, subjected to strict and unquestioned hierarchy, and pressed by their peers in small, highly competitive work groups. "It is a system in which workers strangle themselves," says Shoji Kokichi, a sociologist from Tokyo University.

Union Makes Inroads

Given the spreading disillusionment in the Smyrna workforce, it is not surprising that the UAW has begun to make inroads. Jim Turner, the UAW's Nashville-based regional organizer, has been developing contacts among Nissan workers since the plant began operating, and the union has recently added two full-time organizers. Support for the union and attendance at its

Remember – we work as a Team here, Unit 79041682 ...

monthly meetings have been increasing, but the organizers are taking a cautious "go-slow" approach.

The state of Tennessee, hostile to worker rights and unions, presents problems to the UAW. Not only is it a "right-to-work" state; it also has weak or nonexistent statutory protection for workers who are injured or sexually harassed on the job. A recent study by the Southern Labor Institute rated Tennessee the sixth worst in the United States on worker protection and the fifth worst on overall "labor climate."

But most of the difficulties stem from the plant itself. "Many of the people got their jobs at Nissan through relatives or friends," Turner points out. "They are basically honest and loyal, and the company takes advantage of that. They make them feel guilty, y'know, like you're betraying your father if you take a sick day. But people are coming around to realize this is not the utopia they promised it would be."

The internal structure of the Nissan plant makes unionizing difficult. Management has broken the workforce down into small groups, which keeps workers isolated from other groups. In addition, the smaller the group, the greater the peer pressure. If an employee falls behind in production or takes a sick day, the burden must be shouldered by others in the group.

The pressure intensified after Nissan began a program of awarding merit points in work groups for accident-free production. Instead of reporting injuries to first aid, employees will work with injured wrists, hands, and elbows. And some employees have even been known to report the injuries of workers in other groups.

The union also must contend with the natural impulse of workers to deny they made a mistake. "People don't want to admit they were hogwashed," says Sara Wood, the pseudonym of an assembly worker. "They will tell me privately that they can't stand it, and then go back to work the next day and tell their supervisor, 'I love the challenge of this job.' You look at them with your mouth wide open. You just can't believe it."

What's more, Nissan President Marvin Runyon has a Reagan-like ability to stay above the fray and retain the trust of the workforce. "Runyon has a charisma and magnetism that is unreal," Wood says. "It's hard to keep my balance in my head when I am around him. They think he is like God over there."

The white-haired, folksy Runyon addresses the workforce every three months on a closed-circuit television system that extends throughout the plant. Favored employees are selected for inclusion in the studio audience, and that still has the capacity to thrill some employees.

But Runyon's charm has its limits. He wrapped up a recent address by saying, "I'm sure everyone is enjoying their job." The entire trim-and-chassis line reportedly burst into laughter. When the address was rebroadcast for the night shift, that line had been edited out.

CHOOSING SIDES: UNIONS AND THE TEAM CONCEPT
Labor Notes, 7435 Michigan Avenue, Detroit, MI 48210 313 / 842-6262

Suggestions for Further Reading

Several periodicals will help keep the reader abreast of current developments in the team concept and related areas:

Labor Notes, the monthly newsletter for union activists. Covers U.S. and Canada, includes articles written by participants themselves, resources, and discussions of strategy. For subscription information see the ad at the end of this book.

Labor Research Review, which comes out twice a year, publishes articles and debates on tactics and strategy for the labor movement. Subscriptions are $12 from 3411 W. Diversey, Chicago, IL 60647.

Labor Studies Journal, published three times a year, helps bridge the gap between academic materials and the needs of trade unionists. It includes reviews of recent books. Individual subscriptions are $15 from Transaction Periodicals, Department 8010, Rutgers University, New Brunswick, NJ 08903.

Automotive News, a weekly industry journal, includes insightful coverage of labor-management relations. $55 per year, 965 E. Jefferson, Detroit, MI 48207.

Solidarity is the monthly magazine of the United Auto Workers, 8000 E. Jefferson, Detroit, MI 48214. $5 per year.

The United States Department of Labor, Bureau of Labor-Management Relations and Cooperative Programs, has a mailing list. Many of its regular publications are little more than cheerleading for cooperative programs. Some of the in-depth reports, however, contain valuable information. To be added to the mailing list write to the Bureau at Washington, DC 20210.

Books and Articles

AFL-CIO, *The Inside Game*, available free from AFL-CIO Industrial Union Department, 815 16th St. NW, Washington, DC 20006.

Steve Babson, "Craft, Class, and Culture: Tool and Die Makers and the Organization of the UAW," *Michigan Historical Review*, Spring 1988.

Christian Berggren, " 'New Production Concepts' in Final Assembly: The Swedish Experiences," International Institute for Comparative Social Research/Labor Policy (Wissenschaftszentrum Berlin, Steinplatz 2, D 1000 Berlin 12), November 1987.

Peter Cappelli and Robert McKersie, "Management Strategy and the Redesign of Workrules," *Journal of Management Studies,* September 1987.

Communications Workers of America, *Occupational Stress: The Hazard and the Challenge*, Instructor's

Manual (CWA, 1925 K Street NW, Washington, DC 20006), 1986.

Michael A. Cusumano, *The Japanese Automobile Industry: Technology & Management at Nissan & Toyota*, Cambridge, Harvard University Press, 1985.

Ben Dankbaar, "Teamwork in the West German Car Industry: Management Strategies and the Quality of Work," International Institute for Comparative Social Research/Labor Policy (Wissenschaftszentrum Berlin, Steinplatz 2, D 1000 Berlin 12), 1987.

Knuth Dohse, Ulrich Jurgens, and Thomas Malsch, "From 'Fordism' to 'Toyotism'? The Social Organization of the Labor Process in the Japanese Automobile Industry," *Politics and Society*, Vol.14, No.2, 1985.

CAITS, *Flexibility: Who Needs It?*, London, 1986 (CAITS, Polytechnic of North London, Holloway Road, London N7).

Guillermo J. Grenier, *Inhuman Relations: Quality Circles and Anti-Unionism in American Industry*, Philadelphia, Temple University Press, 1988.

John Junkerman, "We Are Driven," *Mother Jones*, August 1982.

S. Kamata, *Japan in the Fast Lane: An Insider's Account of Life in a Japanese Auto Factory*, London, Allen and Unwin, 1983.

Harry C. Katz, *Shifting Gears: Changing Labor Relations in the U.S. Automobile Industry*, Boston, MIT Press, 1985.

Harry C. Katz, Thomas A. Kochan and Jeffrey H. Keefe, "The Impact of Industrial Relations on Productivity: Evidence from the Automobile Industry," paper presented at the Brookings Microeconomic Conference, Washington, DC, December 3-4, 1987, forthcoming in *Brookings Papers on Economic Activity*, Special Issue.

Nelson Lichtenstein and Stephen Meyer III, *On the Line: A Social History of the Automobile Industry,* Urbana, University of Illinois Press, 1988.

Daniel Luria, "The Relations Between Work Rules, Plant Performance, and Costs in Vehicle Assembly Plants and Parts Production," paper prepared for "The Future of Work in the Automobile Industry," International Institute for Comparative Social Research/Labor Policy (Wissenschaftszentrum Berlin, Steinplatz 2, D 1000 Berlin 12), November 1987.

Eric Mann, *Taking on General Motors: A Case Study of the UAW Campaign To Keep GM Van Nuys Open*, Los Angeles, University of California Institute of Industrial Relations, 1987.

David Moberg, "Is There a Union in Nissan's Future?"

In These Times, April 6, 1988.

Yasuhiro Monden, *Toyota Production System: Practical Approach to Production Management*, Industrial Engineering and Management Press, 1983.

Kim Moody, *An Injury to All*, London and New York, Verso Press, 1988 (available from Labor Notes).

Daniel Nelson, *Frederick Taylor and the Rise of Scientific Management*, Madison, University of Wisconsin Press, 1980.

Greg Nicklas, "Self-Managing Teams and Unions," *The Quality Circles Journal*, International Association of Quality Circles, June 1987.

Mike Parker, *Inside the Circle: A Union Guide to QWL*, Detroit, Labor Notes/South End Press, 1985.

Lee Schore, "Occupational Stress: A Union Based Approach," Institute for Labor and Mental Health, Oakland, California.

Harley Shaiken and Stephen Herzenberg, *Automation and Global Production*, Center for U.S.-Mexican Studies, University of California, San Diego, 1987.

Jane Slaughter, *Concessions and How To Beat Them*, Detroit, Labor Notes, 1983.

Peter J. Turnbull, "The Limits of Japanisation—Just-In-Time, Labor Relations and the UK Automotive Industry," to be published Autumn 1988 in *New Technology, Work, and Employment*, Vol.3, No.2.

Peter Unterweger, "Appropriate Automation: Thoughts on Swedish Examples of Socio-Technical Innovation," Industrial Relations Research Association, Spring 1985.

Peter Unterweger, "Work Organization and Technology in Three Swedish Auto Plants," UAW Research Department, 1987.

Donald M. Wells, *Empty Promises: Quality of Working Life Programs and the Labor Movement*, New York, Monthly Review Press, 1987.

Barry Wilkinson and Nick Oliver, *The Japanisation of British Industry*, Oxford, Basil Blackwell, to be published Autumn 1988.

Tim Wise, "Life on the Fast Line," *Dollars and Sense*, April and May 1987.

Index